Defining the Moment

Understanding Brain Death in Halakhah

Rabbi David Shabtai, MD

Shoresh Press
New York

Copyright © 2012 Rabbi David Shabtai, MD
All rights reserved.

ISBN: 0615560482
ISBN-13: 9780615560489

Library of Congress Control Number: 2011960777
Shoresh Press, New York, NY

For more information about this book or to contact the author, please visit www.definingthemoment.com.

תנו לה מפרי ידיה

המרחם על כל בריותיו ברחמים
הוא יחוס ויחמול וירחם על
נפש רוח ונשמה של האשה

שפרינצא רבקה בת הינדא ע"ה
Roberta Susan Shabtai

רוח ה' תניחנה בגן עדן

ספר זה מוקדש לעלוי
נשמתה ע"י משפחתה
למלאת ט"ו שנה לפטירתה

תהא נשמתה צרורה בצרור החיים

Table of Contents:

Introduction   xv

SECTION I: DEFINING THE MOMENT OF DEATH

Chapter 1: Organ Transplantation and Brain Death   3
Chapter 2: The Science of Brain Death   13
Chapter 3: What it Means to Define Death   35
Chapter 4: Definitions of Death   45

SECTION II: HALAKHIC TEXTS

Chapter 5: Talmud Yoma   69
Chapter 6: Mishnah Ohalot   97
Chapter 7: Talmud Hullin   115
Chapter 8: Hakham Tzvi   139
Chapter 9: Hatam Sofer   161

SECTION III: MODERN OPINIONS ON BRAIN DEATH

Chapter 10: Rabbi Moshe Feinstein – First Responsum   185
Chapter 11: Rabbi Moshe Feinstein – Second Responsum   201
Chapter 12: Rabbi Moshe Feinstein – Third Responsum   217
Chapter 13: Rabbi Moshe Feinstein – Fourth Responsum   245
Chapter 14: Rabbi Moshe Feinstein – Putting it All Together   257
Chapter 15: The Israeli Chief Rabbinate   271
Chapter 16: Rabbi Shelomoh Zalman Auerbach   309
Chapter 17: Cardiac Function and Vital Motion   345
Chapter 18: Challenging ICSR as Determinant of Death   367
Chapter 19: Opposing Brain Death   383

Epilogue   399
Index   401

Acknowledgments

I have been fascinated by the topic of determining the moment of death ever since I began learning about medical Halakhah and bioethics years ago. This project rightfully represents the culmination of many years of sincere support and the dedication of many people.

First, my sincere acknowledgments are reserved for the Almighty, who has guided me, protected me, and profoundly blessed me in innumerable ways. *Odeh la-Hashem be-khol levav, be-sod yesharim ve-eidah*.

Above all others, I must express my deepest appreciation, gratitude, and indebtedness to my wife, Monica. She has stood by me always with unwavering support, complete dedication, indefatigable trust, and uncompromising devotion. Her continuing belief in my success is truly admirable and inspirational. She is the pillar of our family, and I and our children cannot find words to express our gratitude, love, and appreciation.

My father, *avi mori* Gabi Shabtai, has always been there to guide, teach, and support me through thick and thin, being my close confidant. My siblings Simmy and Devora, Donny, and Sara have stood by me for as long as I can remember, and each fills an integral role in our family. Together with my aunt and uncle, Linda and Steven Katz, they have sincerely given of themselves to support this project and make it possible. I am sincerely indebted to them all, for far more than I can share in these few lines.

The memory of my mother *z"l*, to who this book is dedicated, is with me constantly. Although she left this world too soon, her life lessons and determination continue to guide me in nearly everything I do.

I am sincerely indebted to my revered teachers, rabbis, and *roshei kollel*, R. Hershel Schachter, R. Michael Rosensweig, R. Mordechai

Willig, and R. J. David Bleich for not only imparting knowledge, but also for teaching and modeling the sensitive and sacred task of learning Torah and understanding Halakhah. They have all gone beyond their normal calling in devoting their time to ensure understanding and in their willingness to entertain repeated questions and challenges to make sure that I have thoroughly understood what they were trying to convey. I similarly am sincerely grateful to Dr. Abraham S. Abraham, who has taught and guided me in many areas of medical Halakhah.

Dr. John Loike has been both my mentor and colleague ever since he brought me into his lab during my college years. There is rarely a paper that I even consider for publication without asking him for his opinion first. He is a man of vision and clarity and I am fortunate to continue to work with him.

Learning Torah is best accomplished through studying with a partner and hammering out intricate details through conversation and discussion. I have been blessed to learn Torah in the company of eminent scholars, insightful colleagues, and genuinely good friends. In particular, I must acknowledge R. Jonathan Cohen, my colleague and dear friend, for his earnest and unrelenting search for truth. We have worked together on many "end of life issues," and without his insights, comments, and constructive criticisms, this book would not be what it is today.

Many people have assisted and supported me throughout this project. They include, but are certainly not limited to: R. Menachem Genack; R. Gil Student; R. Dr. Richard Weiss; Prof. Leslie Newman for her continued literary support; Dr. Joseph Weisstuch and Dr. Edward Katz for their guidance during my years in medical school; Mrs. Meira Mintz for her superb editing skills; R. Levi Mostofsky and Mr. Peter Kahn for their continued support; R. Yaacov Feit for his creativity; R. Yehudah Turetsky, R. Yaakov Werblowsky, and R. Moshe Stavsky for their insights and indulgences; R. Yaakov Sasson, R. Asher Bush, R. Nachman Cohen, R. Dr. Edward Reichman, Dayyan Shmuel Simons, Dr. Kenneth Prager, and Dr. Elliot Bondi for fascinating conversations and insights;

and Mr. Menachem Butler for his creativity, support, and exceptional resourcefulness.

Rabbi David Shabtai, MD
December 2011
Kislev 5772

Shlomo Moshe Amar
Rishon Lezion Chief Rabbi Of Israel
President of the Great Rabbinical Court

שלמה משה עמאר
הראשון לציון הרב הראשי לישראל
נשיא בית הדין הרבני הגדול

בס"ד, א' כסלו, תשע"ב
ב"ע/140-18-1

לכבוד
הרב דוד יהודה שבתאי שליט"א

שלום רב !

אחיך היקר הרה"ג ר' שמחה הראני את מעשי ידיך חיבור שלם שחיברת בשפה האנגלית על הגדרת רגע המות לפי ההלכה, לא עברתי על הספר, אבל מ"מ ברכתי שלוחה לך, שתצליח להדפיסו לתועלת שוחרי תורה ותושיה. ותמשיך לשקוד באהלה של תורה ולחבר עוד חיבורים יקרים ומועלים, ולאילנא רברבא תתעביד.

בברכה נאמנה מעיר הקודש והמקדש,

שלמה משה עמאר
ראשון לציון הרב הראשי לישראל

BETH DIN ZEDEK
BETH DIN ZEDEK ECCLESIASTICAL JUDICATURE OF THE
CHICAGO RABBINICAL COUNCIL

2701 W. Howard Street · Chicago, Illinois 60645-1303
773-465-3900 FAX: 773-465-6632
e-mail:info@crcweb.org

בית דין צדק דק"ק שיקגו והגליל
דמועצת הרבנים דשיקגו

בס"ד

RABBI ISRAEL M. KARNO, *of blessed memory*
Av Beth Din Emeritus

RABBI C. DAVID REGENSBERG, *of blessed memory*

הרב גדלי' דוב שווארץ, ראב"ד
RABBI GEDALIA DOV SCHWARTZ
Av Beth Din

הרב אברהם מרדכי אברמסן
RABBI ALAN M. ABRAMSON
Menahel

November 15, 2011

י"ח מרחשון תשע"ב, ג' פרשת חיי שרה

Rabbi David Shabtai, M.D.
666 West 188th Street
Apartment 4D
New York City, New York 10040

Dear Rabbi Shabtai,

After examining many parts of your manuscript, "Defining the Moment: Understanding Brain Death in Halakhah," I am extremely impressed by your thorough analysis of all of the halachic problems dealing with this matter, and the in depth understanding and knowledge of all of the medical issues.

Without making any arbitrary statements concerning a halachic-medical decision I would recommend this work to any Rabbinic decisor in order to gain a greater knowledge of these very vital and critical matters.

With all best wishes for your extraordinary endeavors, I remain,

Sincerely yours,

Rabbi Gedalia Dov Schwartz
Av Beth Din

GDS/sm

הרב צבי שכטר
ראש ישיבה ורם כולל
ישיבת רבינו יצחק אלחנן

Rabbi Hershel Schachter
24 Bennett Avenue
New York, New York 10033
(212) 795-0630

מכתב ברכה
_____

לכבוד נאמיה לב ובועז יקירי'
הר"ר אשר שמחו הרו"ה לרגל המוסמך על
קבלת הסמכה וגמר דיפלומה של חידו"ת
דקדקות רב המאות של המקורות
בהלכה. הריני הנני נותן ברכתי
כדרך כתבה שנזכה לעלות מעלה, והנה
ממולא ויהי' ביושבתנו, ולא יצא ?? לא
רן ספרו, ולו תקדר לי דבר שבקדושה
ויגדל מתח' ונ[...]
ברכה לקבל עו"י התורה,
צבי שכטר

פ"ק מלך, ערב חנוכה, תשנ"ה

ב"ה

RABBI J. DAVID BLEICH
400 EAST 77TH STREET
NEW YORK 21, N.Y.

AG 9-0766
RH-4-4406

"Those who are ordained are numerous, but those who know are few." Those words, penned by R. Shlomoh Luria in the sixteenth-century, appear in his *Yam shel Shlomoh, Bava Kamma* 7:58, describing the self-professed rabbinic experts of his day. They are all the more true in the twenty-first century, particularly with regard to issues of medical Halakhah in general and of so-called "brain death" in particular.

Let me be quite blunt: No one has made a credible case for recognition of neurological death both because the concept is alien to halakhic discourse and because the medical phenomenon does not exist in a patient with a beating heart. Neurologists and ethicists candidly concede that physicians have not discovered previously unrecognized medical realia but have simply formulated a new standard for withdrawal of treatment, harvesting of organs, etc. Semantic sleight of hand endows old words with new meaning in what has become a successful bid for societal acceptance.

The halakhic arguments that have been advanced, specious or otherwise, serve to promote respiratory death as a halakhic standard. Neither modern medicine nor contemporary ethics is prepared to accept such an expansive definition of death. Indeed, as our author points out, the very suggestion that a patient such as Christopher Reeve, or indeed a polio victim sustained in an iron lung, may not be alive appears to be a *reductio ad absurdum*. The result is obfuscation and confusion. Truth be told, the problem has its roots in a desire to adapt Halakhah to contemporary mores. The *nisayon* facing today's physician – and rabbinic decisor – should not be minimized. But both intellectual honesty and commitment to *Torah mi-Sinai* demand a different quality of discourse.

Rabbi Dr. David Shabtai has undertaken the formidable task of exhaustively assessing the extensive literature devoted to this topic. His academic credentials make him exceptionally qualified for that endeavor. Rabbi Shabtai brings a keen analytical intellect both to the study of rabbinic texts and to the study of medicine. He has the unique distinction of being the only fellow, past or present, of Yeshiva University's Kollel Elyon, to hold a medical degree. The present work is a *tour de force* representing years of study and investigation.

I regard a cautionary note to be in order. Rambam, *Hilkhot Sanhedrin* 21:1, rules that a member of a *bet din* must reject evidence, including eyewitness testimony, that he knows to be at variance from the truth. In an entirely different context, R. Moshe Feinstein, of blessed memory, *Iggerot Mosheh, Yoreh Deah*, I, no. 54, wrote that, in effect, a halakhic decisor is called upon to rule either on the basis of knowledge or on the basis of belief. Epistemologically, the two are entirely distinct phenomena. Witnesses, documentary evidence, etc., establish a basis for belief. Knowledge is much more subtle and much more idiosyncratic but far more certain than belief. That insight is really what underlies Rambam's ruling. A *dayyan* dare not allow evidentiary presumptions, that can yield only belief, to trump knowledge.

Rabbi Shabtai correctly assumes that Rambam's ruling applies only to actual decisions of a *bet din*, not to presentations of announced opinions. Decisions must be rendered on the basis of conviction. Intellectual discussion is best conducted by presenting an opinion in its most favorable light, both factual and theoretical. The author has succeeded in presenting positions he knows to be erroneous in the most plausible light possible, in presenting arguments he knows to be specious in as cogent manner as possible and in presenting purported facts that strain credulity in as credible a manner as possible.

That is both the weakness and the strength of the present volume. The strength of a dispassionate but thorough presentation of conflicting views is obvious. The weakness is that the reader cannot attain edification by simply reading the work. The reader who hopes to penetrate to the *amittah shel Torah* must read every word with care and reflect diligently upon what he has read. Assuming that the reader brings the necessary intellectual skills to the endeavor, he will be amply rewarded.

Rabbi Shabtai must already be considered a ranking figure in the field of Jewish Bioethics. There is no doubt that he will become an eminent and eloquent proponent of authentic Jewish teaching in this area. The coming generation will be enriched by his erudition and expertise. May the Almighty guide him and shower upon him the blessings vouchsafed to those who uphold and strengthen His Torah.

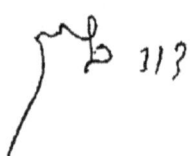

Introduction

In His famous response to Iyov "out of the whirlwind," God admonishes Iyov for questioning Divine Providence, emphasizing the limitations of human ability and human intellect. Cautioning Iyov that mere mortals cannot always understand, nor even sometimes perceive, the Divine plan for humanity, God challenges him, "Were the gates of death revealed to you? Can you see the gates of the shadow of death?" (*Iyov* 38:17). Who is Iyov, with his limited perception and worldview, to challenge God's management of this world? No one can be so haughty as to assume that everything that occurs must be understandable to him. God explains to Iyov that it is only He who created and continues to maintain this world, and it is He alone who determines when a person lives and when he dies. Accordingly, to God, the plan makes perfect sense.

We cannot understand the true meaning of death or why people die at certain times; the Divine calculus lies beyond the grasp of the human mind. But while its meaning eludes us and we cannot precisely comprehend its grasp on humanity, as a matter of Halakhah, we are nonetheless charged with accurately describing and defining when it occurs.

The Challenge

One of the most pressing ethical problems of our day, defining death deeply probes the meaning of what it means to be alive. Aside from philosophical intrigue, determining the precise moment of death has serious practical ramifications, ranging from issues of burial, bereavement, and mourning to withdrawing therapy. Historically, this was a simple procedure – aside from fairly infrequent events, it was obvious when a person was dead. Traditionally, when a person's heart stopped beating and he was no longer breathing, he was declared dead. Even though there is theoretically a time gap between the person's last breath and his heart standing still, before the age of modern medicine, this difference was quite small and almost always imperceptible.

Nonetheless, the technical aspects of making this precise determination in pre-modern times were not quite as straightforward. Without the aid of modern monitoring devices, respiratory failure was particularly difficult to diagnose. Since a patient's last breath can only be identified retroactively – only after it is evident that he has taken no more – the difficulty incumbent upon those attending to his needs is readily apparent. Similarly, in the era before widespread medical monitoring, one wonders how doctors effectively or accurately monitored cardiac activity. Although normally apparent, the heartbeat and pulse can sometimes be difficult to assess, especially in a weak and dying person. When they become no longer palpable or perceptible, the examiner must consider whether in fact the person has died or whether his means of assessment are insufficiently sensitive to detect weak activity even though it exists. The historical lack of effective medical interventions, however, meant that even in the case of irreversible respiratory failure alone, by the time a doctor could be sufficiently convinced that these in fact were the person's very last breaths, it is highly likely that the heartbeat would have already stopped as well.

The significant advances in medical therapies in the last century allowed for teasing apart the moments between the failure of the respiratory and cardiac functions. Separating these events was likely unimaginable in centuries past, prompting a fundamental reexamination of determining the moment of death in the age of modern medicine. While properly "understanding" death may be beyond the ken of human intellect, the serious consequences of determining precisely when it occurs demand our most diligent efforts. We must know when our duties to heal the sick end and when the responsibility of burial ensues; we must be able to state with definitive halakhic clarity when a person's body no longer supports life. It is only when a person dies that we can begin to discuss transplanting his vital organs into another person, whose life may yet be saved. It is this last issue that will be our main focus.

Introduction

Timely Discussion

The issue of brain death has been widely and hotly debated ever since the Ad Hoc Committee of the Harvard Medical School to Examine the Definition of Brain Death published its 1968 seminal article identifying brain death as "a new criterion for death."[1] While now legally accepted in almost all U.S. jurisdictions,[2] scholars have long questioned and examined the definition's ethical and philosophical basis and assumptions. The "consensus" rationale, however, has shifted considerably since 1968. The fundamental question of whether brain death in fact constitutes the death of an individual – and if true, why this should be so – has recently come into sharper public focus. It therefore behooves us to better understand this issue, analyzing both the scientific facts as well as the halakhic postulates, not only to understand how Orthodox Judaism approaches the topic, but to enrich ourselves by becoming interested and engaged members of our own community.

In 2008, responding to several calls in the bioethical literature challenging the *status quo* of recognizing brain death as the death of the individual, the President's Council of Bioethics issued a "white paper," entitled *Controversies in the Determination of Death* (Washington DC, 2008). The President's Council's report paints a clear and thoughtful description of the history of determining death, the various analyses and approaches justifying the new neurological standard, as well as a survey of recent critiques and challenges. Perhaps not surprisingly, the President's Council defends the current standard of considering brain death as the death of the individual, but in doing so, presents a completely novel approach and justification. The Council offers a radical shift in understanding what it means to be dead and how brain death fits in with their new model.

This fundamental reexamination of brain death is not limited to the academic world of bioethics. The Catholic Church has long supported brain death predicated organ donation, conforming to the consensus

---

[1] "A definition of Irreversible Coma," *Journal of the American Medical Association* 205 (1968). 337-40.
[2] President's Council on Bioethics, *Controversies in the Determination of Death* (2008): 6 note.

medical opinion that brain death means that an individual has died, arguing that these questions do "not fall within the competence of the Church."[3] This thinking has begun to change however, with scholars arguing that Catholic doctrine does not necessarily support recognizing brain death as the death of the individual.[4] Similarly, recent Muslim scholarship has begun to challenge the Islamic community's historical acceptance of "brain death" as the death of the individual. Based on their understanding of the nature of the soul and its departure, several Muslim authors have argued against recognizing brain death as religiously significant.[5]

Judaism has also seen its fair share of internal debate on this fundamental issue. While this discussion is quite longstanding in the literature, several recent events, position statements, and pronouncements have engendered renewed interest in understanding this complicated area of Halakhah. In 2008, the Israeli Knesset passed "The Brain and Respiratory Death Law – 2008,"[6] formally recognizing brain death as legal death. Crafting this law brought together members of Israeli legal and halakhic communities, with the Israeli Chief Rabbinate endorsing the final version.[7]

Arriving at the opposite conclusion, the Chief Rabbinate of England recently reviewed the relevant halakhic discussions and issued a statement concluding that brain death does not constitute halakhic death.[8] The Office of the Chief Rabbi is working with the UK Transplant

---

[3] B. Haid, "The Prolongation of Life: An Address of Pope Pius XII to an International Congress of Anesthesiologists," *The Pope Speaks* 4 (1958): 398.

[4] R. de Mattei (ed.), *Finis Vitae: Is Brain Death Still Life* (Italy: Rubbetino, 2006); L. di Scaraffia, "I segni della morte. A quarant'anni dal rapport di Harvard" (Italian), *L'Osservatore Romano* (September 3, 2008).

[5] A. Bedir, S. Aksoy, "Brain death revisited: It is not 'complete death' according to Islamic sources," *Journal of Medical Ethics* 37 (2011): 290-4; M.Y. Rady, I.L. Verheijde, "Brain death is not 'complete death' in Islam: A global call for revising the legal definition of death in Islam," *Journal of Medical Ethics*, electronic letter to the editor (April 26, 2011).

[6] *Sefer ha-Hukkim* 2144, 24 *Adar II*, 5768 (March 31, 2008).

[7] "The Decision of the Israeli Chief Rabbinate from *Tishrei* 5770" (Hebrew), *Assia* 87-88 (2010): 96-99.

[8] "Religion, Organ Transplantation, and the Definition of Death," *The Lancet* 377 (January, 22 2011), p. 271.

Registry to take halakhic considerations into account in enabling a complementary halakhically sanctioned organ donation process that allows for a cardiopulmonary determination of death.[9] Across the Atlantic, the Rabbinical Council of America (RCA) released a study by its Vaad Halacha on "Halachic issues in the determination of death and in organ transplantation including an evaluation of the neurological 'brain death' standard" (June, 2010). Designed to assist its members "in the process of *psak halacha*,"[10] the report stirred much controversy, even while "not intended as a formal ruling." One of its strengths is its careful and methodical recording and presentation of the oral record and history of this important debate.

Speaking in broad strokes, there are three main suggestions for halakhically defining death: the complete and irreversible inability to breathe on one's own (irreversible cessation of spontaneous respiration [ICSR]), the complete and irreversible cessation of all bodily motion (including heartbeat), and the complete absence of the head. Each is carefully articulated by various halakhists independently. What is missing – and what should hopefully help in understanding this important debate – is a composite analysis of all of these positions, how each position relates to the sources, the scientific facts, and the other approaches. The science and Halakhah must meet under one roof to create a "conversation" between these positions, with the goal of guiding our understanding of how each halakhist arrived as his respective conclusion.

In charging judges to properly perform their duties, the Talmud exhorts them to reserve judgment until clarity is reached: "If the matter is as clear to you as knowing that the sun is shining – only then offer a ruling."[11] The Talmud then quotes an alternate, but seemingly similar tradition: "If the matter is as clear to you as knowing that your sister is forbidden onto you – only then offer a ruling." The Vilna Gaon explains

---

9 J. Sacks, "Organ Donor Cards are not Incompatible with Jewish Law: There is Only a Problem When the Duties to Honour Life and to Save Life are in Conflict," *The Guardian* (January 14, 2011).
10 "Halachic Issues in the Determination of Death and in Organ Transplantation, Including an Evaluation of the Neurological 'Brain Death' Standard" (June, 2010), 1.
11 *Sanhedrin* 7b, as per Rashi.

the seeming repetition as highlighting two foci of a judge's requisite expertise. He must not only be well versed in the halakhic tradition – exemplified by the Halakhah of forbidden relationships – but also in worldly factual matters – with the shining sun serving as the parallel example.[12]

Taking the Vilna Gaon's comment to heart, properly understanding how Halakhah approaches the question of brain death requires both halakhic and medical knowledge. The goal of this book is to present and analyze the scientific facts and medical realities as well as the traditional halakhic sources and their possible ramifications for this modern issue. While the science, medicine, and social attitudes of possibly recognizing brain death as death have developed and evolved throughout the last half-century, the historical record is not a primary focus here, although historical circumstances indeed affected and shaped both scientific and halakhic positions during this time.

This discussion neither adopts nor advocates any particular halakhic stance and therefore should not be construed as a substitute for an authoritative decision from one's personal halakhic authority. Similarly, the medical information presented should not be relied on for practical purposes; all medical questions must be referred to a competent and caring physician. The goal is to guide the reader to better understand the science and Halakhah – not to arrive at practical conclusions, whether medical or halakhic.

Organization

The scientific background is the first section discussed. While not necessarily most axiologically important, a thorough understanding of the science provides the most effective means of properly applying halakhic principles. Presenting basic physiological principles as well as relating to recent research in the field should benefit both laymen and medical professionals. This also provides readers less familiar with the field with the language and terminology to engage in further meaningful research and discussion. A survey of contemporary bioethics follows the scientific

---

12 *Aderet Eliyahu, Devarim* 13:15; *Commentary to Mishlei* 6:4.

analysis, so as to place the halakhic "brain death debate" in its current social and ethical context. It is both helpful and enlightening to explore how ethicists, philosophers, physicians, and legal systems outside the halakhic tradition relate to brain death in order to better understand its impact on modern life.

The second and third sections discuss brain death from the halakhic perspective. The second section focuses on the "primary" halakhic sources, including the relevant Mishnaic and Talmudic sources, which serve as the framework and springboard for all modern halakhic discussions. This section also includes two responsa of two post-Talmudic halakhists, *Hakham Tzvi* and *Hatam Sofer*. Writing several hundred years ago, each penned a responsum dealing with determining the moment of death, one of the most crucial elements of the current discussion. Both lived too early to relate to the notion of brain death specifically, but they present and analyze the topic of determining death in broad terms, and these responsa have therefore had an enduring impact on analyses of the modern issues.

The focus in these chapters is understanding how these sources are read, analyzed, and employed in the current debate. Alongside the original texts and their classical commentaries, we present an in-depth analysis of how modern halakhists relate to each particular text and how these texts fits in to each halakhist's broader understanding.

The third section provides a comprehensive overview and thorough analysis of each of the major modern positions. The goal in each chapter is to guide the reader in understanding how each halakhist applies the scientific principles from the first section along with the halakhic traditions and precedents in the second section to arrive at their respective positions.

Because of the enormous influence and authority of R. Moshe Feinstein, his four relevant responsa are presented independently. A summary chapter attempts to put all of these pieces together and relate to the various interpretations of these responsa that have emerged since R. Feinstein's passing in 1986. The Israeli Chief Rabbinate's position is presented next, with a full translation of its official position statement and accompanying explanatory letter. Following the discussion of the Chief Rabbinate's position is a chapter dedicated to the opinion of R. Shelomoh

Zalman Auerbach, who, at least in theory, manages to bridge the gap between some of the other more extreme positions. Because it is vital to properly understanding his opinion, a careful history of his involvement in the debate is highlighted, along with a full description and analysis of the famous "decapitated sheep experiment." The last three chapters focus on what may be termed "the halakhic consensus," relating most directly to the approaches of R. J. David Bleich and R. Eliezer Yehudah Waldenberg, as well as detailing many other related positions.

In analyzing the various positions in the third section, the discussion is almost exclusively limited to written texts. Because texts are universally accessible, these are arguably one of the most objective methods of approaching a particular position. Furthermore, as forming part of the halakhic tradition, the text represents each halakhist's opinion as he wished to make it publically known. While a rich oral record accompanies much of this debate, it is included only in a very limited way. While perhaps admissible as evidence in the discussion, this book will largely eschew almost all oral testimony, especially when a written record exists. Methodologically, this book takes the written word at face value, understanding each text in its particular context and, where possible, relating it to other texts from the same halakhist. It is human nature to approach an issue with preconceived notions and biases, whether consciously aware of them or not. The various discussions therefore present multiple approaches to each text, in an attempt to arrive at the most accurate understanding.

Framing the discussion in this way leads to certain limitations, omitting the opinions of those halakhists who have not left a written record, such as R. Joseph B. Soloveitchik. The decision to exclude these articulated opinions does not reflect assumptions regarding the stature or authority of any particular halakhist and should not be taken as casting aspersions on the authenticity of relevant testimony. It is simply an imperfect method of steering the discussion toward the texts, where the goal of the book – providing an understanding of how modern halakhists arrive at their decisions – is most readily accessible. The interested reader is directed to the previously cited RCA paper for detailed and insightful analyses of these testimonies.

Introduction

The Halakhic Process

As this debate itself forms part of the ongoing halakhic process, it conforms to Halakhah's standards and methods. All positions stem from the Talmudic sources and deal exclusively with Halakhah. In doing so, the debate largely "ignores" emotional and philosophical considerations. This approach does not stem from insensitivity to the plight of donor families and organ recipients or lack of familiarity with and unwillingness to engage in broader philosophical discussion. Indeed, the ability of families to even have these discussions in these difficult times is certainly ennobling, in their desire to do what is proper. It is rather because as a matter of Halakhah, deciding whether or not a certain set of circumstances renders a person dead must be defined exclusively by halakhic constructs and halakhic criteria. The halakhic question of whether brain death qualifies as death is therefore most appropriately distanced from these emotions.

Secular organ donation advocates often urge families to "make the death of their loved one more meaningful" by enabling other sick, but potentially salvageable patients to live. While sincerely motivated, the decision of whether or not a particular patient is alive or dead must be independent of these "utilitarian" concerns. The primary principle for all halakhists is saving lives – *pikuah nefesh* – a principle so central that it overrides almost all prohibitions. But one of the exceptions to the *pikuah nefesh* mandate is the prohibition of taking a life; Halakhah forbids sacrificing one life to save another. Halakhists therefore debate how many lives are at risk in organ transplantation – one or two. Life-saving is so fundamental to Halakhah that both the donor's and the recipient's life must be considered.

Similarly, while Halakhah often refers to death as *yetziat neshamah* – the departure of the soul – metaphysical considerations are not relevant to this discussion. The definitions and criteria for determining death form part of the halakhic tradition; even while the debate as to their detailed parameters ensues, everyone agrees that the halakhic tradition binds us to these definitions and criteria, whatever they might be. While they are almost certainly relevant to the metaphysics of the soul's departure, determining death is a halakhically regulated process and perforce relies on empirical phenomena, not on philosophical or metaphysical considerations.

Hazal did not explain or leave any record about the relationship between their understanding of the *neshamah* and its ultimate departure and the halakhic definitions and criteria for death. Their approach seemingly allows for the notion of the soul departing each and every night, although this does not render a person dead,[13] at the same time that they declare a person to be dead even while his soul has not yet departed.[14] Making any assumptions as to *Hazal*'s theory of *yetziat neshamah* and attempting to reconcile and elucidate these assertions is speculative at best. Even if we could state with confidence that *Hazal* understood *yetziat neshamah* to correspond to a particular philosophical principle, Orthodox Judaism is bound by the strictures of the halakhic tradition, irrespective of their metaphysical underpinnings. The definitions and criteria that *Hazal* employed to determine death are therefore relevant, accurate, and obligatory today – even while the practical applications of these principles is perhaps more complicated than in the past.

It is in this realm that the internal mechanics of Halakhah are played out according to its own methodologies, strictures, and limits – freezing all variables and then carefully shifting each variable independently to study its effects in isolation.[15] While "real life" is far more complex than these theoretical constructs, this process (hopefully) allows for arriving at a proper and correct halakhic conclusion borne out of its own tradition. Having made that determination, practical considerations now become relevant to applying those principles properly. It is only after deriving the Halakhah on its own terms that we can begin to apply it to these "real world" scenarios by presenting new factors and concerns that test its applicability and possible limitations.

Keeping the rigors of the halakhic tradition in mind, there are two sincerely motivated misconceptions that sometimes prevent any

---

13 *Midrash Tehilim* (Buber), *mizmor* 25, no. 2.
14 Rif, *Hilkhot Tum'ah* 2b (Vilna ed.); Rosh, *Hilkhot Tum'ah*, no. 9.
15 Cf. A. Tatz, *Dangerous Disease & Dangerous Therapy in Jewish Medical Ethics* (Southfield, MI: Targum Press, 2010), 28.

discussion of organ donation – even when the donor is unambiguously dead according to all approaches. The first is concern for the prohibition of *nivul ha-meit*, desecrating a corpse. Derived from the Torah,[16] Halakhah forbids tampering with a corpse in any way.[17] Furthermore, Halakhah requires burial of each and every part of a dead body, even at great expense and inconvenience.[18] Modern communal organizations, such as Misaskim and Zaka, have taken it upon themselves to ensure fulfillment of this Halakhah, even in challenging circumstances. How, then, can we even begin to discuss actively removing part of a corpse to transplant into another human being? These are important concerns, motivated by a desire to adhere to the halakhic tradition, often in the face of countervailing social mores. Perhaps borne out of the struggle to prevent automatic autopsies despite their prevalence and permissibility in the general culture, many may find it difficult to take a step back from their (appropriately) strong initial resistance.

As a halakhic question, however, organ donation is certainly unique, as organ donation saves lives and fulfills the mandate of *pikuah nefesh*. Potential recipients are all seriously ill, with minimal life expectancy; their only hope of recovery is through receiving an organ.[19] Saving lives

---

16 *Devarim* 21:23.
17 *Shulhan Arukh*, YD 349:1.
18 Cf. J.D. Bleich, "Survey of Recent Halakhic Periodical Literature – A $25,000,000 Funeral," *Tradition* 40:3 (2007): 49-68.
19 This is also true of kidney recipients; although they can live for a significant period of time in kidney failure while receiving hemodialysis, they could live considerably longer with a transplanted kidney. Depending on the etiology of the patient's end stage renal disease, the benefit of transplantation could be as great as 7-11 additional years (R.A. Wolfe, V.B. Ashby, E.L. Milford, et al., "Comparison of mortality in all patients on dialysis, patients on dialysis awaiting transplantation, and recipients of a first cadaveric transplant," *New England Journal of Medicine* 341 (1999): 1725-30). Extending someone's life for even mere moments, qualifies as *pikuah nefesh*. This is true not only when saving a life from imminent demise, but even extending the life of someone who is otherwise expected to live for some time.

Importantly, these data are relevant to traditional hemodialysis; newer methods, such as nocturnal home hemodialysis, may actually provide comparable benefit to transplantation (R.P. Pauly, J.S. Gill, C.L. Rose, et al., "Survival among nocturnal home haemodialysis patients compared to kidney transplant recipients," *Nephrology Dialysis Transplantation* 24 (2009): 2915-9). If this is true, it would seem that if both options are

permits and often mandates setting aside almost all other prohibitions. While perhaps unsettling to family members, this includes the prohibition against desecrating the body and the charge to bury the body whole. Similarly, the requirement of burying all parts of a person is also set aside when the countervailing pressure is that of *pikuah nefesh*. While these are both certainly appropriately motivated concerns, they are practically inapplicable when it comes to life-saving organ donation.

For both fundamental and technical reasons, modern halakhists describe organ donation as a permissible mitzvah – one that is not obligatory, but certainly praiseworthy. Because this discussion will focus on understanding how Halakhah defines the moment of death, the intricacies of the halakhic aspects of organ donation are beyond its scope.

The Role of Halakhah and Halakhic Authority

Since physicians are the ones tasked with practically determining brain death and facilitating organ donation, physicians and physician groups have appropriately long dominated the discourse on the bioethics and propriety of these endeavors. Taking a step back, however, it should become clear that determining death is not solely a medical task. Physicians and medical professionals are certainly necessary to administer and interpret the tests necessary to determine death – but what is it that they are testing for? How are the criteria for what it means to be dead established? Answering the questions of what it means to be dead and when a person is no longer considered living demands a philosophical, ethical, legal, or religious response.

Medicine is limited to the empirical world. What is the patient's blood pressure? Is he breathing? What is the likelihood that a patient with a given condition will die? These are all questions of fact – some

---

available with equal benefit to some theoretical patient, one should opt for dialysis, as one method entails a prohibition and one does not. Realistically, however, each therapy entails different risks, potential side-effects, and additional benefits, which all may be relevant and vital to resolving this halakhic analysis. This decision should be made in conjunction with a competent and caring doctor and a knowledgeable halakhic authority; further discussion is beyond the scope of this book.

firmly established and others statistically predicated, but all fact. But a different set of questions goes beyond this realm. Is a particular intervention worthwhile? Is it appropriate to refrain from intervening and, in effect, to allow a patient to die? When can/should we consider a fetus to be alive? These are questions of values and ethics. While all good doctors are value-driven and ethical, debating and resolving these questions does not require medical expertise.

Yet, physicians cannot be completely discounted. They may, in fact, be more keenly aware of certain practical nuances or applications, and able to provide important data for these larger discussions. Medical professionals are also crucial to applying these value-driven principles into practice. Having arrived at philosophical, ethical, or religious principles, the question now turns to one of fact – do the current circumstances or does this specific patient meet the criteria established by those principles? To appropriately take this step, medical expertise is both necessary and vital. This question will be discussed in chapter 3 in a broader bioethical framework.

Halakhic Opinions

Halakhah applies equally to each and every person, regardless of their level of understanding and piety. This democratic element is limited, however, to the practice of Halakhah, with each person responsible and required to follow its directives. Determining Halakhah – its nature, scope, and applicability – is far less universal, devolving only upon those most versed and experienced in its depth and breadth. Even while devoid of a formal hierarchical structure, since the time of the Israelites in the desert, there has been an acute awareness that difficult question are not answerable by all. The more complex issues were passed "up the chain of command," eventually reaching Moshe if necessary, as he was universally recognized as the foremost expert. Although the parallel is clearly incomplete and we lack such leadership in modern times, we too must be aware of our limitations. There are some questions that are so complex or whose ramifications are so vast and daunting that they should be left to "the experts." Even while lacking formal credentials for halakhic expertise, there are certain scholars, who by virtue of their tremendous knowledge, experience, piety, and devotion to Halakhah, are widely recognized as eminently qualified to issue such rulings.

There are some areas of Halakhah in which even some of the most pious, knowledgeable, and renowned rabbis shy away from issuing rulings. These have traditionally included resolving the often complex status of *agunot*, married women whose husbands are missing or otherwise unwilling or unable to grant a valid divorce. Resolving such questions erroneously has repercussions for generations – potentially creating *mamzerim*, children of illicit relationships, who, along with their descendents, may not marry within the community. There are generally only a few scholars in each generation willing to accept this daunting responsibility and challenge.

This is also true regarding defining the moment of death, when what hangs in the balance is a question of potential murder. Since it cannot be overstated, killing another human being, no matter what his condition or prognosis, rips at the very heart of our moral fabric and destroys the universal social contract. It is always forbidden, no matter the context or consequence. It is an issue striking at the very heart of who we are as human beings and what it means to be alive. It is therefore most appropriately dealt with by these very same "experts." While the spirit of traditional Jewish learning invites and even encourages individual creativity and debate, questions such as these are meant for the house of study, not for practically deciding matters of life and death.

Therefore, this discussion relates to the halakhic approaches to brain death in an inclusive but realistic manner. It is not encyclopedic and does not attempt to collect any and all positions posited on the issue. Rather, it discusses the opinions of those rabbis and scholars recognized by the vast majority to be "the halakhic experts" and for whom it is both natural and expected to determine questions of life and death. While there are almost certainly other rabbis and scholars deserving of and attaining this distinction, lack of inclusion should not be taken as any slight to their honor or assumption about their status. Such an omission says far more about the author's own ignorance than the particular rabbis' stature.

The author is certainly not qualified to count himself among these experts. The purpose of this discussion rather is to explicate each of their positions, understand how it relates to the halakhic sources, and appreciate how each halakhist weaves the modern medical facts into their final tapestry of practical decision. It is through the prism of these experts' opinions that the Halakhah is crafted. The hope is to guide the reader in understanding how the halakhic sources and scientific facts lead to their conclusions.

SECTION I:

DEFINING THE MOMENT OF DEATH

CHAPTER 1:

Organ Transplantation and Brain Death

When does a person die? The answer seems almost obvious – when he is no longer alive! But when does that transition happen? At what moment does a person go from being alive to being dead?

Until relatively recently, determining the precise moment of death was largely relevant only to determining when a person could and should be buried. Traditionally, a person was deemed "dead" when he stopped breathing and his heart stopped beating (cardiopulmonary arrest). Medical developments, however, have generated a need to reevaluate this crucial measure, and answering this question precisely has become increasingly important over the past few decades.

The advent of "organ replacement therapy" in the mid-twentieth century spawned entirely new fields of bioethics, studying the determination of death, organ procurement, and organ allocation. Early on, physicians, ethicists, and lawyers alike agreed that from a moral and ethical perspective, surgeons may not procure life-sustaining organs from living patients. Harvesting life-sustaining organs by definition necessitates ending the life of the donor, and it is therefore permissible to procure such organs only from the dead. This conclusion became known as the "Dead Donor Rule" (DDR) – life-sustaining organs may only be recovered from the deceased.

From its conception and during most of its tenure, the DDR has been defended at all costs. Sacrificing an innocent life to save another is something the public, as well as the legal, moral, and ethical establishment, is unwilling to accept. Thus, as a matter of course, all transplantable life-sustaining organs – such as hearts, whole livers, and lungs – are procured only through cadaveric donation. Since donors of single kidneys, bone marrow, and liver sections can live healthy lives without these organs, they may be – and often are – preferably procured from living volunteers.

The Dead Donor Rule in Halakhah

The DDR, which was formulated from an ethical and moral perspective, accords completely with normative Halakhah.

The Talmud establishes that *pikuah nefesh*, saving a life, is of prime halakhic importance and overrides almost all halakhic requirements and prohibitions; the few exceptions are the three cardinal sins, including murder.[1] Taking a life is never sanctioned, even in the hopes of thereby saving another. The Talmud predicates this on logic – "Why do you think your blood is redder than your fellow's?" Put more poignantly, it is not our place to judge the value of a person's life, neither in terms of quantity nor quality. Every moment of life is precious and of infinite and inestimable worth, and we are not empowered to choose to save one person's life at the expense of another's.

This notion applies to all people, be they young or old, healthy or ill. Although not liable to the death penalty, Halakhah summarily forbids killing even one who is a *tereifah* (a person with a trauma or illness-induced anatomical defect with which he can survive no longer than twelve months) or a *goses* (a moribund patient).[2] The Mishnah goes so far as to prohibit even gently closing the eyes of a *goses* for fear of inducing even minor stress that could possibly shorten his life by mere moments.[3] *Masekhet Semahot* compares a *goses* to a flickering candle; even when it is about to go out on its own, it can be extinguished more quickly by a person

---

1 *Sanhedrin* 74a.
2 Ibid., 78a.
3 *Shabbat* 23:5.

laying his finger upon it, and snuffing out even short-lasting, ephemeral life is prohibited.[4] While a dissenting voice exists, R. Yehezkel Landau is emphatic that such a position is foreign to mainstream Judaism.[5]

The rabbinic consensus is thus clear in forbidding sacrificing one patient, no matter his medical status, to save another.[6] At issue here is far more than a cost-benefit analysis, in which we could argue that it is worthwhile to sacrifice a dying patient for some greater good. Such a decision is rather a judgment call on the quality of life – deciding that one person's life is inherently less valuable than another's – and that decision is a matter of Divine calculus, to which mere mortals are not privy.

Removing life-sustaining organs from living donors is therefore absolutely forbidden according to Halakhah; even *pikuah nefesh* has its limits.[7]

Organ Harvesting and Halakhah

The first part of the DDR clearly accords with the halakhic conclusion. But what of the converse aspect of the rule? May organs harvested from the dead be transplanted into other patients?

The Torah prohibits delaying burial, and Biblical law prohibits desecrating a corpse.[8] *Hatam Sofer* explains that even after the soul departs, the body in which it was previously housed retains certain aspects of

---

[4] *Semahot* 1:4.
[5] *Responsa Noda bi-Yehudah*, HM 59. This rejected notion was resurrected some years later by *Minhat Hinukh*, mitzvah 296, s.v. *ve-hineh nir'eh li* (sec. 28 in the Makhon Yerushalayim edition) regarding circumstances of indirect murder. Responding to a similar claim by Me'iri (*Sanhedrin* 72b, s.v. *yir'eh li*), R. Ovadiah Yosef (*Responsa Yabi'a Omer*, EH 4:1) is quick to note this limitation. He argues that aside from *Tiferet Yisrael* (*Yoma, Bo'az* 8:2), no authority – including *Minhat Hinukh* and Me'iri – ever permitted killing even a *tereifah* to save another person.
[6] While Halakhah does recognize certain classes of people whose murder, while prohibited, does not incur capital punishment, a thorough reckoning of these cases is beyond the scope of the current investigation.
[7] Live organ donation is another matter entirely. Discussion of the important question that it raises – whether it is forbidden, proper, incumbent, or meritorious to undertake some measure of danger in the hopes of saving another person from certain death – is beyond the scope of this book.
[8] *Devarim* 21:23, *Shulhan Arukh*, YD 349:2.

holiness.⁹ Although prohibited, however, desecrating a corpse is not one of the three cardinal sins, and is therefore permitted for the purpose of saving a life. As R. Landau explains, the prohibition is lifted when the particular action in question directly leads to potentially saving another known person. Although the medical outcome may be tentative – that is, even if the therapy will only possibly, but not certainly, be efficacious – violating this or any other non-cardinal prohibition is not only permissible, but even obligatory. This is true as long as the recipient is clearly identified.[10] As *Hatam Sofer* describes, there must be a *"holeh lefaneinu"* – a sick person in front of us who can only be saved by violating a prohibition; hypothetical patients do not meet such requirements.[11]

Thus, removing an organ from a corpse to save the life of someone awaiting such a transplant is warranted; removing that same organ and storing it for some future patient who has yet to present himself is prohibited.[12]

When it comes to *pikuah nefesh*, it is incumbent upon all those obligated in *mitzvot* to do everything in their power to save a life, even at significant expense. Death, however, relieves a person of *mitzvah* obligations;[13] a dead person has no obligation to save another person. Thus, the permissibility to remove organs clearly devolves upon the living, although using the organs from a person who is no longer obligated by Halakhah.[14]

---

9 *Responsa Hatam Sofer*, YD 336. This is the starting point of the rich halakhic literature discussing the prohibition of autopsies in Halakhah. See A. Steinberg, *Entzyklopedia Hilkhatit Refu'it* (Jerusalem: Schlesinger Institute, 5766), vol. 5, s.v. *nitu'ah ha-met*, col. 560-1.

10 *Responsa Noda bi-Yehudah*, YD 200.

11 *Responsa Hatam Sofer*, YD 336.

12 The cornea of the eye, unlike other organs, is viable for transplant for several hours after cardiac arrest, and the question of the permissibility of a corneal transplant therefore avoids the problem of precisely determining the time of death. Corneas cannot, however, necessarily be described as life-saving or life-sustaining, and the question of the permissibility of desecration of a corpse is therefore particularly relevant. Discussion of this issue can be found in R. Ovadiah Yosef, *Responsa Yabi'a Omer*, YD 3:20-23, and the many references cited therein.

13 *Shabbat* 151a.

14 In his discussion of corneal transplants (see n. 14 above), R. Ovadiah Yosef assumes that in the absence of additional mitigating factors, harvesting the cornea may be

R. Yaakov Ettlinger notes that it is permissible to seize and utilize another person's property in the course of saving a life, but only on condition that the property owner is reimbursed for his loss. When reimbursement is not possible, however – such as when the property owner is deceased – commandeering the property is forbidden, as the condition cannot be fulfilled.[15] R. Yitzchak Ya'akov Weisz largely accepts this approach and compares a person's internal organs to his property; neither may be taken when repayment is not possible. Once a person dies, reimbursement is no longer relevant, and the acquisition of his organs is therefore forbidden even in the context of *pikuah nefesh*. R. Weisz notes, however, that if a person consents to having his organ's harvested after his death, his consent is tantamount to forgiving the repayment, thereby permitting organ recovery. While the possibility of repayment is a necessary condition to seizing someone else's property, when the latter agrees to have his property taken, the condition is considered fulfilled.[16]

Both R. Shelomoh Zalman Auerbach[17] and R. Moshe Feinstein[18] assume that organ donation from the dead is certainly permissible and, although not compulsory, is likely a mitzvah. Siding with *Noda bi-Yehudah*, they argue that while it is generally prohibited to desecrate a corpse, that prohibition (as well as all others, save the three cardinal sins) is set aside in the context of *pikuah nefesh*. As long as harvested organs are intended for transplant into a currently ill patient, the practice is permitted and even encouraged. The only question is one of consent. R. Auerbach claims that since the organs are being used for *pikuah nefesh*, consent is not necessary, while R. Feinstein requires the consent of the recently deceased's family.

---

forbidden even it can be proven that the recipient's life will be saved or extended in some way. In other words, the prohibition stands even in the face of *pikuah nefesh*. Based on similar principles, R. Yosef recommends that families not consent to organ donation from their recently deceased relative (personal communication with R. Ya'akov Sasson, R. Yosef's grandson, July 26, 2011).

15 *Responsa Binyan Tziyon* 1:270.
16 *Responsa Minhat Yitzhak* 5:8.
17 *Responsa Minhat Shelomoh, Tinyana* 86:5:1.
18 *Responsa Iggerot Mosheh*, YD 2:174:4.

Despite this halakhic conclusion, there is a popular misconception that permitting removing organs for donation denies the principle of eschatological resurrection, the belief that souls will return to their complete bodies at the time of the Messianic redemption. This apprehension, however, is misplaced. The very faith in resurrection is a belief that God can give new life to dead flesh; even a few short months after burial, most corpses are no longer whole. One should not think that he can somehow limit God's ability to revive the dead by removing an organ with appropriate halakhic sanction – especially when performing a life-saving procedure. Just as God can resurrect the dead – the ultimate miracle – He can manage to do so with less than complete bodies.

The Need to Reassess the Definition of Death

Since all transplantable hearts, whole livers, and lungs are procured only from the dead, the advent of organ replacement therapy forced the discussion of the moment of death to center stage. The traditionally accepted cardiopulmonary standard presented significant challenges for organ transplantation, since once circulation stops, many organs – particularly the heart – quickly lose their potential for transplantation. Without a continuous supply of oxygenated blood, cardiac cells quickly necrose ("die" from a lack of cellular metabolism and subsequently rupture), making it unlikely for the heart to ever beat again, even if transplanted into another person. To make the heart usable in the recipient, the ischemic time (time without blood flow) must be minimized.[19] Waiting until the heart stops and only then starting the harvesting procedure will not provide for a transplantable heart.

In practice, this means that a heart is only transplantable when it is removed from a body in which blood flow continues up until the point that the surgeon actively stops the flow of blood immediately prior to excising the heart. Under bioethical principles at the time that transplantation became feasible, however, a patient in whom a heartbeat and circulation continued was considered alive – and therefore an ineligible

---

[19] The procedure established to avoid this problem is described in greater detail at the end of this chapter.

donor under the DDR. Heart transplantation demanded a "heart-beating cadaver."

It was during this time that the legal, ethical, and moral definition of death was challenged. The true impetus for this reevaluation is subject to debate. Some argue that it was a utilitarian attempt to increase the availability of transplantable organs, while others claim that it was necessary in light of the major advances in critical care medicine and the need to determine when it is appropriate, permissible, and/or advisable to pursue or discontinue medical treatments.[20] Regardless of the immediate cause, however, perspectives began shifting from the traditional cardiopulmonary standard for death to neurologically based approaches.

At this time, the newly developed mechanical ventilator, a machine able to substitute for a patient's endogenous breathing, created a new category of patients who were irreversibly neurologically devastated but still maintained certain vital vegetative functions. While irreversibly unconscious, these patients could be sustained in their current state for weeks and even months. In 1959, French neurologists Drs. Pierre Mollaret and Maurice Goulon were among the first to clinically characterize this condition, coining the descriptive term, *"coma dépassé,"* "beyond coma."[21] Other physicians as well began wondering whether, in fact, these patients could – and perhaps should – be more accurately characterized as "dead," with their remaining biological functions not truly natural, but merely artifacts of intensive technological support.

One of the most influential effects of these musings was the creation of the Ad Hoc Committee of the Harvard Medical School to Examine the Definition of Brain Death, which published its famous "A Definition of Irreversible Coma" in the *Journal of the American Medical Association*

---

20 Cf. M. Pernick, "Brain Death in Cultural Context: The Reconstruction of Death, 1967-1981," in *The Definition of Death: Contemporary Controversies*, ed. S.J. Younger and R.M. Arnold (Baltimore: Johns Hopkins University Press, 1999), 3-33; C. Machado, J. Korein, Y. Ferrer, et al., "The concept of brain death did not evolve to benefit organ transplants," *Journal of Medical Ethics* 33 (2007): 197-200.
21 "Coma dépassé et nécroses nerveuses centrales massives" (French), *Reviews in Neurology* 101 (1959): 116-39.

in 1968.[22] Without explaining precisely why it should be the case, the Committee argued for identifying the permanent loss of brain function with death. What became widely known as the "Harvard criteria" included characteristics of a permanently non-functioning brain, such as unreceptivity and unresponsiveness, no movements or breathing, and no reflexes. These criteria, together with a confirmatory flat electroencephalogram (EEG) showing no discernable electrical activity in the cerebral cortex, were considered diagnostic of death once doctors excluded any and all confounding variables and verified the results by repeating all these tests 24 hours later.

Crafting the definition with these limiting criteria was intended to effectively rule out any possibility that the loss of brain function was merely temporary and subject to possible reversal. Since certain reversible conditions, such as hypothermia and some drug intoxications, may mimic the signs and symptoms of brain death, proper diagnosis demands a rigorous search for these possibilities, ensuring that whatever has happened to the patient is actually permanent. Indeed, although the definition and criteria of brain death have been somewhat modified since the Harvard Committee's description in 1968, these limitations, for good reason, have remained intact.

Largely accepted in the medical world, the Harvard report ushered in the era of brain death-based organ donation. The results were horrendously unsuccessful at first; all heart transplant recipients died shortly after surgery, many within hours and all within days. These morbid outcomes eventually led to a professional moratorium on cardiac transplants, lifted only with the discovery and introduction of cyclosporine therapy and the implementation of immunosuppression in the late 1970's and early 1980's. The discovery that the key to survival depends upon the recipient not rejecting the transplanted organ led to increased vigilance in matching donor-recipient pairs and development of immuno-modulating agents, such as cyclosporine.

---

22 "A definition of irreversible coma: Report of the Ad Hoc Committee of the Harvard Medical School to Examine the Definition of Brain Death," *Journal of the American Medical Association* 205 (1968): 337-40.

The Current Picture

In 2011, transplants have become commonplace, occurring regularly in large medical centers. In the United States alone, there were 7,943 deceased donors in 2010, offering a total of 28,458 transplanted organs, including 2,406 hearts.[23] Rapidly advancing technologies now enable kidney, pancreas, liver, heart, lung, and intestine transplants.

These organs each react differently to warm ischemia – the cessation of blood flow that results from warmer temperatures. At issue is how long each organ can survive without any blood supply so that it can still function effectively when transplanted into a recipient. As a result, different institutions have implemented their own policies regarding whether these organs must be recovered from "heart-beating cadavers" or from the more traditional, non-heart beating cadavers.

Cardiac muscle in particular is notoriously susceptible to ischemia, especially warm ischemia. Even when removed from a "heart-beating cadaver," ischemia is present for at least some time, and various methods of cardiac cell protection are therefore employed before and during transplantation. This is frequently accomplished by infusing cold cardioplegia solution, inducing hypothermic cardiac arrest. The solution stops the heart from contracting and the cold environment slows the rate of enzymatic reactions, limiting the rate of cellular metabolism. When utilizing less energy, the cells manage to survive longer without an oxygen source, increasing their potential transplantability window.

Once removed from the donor, the heart is transported to the recipient's location. The length of the ischemic period has important ramifications for the recipient, with a recent study showing that longer ischemia times increase the risk factor for 30-day mortality after heart transplant.[24] As a result, several physicians have suggested trying to keep the heart

---

23   http://optn.transplant.hrsa.gov/latestData/rptData.asp filtering for "Donors Recovered in the U.S. by Donor Type" and "Organ" type.

24   Each additional 15 minutes between the onset of ischemia and eventual reanimation was shown to increase the odds ratio of 30-day mortality by 1.06 – 1.11. See N.R. Banner, H.L. Thomas, E. Curnow, et al. "The importance of cold and warm cardiac ischemia for survival after heart transplantation," *Transplantation* 86:4 (2008): 542-7.

"pumping" during its transport, thereby almost completely eliminating the warm ischemia time. One such novel suggestion is the "Organ Care System" (TransMedics, Inc.), an experimental chamber in which the explanted heart is connected to "mobile lungs" that provide it with oxygenated blood and allow the heart to continue beating until the recipient's surgical team is ready to implant it.[25]

In the United States, all organ transplants are coordinated through the United Network for Organ Sharing (UNOS), under contract from the federal Organ Procurement and Transplantation Network (OPTN), with the practical aspects managed by 58 regional organ procurement organizations (OPO). Transplant surgeries are performed at 249 centers throughout the country. Patients suffering from diseases that indicate potential benefit from an organ transplant are referred to a transplant center for a thorough evaluation, and upon acceptance, the patient's profile is added to the national database. When a donor is identified, the regional OPO compiles a list of patients in the UNOS database in the donor's vicinity who match the donor's characteristics. Following algorithms established by the OPTN, a computer generated rank list is created and potential recipients are then contacted according to rank to assess their immediate suitability for transplant.[26]

As we have seen in this chapter, modern advances in organ replacement therapy have opened entirely new vistas of medical potential, with the halakhic guidelines theoretically endorsing the endeavor. Practically, however, organ transplants are nearly impossible without relying on brain death as the determination of death. The halakhic ramifications of this point are far less clear and are what this book intends to explore. In order to do so, we must first understand what brain death actually means from a medical perspective.

---

25 The proposal is currently in clinical trials (the PROCEED trial).
26 UNOS maintains a highly informative website (www.UNOS.org), describing its mission, its many policies and policy development protocols, and a wealth of transplantation data. Interested readers are encouraged to read more about UNOS policies and procedures at their website, particularly regarding the system of organ allocation, which will not be addressed here.

CHAPTER 2:

The Science of Brain Death

A basic understanding of the science and physiology of respiration and circulation is vital to understanding the concept of "brain death." The President's Council on Bioethics' 2008 "White Paper," *Controversies in the Determination of Death*, provides a basic yet impressively thorough scientific overview, and much of it is borrowed for the discussion below.

While respiration and circulation are two distinct physiological systems, they are interrelated and interdependent. For breathing to have any physiological meaning, the heart must be circulating blood throughout the body; for circulation to be effective, it must be supported by the oxygen derived from continuous respiration. Analyzing each system independently will clarify how they work in tandem and how the deterioration of one affects the other.

Respiration

A normal healthy person takes approximately twelve to twenty breaths each minute. Respiration begins with the muscular contraction of the diaphragm (a flat to bell shaped muscle separating the lungs from the abdominal cavity), as well as other secondary muscles of respiration, expanding the chest cavity and causing the body to inhale air from the surrounding environment. Air enters the mouth and nose, travelling down the trachea toward and into the lungs by dispersing through the branched respiratory tree, beginning with the large-diameter bronchi and eventually ending at the single-cell alveoli. The alveoli are thin, small spheres surrounded by blood vessels, enabling the diffusion and exchange of gases across their membranes to and from the blood.

Inhalation brings oxygen-rich air to these alveoli, where oxygen diffuses into the blood. In exchange, carbon dioxide, a byproduct of cellular metabolism, diffuses out of the blood into the alveoli. Exhalation entails moving the now carbon dioxide-rich air from the alveoli out to the environment. It is accomplished through the relaxation of the diaphragm and associated muscles, which shrink the chest cavity and force air out through the mouth and nose.

Both components of respiration are critical; all cells need oxygen to effectively produce energy, and all cells must rid themselves of carbon dioxide, which can be toxic when accumulated.

Circulation

The circulatory system is tasked with supplying oxygen-rich blood to the body's tissues (perfusion). To this end, the heart maintains two separate circulatory circuits. The first – the pulmonary circuit – interacts with the lungs to facilitate gas exchange; the second – the systemic circuit – distributes blood to the rest of the body.

Depleted of much of its oxygen and carrying carbon dioxide and other cellular metabolic waste products, blood travels through the veins and arrives at the right side of the heart. From there, the heart pumps the blood through the branching pulmonary vasculature, eventually flowing through pulmonary capillaries (tiny blood vessels with single cell membranes) surrounding the lungs' alveoli, where gas exchange occurs. The blood releases its carbon dioxide into the alveolar spaces and absorbs oxygen from the inhaled air. The newly oxygenated blood then travels to the left side of the heart, from which it is forcefully pumped to the rest of the body.

Neurological Control

Both respiration and circulation are tightly controlled by the brain, albeit very differently.

The brain controls breathing by "sensing" the concentration of carbon dioxide in the blood. When the concentration reaches a critical level, the respiratory center of the brain – the medulla of the brainstem (so named after its anatomical location) – sends a signal through the phrenic nerve that causes the muscles of respiration to contract and begin the process of replenishing the body with oxygen.

The control of respiration is involuntary, promoting breathing even during periods of sleep and unconsciousness and automatically responding to an increased demand for oxygen, such as during vigorous exercise. Other parts of the brain can also influence respiration in what is known as conscious breathing, through which a person can deliberately control the pace and depth of each breath, taking voluntary control over the respiratory muscles.

In stark contrast to respiratory control, the heart does not require any neurological input to initiate a beat. Without any external stimulation at all, the heart beats on its own through an inherent rhythmic flow of "electric currents" (the flow of charged molecules), displaying a property known as automaticity. Although the brain cannot initiate a beat – and is not necessary to do so – it can influence the **rate** of the heartbeat, slowing it down by stimulating the vagus nerve or speeding it up by stimulating certain sympathetic nerves (part of the autonomic nervous system). Similarly, hormones secreted as part of the "flight or fight response" can also affect the heart rate, increasing it when the demand for oxygenated blood is great. The endocrine (hormonal) control is substantially slower, however, than the neurological component.

The unique property of automaticity is readily demonstrated. Hearts removed from animals can be stimulated to begin to beat rhythmically when merely placed in an appropriate environment, without any neurological stimulus whatsoever (an observation taken full advantage of by the "Organ Care System," as described in chapter 1). In embryos, the heart is one of the first organs to form, starting to beat well before the nervous system has developed. Finally, a heart transplanted into a recipient works completely normally (hopefully) – beating and circulating blood throughout the body despite the fact that there is no connection whatsoever between the recipient's neurological system and his newly transplanted heart. As a result, when a cardiac transplant recipient begins running or doing some other exercise, his heart rate does not increase until the endocrine response kicks in, stimulating the heart muscle to contract more quickly and vigorously.

Because of the different role that the brain plays in respiration and heart function, a person whose brain is not properly functioning will sometimes not be able to breathe on his own, but may still maintain a heartbeat so long as gas exchange continues. While such a situation was purely hypothetical not very long ago, the advent of the mechanical ventilator has made it quite plausible and not uncommon.

The Role of the Ventilator

A mechanical ventilator helps a patient who is having difficulty breathing or cannot breathe on his own. The ventilator is attached to a tube placed in the patient's trachea and surrounded by an inflated cuff to create a closed system. Modern ventilators have many possible settings, controlling for volume and pressure, and can either assist a patient's native breathing or completely substitute for it. The ventilator supplies oxygenated air to the lungs, allowing gas exchange to take place on its own.

While mechanical ventilators cannot cure any disease directly, they are often used to temporarily assist a patient suffering from a respiratory condition so that he may recover and eventually no longer require ventilator support. Sometimes, recovery is impossible; ventilation can then indefinitely help support or substitute for the patient's own breathing. Patients of this type often suffer from a disease or lesion along the brain-lung axis, somewhere between the respiratory center in the brainstem and the diaphragm. Included in this group are patients with dysfunctional brainstems, as well as spinal cord trauma victims whose phrenic nerves have been injured.

Importantly, the ventilator does not and cannot directly affect the heartbeat. Since the heart does not rely on the brain for its continued function, it continues beating as long as sufficient gas exchange occurs, regardless of the reason that the patient can no longer breathe on his own or how oxygenated air reaches his lungs. Without a heartbeat, however, any form of ventilation – natural or mechanical – is meaningless, as gas exchange depends on effective blood flow.

The only situation in which respiration continues without a heartbeat is during the cardiopulmonary bypass portion of heart surgery. During certain cardiac surgical procedures, in addition to sedation, the patient is also paralyzed in order to absolutely prevent even reflexive movements. Under such conditions, the patient's brainstem continues to send signals to the diaphragm to contract, but it cannot do so, necessitating mechanical ventilation. Additionally, the heart must also often be stopped in order to allow for precise surgical technique.

To allow for the continued perfusion of oxygenated blood to the body's organs during cardiac surgery, the patient is therefore connected to a "heart-lung machine," which, as its name suggests, substitutes for both the patient's heart and lungs. Collecting blood from the right atrium just as it enters the heart and returning it directly to the aorta (the artery that exits the heart), the heart-lung machine bypasses the heart entirely.

The heart-lung machine is substantially different from a ventilator, and the distinction between the two is critical in order to properly interpret and apply halakhic rulings. A ventilator does not regulate the heartbeat at all, but rather allows for intrinsic cardiac function to continue. A heart-lung machine, in contrast, substitutes completely for the function of the heart, since while connected to the bypass machine the patient's heart does not beat at all.

When connected to a heart-lung machine, a patient's circulation can certainly be described as artificially maintained. The status of circulation when connected to a ventilator however, is more difficult to describe. The source of the oxygen reaching the lungs is irrelevant to the heart's continued beating; as long as gas exchange occurs, whether as a result of spontaneous respiration or mechanical ventilation, oxygenated blood is pumped through the body. From a respiratory perspective, however, the source of constant oxygen necessary for the heart's continued functioning is completely artificial. How, then, should the continued heartbeat of a ventilated patient be described — as natural and intrinsic (as the heart beats on its own) or as artificially maintained (since the oxygen is artificially supplied)? This and similar questions form the core of analyzing what brain death means in terms of both bioethics and Halakhah.

Terminology

Before discussing the diagnosis and criteria of brain death, it is important to clarify the very use of the term. The notion of brain death is rather misleading, as it seemingly implies that there is more than one kind of death. This usage is frequently further obfuscated by the media, often reporting the time of brain death followed by the time that the patient "finally" died. Additionally, the term seems to equate the "death" of a particular organ with the death of an individual. Cells die all the time, but because many tissues are able to regenerate themselves, we assign little meaning to these events. The concept of brain death assumes that the "death" of the brain is far more significant, possibly even indicating the death of the individual.

The President's Council on Bioethics report further elaborates on the problematic term:

> Death itself is not a diagnosis; that is, the phenomenon of death and the selection of the appropriate standard for determining it are **not strictly medical or technical matters** [emphasis added]. Thus, any term chosen as a label for a medical diagnosis should not contain the word "death." It is not death that is diagnosed, but rather a clinical state or condition made evident by certain ascertainable signs. Calling the condition of the patient who meets a set of diagnostic tests "brain death" begs the question of whether this condition does or does not warrant a determination that the patient has died. What is needed is a separate, non-prejudicial name for the condition that describes the state of the patient: a name that does not, by its use, commit one to any judgment about whether the death of the human being has occurred.[1]

Responding to these challenges, various authors have suggested different terms to describe the same phenomenon. As noted in chapter 1, one of the first descriptions used was *coma dépassé* (beyond coma), with

---

1 President's Council on Bioethics, *Controversies in the Determination of Death* (2008): 18.

the Harvard Committee preferring "irreversible coma." Others have suggested more technically descriptive terms, such as "irreversible apneic [inability to breathe] coma" or "brain arrest."[2] Since each description assigns differing importance to various elements of the diagnosis, the President's Council prefers the term "total brain failure." As descriptions predicated upon definitions of death, the various choices reflect different value judgments as to what it means to be dead. We will discuss this at greater length in the next chapter.

Despite the reservations regarding its use, the more ambiguous term "brain death" is more familiar and prevalent in both the lay and scientific literature. Thus, throughout this book, we refer to the state as "brain death" – the quotation marks a constant reminder of the ambiguity and imprecision of the term.[3]

It is also important to emphasize that "brain death" differs from two ostensibly similar but fundamentally different conditions: the persistent vegetative state (PVS) and the minimally conscious state (MCS). While many patients with these diagnoses may lie in intensive care units and be mechanically ventilated, both PVS and MCS patients are capable of spontaneous respiration, as well as other basic vegetative functions. Even when requiring respiratory assistance, all PVS and MCS patients are able to initiate a breath on their own, whereas "brain dead" patients cannot. (MCS patients differ from PVS patients in retaining some inconsistent ability for meaningful voluntary communicative motion, being able to react minimally to stimuli.) The discussion of organ donation refers exclusively to "brain dead" patients, not persistently vegetative or minimally conscious patients.

---

2 Ibid., 19.
3 For others' uses of the term, see D.A. Shewmon, "The brain and somatic integration: Insights into the standard biological rationale for equating "brain death" with death," *Journal of Medicine and Philosophy* 26 (2001), n.1; R.M. Veatch, "The impending collapse of the whole-brain definition of death," in *Transplantation Ethics* (Washington DC: Georgetown University Press, 2000), 103.

Diagnosing "Brain Death"

Protocols for diagnosing "brain death" are hospital specific in the United States, but all contain certain core elements.[4] The following are the basic principles of diagnosis, which are similar to those established by the original Harvard Committee (see chapter 1) and almost universally accepted:[5]

1. The patient is verified to be in a completely unresponsive coma.
2. The patient has a documented history of injury that does not suggest a potentially transient cause of symptoms, such as hypothermia or drug intoxication.
3. The patient demonstrates no brainstem reflexes.
4. The patient shows no drive to breathe during the apnea test.

A patient must meet each and every one of these criteria, as each represents a significant factor in the final determination. The first element requires that the patient exhibit no signs of consciousness, completely lacking communicative ability and not responding to any verbal or painful stimuli. The second requirement demands that the diagnosis be irreversible. As noted in chapter 1, various metabolic derangements, such as hypothermia or poisoning, can mimic the effects of "brain death," but they are often only transient; the "brain death" mimicking effects often subside with the reversal of the metabolic condition. It is therefore imperative to carefully comb through the patient's history for any potentially reversible etiologies, so as to preclude diagnosing as "brain dead" a patient who may possibly recover.

Having satisfied the first two requirements, the latter two prescribe clinical and laboratory tests that assess particular elements of the

---

[4] In New York State, the Task Force on Life and Law issues guidelines for determining "brain death" to be used throughout the state. These were last published in 2005 and are currently undergoing additional revisions. The Task Force's recommendations parallel the discussion below.

[5] These criteria are largely borrowed from the President's Council's Report; *Controversies*, 30.

diagnosis, in particular evaluating the functioning of the brainstem. The lack of brainstem function is a necessary component of the larger "brain death" diagnosis. Proof of its non-function is meant to indicate the scale of the brain damage – having not just devastated the cerebral hemispheres, but even extending farther toward more distant structures.

In addition to its role in controlling respiration, the brainstem also maintains wakefulness cycles and controls certain reflexes, including the gag reflex, the cough reflex, the vestibulocular reflex, and the oculocephalic reflex. The first two describe throat reactions to various stimuli, while the third and fourth cause the eyes to move under particular conditions – when cold water is injected into the ear canal in the former and when turning the head to one side in the latter (the "doll's eyes" phenomenon). If the patient evidences any of these reflexes, his brainstem is clearly functional.

The final condition tests the patient's drive to breathe (apnea is the technical term for the inability to breathe, and a patient with such a condition is described as apneic). While all ventilated patients clearly need at least some respiratory support, the apnea test establishes that the patient has absolutely no drive to inhale even when the body unambiguously signals for it to do so. The fact that the patient cannot breathe spontaneously and does not exhibit brainstem reflexes indicates that his brainstem is non-functional.

Because the technique of the apnea test may have halakhic ramifications, it is important to describe it in detail. The ventilator is disconnected for a period of 2-5 minutes, and the level of carbon dioxide in the blood is permitted to increase well beyond the point that would normally trigger inhalation. The carbon dioxide concentration in the arterial blood is measured both before and after the test to determine if the patient managed to perform any respiration on his own. During the test, clinicians also watch the patient for any signs of chest movement, which, if present, would indicate that the brainstem retains at least some viability, as it has triggered an attempt at inhalation.

In order to prevent damage caused by low levels of oxygen during the test, the patient is "prepared" beforehand by receiving elevated levels of oxygen (usually 100%) for some time, thereby completely saturating the system with oxygenated blood. Since it is the rising level of carbon dioxide, not oxygen loss, that stimulates the brainstem to initiate inhalation, pre-oxygenation protects oxygen levels while not affecting the test results.

While the ventilator is disconnected, the endotracheal tube to which it is normally attached remains in the patient's throat. As a result, reconnecting the ventilator after the five minutes have passed and a second sampling of blood is obtained is a rather simple process. Furthermore, while disconnected, oxygen continues to flow passed the open end of the tube, so that should the patient take a breath, it will be high in oxygen. Leaving the endotracheal tube in place does pose one limitation, as the diameter through which air can flow is smaller than the patient's natural throat diameter, requiring an increased effort to produce a breath than had the tube been completely removed. However, the difference in breathing ability that results is small and of unclear physiological significance, leading to it being summarily disregarded by almost all clinicians.[6]

In almost all facilities and jurisdictions, both the reflex and apnea tests must be repeated after some time interval, ranging between two and twenty-four hours. Similar results at the later time are considered proof that the patient's current state is irreversible. The American Academy of Neurology, in surveying the literature and making policy recommendations, recommends a six-hour interval, although it readily admits this to be an arbitrary time point.[7] Studies examining the sensitivity of different waiting periods are highly impractical and seriously lacking. Thus, although there is a general framework for diagnosing "brain death," institutional variability is widespread, with little oversight or impetus to establish uniform protocols.[8]

---

6 For an additional perspective of the technical issue, see Y. Neuwirth, A. Nebenzahl, M. Halperin, "Timers in Ventilators – Responsa" (Hebrew), *Assia* 81-82 (2008): 99-104.
7 American Academy of Neurology, Quality Standards Subcommittee, "Practice parameters for determining brain death in adults (summary statement)," *Neurology* 45 (1995): 1014.
8 D.M. Greer, V.N. Panayiotis, E.F.M. Wijdicks, "Variability of brain death determination guidelines in leading US neurological institutions," *Neurology* 70 (2008): 284-9; D.J. Powner, M. Hernandez, T.E. Rives, "Variability among hospital policies for determining brain death in adults," *Critical Care Medicine* 32 (2004): 1284-8.

Some recent studies have questioned whether the second exam is necessary at all. In one large study, none of the patients found to be "brain dead" during the first exam were found to regain function upon reexamination.[9] The New York Task Force on Life and the Law is considering eliminating the need for the second exam, but it has not yet released its final report.

"Brain Death" – Diagnosis or Prognosis

In an article published in *Neurology*, Dr. D.A. Shewmon calls the validity of these tests into question. He notes that "brain death" is often thought to "inexorably and imminently deteriorate to cardiovascular collapse despite the most aggressive therapy and resuscitative efforts," with descriptions of survival from "no longer than several days," to "as long as 10 days," to the increasingly vague "within a relatively short time."[10] A more thorough analysis, however, reveals rather remarkable data. In a survey of 56 patients who continued to be ventilated even after being diagnosed as "brain dead," half survived for more than a month, nearly a third survived for more than two months, 13% survived more than six months, and 7% for more than a whole year. While it is true that "brain dead" patients with prolonged survivals comprise only a small proportion of all "brain dead" patients, "the small proportion of prolonged survivals … in no way diminish[es] … their conceptual importance." Additionally, "many more *potential* cases have never been manifest because brain death is nearly always a self-fulfilling prophecy of somatic demise through organ harvesting or discontinuation of support." In other words, many more "brain dead" patients may have the ability to survive for longer periods, but we have no way of knowing because their organs are harvested before they are given a chance. While a significant percentage of "brain dead"

---

9 D. Lustbader, D. O'Hara, E.F.M. Wijdicks, et al., "Second brain death examination may negatively affect organ donation," *Neurology* 76 (2011): 119-24. Others have questioned the methods and inherent limitations of this study; see A.R. Joffe, M.Y. Rady, J.L. Verheijde, "Letter to the editor," *Neurology* 77 (2011): 1314-5; D.J. Gelb, "Letter to the editor," ibid.
10 D.A. Shewmon, "Chronic 'brain death' – Meta-analysis and conceptual consequences," *Neurology* 51 (1998): 1538.

patients certainly do quickly succumb to cardiovascular collapse, they are often unsuitable organ donors. It is precisely "the best donor candidates [who] have the most intact organs and therefore also the greatest survival potential."[11]

Thus, it is important to avoid conflating a prognosis of eventual death with the diagnosis of present death. For "brain death" to qualify as the death of the individual, it must satisfy the criteria that define death presently, not merely prognosticate a future event. The data gleaned from medical tests should therefore be used cautiously in attempting to understand the nature of the limited functionality of a "brain dead" patient and what these remaining functions indicate about a presumptive declaration of death – but not necessarily much more.

Children and Infants

It is important to note a serious practical limitation of this entire discussion. The clinical presentations of "brain death," as well as the pathophysiological mechanisms involved, differ in children and adults. A child's brain is far more resilient and able to adapt and recover from

---

11 Ibid., 1542. In subsequent letters to the editor, a number of respondents challenged Dr. Shewmon's data on several grounds, mostly related to the appropriate allocation of resources (A. Lopez-Navidad, "Letter to the editor," *Neurology* 53 (1999): 1369; C. Crisci, "Letter to the editor," ibid.: 1370). Drs. Wijdicks and Bernat ("Letter to the editor," ibid.: 1369) question the accuracy of Shewmon's data, expressing skepticism "about whether all the reported cases represent valid B[rain] D[eath] determinations." They note that in his survey of the medical literature, Shewmon did not provide details of the measurements of each apnea test, nor provide consistent "documentation of the details of neurological examination."

Responding to these charges, Dr. Shewmon ("Reply from the author," ibid.: 1371-2) notes that the diagnoses of nearly all patients "were confirmed by at least one neurologist or neurosurgeon." He argues that "if a neurologist tells me (or tells a reporter) that a patient fulfilled standard diagnostic criteria for B[rain] D[eath], I have no a priori reason to doubt it. To accept [this conclusion] if the patient was an organ donor or had support terminated, but to reject it if somatic survival lasted longer than a week, represents a question-begging double standard." Limiting the discussion to physiological facts and leaving aside the possible moral and ethical questions involved, Dr. Shewmon's data appears to be solid, and is therefore presented here as fact.

injuries that would irreversibly devastate an adult brain. In light of these differences, many have advocated for stricter "brain death" criteria and testing in children, including additional imaging and an increased time interval between the tests. Actual practice varies from institution to institution, however, and because of the difficulty in accurately making this diagnosis, throughout this book, we will refer exclusively to adults (even when not stated explicitly). While the differing diagnostic requirements may indeed have important halakhic ramifications, a more thorough scientific and medical study is necessary, and this is beyond the scope of the current endeavor.

Additional Testing

Some authors and protocols advocate for additional testing to confirm the irreversibility of the diagnosis by more precisely identifying the brain damage incurred, particularly that of the brainstem. Since the standard criteria for "brain death" define death in many legal jurisdictions, the diagnosis must be both sensitive and specific, and further testing provides confirmatory support to the diagnosis.[12]

The original Harvard Committee recommended EEG testing to confirm the lack of any cerebral electrical activity, which may not be apparent upon clinical exam. This criterion has somewhat fallen out of favor today for both fundamental and technical reasons. An EEG only assesses the very outer cortex of the brain, leaving the deeper elements unexplored. Even in the realm of the outer cortex however, the test often provides confounding results because of excess "background noise;" this "noise" is sometimes proof of scattered cellular activity, but it can also be caused by the various noises and machines in the patient's vicinity. More accurate and updated tests of electrical activity include tests for evoked potentials (an electric response of the nervous system to a stimulus). Neurological electrical activity is measured through somatosensory evoked potentials

---

12 From a statistical perspective, sensitivity measures the percentage of people who are actually "brain dead" who are accurately diagnosed by these standards; specificity measures the percentage of non-"brain dead" patients who are correctly identified as such.

(stimulating the median nerve in the forearm) or by brainstem evoked potentials (BAER, an auditory test).

Some advocate for more specific testing aimed as assessing **structural** damage by examining intracranial blood flow. Non-perfused brain cells (cells that are cut off from blood supply) "die" very quickly. Thus, angiography based exams measuring arterial blood flow – such as classic angiography, CT (computed tomography) scans, MRI (magnetic resonance imaging) scans with angiography, and transcranial doppler studies – are often used to confirm the lack of blood flow and clinch the diagnosis.

As a result of the Israeli Chief Rabbinate's insistence on additional, non-physician based assessment of the irreversibility of the brainstem's dysfunction (discussed in detail in chapter 15), current Israeli law requires one of these tests.[13] In the United States, however, standard practice "dictates that these tests should be optional, to be used by the clinician in difficult cases."[14] These additional tests attempt to verify the destruction of brain tissue as evidence for the irreversible nature of the current condition. But because they are unnecessary to legally declare death, they are used in practice only in cases in which the diagnosis of "brain death" is questionable for some reason. The specifics of actual practice differ throughout the country, as noted earlier.

The American Academy of Neurology actually finds no basis to support performing these exams, and in fact argues against their routine use, as a significant portion of patients (studies ranging from 30% to 56%) exhibit cerebral blood flow even when clinically diagnosed as "brain dead." Blood flow is thus non-indicative of the clinically diagnosed state.[15]

---

13 "Brain and Respiratory Death Law – 2008."
14 *Controversies*, 34; E.F.M. Wijdicks, P.N. Varelas, G.S. Gronseth, et al. "Evidence-based guideline update: Determining brain death in adults – Report of the Quality Standards Subcommittee of the American Academy of Neurology," *Neurology* 74 (2010): 1911-8.
15 E.F.M. Wijdicks, "The case against confirmatory tests for determining brain death in adults," *Neurology* 75 (2010): 77-83.

The Danger of Misdiagnosis

It is important to note that the diagnosis of "brain death" itself, even with these additional tests, is not completely failsafe. The highly publicized 2008 case of Zack Dunlap, a 21 year old man from Oklahoma, brought this issue to the center of media attention. Mr. Dunlap was the victim of a terrible accident who was declared "brain dead" 36 hours later. The diagnosis was reportedly confirmed twice by PET scan (positon emission tomography, providing a three-dimensional image often used in ascertaining function). Mr. Dunlap's parents report that physicians told them that these scans showed "no blood flow at all" in the brain. Since Mr. Dunlap indicated on his driver's license that he wished to be an organ donor, UNOS was contacted, and the standard procedure for organ transplantation was initiated. While awaiting surgery, however, a relative who came to say goodbye pressed his fingernail under Mr. Dunlap's, causing Mr. Dunlap to retract his arm in pain – clear evidence that he was certainly not "brain dead." After cancelling the organ harvest, Mr. Dunlap was treated more aggressively and underwent months of rehabilitation and physical therapy; he later appeared on NBC's "Today Show" to talk about his story.[16]

Since Mr. Dunlap's medical records were not made public, it is hard to know what really happened from a medical perspective, and any suggestions are therefore merely speculative. If the story he and his family tell indeed presents an accurate description of what occurred, it should shock the entire medical establishment into rethinking the ethical criteria of the last 50 years. It would appear that a "brain dead" patient can come back to life!

But even if Mr. Dunlap was originally misdiagnosed as "brain dead" as a result of physician error or inaccurate testing, the ramifications are no less shocking. This would mean that Mr. Dunlap was never actually "brain dead," even though some physicians thought he was. The diagnosis of "brain death" in his case may have been a product of poor technique, but it leads one to wonder how often similar mistakes occur and are not detected. Perhaps such errors are actually frequent occurrences,

---

16 http://today.msnbc.msn.com/id/23775873/

which are underreported because a diagnosis of "brain death" is a self-fulfilling prophecy, leading to the rapid withdrawal of treatment and/or organ donation. Accordingly, while an accurate diagnosis of "brain death" most certainly reflects an irreversible condition and this case is irrelevant to the fundamental underpinnings of determining death,[17] Mr. Dunlap's story should raise serious practical concerns as to the broader reliability of the organ donation enterprise.

More recently, a group of neurologists from Emory University School of Medicine reported about one of their patients, who had experienced a heart attack and was diagnosed as "brain dead" as per the American Academy of Neurology guidelines. The exam was repeated again six hours later by separate board certified neurologists, followed by a 10-minute apnea test, and the patient was pronounced dead. After obtaining family consent and finding an appropriate donor, the patient was taken to the operating room for organ harvest 20 hours after being pronounced dead. Upon arrival, the anesthesiologist noted that the patient was coughing and able to breathe on his own. The patient was immediately rushed back to the intensive care unit, much to the surprise of the medical team that had recently bid him a final farewell. The patient regained a cough reflex, bilateral corneal reflexes, and spontaneous respirations – all of which were absent during both "brain death" exams less than one day earlier. The patient's neurological prognosis was still rather poor, however, and he was once again diagnosed as "brain dead" approximately two days later. Given the circumstances, the medical team did not approach the family again about organ donation, and together decided to terminate all therapies, after which death was finally declared by cardiopulmonary criteria.[18]

While certainly alarming, the authors note that there may be several confounding variables in this case that may have led to the fact that the patient only **appeared** initially as "brain dead" and that masked the continued signs of neurological function. Because of initial high hopes for neurological recovery, therapeutic hypothermia was attempted for neural protection after the patient's initial cardiac arrest and low dose sedatives

---

17 "Evidence-based guideline update," 1912.
18 A.C. Webb, O.B. Samuels, "Reversible brain death after cardiopulmonary arrest and induced hypothermia," *Critical Care Medicine* 39 (2011): 1538-42.

were administered. However, because of the particular timing of each of these interventions, neither is likely in and of itself to have led to a misdiagnosis of "brain death;" "brain death" was only declared 72 hours after the patient's body returned to normal temperature, and lack of brainstem reflexes was noted many hours after the sedatives had worn off.[19] It remains unclear whether the combined effects of the various therapies, the patient's initial cardiac event, or some other coincidental factors had any influence on the transient return of limited brainstem function.[20]

Whether this represents a case of a complicated misdiagnosis or fundamentally questions the irreversible nature of a "brain death" diagnosis, this case should certainly add to the uncertainty spurned by Zack Dunlap's story. The authors lament that "this sequence of events undermined the credibility of the medical team by raising serious doubts in the minds of the patient's family about the ability to establish when life has permanently ended"[21] – as it indeed should.

Pathophysiology of "Brain Death"

To properly analyze the various approaches to what "brain death" should mean, it is important to understand the nature of the destruction of the brain that occurs in "brain death." Many arguments for and against recognizing "brain death" as the death of the individual rest upon the different descriptions of the actual state of the brain and its components during this state. To avoid an overly technical discussion, the President's

---

19 S. Streat, "'Reversible brain death' – Is it true, confounded, or 'not proven'?" *Critical Care Medicine* 39 (2011): 1601-3.
20 Several letters to the editor challenged these data on various grounds, arguing that there must have been some confounding variables that were unaccounted for, although not indicating what those variable might have been (E.F.M. Wijdicks, P.N. Varelas, G.S. Gronseth, et al., "Letter to the editor," *Critical Care Medicine* 39 (2011): 2204-5) or that misdiagnosis would have been avoided by increasing the waiting period between exams (C.J.G. Lang, "Letter to the editor," ibid.: 2205-6). In response, the authors note that they took all standard precautions for excluding confounding variables. They also argue that since increasing the observation time between "brain death" exams has never been shown to affect diagnosis (see note 9 above), there was no reason to implement such a policy in this case (A. Webb, O.B. Samuels, "The authors reply," ibid.: 2206).
21 Webb, "Reversible brain death," 1540.

Council report,[22] a well-written description for the non-pathologist, will once again serve as a guide.

While the diagnosis of "brain death" describes the brain's irreversible loss of functional capacity, this is often not the result of the initial injury to the brain, but rather brought about through a self-perpetuating cascade of events. The cycle often begins with a brain injury that causes severe damage to the cells of the brain, which leads to edema, the abnormal accumulation of fluid within the brain. With the rigid skull providing little or no space in which to expand, the swelling brain suffers a steady increase in intracranial pressure (ICP). The elevated ICP makes it more difficult for blood to flow to the brain, further depriving the brain tissue of oxygen and other nutrients. This, in turn, leads to additional damage, which leads to more edema and more swelling. Eventually, the ICP increases to such a degree (more than the systolic blood pressure) that it prevents blood from flowing into the brain at all. When death is declared by neurological criteria, this self-perpetuating cascade should have run its full course – blood should no longer be reaching the brain, at least in theory.

Importantly, and certainly not intuitively, in many patients, certain areas of the brain remain intact and quite viable despite this diagnosis. Somehow, oxygenated blood is still reaching these brain structures in spite of the extensive damage.[23] These may be random, isolated cells, incapable of coordinated function, or even more cohesive segments that are still capable of physiological function. The most notable of the latter is the hypothalamus, the part of the brain responsible for thermoregulation (the control of body temperature) and blood pressure maintenance. Even after "brain death," some patients continue to maintain body temperature within reasonable physiological limits, exhibiting the ability of the brain to both sense body temperature and to integrate that

---

22 *Controversies*, 35-38.
23 Dr. D.A. Shewmon explains that "islands" of cells may remain viable due to "inhomogeneities of intracranial pressure and/or blood supply from extracranial collateral vessels" (quoted ibid., 36).

information into practical physiological consequences.[24] Similarly, the secretion of the hormone ADH (anti-diuretic hormone, also known as arginine vasopressin) from the posterior pituitary gland is evidence of hypothalamic function; the brain senses blood volume and integrates that information to react appropriately, preventing the condition of diabetes insipidus (the inability to excrete water from the kidneys).[25]

Pathological features of brains from "brain dead" patients appear throughout the brain, although lacking sufficient distinctive characteristics to qualify as a unique pathological diagnosis of "brain death." Autopsy studies on such brains are rare, with the landmark Collaborative Study of Cerebral Death in 1975 describing "pericellular edema, necrosis, neuronal loss and infarction" in the cerebral cortex of brains from "brain dead" patients.[26] These characteristics and descriptions formed what was then called "respirator brain," referring to dusky, congested, discolored brain tissue, containing liquid portions and often brain fragments when removed from the skull, but even then preserving various brain areas.[27]

Today, however, the pathological picture is far different, likely due to the much reduced time between declaration of "brain death" and organ procurement or withdrawal of therapy. A recent study of brains from patients clinically diagnosed as "brain dead" revealed far less macroscopic (visible to the naked eye) damage and diffuse, inconsistently located microscopic cell damage at varying degrees of severity. The brain lobes showed microscopic moderate to severe ischemic change (caused by lack of blood perfusion) in 68% of cases, with moderate to severe neuronal

---

24 "Brain dead" patients often have body temperature less than the normal 37C, but this lower temperature is continuously maintained. This means that, for some reason, the "set point" for appropriate body temperature is reset to a lower level, and the body actively maintains that temperature in the face of changing conditions. It is the ability for maintaining homeostasis that is the current focus, not the "set point" around which homeostatic mechanisms respond.
25 *Controversies*, 37-38.
26 A. Walker, E. Diamond, J. Moseley, "The neuropathological findings in irreversible coma," *Journal of Neuropathology and Experimental Neurology* 34 (1975): 295-323.
27 M.K. Herrick, D.F. Agamanolis, "Displacement of the cerebellar tissue into spinal canal. A component of the respirator brain syndrome," *Archives of Pathology* 99 (1975): 565-71.

ischemic change of the thalamus in 34%, and of the various brainstem structures in around 40% of patients.[28] In this series, organ harvesting occurred less than 36 hours after the clinical determination of "brain death," with a third of transplants less than 12 hours after making the diagnosis – something quite unheard of 35 years ago.[29] Today, a "dead" brain should thus more properly be described as having little if any macroscopic damage (other than from previous trauma), with microscopic neuronal injury at varying degrees found diffusely but inconsistently in various brain segments.

A number of reports purport to demonstrate that the brain cells of "dead" brains should be described as dead. These include studies of glucose utilization,[30] oxygen levels,[31] and temperature assays,[32] among others, all identifying the brain cells as completely "dead." A closer look, however, reveals that these studies probe only the outermost 1-3 cm of brain tissue (known as the neocortex). Since, as noted above, up to 68% of cells in the cortical areas may in fact be classified as dead and considering that the outermost layers of brain tissue would logically "die" first given low or even apparently absent cerebral perfusion, it is likely that the samples were taken from these "dead" areas. Thus, while perhaps accurately reflecting the state of most of the cells in the neocortex as "dead," none of these biochemical studies have any relevance to deeper brain structures,

---

28 E.F.M. Wijdicks, E.A. Pfeifer, "Neuropathology of brain death in the modern transplant era," *Neurology* 70 (2008): 1234-7.

29 See also an editorial in the same journal, G. Saposnik, D.G. Munoz, "Dissecting brain death: Time for a new look," ibid.: 1230-1, analyzing the choice of criteria for determining cell death and speculating that choosing different criteria may lead to somewhat different results. These authors do not, however, offer a philosophical, ethical, or medical basis for selecting one set of criteria over another.

30 A.B. Valadka, J.C. Goodman, S.P. Gopinath, et al., "Comparison of brain tissue oxygen tension to microdialysis-based measures of cerebral ischemia in fatally head-injured humans," *Journal of Neurotrauma* 15 (1998): 509-19.

31 S. Palmer, M.K. Bader, "Brain tissue oxygenation in brain death," *Neurocritical Care* 2 (2005): 17-22; J.C. Rose, T.A. Neill, J.C. Hemphill, "Continuous monitoring of the microcirculation in neurocritical care: An update on brain tissue oxygenation," *Current Opinion in Critical Care* 12 (2006): 97-102.

32 C.S. Rumana, S.P. Gopinath, M. Uzura, et al, "Brain temperature exceeds systemic temperature in head-injured patients," *Critical Care Medicine* 26 (1998): 562-7.

such as the hypothalamus or the brainstem, and to whether any part of the brain remains viable in "brain death."

What to Make of All of This?

Understanding the physiology and pathology of "brain death" is the basis for analyzing what role, if any, "brain death" should play in determining the death of the individual.

Clinically, "brain dead" patients are quite similar to each other; they are irreversibly unconscious and have irreversibly lost the ability for spontaneous respiration. From a physiological and pathological perspective, however, differences between patients abound. Many patients continue to maintain various brain functions, most notably of the hypothalamus, and many preserve areas of blood perfusion. Assuming that the viability of the brain is determinant of life, are these functions evidence of a living brain, or perhaps best described as "residual" and not of particular significance?

Furthermore, there is no pathological uniformity among "dead" brains; pathological change is demonstrated in mostly microscopic damage of various degrees, inconsistently found throughout the brain. This certainly excludes the possibility of diagnosing "brain death" pathologically. Should these structural differences matter? Are they indicative of viability, or simply irrelevant in the larger scheme?

Additionally and most importantly, as long as the patient remains ventilated, his heart continues to beat. How should this sustained function be described – as independent because of its inherent automaticity, or as artificial because of its reliance on artificially supplied oxygen?

One's approach to "brain death" depends on how one answers these questions. This discussion is taken up in the next chapter.

CHAPTER 3:

What it Means to Define Death

One of the unifying themes across discussions of organ donation has been respect for the Dead Donor Rule (DDR), which has remained a firm guiding light in bioethical discourse and practice.[1] By incorporating neurologically dependent definitions of death, as described in chapter 2, the medical establishment allowed the organ transplantation enterprise to flourish while continuing to respect the DDR.

In the early years of its conceptualization, efforts were almost exclusively focused on identifying and accurately describing the term "brain death" and differentiating it from other potentially reversible conditions. Even the truly seminal paper by the Ad Hoc Committee of the Harvard Medical School to Examine the Definition of Brain Death, while detailing a proposed diagnosis of "brain death," did not offer an explanation or rationale for **why** "brain death" should qualify as the death of the individual.[2] Nonetheless, taking its conclusion as a given, the Committee's

---

1 This *status quo* has recently come under increasing challenge. The August 2011 of *American Journal of Bioethics* (11:8) contains a symposium of articles debating whether or not the DDR should remain optimal public policy.

2 "A definition of irreversible coma: Report of the Ad Hoc Committee of the Harvard Medical School to Examine the Definition of Brain Death," *Journal of the American Medical Association* 205 (1968): 337-40.

"Definition of Irreversible Coma" was almost universally accepted as definitively describing the death of a person – not just his brain.

From a philosophical perspective, however, what justification was there for redefining death? Even granting that the change was prudent and justified, why identify "brain death" with the death of the individual and not just of a particular organ? Furthermore, is it, in fact, the role of the medical establishment to offer such a definition at all?

"Uniform Determination of Death Act"

Since the late 1960's, all American jurisdictions have adopted updated determinations of death that include traditional as well as neurologically based criteria. Interestingly, it was not until 1981 that the President's Commission for the Study of Ethical Problems in Medicine and Biomedical and Behavioral Research produced *Defining Death: Medical, Legal and Ethical Issues in the Determination Death*, analyzing the matter from a public policy standpoint and recommending the adoption of a universal statute for legally determining death. Aside from proposing the statute, the President's Commission analyzed the various approaches as to what might qualify as determinant of death, aside from the traditional cardiopulmonary arrest. Their proposed "Uniform Determination of Death Act" (UDDA) was subsequently accepted across the country, with only minor variations between jurisdictions. It reads:

> An individual who has sustained either (1) irreversible cessation of circulation and respiratory functions or (2) irreversible cessation of all functions of the entire brain, including the brainstem, is dead. A determination of death must be made in accordance with accepted medical standards.[3]

Complementing the traditional approach, the statute incorporates the newly developed neurologically oriented definition as well.

The UDDA is legally binding, leaving no room for personal variance. Because "brain death" is legally defined as death, regardless of how one

---

3 *Defining Death: Medical, Legal and Ethical Issues in the Determination Death*, 2.

personally feels about the issue, physicians and hospitals may stop treating such patients unilaterally – that is, despite a patient's or his proxy's objections. While many doctors normally postpone pronouncing death in these patients for some time, so as to allow family members to say goodbye, once a patient is declared "brain dead," his health insurance may – and likely will – refuse to compensate the hospital for any continued care.

Responding to the lack of philosophical consensus on the matter, some have argued for including a "conscience clause" in the law, which would allow personal freedom in choosing one of several options for defining one's death. This idea has gained little support on the ground, however. In the United States, only the state of New Jersey allows for a religious exemption as part of its "Declaration of Death Act," prohibiting a physician from declaring death by neurological criteria when "such a declaration would violate the personal religious beliefs of the individual." Rather, "in these cases, death shall be declared, and the time of death fixed, solely upon the basis of cardio-respiratory criteria."[4] While not codified as law, the New York State Task Force on Life and the Law (2005) recommends that hospitals develop policies that "reasonably accommodate the beliefs of those who reject the brain death standard on religious or moral grounds,"[5] and this recommendation has been adopted by the New York State Hospital Review and Planning Council. How this is carried out in practice, however, varies by institution and is largely dealt with outside of the court system, leaving the legal ramifications of this regulation ambiguous.[6]

Definition of Death vs. Criteria for Determining Death

In 1981, Drs. Bernat, Culver, and Gert published a seminal paper that helped shape the debate over "brain death" in the world of bioethics. They argue for the

---

4 *New Jersey Statutes Annotated*, Title 26, 6A-1-6A-8. Israeli law incorporates a similar clause; see chapter 15.
5 http://www.health.state.ny.us/nysdoh/taskfce/taskbio.htm, accessed July 1, 2010.
6 The philosophical notion of accepting a pluralistic definition of death as a matter of public policy has been analyzed elsewhere. See, for example, K. Zeiler, "Deadly pluralism? Why death-concept, death-definition, death-criterion, and death-test pluralism should be allowed, even though it creates some problems," *Bioethics* 23 (2008): 450-9.

rigorous separation and ordered formulation of three distinct elements: the **definition** of death, the medical **criterion** for determining that death has occurred, and the **tests** to prove that the criterion has been satisfied... Providing the definition is primarily a philosophical task; the choice of the criterion is primarily medical; and the selection of the tests to prove that the criterion is satisfied is solely a medical matter.[7]

Explaining these terms more precisely, Bernat writes that "defining death is the conceptual task of making explicit our understanding of it," while a criterion of death is "the general measurable condition that satisfies the definition of death by being both necessary and sufficient for death."[8] Tests are necessary when the job of assessing the criteria is less than straightforward, with ambiguities frequently caused by technological intervention.

In defining and defending theories of "brain death," most authors have relied on this framework as most helpful in describing their positions, as we will see in chapter 4. Furthermore, the same structure is instructive for understanding the various Mishnaic and Talmudic discussions, as we will see in chapters 5-6.

Who Should Define Death?

The tripartite division distinguishing between the definition of death, criteria of death, and testing for death touches on an important issue. Who should be responsible for determining the meaning of "death"?

Physicians, ethicists, lawyers, and religionists alike have offered various proposals for identifying the moment of death. Each brings a different perspective to the discussion, reflective of different core values, assumptions, and methodologies. Under whose auspices does this question fall? Is it purely medical/biological, or should it depend upon ethical/legal issues? What role, if any, should religion play in the discussion?

---

7 "On the definition and criterion of death," *Annals of Internal Medicine* 94 (1981): 389.
8 "The whole-brain concept of death remains optimum public policy," *Journal of Law Medicine & Ethics* (Spring 2006): 35-43.

Neither the Harvard Committee of 1968 nor the President's Commission in 1981 broached the subject of who should define what death means or under which discipline or purview this type of question even belongs. Both groups looked toward the medical establishment for guidance, assuming that physicians and scientists were the most qualified to render judgment on this issue. Throughout the controversies surrounding the determination of death, however, tensions between the legal and medical communities persisted.[9]

Even if one argues for defining death biologically, as the medical community generally does, the larger issue of identifying the biological features compatible with death remains to be resolved. Dr. James Bernat argues that

> [a]lthough the totality of beliefs, customs and practices surrounding death throughout cultures in recorded human history can be viewed as a rich and colorful tapestry composed of social, cultural, anthropological, religious, spiritual, and legal threads, death, like life, always has been fundamentally a biological phenomenon. Thus, only living organisms can die, and all living organisms must die.[10]

Yet, one should not take the determination of death by precise biological events to mean that the biologist (scientist or physician) is the most appropriate arbiter of this decision, although he may have the greatest familiarity and expertise with biological phenomena. Doing so would mean falling into the trap obviated by Bernat's own tripartite description of the whole enterprise – confusing the **definition** of death with the **criteria** necessary to fulfill that definition. Determining when death occurs requires identifying what death means – what, essentially, is the difference between the "living" and the "dead." Selecting this appropriate

---

9 M. Pernick, "Brain death in cultural context: The reconstruction of death, 1967-1981," in S.J. Younger and R.M. Arnold (eds.), *The Definition of Death: Contemporary Controversies* (Baltimore: Johns Hopkins University Press, 1999), 3-33.
10 "A defense of the whole-brain concept of death," *Hastings Center Report* 28 (1998): 14-23.

meaning is a matter of value judgment and ethics, not science. Answering the question of why a particular clinical state should constitute death requires a philosophical, ethical, moral, or religious response, not a scientific one.

Science and medicine can answer questions that have observable or provable answers. They can explain physiological relationships, diagnose a disease state, statistically prognosticate a course of a disease, and posit and administer treatment aimed at curing what we think or know is wrong in a particular patient. These are answers based on fact; they have numerical relationships and can be proven or statistically modeled. Science and medicine cannot, however, make value judgments or answer philosophical questions.

Thus, while medicine can provide the prognosis of a given cancer and the statistical probability that a variety of treatments will succeed, it cannot answer whether or not the possible benefits of those treatments outweigh potential side effects for a particular patient. This requires a judgment call – assigning a value to each of these elements before calculating them together. This judgment is relegated to the realm of ethics and philosophy, not science. Similarly, medicine can describe the gestational progress of a fetus in remarkable detail – when its heart begins to beat, when it can begin to move its limbs, and when it can survive outside of its mother. None of these determinations, however, can answer the question of whether or not we should consider a fetus to be an independent life, and if so, at what point in gestation should that occur. Determining when a fetus is considered a living being requires positing what it means to be alive – what are the essential characteristics shared only by the community of the living? These questions demand a value judgment – one made based on moral, ethical, or legal principles, not mere physiological facts.

Given that the question of determination of death is essentially one of searching for a **definition** of death, it must perforce be reflective of certain values and attitudes, and the answer therefore differs among societies and cultures of varying values and ethics. As Dr. Robert Veatch notes:

> Although it may be the case that patients in irreversible coma, according to Harvard criteria, have shifted into that status where they are no longer considered living, the decision that they are

"dead" cannot be derived from any amount of scientific investigation and demonstration. The choice among the many candidates for what… is to be called "death" is a philosophical or moral question, not a medical or scientific one.[11]

Echoing Veatch's claim, R. J. David Bleich observes that

A definition of death cannot be derived from medical facts or scientific investigations alone. The physician is eminently qualified to describe the physiological state which he observes. But he can do no more than report his clinical observations… The question of whether a human organism in any particular physiological state is to be regarded as a living person … or as a corpse which may be medically abandoned with moral equanimity, is an ethical, religious, and legal question, not a medical one.[12]

The **criteria** for death bridge the gap between the philosophical constructs and physical reality; they provide a physical representation of when the ethical definition has been met. They are the physiological processes that represent a particular philosophical or ethical **definition**. If death is **defined** as the inability to breathe, then the **criterion** would be irreversible apnea. Alternatively, if the **definition** is the inability to perform conscious thought, then the **criteria** would be the "death" of the areas of the brain responsible for thinking (cerebral hemispheres).

Tests are necessary to assess whether or not the **criteria** have been fulfilled; they answer a question of reality and fact. No matter how one determines the criteria, the test identifies whether this particular patient's clinical presentation fits these criteria or not. Thus, as an objective question of fact, testing falls exclusively to the realm of medicine and science.

For example, if the **criterion** for death is irreversible apnea, the most appropriate **test** to determine whether a particular patient is apneic is a

---

[11] R.M. Veatch, *Transplantation Ethics* (Washington DC: Georgetown University Press, 2000), 46.
[12] *Contemporary Halakhic Problems*, vol. IV (New York: Ktav Publishing and Yeshiva University Press, 1995): 316.

comparison of arterial carbon dioxide concentration when connected vs. disconnected from a ventilator. Similarly, if the **criterion** for death is the irreversible cessation of heartbeat, then an appropriate **test** would be an EKG.

Since the **definition** of death is a value or judgment based determination, it should not change with technological changes and advancement. Medical advances certainly create many new ethical problems, but the principles of morality and ethics that guide these decisions are unaffected by scientific progress. Depending on the **definition**, the **criteria** may sometimes be updated; advances in science and medicine may reveal previously unknown physiological parameters that more accurately reflect and represent the particular definition, and should therefore replace previous criteria. Essentially, however, the **definition** of death and the **criteria** linked to it should be unresponsive to change.

Tests are very different. Since tests answer a factual question – have the **criteria** been met? – they must always employ the most updated means to make that assessment. They do not reflect particular values or judgments, and therefore must incorporate scientific and technological advancements as crucial elements in most accurately assessing particular situations. In Talmudic times, breathing was measured by placing a feather to a person's nose; we would not rely on such a crude assessment today. In order to answer the question of whether or not a patient is breathing – a question of fact – we must use the most accurate means at our disposal, such as measuring oxygen saturation levels. Similarly, in Talmudic times, a heartbeat was assessed by palpation or placing an ear to a person's chest. Today, we know that these tests are far less sensitive and specific than an EKG. If we are interested in determining whether or not a patient has a heartbeat, we cannot make that decision without invoking modern technology.

Ethics and Halakhah

Many ethicists have analyzed what society means when it refers to a person as "dead" and when a legal, moral, or ethical society may or should cease to afford a person the rights, privileges, and responsibilities of living members of that society. The question of "brain death" pushes this exercise to the extreme. In the normal "course of human events," society does not encounter people who in some ways resemble the living (maintaining a heartbeat and other vegetative functions), but in others resemble the deceased (unresponsive and irreversibly unable to breathe on their own). The question is where it is most appropriate to draw the line. How should society define what it means to be alive and what it means to be dead?

This dilemma is expressed in a famous anecdote recorded in the epigram to *The Definition of Death – Contemporary Controversies*,[13] a collection of scholarly articles on the topic:

> A young boy attending his first baseball game asked his father, "How can the umpires tell a ball from a strike?" The father suggested that after the game, the boy pose the question to the three umpires. When the boy asked the first umpire, he responded, "I call them as I see them." The second umpire answered, "I call them as they are." But the third umpire stepped back and stared at the boy. "Son," he said, "they ain't anything till I call them!"

Halakhic decision-making stands in stark contrast to the position of the last umpire. It is not the halakhist's role to postulate a certain definition of death to which reality must conform, but rather to analyze, isolate, and derive what Halakhah identifies as death. The halakhist assumes that Halakhah contains the appropriate definitions, and often criteria, awaiting the relevant data so as to properly apply the *halakhah* in question. The task is thus one of combing the halakhic corpus and distilling a halakhic definition of death, and thereby formulating appropriate criteria. It is at that point that the halakhist turns to the physician or scientist to establish and evaluate these criteria from their perspective and propose appropriate clinical tests to assess whether or not they have been met.

This methodological approach pervades all areas of halakhic application and will be evident throughout the discussions in the coming chapters.

---

13 Baltimore: Johns Hopkins University Press, 1999.

CHAPTER 4:

Definitions of Death

As we noted in the previous chapter, although "brain death" is almost universally legally accepted as the definition of death, the ethical, moral, and philosophical basis for this determination remains unsettled and subject to continued challenge and controversy. We will briefly summarize various approaches that appear in the medical and bioethical literature, noting their salient points and some of their strengths and weaknesses. These synopses are most certainly incomplete, however, and the interested reader is directed to the primary literature to explore these positions in greater detail.

The "Whole Brain" Approach

The first approach is the "whole brain definition" of death, which views the brain as "the hallmark of life because the brain is the regulator of the body's integration."[1] This was the approach endorsed by the President's Commission for the Study of Ethical Problems in Medicine and Biomedical and Behavioral Research in 1981, and it is reflected in the UDDA's requirement of the "irreversible cessation of **all** the functions

---

1 President's Commission for the Study of Ethical Problems in Medicine and Biomedical and Behavioral Research, *Defining Death: Medical, Legal and Ethical Issues in the Determination Death* (1981): 32.

of the **entire** brain" (emphasis added). Since "systemic integrated function" demands organized and directed neurological activity, isolated "electrical and metabolic activity at the level of individual cells… cannot contribute to the operation of the organism as a whole,"[2] and is therefore discounted.

In detailing this approach more precisely, Dr. J.L. Bernat argues that death is **defined** here as "the permanent cessation of functioning of the organism as a whole," the **criterion** for which is "permanent loss of functioning of the entire brain," relying on **tests** proposed by the Harvard Committee and updated by the American Academy of Neurology. Bernat attempts to identify what represents the "whole" person, or more precisely, what gives meaning to the myriad subsystems within the human body, arguing that it is the brain's role in somatic integration that justifies its representing the "organism as a whole."[3] According to this logic, when the brain's ability to integrate and regulate the various subsystems ceases, the person is dead. Accordingly, the Commission concludes:

> Continued breathing and circulation are not in themselves tantamount to life. Since life is a matter of integrating the functioning of major organ systems, breathing and circulation are necessary but not sufficient to establish that an individual is alive. When an individual's breathing and circulation lack neurological integration, he or she is dead.[4]

Since Bernat penned his conclusions in 1981, numerous physiological functions have been discovered to continue even after "brain death,"

---

2 Ibid., 75.
3 J.L. Bernat, "On the definition and criterion of death," *Annals of Internal Medicine* 94 (1981): 389.
4 *Defining Death*, 33. Although providing two separate avenues of defining death, the Commission preferred to think of their proposal as merely providing "legal recognition for new diagnostic measures of death," not offering "a wholly new concept of death" (ibid., 41). They argue that the "whole brain" definition of death is what the traditional cardiopulmonary definition really attempted to identify, although doing so by proxy. The Commission does not elaborate on this notion, however, and it will not be further discussed here.

many of which are related to the "functioning of the organism as a whole" and therefore pose serious challenges to Bernat's position. In fact, it was on this basis that the Commission's successor, the President's Council of Bioethics of 2008, called the Commission's position into question. In their *Controversies in the Determination of Death: A White Paper by the President's Council on Bioethics*, the Council questions the scientific basis of the Commission's approach and justifies re-examining the issue based on increasing evidence for continued integrative functioning of a "brain dead" brain. The Council quotes extensively from Dr. Alan Shewmon's research, in which he identified multiple integrative physiological functions that continue in patients clinically diagnosed as "brain dead."[5] These include:

> [homeostasis (maintenance of current conditions) of] mutually interacting chemicals… and physiological parameters, through the functions of… the liver, kidneys, cardiovascular, and endocrine systems; elimination, detoxification, and recycling of cellular waste; energy balance; maintaining body temperature (thermoregulation); wound healing; fighting infection; developing fever in response to infection; gestation of a fetus; as well as proportional growth and sexual maturation of a child.[6]

With this information in hand, the Council was faced with two possible options – either declaring "brain dead" patients alive, as they exhibit integrative functions and therefore do not fulfill the rationale of the 1981 Commission, or redefining death by offering a different philosophical basis for it, thereby maintaining the practical and clinical *status quo*. The Council chose the latter option, which will be explored more fully later in this chapter.

Attempting to preserve his approach in light of these discoveries, Bernat updated it somewhat to **define** death as "the permanent cessation of the *critical* functions of the organism as a whole," with the **criterion** for death best fulfilling this definition as "the irreversible cessation of all

---

5 "Chronic 'brain death,'" 1541.
6 *Controversies*, 56.

clinical functions of the entire brain"[7] – not necessarily all functions.[8] Bernat maintains that his reference to "clinical functions" accurately reflects the intention of the President's Commission's description of "systemic integrated functioning."

In focusing the criteria on "clinical functions," Bernat disregards evidence of residual spontaneous electroencephalographic (EEG) activity, since "the whole-brain criteria of death... does not require the cessation of functioning of every single neuron." He argues that these isolated neurons provide no **critical** role and "this random and purposeless cellular physiologic activity has no bearing on the status of the organism as a *whole*."[9] In further elaborating on his position, Bernat explains that "clinical functions" include "physical signs of brain functions that are detectable on ordinary bedside neurological examination," specifically excluding "meaningless cellular activities of isolated nests of surviving neurons, as well as those brain activities that cannot be measured at the bedside."[10] He therefore considers the continued secretion of ADH (a regulator of water balance) a non-clinical function, "because its presence or absence is not assessed or detected on a usual clinical examination and requires a laboratory test for diagnosis."[11] It thus cannot qualify as evidence for the continued "function of the organism as a whole." Nonetheless, Bernat still advocates requiring the standard apnea test, which does require minimal technological intervention. He argues that this test is different since it amounts to nothing more than "simply observing an unventilated patient for the prolonged absence of breathing... The technological portion is not necessary to prove apnea or determine death."[12]

---

7 J.L Bernat, "A defense of the whole-brain concept of death," *Hastings Center Report* 28 (1998): 17.
8 Importantly, this distinguishes Bernat's "whole brain" approach from that of R. Shelomoh Zalman Auerbach, as described in chapter 16.
9 Ibid.
10 "Refinements in the Definition and Criterion of Death," in S.J. Younger, R.M. Arnold, R. Schapiro (eds.), *The Definition of Death – Contemporary Controversies* (Baltimore: Johns Hopkins University Press, 1999), 87.
11 Ibid., 88.
12 Ibid.

Bernat's position raises many serious issues. First and foremost, it evokes serious concern that strict adherence to the UDDA's description of "irreversible cessation of all functions of the *entire* brain" is not possible, and certainly not practiced in many or even most circumstances. This is, in fact, why the President's Council (2008) qualified their own descriptive term, "total brain failure," as somewhat less than "total," referring not to the actual functioning of each and every neuron, but rather to "the fact that the brain injury has reached the *endpoint* of a process of self-perpetuating destruction of neural tissue."[13]

Second, Bernat's own assumption should lead to the opposite result. In his 1981 paper, Bernat suggests that "[t]emperature regulation is one example of an activity of the organism as a whole" because it "is important for normal maintenance of all cellular processes."[14] The problem is that Shewmon has demonstrated that thermoregulation does, in fact, persist in many "brain dead" patients.[15] From Bernat's own analysis, it would appear that he would need to distinguish amongst "brain dead" patients, treating those maintaining thermostatic homeostasis as alive and those no longer capable of such regulation as dead. Bernat never puts this element of his theory into practice, however, and no current regulations anywhere require a loss of thermostatic homeostasis as a prerequisite for diagnosing "brain death."[16]

Furthermore, Bernat's earlier and later theses seem to contradict each other somewhat. Why should there be a distinction between thermoregulation – "an activity of the organism as a whole," the presence of which would indicate "life" – and ADH secretion – "an example of a function of the organism as a whole [that] it is not an example of a critical function,"

---

13 *Controversies*, 38.
14 "On the definition," 390.
15 "Chronic 'brain death,'" 1541.
16 Almost all protocols do require that the patient not be hypothermic, but this is not necessary to prove homeostatic ability, but rather an attempt to exclude a confounding variable. Hypothermic patients may have muted brainstem reflexes because of their abnormal body temperature, and not necessarily because of organic brain damage. To ensure an accurate diagnosis of "brain death" as reflective of actual brainstem pathology, a patient must be warmed prior to testing his brainstem-mediated reflexes. This says nothing at all, however, about the patient's ability to maintain a body temperature.

and therefore not indicative of life? Bernat explains that ADH is not a "critical function" because it is possible to "survive for long periods without ADH" given the proper nutrient environment.[17] This argument is rather difficult, however, because according to this logic, even spontaneous respiration can be described as non-critical, since a person can live for quite a while without breathing on his own given the appropriate ventilator environment. This is a proposition that Bernat most certainly does not accept.

Finally, while Bernat asserts that "death determination is and should remain a clinical procedure,"[18] he offers no rational or philosophical basis for why the *critical* functions of the brain must be manifest in what he describes as *clinical* functions. Why should that which is critical necessarily be clinically observable on a bedside exam? In other words, choosing "*clinical* functions" as the **criteria** does not necessarily reflect the **definition** of "all *critical* functions" of the brain.

Despite these shortcomings, Bernat argues that the "whole-brain" oriented definition of death is still the best option, since it "comprises a concept and public policy that make intuitive and practical sense and have been well accepted by the public throughout many societies." He quite forcefully declares that "while I am willing to acknowledge that whole brain death formulation remains imperfect, I continue to support it because on the public policy level its shortcomings are relatively inconsequential."[19]

Dr. Bernat's argument may be a plausible defense from a bioethical or public policy perspective, but in evaluating the halakhic acceptability of the "whole brain" approach, we must consider whether such utilitarian motives for determining death are appropriate in halakhic discourse.

---

17 Ibid., 86.
18 "Refinements," 88.
19 "The whole-brain concept of death remains optimum public policy," *Journal of Law Medicine & Ethics* (Spring 2006): 41.

The "Higher Brain" Definition

Recognizing that the "whole-brain" definition is problematic, Dr. Robert Veatch proposes a definition of death as "the irreversible loss of that which is essentially significant to the nature of humans."[20] Declaring a person dead, Veatch argues, is far more than just describing cellular status. It is rather a practical statement with profound consequences – allowing relating to an individual as no longer living – and the definition of death should therefore reflect the death of "that which is essential to the nature of the human."

In Veatch's view, this essential quality of humans is "the capacity for experience or social interaction,"[21] most closely represented by the capacity for consciousness. While determination of "life" does not require **actual** social interactions – if it did, a person's death would be dependent on the desire of others to interact with him – it is the **ability** to interact that Veatch argues most closely identifies what makes a human being a living organism.

This approach has been termed the "higher brain" definition, since the capacity for these abilities lies within the cerebrum and cerebral cortex, areas of the brain located closer to the scalp. The anatomical location of the brain damage, however, is not the crucial factor, but rather the capacity for experiencing the world and engaging in it socially.

Essentially, Veatch argues that death should be defined from a social, and not biological, perspective; it should reflect that which is uniquely human, which is not necessarily reflective of purely biological cellular functions. He leaves the precise **criteria** that satisfy this **definition** somewhat vague, aware of possible and appropriate philosophical debate regarding which functions, attributes, or characteristics should qualify. The physiological parameters that most accurately reflect the characteristics of the "capacity for experience and social interaction" should clearly be decided by medical and legal consensus – an as of yet unrealized goal.

---

20 R.M. Veatch, *Transplantation Ethics* (Washington DC: Georgetown University Press, 2000): 87.
21 Ibid., 94-95.

The President's Commission charged that the "higher brain" definition is simply not workable, since physicians are unable to measure the irreversible loss of higher functions with much precision.[22] Defending his approach as not only philosophically sound, but also practically appropriate, Veatch responds that "even if we could not presently measure accurately the loss of key higher functions such as consciousness, that would have bearing only on the clinical implementation of the higher-brain-oriented definition, not the validity of the concept itself."[23] The definition of death is valid, even if it is difficult to implement in practice. Veatch is also quick to note that the accuracy with which "irreversible unconsciousness" is presently diagnosed at least equals, if not surpasses, the accuracy in determining the "irreversible loss of all functions of the entire brain," the definition proposed by the very same Commission critical of his approach.

The more substantive challenge to the "higher brain" definition is the "slippery slope" argument. Once the insistence on the loss of **all** functions is abandoned (even though it was never truly insisted on in its totality even in its current state), "there seems to be no stopping the slide of eliminating functions considered insignificant."[24] Patients meeting the "higher brain" definition of death maintain important biological functioning – most notably, spontaneous respiration – lacking only the capacity for consciousness. How firm is the "line in the sand" between permanently unconscious patients and those with only marginal consciousness? What stands in the way of one day treating people with merely impaired consciousness as satisfying a somewhat looser understanding of what constitutes the "higher brain" definition of death?

Essentially, this argument boils down to the fact that the "higher brain" definition makes a certain value judgment about what is important to human life and what is tangential to it, leaving open a Pandora's box of flexibility and options regarding where to draw the arbitrary line in increasingly more uncomfortable places. Veatch notes, however, that

---

22 *Defining Death*, 40.
23 *Transplantation Ethics*, 108.
24 Ibid., 109.

the same argument can be levied against proponents of the "whole brain" definition of death, who, to his mind, arbitrarily draw a line between the "top of the spinal cord and the base of the brain," differentiating between brainstem mediated reflexes, the absence of which indicate death, and those controlled by the spinal cord.[25]

Dr. Robert Truog, a long time opponent of all neurologically based determinations of death, repeatedly pushes Veatch's argument to its limits, noting that it proposes to declare spontaneously breathing individuals dead:

> No matter how philosophically attractive the higher brain option might be, the notion that a spontaneously breathing patient who is surviving with only minimal nursing care is actually dead is extremely counterintuitive... Declaring these patients as dead "by definition" would seem to contradict all of our common sense notions of what it is to be alive. To make matters worse, if we were to commit ourselves to the idea that they are dead, then we should logically be committed to treating them as dead people. The common practice in our society is to bury or cremate dead people. Could we even imagine cremating people who are still breathing, even if we are philosophically convinced that they should be considered dead?[26]

More than simply presenting a *reductio ad absurdum*, Truog argues that by Veatch's own definition of what it means to be human, his position cannot stand. It simply counters common sense to assert that breathing is not part of what it means to be human, leaving Veatch's essential definition of death as "irreversible unconsciousness" somewhat wanting.[27]

---

25 Ibid., 110.
26 R.D. Truog, "Brain death – too flawed to endure, to ingrained to abandon," *Journal of Law, Medicine & Ethics* (2007): 276.
27 Idem., "Is it time to abandon brain death?" *Hastings Center Report* 27 (1997): 29-37.

Brainstem Death

While the United Kingdom has no statutory definition of death, the courts of England and Northern Ireland have adopted a third definition of death, accepting the "irreversible loss of the capacity for consciousness, combined with irreversible loss of the capacity to breathe" as criteria.[28] This approach focuses on particular physiological functions, accepting the "higher brain" definition with an additional essential caveat, thereby mitigating much of the criticism of Dr. Veatch's approach. In addition to demonstrating permanent lack of consciousness, the patient must also be irreversibly unable to breathe, which, as the British Guidelines explain, is predicated upon the destruction of the brainstem.

The British Code of Practice argues that "death entails the irreversible loss of those essential characteristics which are necessary to the existence of a living human person," focusing particularly on consciousness and breathing.[29] Brainstem death is equated with death because it produces a state of "irreversible loss of the capacity for consciousness, combined with irreversible loss of the capacity to breathe." There is no real attempt, however, to propose a comprehensive **definition** of death for which brainstem death qualifies as a satisfying **criterion**.

The President's Council's Definition

The President's Council of 2008 also adopts a combined approach, arguing for a modified "whole brain" definition that includes the concomitant irreversible incapacity for spontaneous respiration. Practically,

---

28 Working Party of the Royal College of Physicians on behalf of the Academy of Medical Royal Colleges at the request of the Health Department, *A Code of Practice for the Diagnosis of Brain Stem Death – Including Guidelines for the Identification and Management of Potential Organ and Tissue Donors*, p. 7.

The UK approach was significantly influenced by the thought of British neurologist Dr. Christopher Pallis, who argued tirelessly for a brainstem based determination. See C. Pallis, "ABC of brain stem death: From brain death to brainstem death," *British Medical Journal* 285 (1982): 1487-90, as well as the rest of the journal's "ABC of brainstem death" series throughout 1982.

29 *A Code of Practice*, p.7.

the Council's reformulation of the "whole brain" definition is parallel to the "higher brain" definition, but in including the irreversible capacity for respiration, the President's Council proposes a new **definition** of death. The President's Council agrees that death is the point at which the organism can no longer be considered whole. The Council differs with its predecessors, however, in abandoning reliance on the concept of integration and the brain's primacy in affecting these vital functions. Rather, the Council argues:

> Determining whether an organism remains a whole depends on recognizing the persistence or cessation of the fundamental vital work of a living organism – the work of self-preservation… When there is good reason to believe that an injury has irreversibly destroyed an organism's ability to perform its fundamental vital work, then the conclusion that the organism as a whole has died is warranted.[30]

The Council identifies life with the persistence of self-preservation, defined as the **need** to engage the surrounding world, to be receptive to the world (consciousness), and to maintain ability to act on one's own behalf. The Council therefore firmly distinguishes between the mechanical, muscular work of breathing, and even the ensuing gas exchange that it promotes, and the **drive** to breath, describing the latter as the most primitive "inner experience of need."[31] This drive need not be consciously appreciated, since its presence is reflective of the "organism's own impulse, exercised on its own behalf, and indispensable to its continued existence."[32]

The Council is quick to note that it is not the inability to breathe alone that qualifies as death; according to the Council's definition, any interaction with the surrounding environment is evidence of a living being. Thus, spinal cord trauma victims who have irreversibly lost the capacity for spontaneous respiration are most certainly alive by virtue of

---

30 *Controversies*, 60.
31 Ibid., 64.
32 Ibid.

their capacity for consciousness – equally valid evidence that the person engages in the essential work that defines living things.

In explaining their hesitance to rely solely on a brainstem standard, as per the UK Code, the Council explains that the latter is not only "conceptually suspect... [but also] clinically dangerous because it suggests that the confirmatory tests that go beyond the bedside checks for apnea and brainstem reflexes are simply superfluous" even when "the irreversibility of the patient's condition [cannot] be known with confidence."[33]

While not dictating any change in clinical practice, since traditionally diagnosed "brain dead" patients still qualify as dead even according to this new approach, the President's Council's proposal is a radical shift from the past. It is a complete redefinition of what it means to be dead, philosophically distinct from the reigning *status quo*.

In a rather ferocious attack on this newly proposed position, Drs. Miller and Truog argue:

> Since, according to the Council, neither loss of the capacity for consciousness (as in PVS) nor loss of the capacity for spontaneous breathing (as in cervical quadriplegia) by itself makes a patient dead, why does the combination constitute death in patients with total brain failure when a host of other biological functions are maintained? In short, a coherent account of why patients with "total brain failure" are dead has not been supplied.[34]

Truog and Miller have long been staunch opponents of all neurologically based criteria for death, arguing for the incoherence of describing a person maintaining multiple physiological functions as a corpse. They find the President's Council's "bizarre language," describing "brain dead" patients as alternatively both dead and alive, as "conceptually muddled."[35] The Council

---

33 Ibid., 66-67.
34 "The incoherence of determining death by neurological criteria: A commentary on *Controversies in the Determination of Death*, a white paper by the President's Council on Bioethics," *Kennedy Institute of Ethics Journal* 19 (2009): 189.
35 Ibid., 187.

refers to "somatic survival"[36] and "somatic health"[37] of patients they themselves describe as dead. This conceptual vacillation culminates in the paradoxical claim that, "If the body is a cadaver, then, of course, it is no longer fitting to speak about its 'health.' Nonetheless, *something like heath* is still present in the body of a patient with this diagnosis"[38] – leading Miller and Truog to wonder, "How can even something like health be present in a cadaver?"[39] Bolstering their point, they quote Dr. H. Tristam Engelhardt's 1986 *Foundation of Bioethics* description of "brain dead" patients: "They appear to be alive because they are in fact alive. It is because human biological life continues unabated that transplant surgeons are interested in such bodies as an ideal source for harvesting organs."[40]

John Lizza takes Miller and Truog to task, arguing that they mistakenly view the definition of death in strictly biological terms.

> [I]t is not in terms of human beings as strictly biological beings that one is interested in an answer to the question. Rather one is interested in the life and death of human beings understood as psychological, moral, and cultural beings, as well as biological beings.[41]

---

36 *Controversies*, 45.
37 Ibid., 49.
38 Ibid., 39.
39 "Incoherence," 187.
40 Ibid., 188. At first glance, it may appear that Miller and Truog arrive at a different conclusion from the President's Council because they approach the definition of death from a different perspective. Miller and Truog attempt to identify dead patients as cadavers or corpses and compare "brain dead" patients to that standard – a person is alive if he is not dead. The Council, on the other hand, appears to be more interested in what it means to be alive, defining death as lacking that or those vital characteristics – a person is dead if he is not alive. While appealing, however, this distinction cannot be true. Miller and Truog, as well as the President's Council, assume death to be a discrete phenomenon. Life and death are dichotomous; a person can be either alive or dead – there is no in between. Regardless of the direction one takes to approach the matter, given this assumption, the definition should not differ. For a different perspective on the nature of life and death, see the text at n.45 below.
41 "Commentary on 'The incoherence of determining death by neurological criteria,'" *Kennedy Institute of Ethics Journal* 19 (2009): 395.

Lizza argues that defining death solely by biological criteria, as per Miller and Truog, would lead to the "incoherent" and "absurd implication that decapitation would not necessarily entail death" were such a person to be artificially supported so that he maintained integrated bodily function.[42] Because such a conclusion is inconceivable, Lizza argues, the premise must be flawed and incompatible with truth.

Responding to Lizza's attack, Truog and Miller emphasize their insistence on defining death biologically, undermining Lizza's implicit assumption that it must be defined otherwise: "The hypothetical case of a live decapitated human being with biological functioning otherwise being artificially sustained is repugnant, but by no means absurd."[43] Elaborating their position according to Bernat's tripartite structure, they argue:

> [Death is] a fundamental[ly] biological phenomenon, not a social construction... We are biological organisms, despite the fact that what is meaningful about human life is not defined in biological terms... In contrast, a determination of exactly when death has occurred, required to serve various social purposes, combines social and normative considerations with biological facts. The determination of death, therefore, is not strictly a biological matter.[44]

Truog and Miller point out that Lizza's essential argument of *reductio ad absurdum* misses the mark, since Lizza's real thesis is about the more fundamental notion of whether death should be defined biologically or socially.

Other Options

In a unique approach to the matter, Drs. Baruch Brody and Amir Halevy challenge one of the basic tenets of this entire discussion, arguing

---

42 Ibid., 393.
43 This is very similar to R. J. David Bleich's approach, analyzed in chapter 17.
44 "The incoherence of determining death by neurological criteria: Reply to John Lizza," *Kennedy Institute of Ethics Journal* 19 (2010): 398.

that death is a "process, rather than an event that occurs at a particular point in time."[45] They claim:

> [T]he world does not easily divide itself into sets and their complement. Death and its complementary property, life, determine mutually exclusive but not jointly exhaustive sets. Although no organism can fully belong to both sets, organisms can be in many conditions (the very conditions that have created the debates about death) during which they do not fully belong to either. That is why you cannot find the answers to the questions by finding the right moment in the process to serve as the moment for belonging to the set of the dead. Death is a fuzzy set.[46]

In answering the diverse questions of when life-support may be unilaterally withdrawn (without patient or proxy consent), organs procured, and burial initiated, Halevy and Brody suggest that each question be answered on its own – "with the answer to one question (some point in the process) not necessarily being the answer to the other questions."[47] They argue that life-support be withdrawn when "the organism no longer composes a person," which they identify as the loss of the cerebral cortex, but that burial be delayed until the heart stops beating (cardiac asystole). While the former criteria, they argue, respects "appropriate stewardship of society's resources," the latter respects "the traditional definition… [recognizing that] the organism is fully dead at that point."[48] Organ harvesting, they propose, may commence once the person can no longer breathe, as that criterion "preserves the proper balance between trying to maximize the supply of organs to save lives and trying to preserve public support for organ transplantation by not harvesting organs in cases that would be socially unacceptable."[49]

---

45 "How much of the brain must be dead?" in *The Definition of Death – Contemporary Controversies*, 71.
46 Ibid., 72.
47 Ibid., 79.
48 Ibid., 80-81.
49 Ibid., 80. Interestingly, *Tosafot Rid* (*Bava Batra* 137a) also describes a "beginning" and "end" to death. *Sema* (*HM* 248:16) notes, however, that the Talmud there actually describes a *goses*, and thus refers to a beginning and end to the *gesisah* process, not death.

Aside from the philosophical novelty of abandoning the notion of defining death as a precise moment in time – an idea that is rejected by almost all ethicists and religionists alike – Halevy and Brody's proposal raises eyebrows. Of particular note is their justification of identifying the loss of the ability to breathe as the moment at which to permit organ retrieval on purely utilitarian grounds – balancing that which is socially acceptable against that which will maximize available organs. Accepting these two notions as the terminals between which a balance must be sought certainly borders on the morally questionable. Utilitarian motives and suggestions for the definition of death are simply restatements of the willingness to sacrifice one patient to save another, a sentiment strongly rejected by the DDR. Indeed, the medical establishment felt so strongly about preserving the DDR's primacy that it preferred to redefine death rather than abandon the principle, insisting that death be defined objectively and independently. The flipside is equally troublesome – allowing societal attitudes to dictate death determinations implies that physicians should try to "get away with" whatever they can manage to dupe society into believing.

Rejection of "Brain Death" Criteria

Aware of the limitations of each of these approaches, Drs. Miller and Truog have opposed neurologically based criteria for death from their inception, as can be seen in their criticisms and critiques cited in the previous sections. Similarly, Dr. Alan Shewmon, who was at first a proponent of the "higher brain" definition and later advocated for a "whole brain" definition, has since become one "of the most important opponents of brain-based criteria for human death, important in part because of his status as a professor of pediatric neurology at the UCLA School of Medicine… [who] cannot be justly accused of ignorance of how the brain works."[50]

---

[50] M. Potts, "A requiem for whole brain death: A response to D. Alan Shewmon's 'The brain and somatic integration,'" *Journal of Medicine and Philosophy* 26 (2010): 480.

Truog is a staunch advocate for completely abandoning the notion of "brain death," as it is "theoretically incoherent and internally inconsistent":[51]

> The status of "brain death" is, in this sense, not dissimilar from the status of "legally blind." Both represent a point on a continuum of organ dysfunction... By social convention, however, both signify a threshold with important medical, legal, and social implications. Patients who are legally blind are treated as if they are blind (even if they retain some rudimentary sight), and patients who are brain dead are treated as if they are dead (even if they retain some neurological functioning and other characteristics of the living).[52]

Although they deny that "brain dead" patients are actually dead, Truog and Miller do not give up entirely on the prospect of organ transplantation, instead advocating for abandoning the DDR to allow donation from living patients. They propose specifically limiting donation to patients suffering from severe neurological injury whose brains have up until now been characterized as "dead," although they argue that these individuals remain fully alive. Despite the fact that removing a life-sustaining organ harms the donor, Truog believes:

> [When the patient] is either permanently unconscious or imminently dying... [he] should be allowed to decide whether... [he] want[s] to accept the harm of an earlier death in order to bestow the benefits of transplantable organs to others in need. This approach seeks to balance concerns about nonmaleficence [not inflicting harm on patients] with respect for autonomy [allowing patients to choose]. This view is consistent with many other practices in our society that permit individuals to

---

51 "Time to abandon," 29.
52 R.D. Truog, W.M. Robinson, "Role of brain death and the dead-donor rule in the ethics of organ transplantation," *Critical Care Medicine* 31 (2003): 2393.

choose certain harms for themselves in order to provide benefits to others.[53]

Expanding on this notion, Truog and Miller compare the case of organ donation from a living patient to that of a patient (or his proxy) consenting to withdrawing life-sustaining treatment even though this will inevitably bring about the patient's death. While some claim that it is not the removal of treatment *per se* that causes the patient's death, but rather the underlying disease or condition, this stance cannot withstand critical scrutiny:

> Causes are events or circumstances that *make the difference* in explaining a particular occurrence. Assuming that a patient who is on life support will normally continue to live for some period of time... the withdrawal of life support brings about death... The withdrawal makes the difference.

> If it is acceptable to cause the death of a brain dead patient by stopping life support, subject to valid consent, then why is it not acceptable to extract organs before treatment is stopped? In this situation, whether death is caused by stopping treatment or by extracting vital organs is ethically immaterial.[54]

Essentially, Truog and Miller argue that there is no difference between withdrawing treatment and actively terminating the life of a patient who is irreversibly unconscious or imminently dying through organ harvesting. Society, however, as reflected in American law, strongly distinguishes between the two options, considering the removal of therapy permissible and active euthanasia criminal. While the philosophical difference between the two practices is intriguing, from a legal perspective, withdrawing treatment is predicated upon the patient's autonomous right to refuse therapy, while forbidding eutha-

---
53 "Too flawed to endure," 278.
54 "Rethinking the ethics of vital organ donations," *Hastings Center Report* 38 (2008): 40-41.

nasia is founded on the prohibition of suicide. Removing organs from a living patient more closely parallels active euthanasia than removal of therapy.

The consent of the patient to ending his life for the sake of helping others is further immaterial. While society allows (and often encourages) people to accept certain risks and even harms in the hopes of benefitting others, it nonetheless forbids suicide. Accepting risks or harms is appropriate; accepting certain death is not.

The question of withdrawing treatment in Halakhah is not the subject of this discussion; for our purposes, it suffices to say that most rabbinic decisors forbid withdrawing therapy that will imminently bring about the death of the patient.[55] Nonetheless, Halakhah may and often does differentiate between withdrawing and withholding treatment, the former being active and the latter being passive, a distinction that is largely disregarded in the world of secular bioethics. For religious Jews, accepting or rejecting the DDR is a matter of Halakhah, as discussed in chapter 1, as is acceptance or rejection of "brain death;" the conclusion is not determined by bioethicists. It is important to keep in mind that Truog and Miller's analysis of "brain death," which is pertinent to the halakhic discussion, is completely independent from their position on the DDR, which is halakhically untenable.

Irreversibility and "Donation After Cardiac Death"

No matter what definition of death we adopt – whether cardiopulmonary or some form of "brain death" – the state must be **irreversible**. If the cessation of particular biological functions is the criteria for death, they must have irreversibly ceased. This is one of the basic assumptions of all ethical and halakhic discussions of "brain death;" it is explicitly taken for granted, for example, by both R. Shelomoh Zalman Auerbach and R. Moshe Feinstein.

If the condition is reversible, the patient is, by definition, not dead. Thus, if one defines death as the absence of a heartbeat, were a person's

---

55 For a fuller analysis, see D. Shabtai, "End of Life Therapies," *Journal of Halacha and Contemporary Society* 56 (2008): 22-48.

heart to stop but then to be restarted through CPR and/or electric defibrillation, the heart attack victim is considered to be resuscitated – having been brought back from **dying** – and not resurrected – having been brought back from **death**. The latter requires divine intervention and is within the domain of the prophet, while the former requires proper technique and equipment, falling under the purview of the medical professional. The heart attack victim never died because his heart never **irreversibly** stopped working, as evidenced by its eventual reanimation. The fact that this can only be known retroactively does not detract from its truth.

When physiological functions stop, many maintain the potential for reversibility for a short while thereafter. As long as that potential exists, the function cannot be described as "irreversibly ceased." Therefore, even when resuscitative efforts fail, or even if they are never attempted, a person can only be described as dead when the potential for reversibility passes, whether or not it was actualized.[56]

This point has important ramifications for "donation after cardiac death" (DCD) protocols, a recent innovation to attempt to procure organs from patients who are terminally ill but not quite "brain dead." DCD protocols call for voluntarily withdrawing life-support from a patient (through proxy or prior patient consent), allowing the heart to eventually stop beating on its own. Once asystole (no heartbeat) ensues, the surgical team waits 2-5 minutes (depending on the institution) and then begins the harvesting procedure. The enterprise depends on determining death by the irreversible cessation of cardiac activity, with the waiting period intended to rule out any possibility of autoresuscitation (without any intervention). Once the heart can no longer restart spontaneously, the patient is declared dead. Using this method, the heart is often not transplantable because of the extended warm ischemia time, but many other organs retain their transplant potential.[57]

---

56 See *Shulhan Shelomoh, Erkhei Refuah* 2, p. 35 and *Responsa Tzitz Eliezer* 17:11 (also 16:24, 64) for further discussion of this issue.

57 If the waiting period were to be shortened, even hearts might be potentially transplantable. See M.M. Boucek, C. Mashburn, S.M. Dunn, et al., "Pediatric heart transplantation after declaration of cardiocirculatory death," *New England Journal of Medicine* 359 (2008): 709-14, in which physicians waited only 75 seconds prior to harvesting babies' hearts, enabling transplant into waiting recipients.

Some ethicists have noted that although autoresuscitation may no longer be possible after the waiting period, interventional methods (CPR and electronic defibrillation) might still be fruitful in returning the patient's circulation.[58] If this is true, the patient's state is still potentially reversible when the organ harvest begins, as his heartbeat could in theory be regenerated – raising thorny and uncomfortable questions for the transplant surgeon of whether DCD violates the DDR.

Some have attempted to argue for differentiating between the "**irreversible** cessation of cardiac function," implying that it **cannot** be reversed, and the "**permanent** cessation of function," implying that practically, it **will not** be reversed.[59] The latter is true of DCD donors, as they must have "do not resuscitate" (DNR) orders in place prior to beginning the procedure.[60] Once the time for potential autoresuscitation passes, the patient's heartbeat can be described as permanently, although not necessarily irreversibly, ceased, because interventional methods are considered an assault on a DNR patient and will not be used. This, these bioethicists argue, is sufficient to declare death.

DCD is a novel and thought-provoking enterprise, requiring a separate treatise for discussion. The interested reader is directed to the many

---

58 M.Y. Rady, J.L. Verheijde, J. McGregor, "Organ procurement after cardiocirculatory death: A critical analysis," *Journal of Intensive Care Medicine* 23 (2008): 303-12; F.G. Miller, R.D. Truog, D.W. Brock, "The dead donor rule: Can it withstand critical scrutiny?" *Journal of Medicine and Philosophy* 35 (2010): 299-312; R.M. Veatch, "Transplanting hearts after death measured by cardiac criteria: The challenge to the dead donor rule," *Journal of Medicine and Philosophy* 35 (2010): 313-29.
59 J.L. Bernat, "Contemporary controversies in the definition of death," *Progress in Brain Research* 177 (2009): 21-31.
60 A practical difference between DCD based organ donation and "brain death" dependent organ donation is that a DCD patient is considered alive up until the moment prior to the harvest. Because of this, were the patient to suffer sudden cardiac arrest during transport from the ICU to the operating room, the DCD donor would not be resuscitated, as he is a living patient with a valid DNR in place. The "brain dead" donor, however, is legally considered dead, and thus CPR may be initiated despite a valid DNR. The DNR order is irrelevant after the patient's death because the very same actions that were considered resuscitative during life are now described as tools for promoting organ survival in a corpse. See B. Cummings, N. Noviski, M.P. Moreland, et al., "Circulatory arrest in a brain-dead organ donor: Is the use of cardiac compression permissible?" *Journal of Intensive Care Medicine* 24 (2009): 389-92.

recent reviews on this controversy.[61] Without engaging in a rigorous halakhic analysis, however, from a superficial perspective, this argument does not appear to conform to halakhic standards.

A thought experiment highlights the importance of the notion of irreversibility and the dilemma that results if we abandon it. Imagine a patient for whom a DCD protocol is performed and the waiting time post-asystole has passed. What would this patient's status be if circulation was somehow restarted? Should he be considered alive, which would obviously seriously threaten the previous declaration of death? Or should artificially supported circulation be considered inconsequential in the overall scheme? This situation is no longer in the realm of science fiction. DCD patients can be connected to ECMO (extra corporeal membrane oxygenation) prior to removal of therapy, which, after the heart has stopped, can supply the body with a continuous flow of oxygenated blood, effectively constituting a portable heart-lung machine that preserves blood flow to the organs to aid the harvesting process. Leaving the presence of circulation aside, when the heart muscle is exposed to oxygenated blood, it can often start beating spontaneously – throwing the recent declaration of death into turmoil.

To alleviate these ethical "problems," some have suggested loading the ECMO apparatus with high doses of lidocaine in order to prevent the heart from reanimating when exposed to oxygenated blood, or alternatively placing an aortic balloon to completely prevent cardiac reperfusion. These protocols are highly questionable practices, leaving one wondering as to the role of utilitarian theory in determining death.[62] While effectively solving the problem of a reanimated heart, these "solutions" do nothing to quell the vexing ethical problems raised by this protocol – other than for someone who wishes to completely ignore them. While these and other questions have been hotly debated in the academic literature, however, the discussion has had little to no impact on actual clinical practice.

---

61 See, for example, J.L. Bernat, A.M. Caprom, T.P. Bleck, et al., "The circulatory-respiratory determination of death in organ donation," *Critical Care Medicine* 38 (2010): 963-70.
62 Cf. C. DeJohn, J.B. Zwichenberger, "Ethical implications of Extracorporeal Support for Organ Retrieval (EISOR), *ASAIO Journal* (2006): 119-22.

SECTION II:

HALAKHIC TEXTS

CHAPTER 5:

Talmud Yoma

The starting point for almost all halakhic discussions of "brain death" is analysis of a *mishnah* and ensuing Talmudic discussion in Talmud *Yoma* (83a, 85a):

> A person upon whom a building collapsed [on Shabbat] and it is questionable [or uncertain] whether or not he is [actually] there or not, or whether he is alive or dead… they must clear the rubble to excavate the victim. If they find him alive – they must [continue] the [rescue] efforts; if [they find him] dead – they must leave him [there]. (Mishnah, *Yoma* 8:7)
>
> The Rabbis taught: [When clearing the rubble], until where [on the victim's body] must one examine [to determine if he is alive or dead]? Up to his nose [*hotmo*]; and some say, up to his heart [*libbo*] …
>
> Perhaps this Tannaic dispute is similar to a parallel dispute: A *beraita* teaches: From where is the fetus formed? From his head… Abba Shaul says from his navel (*tabburo*)…
>
> [However,] you can even say that Abba Shaul [agrees with the view that we examine the building collapse victim up until his

nose, since] Abba Shaul was only discussing fetal formation, for everything is formed from its center; however, with regard to saving a life (*pikuah nefesh*), even Abba Shaul agrees that the central life force (*ikkar hiyyuteih*) is in the nose, as it is written, "All in whose nostrils was the breath of the spirit of life" (*kol asher nishmat ru'ah hayyim be-appav*) (*Bereishit* 7:22).

R. Pappa said: The dispute [regarding up until where one must examine the avalanche victim] pertains only [to when the victim was discovered] from the bottom [feet-first] and the examination proceeds towards the head. However, when [clearing rubble] from the head down, [all agree that once] he has checked the nose [*hotmo*], he may not proceed further, as it is written, "*kol asher nishmat ru'ah hayyim be-appav.*" (Talmud, *Yoma* 85a)

The context of the passage is a larger discussion of necessary and permitted life-saving efforts on Yom Kippur and Shabbat; the issue of determining death is related to through roundabout means, and even then only in extreme circumstances.

Indeed, Dr. Avraham Steinberg notes that there is no list of criteria, or even discussion, in any Mishnaic or Talmudic source of determining death under "routine" circumstances.[1] This is likely due to the fact that in ancient times (and even as little as 100 years ago), these questions were irrelevant in "normal" situations; determining death was not overly complicated. Without intensive medical therapies, in most "standard" cases, organ systems shut down within moments of each other, if not simultaneously, and identifying when that occurred was not particularly challenging.

Text

The text as quoted above is that which appears in the modern printings of the Talmud, known as the "Vilna Shas," published by the Romm

---

1 *Entzyklopedia Hilkhatit Refu'it* (Jerusalem: Schlesinger Institute, 2006), vol. 6, s.v. *rega ha-mavet*, col. 834.

family in 1881; this was the text in Rashi's library as well.[2] However, most prior editions, including those of the majority of the classic medieval commentators,[3] contain an important textual variant. While the importance of textual variations is often debated in halakhic literature, the differences in this context are amplified, as it appears that Rashi and *Me'iri* alone assumed that the text that we have today is in fact correct.

In Rashi's version, the two options of where one must check for signs of life in an avalanche victim are the nose/face (*hotmo*) and the heart (*libbo*). The more common medieval version, however, substitutes *tibburo* – generally translated as abdomen, stomach, or navel – for *libbo*.[4] In its parallel (but slightly different) version of the discussion, the Talmud *Yerushalmi* also describes the disagreement as *hotmo* vs. *tibburo*.[5]

It is noteworthy that the *tibburo* text appears to fit more smoothly into the broader discussion. The Talmud develops a parallel between two Tannaic disputes – the first debates which part of the victim's body must be examined in order to ascertain if he is alive, while the second debates the origins of fetal development. In the latter discussion, the Talmud records two opinions regarding the point from which the fetus develops – the head or the *tabbur* – each with a respective Biblical proof-text. The textual version that includes *tibburo* as an option in the first debate more elegantly completes the parallel than the alternate (modern) text, according to which we must explain the comparison between the heart (*libbo*) in the first dispute and the navel (*tabbur*) in the second.

Some have argued that the modern text (Rashi's version) is less likely to be authentic in light of the fact that the alternate text (the *Yerushalmi* version) more seamlessly creates a coherent discussion.[6] This would entail eliminating any mention of the heart from the Talmud's discussion

---

2 Rashi, *Yoma* 85a, s.v. *hakhi garsinan*.
3 Rabbeinu Hananel, ad loc.; Rif, *Yoma* 5a (Rif pagination); Rosh, *Yoma* 8:16; Ramban, *Torat ha-Adam, sha'ar ha-meihush, inyan ha-sakkanah* (p. 33 in the Mossad ha-Rav Kook edition); Rabbeinu Yeruham, *Toldot Adam ve-Havah*, *netiv* 12, *helek* 9.
4 *Dikdukei Soferim* (*Yoma* 85a) notes that the British Museum's Talmudic manuscript, as well as an older manuscript found in Munich, also quotes *tibburo* instead of *libbo*.
5 Talmud *Yerushalmi*, *Yoma* 8:5. This source will be discussed further below.
6 A. Steinberg, "Determining the Moment of Death and Heart Transplants" (Hebrew) in M. Halperin (ed.), *Kevi'at Rega ha-Mavet*, 2nd edition (Jerusalem: Schlesinger Institute,

entirely, which would seemingly support discounting its role in determining death. According to this approach, the Talmud presents only two possible evaluations to determine death – examination of the *tabbur* or *hotem*.

Despite the lack of elegance in Rashi's text, R. J. David Bleich notes that Rashi does not even make mention of the discrepancy between *libbo* and *tibburo*, even though he was keenly aware of the explicit mention of *tabbur* as an option for the origin of fetal development in the subsequent discussion.[7] While not necessarily proof of either conclusion, Rashi's silence on the matter should mitigate possible ramifications derived from the alternate text. In fact, *Yefeh Einayyim* comments that when the Talmud employs the term *libbo*, it actually intends to refer to the *tabbur*; it simply chose to provide a more localized landmark where the heartbeat can be assessed more accurately, as this is "*ha-regesh ha-hiyuni*," the "vital sensation." In his view, *tabbur* is a general term that incorporates *libbo* within its spectrum, and the textual differences between the variant texts are irrelevant. The Talmud presents two possible evaluations to determine death – examination of *libbo/tibburo* or *hotmo*.[8]

Hotmo and Libbo

The Talmud ultimately rejects the comparison between the two Tannaic disputes, moving on to more clearly analyzing *hotmo* vs. *libbo/tibburo*. In delineating this disagreement, the Talmud is less descriptive as to the significance of these landmarks and what one should be checking for once having uncovered them. The simplest explanation is that checking **hotmo** indicates looking for signs of **respiration**, while checking **libbo** indicates looking for signs of a **heartbeat** or pulse, these landmarks having been selected as the most sensitive locations for detecting each respective function. R. Pappa concludes that both opinions agree that if the victim is discovered head-first, only his respiration need be examined;

2007) (henceforth, *KRhM*), 46; Y. Sheilat, "Determining the Moment of Death for Organ Donation" (Hebrew) in *KRhM*, 282.
7 R. J. David Bleich, *Bi-Netivot ha-Halakhah* 3 (henceforth *BNhH*), 132-3.
8 *Yefeh Einayyim, Yoma* 8:5.

they disagree only regarding a case in which he is discovered feet-first. In such a case, is evaluating his heartbeat (*libbo*) sufficient, or may/must the rescuers continue to uncover him in order to check for respiration (*hotmo*)? According to this reading of the passage, cessation of respiration certainly establishes that the victim is dead, while one opinion maintains that cessation of heartbeat does as well.

The meaning of the term *libbo* appears quite straightforward, especially according to the modern (Rashi's) text. The term *libbo* refers to the heart; according to the opinion that maintains that evaluation of *libbo* is sufficient to determine death, recovery efforts must continue until the upper chest is revealed so as to enable an effective cardiac exam. In an age before stethoscopes, this most likely included palpating for the point of maximal impact (PMI, at approximately the fifth rib space between the anterior axillary and mid-clavicular lines), and possibly even auscultating by placing an ear on the victim's chest.

The alternate text of *tibburo*, however, leaves room for far more ambiguity. The term refers to the abdomen, stomach, or navel, and there are no vital signs traditionally examined in those areas. While R. Bleich suggests that it refers to palpating the abdominal aorta and searching for a pulse,[9] this is unlikely; the abdominal aorta is often difficult to feel and is a rather insensitive indicator of continued heartbeat. Rejecting this approach, Dr. Steinberg suggests that *tabbur* is intended as a means of assessing respiration, possibly referring to the movement of the anterior abdominal wall or possibly the diaphragm.[10]

Dr. Steinberg notes that according to his interpretation that *tibburo* also refers to breathing, almost all Talmudic commentators throughout the ages who had the text of *tibburo* in hand operated under the assumption that the sole criteria for determining death is the lack of breathing – in modern medical terms, "the irreversible cessation of spontaneous respiration" (ICSR). Their version of the Talmudic text does not entertain any other positions, only considering evaluation of *tibburo* or *hotmo*. While Rashi does allow for another position as a result of his text, it is only Rashi and *Me'iri* who even entertain such a stance; all the other

---

9 *BNbH*, 133.
10 "Determining the moment of death," 46.

commentators, by citing the *tibburo* text and thereby eliminating that possibility, implicitly disagree with it. Dr. Steinberg argues that in deciding matters of practical Halakhah, one should follow the great majority of the Talmudic commentaries, as opposed to relying on Rashi alone, and therefore completely reject any criteria other than ICSR as determinant of death.[11]

R. Bleich notes, however, that even if we were to accept Dr. Steinberg's suggestion and rely solely on respiration in determining death, we must still analyze what the Talmud means when it refers to examining respiration. Does it necessarily refer to criteria for how death should be defined, or as a means to assess some other criteria?[12] This difference is fundamental to understanding the Talmudic discussion.

Meanings and Significance: Criteria and Tests

Analyzing this discussion within the bioethical framework described previously – distinguishing between **definitions** of death, physiological **criteria** that satisfy those definitions, and **tests** that prove fulfillment of those criteria – provides for a structured understanding of the Talmudic debate. Are the alternate Talmudic opinions suggesting different possible **criteria** for establishing death – cessation of respiration or cessation of heartbeat? Or do the opinions debate the appropriate **tests** – feeling the nostrils for breathing or palpating the upper chest for heartbeat – that could establish fulfillment of **criteria** that the Talmud takes for granted?

Furthermore, what is the reasoning behind these different positions? According to R. Pappa, both opinions agree that *hotmo* is sufficient to determine death; when uncovering a buried victim head-first, one should stop at the nostrils and evaluate respiration. The position advocating *libbo* argues only in a case of discovering the victim feet-first. Once the chest is revealed, a negative cardiac exam is sufficient to determine death and prohibit any further recovery efforts, but even this position agrees that a negative respiratory exam is also sufficient to determine death.

---

11 Ibid.
12 *BNhH*, 132, 146.

At first glance – and as argued by Dr. Steinberg – R. Pappa argues in favor of determining death based solely upon respiratory criteria. Understanding the previous Talmudic discussion as debating the **criteria** for death, R. Pappa concludes that there is actually no real disagreement; even the *libbo* position admits that a negative respiratory exam is sufficient to determine death. When the victim is found feet-first, however, the *libbo* position argues that since breathing cannot continue without a heartbeat, evidence for no heartbeat, sufficiently proven by a negative cardiac exam, is also indicative of death – but, according to Dr. Steinberg, **the true criteria is lack of respiration according to all opinions**. This is certainly true if the alternate option to *hotmo* is *tibburo*; in that case, the opinions only differ regarding whether an evaluation of *tibburo* sufficiently indicates a lack of respiration.

Assuming that the Talmud is debating appropriate criteria for death, Dr. Steinberg argues that the conclusion supports universal agreement that ICSR is the appropriate halakhic criteria for death. This contention is further supported by the fact that the only evidence cited by the Talmud (in the form of a Biblical proof-text) supports relying on respiration.[13]

This understanding of the debate however, is difficult to read into the Talmudic text. If both opinions maintain that cessation of respiration is a sufficient **criteria** to establish death, why doesn't the *hotmo* opinion rely on cessation of heartbeat, as the *libbo* opinion does, when the victim is uncovered feet-first? If there is no heartbeat, the victim cannot be breathing; why then require continued checking until *hotmo* if breathing is not physiologically possible? Reading the Talmud as debating the **criteria** for death invariably leads to this conundrum.

Rashi therefore explains that the Talmud is not debating the actual **criteria** for death – cessation of heartbeat or respiration – but only the particular **tests** used to determine whether some previously agreed upon criteria have been met. Both opinions agree that a person cannot breathe without a heartbeat; the question is only whether a chest exam is sufficiently sensitive to diagnose a heartbeat.

---

13 *KRhM*, 47. Thus, according to R. Steinberg, ICSR is certainly the conclusion of the Talmud according to the *Yerushalmi* text and even according to his understanding of Rashi's version of the *Bavli*.

Rashi explains that when uncovering the victim feet-first, the *ḥotmo* opinion requires continuing the recovery until reaching *ḥotmo* because "sometimes life (*ḥiyyut*) is not perceptible in the heart, but is perceptible in *ḥotmo* (*de-zimnin de-ein ḥiyyut nikkar be-libbo ve-nikkar be-ḥotmo*)."[14] According to the *ḥotmo* opinion, a superficial chest exam is simply insufficiently sensitive to diagnose a heartbeat. *Hakham Tzvi* explains that a negative cardiac exam can often be quite misleading; because the heart is buried beneath the chest wall, a palpable heartbeat cannot always be detected even though the heart continues to pump blood throughout the body.[15] Because of the difficulty and lack of reliability of a cardiac exam, this opinion allows and mandates that when discovering a victim feet-first, recovery efforts continue towards uncovering *ḥotmo* so that a more sensitive, reliable, and accurate determination of **cardiac** activity – namely, a respiratory exam – can be performed.

Rashi thus assumes that even the opinion that requires checking *ḥotmo* agrees that **the criteria for death requires the irreversible cessation of heartbeat**; the Talmudic argument relates only to which anatomical location allows for a more accurate diagnosis. The *libbo* opinion merely disagrees as to the requisite sensitivity necessary to make this determination. Acknowledging the limitations of a superficial chest exam to ascertain a heartbeat, this opinion believes that the diagnosis is nevertheless sensitive enough to determine death, essentially arguing for a lower sensitivity threshold.

When the victim is uncovered head-first, R. Pappa argues that even the *libbo* opinion agrees that a negative respiratory exam is sufficient to determine death – not because he essentially accepts respiratory **criteria** for death, but because he agrees that a negative respiratory exam is sufficiently sensitive and reliably accurate to ascertain the irreversible

---

14 Rashi, *Yoma* 85a, s.v. *hakhi garsinan amar Rav Pappa*.
15 *Hakham Tzvi*, responsa no. 87; this approach is discussed in chapter 8. R. Moshe Feinstein (*Responsa Iggerot Mosheh*, YD 2:146) takes issue with *Hakham Tzvi*'s approach and offers an alternative physiological explanation, although Dr. Abraham S. Abraham notes (*Nishmat Avraham*, YD 2d ed., 481) that R. Feinstein's interpretation of the debate is similarly fraught with difficulty. R. Feinstein's position on this matter will be more carefully analyzed in chapters 10-11.

cessation of **cardiac** function. Since the rescuer can effectively prove that the heart is not beating by examining for breathing, when finding the motionless victim head-first and finding no signs of respiration, a rescuer may not continue his recovery efforts; the victim is considered dead based on **cardiac** criteria. The *hotmo* position agrees with this argument because he also ultimately agrees that death requires the heart to stop. He only argues that an evaluation of heartbeat is insufficiently sensitive to make such a determination; thus, even when uncovering the victim feet-first, we require checking for respiration, the most sensitive means of assessing **cardiac** function.

Hakham Tzvi follows Rashi's line of thought and asserts that respiration assists the heart in its vital work, and therefore functions as a reliable indicator of cardiac activity. Quoting from R. Abraham ibn Ezra,[16] R. Yehudah Ha-Levi,[17] and *Sefer Sha'ar ha-Shamayim*,[18] *Hakham Tzvi* reports that the "purpose" (or goal) of inhalation is to bring cool air to the heart, preventing it from overheating from its continuous pumping, while exhalation works to rid the body of the now-warmed air. Indeed, this was the popular scientific consensus for much of human history.[19] (Due to its importance and significance in the discussion of "brain death" in Halakhah, *Hakham Tzvi*'s responsa will be analyzed separately in chapter 8.)

In summary, Dr. Steinberg maintains that *hotmo* and *libbo* are disparate **criteria** for death and that R. Pappa concludes that both opinions essentially agree that **cessation of respiration** is the determining factor. Rashi, on the other hand maintains that the Talmud's question relates to the accuracy and sensitivity of different possible **tests** of cardiac function – assuming that **cardiac criteria** and cardiac criteria alone determine death.

---

16 Commentary to *Bereishit* 2:7.
17 *Kuzari* sec. 4.
18 Sec. 9, s.v. *ha-lev*.
19 For a thorough discussion and analysis, as well as details of the historical record, see E. Reichman, "The Halakhic Definition of Death in Light of Medical History," *Torah U-Madda Journal* 4 (1993): 148-74.

The Meaning of Hotmo

Offering an alternate approach to the entire dispute, R. Hayyim David Ha-Levi[20] and R. Shemuel Wosner[21] posit an expansive interpretation of *hotmo*. They claim that examining *hotmo* includes not only checking for respiration – assessed through signs of nose breathing – but also for signs of a continued heartbeat – assessed by examining the carotid (neck) and/or temporal (temple) pulses. Understanding *hotmo* more expansively forces a reinterpretation of the entire Talmudic debate. According to Rabbis Ha-Levi and Wosner, the opinion arguing for ***libbo*** claims that **a test for continued heartbeat is always necessary** – through examining the actual heart when the victim is uncovered feet-first and by examining the carotid and temporal pulses when uncovered head-first. Conversely, the opinion arguing for ***hotmo* always requires both a respiratory and cardiac exam** before abandoning recovery efforts. According to Rabbis Ha-Levi and Wosner, all opinions require checking for signs of cardiac/circulatory function; they only debate whether checking for respiration is necessary as well.

This approach is quite novel and lacks much support, textual or otherwise. R. Yitzhak Sheilat argues that the simple meaning of the term *hotmo* refers to respiration and no one has ever interpreted it so broadly so as to encompass checking pulses as well. All other interpretations therefore allow for a Talmudic opinion that relies **solely on checking respiration** in determining death – although they may disagree as to what this position signifies (an independent **criterion** of respiration or a **test** of cardiac function).[22] The complete silence of the commentators regarding any mention of checking for pulses in the head and neck is sufficient proof, argues R. Sheilat, that they rejected such an approach.

Moreover, R. Sheilat notes, in context, the Talmud is detailing the extent of permissible recovery efforts on Shabbat and probing their limits. When the Talmud describes discovering the victim's head first and removing enough rubble to uncover his nose, it means precisely that – it is permissible to uncover up until the nose, not quite revealing the neck (where the

---

20 *Responsa Aseh Lekha Rav* 8:64.
21 *Responsa Shevet Ha-Levi* 7:235.
22 KRhM, 286.

carotid arteries are located). This effectively limits the exam to respiration alone, specifically excluding an additional cardiac/circulatory exam. This second critique is not quite as strong, as Rabbis Ha-Levi and Wosner would argue that the Talmudic term *hotmo* refers to the nose area more broadly, encompassing the temporal and carotid regions, and is not limited to the nostrils specifically. (To avoid any ambiguity in our discussion, from here on we will use the term *hotmo* to refer to the nose, face, and possibly neck.)

R. Shaul Yisraeli also takes issue with this position, noting that it appears to contradict the Talmud's conclusion.[23] According to Rabbis Ha-Levi and Wosner, checking for carotid/temporal pulses (implied by *hotmo*) is equivalent to checking the heartbeat directly. In their view, the opinion arguing *libbo* requires checking the heartbeat by evaluating the heart when the victim is discovered feet-first and the carotid and temporal pulses when discovered head-first, while the opinion arguing *hotmo* requires checking for respiration as well in both instances. Accordingly, the debate exists regardless of the direction in which the victim is found; when discovered head-first, the opinion arguing *libbo* requires examining only the pulses, while the opinion arguing *hotmo* requires checking breathing as well – contradicting R. Pappa's assertion that both opinions agree on *hotmo* in such a case.[24]

---

23 "Regarding Permitting Heart Transplants Today" (Hebrew) in *KRhM*, 301.
24 This critique can also be somewhat mitigated by analyzing more specifically what each Talmudic opinion means according to Rabbis Ha-Levi and Wosner. Even in their view, the opinion arguing *libbo* does not necessarily agree that checking the carotid and temporal pulses is **equivalent** to examining the heart itself. A carotid and/or temporal pulse check, although indicative of cardiac/circulatory function, is not as sensitive as a direct cardiac exam. Thus, when uncovering the victim feet-first, having reached the heart and found no heartbeat is sufficient to declare the victim dead and prohibit any further recovery efforts on Shabbat. When uncovering the victim head-first, evidence for lack of heartbeat is also necessary to determine death, as assessed through a carotid/temporal pulse exam, but since it is not quite as sensitive as a direct cardiac exam, that evaluation is sufficient to determine death only in conjunction with a negative respiratory exam – *hotmo* – as R. Pappa concluded. The negative respiratory exam increases the sensitivity of the pulse check sufficiently to allow for a valid determination of death.

While defending the approach of Rabbis Ha-Levi and Wosner, this suggestion similarly has no basis in Talmudic or commentarial literature. Neither R. Ha-Levi nor R. Wosner offer any suggestion as to how to appropriately assess the sensitivity of the

Criteria, Tests, and Definition

As we have noted, **criteria** for determining death are selected as representing particular **definitions** of what death means.

For those who assume that the *hotmo* position advocates adopting respiratory criteria for death, the **definition** of death is the inability to breathe on one's own, the **criterion** meeting this definition is the ICSR, and the **test** that establishes the fulfillment of that criteria is a nose/face exam.

The opposing position is slightly more complex. According to Rashi, the **criterion** for death is cessation of cardiac function, and the most accurate **test** that establishes the fulfillment of that criteria is a respiratory evaluation. But what is the **definition** of death?

Some argue that determining death depends entirely upon the heartbeat and cardiac activity. *Hakham Tzvi*[25] cites the *Zohar*,[26] which states that all life force ("*hiyyut*") derives from the heart; were the heart to stop for even a moment, a person could not live. Many, in particular those who are opposed to recognizing "brain death" as halakhically meaningful, frame the issue in these terms. Upon deeper reflection, however, this position presents many difficulties, as it cannot account for many new technological advances in an acceptably coherent fashion.

If cessation of cardiac activity defines death, how should we define a patient during open-heart surgery, who is maintained on a heart-lung machine? His heart is stopped and oxygenated blood is circulated through his body by intricate machinery – is he dead? For most patients, relying on the requirement for irreversibility in any determination of death resolves this problem. Most patients will make it through surgery and ultimately be disconnected from the heart-lung machine. When their hearts were stopped intra-opertatively, it was not tantamount to death because the cessation was not irreversible. What would be the status of this patient,

---

carotid/temporal pulse check vis-à-vis a direct cardiac exam, or even if insufficient, how a negative respiratory exam overcomes this problem. Although technically plausible, their interpretation is certainly highly unlikely, and possibly the reason that this approach is rejected – either implicitly or explicitly – by almost all others authorities.
25 Responsum no. 87.
26 *Pinhas* 221b.

however, if he were unable to come off of the machine? When would we considered him to have died – when he was initially placed on the heart-lung machine or when it was ultimately removed?

This position similarly has difficulty explaining the status of a patient with an artificial heart, whose natural heart was (irreversibly) stopped, removed and replaced by a substitute. (The transplant is, in effect, simply a heart-lung machine that can remain in a patient for long periods.) This person no longer has any innate cardiac activity. Should he be considered dead even though he walks and talks?

Two possible solutions to this problem require broadening what "cardiac" criteria for death really mean. The first proposes that the focus should not be on the action of the heart *per se*, but rather on the outcome of the heartbeat – namely, effective circulation of oxygenated blood. The lack of heartbeat is a criterion of death only when it no longer accomplishes that goal. Accordingly, the **definition** of death is the absence of effective circulation and the true **criterion** of death is not the cessation of the pumping action of the heart, but rather the (irreversible) cessation of oxygenated blood flow. When circulation is maintained through a heart-lung machine or an artificial heart, the patient does not meet the criteria for death – even if his natural heart never returns to healthy functioning – because oxygenated blood continues to circulate through his body.[27]

R. Bleich advocates a second approach. In his view, the lack of a heartbeat *per se* is not a **criterion** for death, but instead merely an example of something broader. R. Bleich proposes that the true **definition** of death is the irreversible cessation of "vital motion," defined by perceptible spontaneous movements. As long as the body maintains any function that spontaneously produces motion that promotes health – be it heartbeat, respiration, circulation, or any other movement – **criteria** meeting this **definition** of death have not been met. As long as this motion can be described as "vital," the patient is alive, regardless of whether he is connected to a heart-lung machine or supported by an artificial heart. The

---

27 R. Hershel Schachter (*Be-Ikvei ha-Tzon*, 37) adopts this approach to explain Mishnah *Ohalot* 1:6, which describes decapitation as death – the immediate exsanguination caused by forceful decapitation renders circulation ineffective. This idea will be further elaborated in the next chapter.

heartbeat is important inasmuch as it is an example of "vital motion" and often the last vestige of such motion in a dying patient. R. Bleich argues that this is in fact the source for Rashi's underlying assumption of cardiac criteria for death.[28] This approach will be analyzed more extensively in the next chapter and in chapter 17.

The different approaches to understanding the nature of the Talmudic debate – as a dispute about criteria or a disagreement regarding valid tests – interpret the cited proof-text in different ways.

The Talmud cites a Biblical verse as a proof that "the central life force is in the nose" and that all opinions agree that evaluation of *hotmo* alone is sufficient (and permitted) when the victim is uncovered head-first. In context, the verse describes the devastation of the Deluge, which killed *"kol asher nishmat ru'ah hayyim be-appav"* (Bereishit 7:22). Ostensibly, the Torah describes the demise of both humans and animals. Rashi, noting the slight redundancy of *"nishmat"* and *"ru'ah,"* comments that the verse describes "the soul of the spirit of life" (*neshamah shel ru'ah hayyim*),[29] leading some of Rashi's supercommentaries to question to whom specifically the verse refers.[30] These linguistic difficulties lead to significant variations of English translations, ranging from "all who have the soul of the breath of life" to "all in whose nostrils [is] breath of a living spirit." To avoid confusion or possible misinterpretation, the verse will subsequently be cited in transliteration.

---

28 *BNhH* 121-2, 140.
29 Rashi, ad loc. s.v. *nishmat*.
30 Ibn Ezra, s.v. *ve-yitakhen*, notes that a *neshamah* (loosely translated as soul) resides only in humans, while an animal's "life-force" is described in different terms. With this in mind, R. Eliyahu Mizrahi, ad loc., suggests emending the text of Rashi's comment to read, "the breath of the spirit of life" (*neshimah shel ru'ah hayyim*) – the word for breathing (*neshimah*) differing from soul (*neshamah*) by only one letter. This is the preferred approach of other supercommentaries as well; accordingly, the verse describes "all those who breathe" and refers to both people and animals. R. Menachem Kasher (*Torah Sheleimah, Bereishit* 7:22, n. 91) suggests that it is not the word *nishmat* alone that refers to breathing, but rather the entire phrase, *"nishmat ru'ah hayyim."* This is the reason, he suggests, that Talmud *Yoma* selected this verse to describe respiration, rather than the earlier verse (*Bereishit* 2:7), "And He blew into his nose [face] the soul of life" (*va-yipah be-appav nishmat hayyim*); in omitting the term *ru'ah*, that phrase refers to the soul (or some other metaphysical reality), rather than to respiration.

Viewed through the lens of the first approach described above, the verse defines the **criteria** for death, focusing exclusively on respiration. Accordingly, R. Pappa specifically notes that respiration is the accepted **criteria** for death according to both Talmudic opinions. As we noted, however, Rashi understands that irreversible cessation of cardiac activity (or of "vital motion") is the universally accepted **criteria** for death; the Talmudic debate only refers to the most appropriate **test** to evaluate whether these criteria have been met. Accordingly, R. Pappa cites the verse to support relying on a respiratory exam as proof of irreversible cardiac arrest. Since, in Rashi's view, the debate is about which **test** is more sensitive, reliable, or accurate in assessing the irreversible cessation of cardiac function, the Biblical verse serves only to verify that a respiratory exam meets these standards. It does not define any Biblical notion of death or provide actual criteria, but rather only supports the practical notion that examining *hotmo* is a more sensitive, accurate, and reliable **test** in assessing cardiac function than a chest exam.[31]

Indeed, in Talmudic times, a negative **respiratory exam** – presumably performed by placing an object (perhaps a hand or a feather) near the victim's nose and looking for movement – was a certain sign of death, as it indicated irreversible **cardiac failure** (or perhaps more precisely, the irreversible cessation of all "vital motion"). However, the Talmudic debate as to which test is more sensitive or what is the appropriate sensitivity threshold indicates that the choice of test depends upon statistics and probability, allowing for some fluidity in ascertaining which is most appropriate.

The question of which test is superior is a matter of *practical* concern – which is the most accurate measure of cardiac function? – and should therefore be scientifically determined. This is true regardless of which **criteria** is being tested. While the ultimate halakhic **definition** of death has certainly endured, the **tests** that assess whether it has been met – and even more importantly, the irreversibility of such a state – have most certainly been updated. Major advances in resuscitative and critical care medicine have allowed and guided recovery from what in years past would have been described as lethal injuries (especially in cases of trauma, such as a

---

31 Rashi's understanding of the proof-text is discussed further in chapter 17.

building collapse). Today, far more sensitive and specific tests are available and, as R. Shelomoh Zalman Auerbach[32] and R. Ovadiah Yosef[33] have argued, must be used. According to Rashi's understanding, since current technology can detect cardiac function that can be imperceptible to direct palpation, it should substitute for the Talmudic recommendation for a respiratory exam.[34] According to this approach, it is not the irreversible lack of a palpable heartbeat that defines death, but rather the objective lack of cardiac function, and as R. Moshe Feinstein argues,[35] proper evaluation demands the most precise, accurate, and reliable tests available.

Applying the Framework: Circumstances

As noted above, the Talmud describes an extreme case of determining death – a trauma complicated by potential Shabbat restrictions. Can these principles be applied to other situations as well?

Rashi offers general guidelines for employing the Talmud's principles in broader circumstances, explaining that they apply when the ill person appears similar to a corpse (*domeh le-meit*) and no longer moves his limbs (*she-eino meiziz eivarav*).[36] When a victim of a building collapse appears

---

32 *Nishmat Avraham*, OH, 2d ed., 502

33 *Livyat Hen*, no. 93.

34 The Rabbinical Council of America's recent study (Vaad Halacha of the Rabbinical Council of America, "Halachic Issues in the Determination of Death in Organ Transplantation – Including an Evaluation of the Neurological 'Brain Death' Standard" [Sivan 5770/June 2010], 26, argues that the verse is cited as an *asmakhta* – "scriptural support for a rabbinic enactment" (as per Jastrow Dictionary, s.v. *asmakhta*) – connoting that it is simply an indication that one test is superior to another. The term *asmakhta*, however, can often have normative connotations as well – such as an "enactment" – possibly giving the impression that the requisite tests to ascertain whatever criteria is being argued are static and mandated by rabbinic fiat. As R. Auerbach and R. Yosef argue, however, since the matter is one of determining the accuracy, sensitivity, and reliability of a scientific conclusion, the selection of such a test amongst various options should rest on scientific and medical evidence, not rabbinic decree. Given this possible interpretation of *asmakhta*, using that term may be misleading and is therefore avoided in this text.

35 *Responsa Iggerot Mosheh*, YD 2:146.

36 *Yoma* 85a, s.v. *ad heikhan*. R. Moshe Tendler, "Halakhic Death Means Brain Death," *Jewish Review* (January-February 1990): 6-7, 20, focuses on Rashi's usage of the term

so incapacitated, an onlooker might be seriously uncertain whether or not the victim is still alive and possibly requires further recovery efforts, prompting the Talmudic debate as to the appropriate (or permitted) extent of these efforts on Shabbat. In similar situations of uncertainty, the same principles apply.

A questioner (whom we now know to have been R. Tzvi Hirsch Chajes) suggested to *Hatam Sofer* that the Talmudic criteria are limited to a case of a building collapse. In "normal" circumstances, however, such as an elderly person dying from a chronic disease, R. Chajes argues, a pronouncement of death should not be made so quickly. *Hatam Sofer* notes the irony of such an argument, as in traumatic circumstances, it is far more likely for a person to appear dead even though he would not in more mundane situations. In fact, *Hatam Sofer*, argues, the Talmud's discussion is applicable to all ill patients, as indicated by the fact that the Biblical proof-text cited by the Talmud is general in its scope and in no way suggests limiting these principles to avalanche or other trauma situations.[37]

Yerushalmi

As we noted above, the Talmud *Yerushalmi*[38] contains a parallel discussion to the Talmud *Bavli*, albeit with some variation – the most significant being the *Yerushalmi*'s substitution of *tibburo* for *libbo*. The first opinion argues that *hotmo* should be the determining factor, since it is where "existence" is maintained (*be-hu de-hava kayyam*), while the counter opinion maintains that *tibburo* should be determinant, since it is the location from which a person is created (*be-hu de-hava rabbon*). A textual note from *Masoret ha-Shas* in the "standard" printed version of the *Yerushalmi* notes that older editions contain a variant reading, substituting *rakkon*

---

meiziz (he moves), an active form of the verb, as opposed to describing the limbs passively as "moving." R. Tendler argues that this indicates that Rashi only regarded movement as relevant when caused or induced by the central nervous system. This position is analyzed more carefully in the next chapter.

37 *Responsa Hatam Sofer*, YD, 339.
38 *Yerushalmi*, *Yoma* 8:5.

(soft) for *rabbon* (a one letter difference that, due to similarities between a *bet* and a *kaf*, could easily lead to typographical error).

Korban ha-Eidah elaborates that identifying *hotmo* as the "place of existence" is predicated upon the Biblical verse, *"kol asher nishmat ru'ah hayyim be-appav,"* which indicates that *hotmo* is where existence lies. *Tibburo*, on the other hand, represents the first formed part of the fetus, from which the rest of the body "sprouts." According to *Korban ha-Eidah*'s reading, the discussion in the *Yerushalmi* parallels the first suggestion made in the *Bavli* comparing the two Tannaic disputes, which was subsequently rejected. While the *Yerushalmi* does not record a rejection of this approach, nor even mention the Biblical verse in support of *hotmo*, it is difficult and likely inappropriate to derive anything from the *Yerushalmi*'s silence on the matter. In sum, *Korban ha-Eidah*'s reading does not add very much to that which was already known from the *Bavli*.

Penei Mosheh, however, takes a somewhat radical position, arguing that the two opinions in the *Yerushalmi* are not in conflict; rather, each is relevant for particular circumstances. With the text of *"rakkon"* in hand, *Penei Mosheh* argues that what *Korban ha-Eidah* understood as rationales for each approach should instead be interpreted as limitations on their applicability. Both opinions agree that checking until *hotmo* is appropriate in circumstances in which the victim can be described as *"kayyam"* – meaning "when" he is *kayyam*, not "since it indicates" when he is *kayyam*. *Penei Mosheh* interprets *kayyam* to mean strong and hard (*"hazak ve-kasheh"*). As one of several plausible definitions, *Penei Mosheh* seemingly intends to describe a person who otherwise seems healthy (*hazak*) and intact (*kasheh*). However, when the victim can be described as *rakkon*, which he interprets to mean soft to the touch, respiration is unlikely to be discovered in his *hotem*, but signs of life may be present and perceptible elsewhere, such as at his *tabbur*. While *Penei Mosheh* describes *rakkon* as soft to the touch (*rakh ke-she-memashmeshin bo*), he is possibly more generally describing a weakened or severely injured person, whose breathing might be so shallow as to be virtually undetectable without technological means.

Dr. Avraham Steinberg has made much of the *Yerushalmi*'s text. As we noted above, given his reading of *tibburo* as also indicative of respiration, the *Yerushalmi* further isolates Rashi as unique in his insistence on including any mention of the heart in the discussion at all. Dr. Steinberg further argues that the *Bavli* debates the **criteria** for death, firmly arguing for respiratory criteria alone, while, as the *Pnei Mosheh* explains, the *Yerushalmi* discusses the most appropriate **test** to ascertain that this criterion has been fulfilled. Dr. Steinberg argues that the overwhelming majority of commentators, as well as the *Yerushalmi*, never even entertained the possibility of *libbo* having any relevance to this discussion. Therefore, even granting that Rashi disagrees, his opinion should carry little halakhic weight in the face of such staunch opposition. Moreover, irrespective of which text of the *Bavli* is correct, all authorities agree that Halakhah accepts *hotmo*; regardless of what the alternative may be, it should not matter in terms of practical Halakhah.[39]

While seemingly quite straightforward and logical, Dr. Steinberg's approach is not quite as smooth as it might appear. *Korban ha-Eidah*'s reading of the *Yerushalmi* could certainly accord with Rashi's approach, pitting a *hotmo* test against a *tibburo* test, the latter of which may, as we have argued previously, refer to the same evaluation as a *libbo* test. This would clearly seriously hinder the *Yerushalmi* from counterbalancing Rashi's position. Second, while the *tibburo* text was far more prevalent in medieval times, the halakhic codifiers (Rambam and *Shulhan Arukh*) clearly favored Rashi's text and established it as halakhically normative. Finally, R. Bleich notes that Dr. Steinberg is essentially arguing that although agreeing in conclusion, the *Yerushalmi*'s discussion is at odds with that of the *Bavli*. R. Bleich notes that no one has ever reached a similar conclusion, leaving Dr. Steinberg's conclusion with little support.[40]

Rambam's Codification

In codifying the *halakhah* in *Hilkhot Shabbat*, Rambam cites the Talmudic text, with little variance:

(18) A person upon whom an avalanche falls [and it is] questionable whether or not he [buried] there – we must [initiate] recovery efforts on his behalf (*mefak'hin alav*). If they find him alive,

---

39 *KRhM*, 47
40 *BNhH*, 132.

even though he [may be] smashed (*nitrotzetz*) and he cannot [fully recover] (*ve-i efshar she-yavri*), we must [initiate] recovery efforts on his behalf (*mefak'hin alav*) and remove him [from there] for the sake of those moments [that he can survive].

(19) If they check until *hotmo* and cannot detect a *neshamah* [loosely translated as soul], they leave him where he is, as he is already dead.[41]

In not greatly deviating from the Talmudic text, the lack of any mention of R. Pappa's claim seems startling. What emerges is that Rambam clearly sides with the position of *hotmo* regardless of the physical orientation in which the rescuers find the victim; since *hotmo* is accepted as normative, R. Pappa's assertion is largely irrelevant.[42] *Maggid Mishnah* explains that Rambam indeed sides with the first opinion cited in the Talmud – *hotmo*. *Kesef Mishnah* notes that his text of the Talmud differs from that of *Maggid Mishnah*; his version cites *libbo* as the first opinion and *hotmo* as the second. He argues that given that Rambam usually sides with the second opinion cited in the Talmud, the conclusion is not surprising according to this text. *Kesef Mishnah* explains that even according to *Maggid Mishnah*'s (and our) text, Rambam opted for the first option in this case because in matters of *pikuah nefesh*, we are lenient when it comes to matters of doubt (*safek nefashot le-hakel*). Thus, Rambam chose the more expansive approach, requiring extensive recovery efforts regardless of the direction from which the rescuers encounter the victim.

R. Moshe Feinstein analyzes in particular detail the various positions and assumptions made by *Maggid Mishnah* and *Kesef Mishnah* and how the reliance on the principle of *safek nefashot le-hakel* affects these assumptions

---

41 *Hilkhot Shabbat* 2:18-19.
42 In quoting Rambam almost verbatim, *Shulhan Arukh* (OH 329:4) adds the phrase, "regardless of whether the rescuers encountered the victim's head first or his feet first," eliminating any possible confusion. See R. Moshe Feinstein, *Responsa Iggerot Mosheh*, YD 2:146.

and presuppositions.[43] R. Feinstein is one of the few authorities who offer insight into this debate, which will be analyzed more fully in chapter 10.

Many note that this description is the only method provided by Rambam for determining the moment of death. Even in delineating the laws surrounding the moment of death (not necessarily on Shabbat), including what is permitted prior to death and that which must wait until death has occurred, Rambam does not provide a method for ascertaining that moment. In *Hilkhot Avel*, Rambam describes a *goses* – a moribund patient about to die – and states that such a person is considered to be alive, but he does not detail at which point he is considered to be dead:

> One who touches him [a *goses*] is a murderer (*harei zeh shofeikh damim*). To what is this compared? To a flickering candle, where [even a slight] touch, [can cause it to] extinguish. Anyone who closes the eyes (*me'ametz*) [of a *goses*] during the departure of the soul (*im yetzi'at ha-nefesh*) is a murderer; rather, one should wait a short while (*yishheh me'at*) [so as to rule out the possibility] that the person may have [only] fainted (*shema nit'alef*).[44]

Rambam derives the bulk of this *halakhah* from Talmud *Shabbat* 151a and draws on the analogy cited in *Semahot* 1:4. However, his requirement of a "short waiting period" is not found elsewhere and appears to be Rambam's novel addition. Although he explains why it is necessary – in case the patient is not yet truly dead and one's actions would hasten his death – nowhere does Rambam indicate how "short" this interval must be, nor even when it should begin!

Hatam Sofer argues that Rambam intended for his statements in *Hilkhot Shabbat* and *Hilkhot Avel* to complement each other. Thus, the "short while" delineated in *Hilkhot Avel* should be calculated from the moment that the victim no longer appears to be breathing and should last as long as is necessary to ensure that the victim has not merely fainted (or

---

43 *Responsa Iggerot Mosheh*, YD 2:146.
44 *Hilkhot Avel* 4:5.

experienced any other reversible condition).[45] According to *Hatam Sofer*, Rambam claims that when encountering a non-breathing victim, a rescuer should not presume that he is dead until such time has passed that it is clear that the victim is irreversibly no longer breathing. The ultimate purpose of the "short interval" is specifically to determine whether or not the victim's lack of respiration is irreversible.

From a methodological perspective, this "short while" is crucial, as Rambam's instructions for determining death require proving a negative – that is, showing evidence that the victim is no longer breathing. When encountering an avalanche victim, or any other dying patient for that matter, finding that he is not breathing at that very moment is certainly not reassuring, but it is most definitely not a sure sign of death. Perhaps the victim is not breathing now because he has died, but it is also possible that he is merely in between extended breaths. Only the passage of time can dictate that the victim's breathing has completely and irreversibly ceased. This is true regardless of whether the lack of respiration functions as the actual **criterion** for death or simply as a **test** to ascertain the fulfillment of some other criteria.

Rambam offers no reasoning for siding with the *hotmo* position, failing to cite Rashi's explanation of the Talmudic debate and even omitting the Biblical proof-text, thereby leaving himself open to the various interpretive positions offered for the original Talmudic discussion. Thus, in demanding checking the *hotem*, Rambam may either be endorsing the irreversible cessation of respiration as a **criteria** for death or as a **test** to assess the fulfillment of cardiac criteria. It is noteworthy that whereas the Talmud mentions only checking the *hotem*, Rambam adds that the rescuers are checking for signs of the *neshamah* and that when it cannot be detected, the person is dead. While a superficial reading would seem to equate the *neshamah* with breathing, thus arguing for respiratory **criteria** of death, this phrase can also refer to the place in which the *neshamah* is most easily detected, thus referring to a **test** to determine that the criteria for death have been met. Other than this slight addition, Rambam's

---

45 *Responsa Hatam Sofer*, YD, 339. *Hatam Sofer*'s approach is discussed extensively in chapter 9.

language does not appear to lend itself to preferring one option over the other in a convincing manner.[46]

R. Moshe Feinstein expends great effort in analyzing Rambam's additional "short waiting period," as will be discussed in some depth in chapter 10. More relevant to the current discussion is a specific instance of practical implementation of Rambam's novel notion.

The Talmud rules[47] and *Shulhan Arukh* codifies[48] that if a woman dies in childbirth, Shabbat restrictions are set aside in the attempt to save the life of her baby, even to the point of attempting a surgical extraction of the fetus. Rama, however, argues that "today," we no longer follow this practice even on weekdays, since we "are insufficiently expert in [determining] the death of the mother precisely enough for the fetus [to have a chance] to live (*de-ein beki'in le-hakkir be-mittat ha-em be-kiruv kol kakh she-efshar la-velad lihyot*)."[49] *Magen Avraham* explains that this problem

---

46 Rambam does not provide the reasoning behind the decisions he codifies except in rare instances, prompting the commentators to explain the deviation from the norm in those instances. Rambam's omission of Rashi's explanation as the rationale for checking until *hotmo* is therefore certainly not indicative that he disagrees with Rashi. Perhaps Rambam felt that Rashi, in suggesting that a test of respiration establishes cardiac death, only clarifies the physiological assumptions that guided the Talmud in arriving at its conclusion. He may have indeed agreed with Rashi, but did not mention his point, as it is no longer relevant after the Talmud arrived at its final decision.

Some have argued, however, that the simple understanding of the Talmud clearly advocates adopting respiratory **criteria**; Rashi's explanation is novel, and had he not made his comments, alternate interpretations would not be plausible. Thus, all commentators and decisors who quote the Talmud simply, without citing Rashi's explanation – including Rambam – necessarily disagree with him. Accordingly, Rambam specifically quoted the Talmud as is, without even hinting at Rashi's interpretation, to rule that ICSR is the sole halakhic criterion for death. Such an argument from silence is far from certain, however, and lacks supporting evidence. While possible, Rambam's formulation does not indicate a preference for either interpretation. For further discussion of this point, see chapter 17.

47 *Erkhin* 7a.
48 *OH* 330:5.
49 Ibid. and Responsa of Rama 40. Rama's position was advocated many years earlier by the *Ge'onim* (*Teshuvot ha-Ge'onim* [Mantoba], 248, quoted slightly differently in *Kenesset ha-Gedolah*, *Hagahot ha-Tur*, *OH* 330). For an analysis of this work's eclectic selection of responsa, see S. Immanuel, "The Short Responsa of the *Ge'onim*" (Hebrew) in D. Boyarin, M. Hirshman, Sh.Y. Friedman, et al. (eds.), *Atarah le-Hayyim – Mehkarim*

stems from the practical difficulty presented by Rambam's demand for a waiting period before assuming that a patient is dead.[50] Since a surgical extraction of the fetus would certainly hasten the mother's death and Halakhah forbids killing one person to save another, the surgery must wait until the mother's death can be ascertained with a substantial degree of certainty. Our inability to precisely identify when the mother has taken her last breath, however, leads to uncertainty as to when Rambam's "short waiting period" should begin, let alone when it should end. In Talmudic times and through the middle ages, there was virtually no chance for a fetus to survive in a non-breathing mother for that long; by the time the mother's death could finally be established, the fetus would certainly have expired as well. Rama therefore concludes that surgical extraction of the fetus is no longer performed.

From Rama's comments, it seems that death simply cannot be precisely determined. Based on this, some have expressed concern with any modern determination of death. Rama's concern however, is predicated on practical, and not purely halakhic, grounds. Changing realities therefore greatly affect the halakhic determination in this matter.

For example, *Shevut Ya'akov* was asked about the tragic case of a pregnant woman who was beheaded on Shabbat. A bystander leaped to his feet and incised the woman's abdomen to try to save her fetus, but he was unsuccessful and delivered a stillborn. This bystander wanted to know if his actions violated Shabbat restrictions and therefore required atonement. *Shevut Ya'akov* argues that Rambam would never have required a "short waiting period" after decapitation. Rambam's concern is practical – a person may only appear to no longer be breathing, even when actually still breathing shallowly. Rambam's ruling and Rama's extension of it are only applicable, argues *Shevut Ya'akov*, when there is some room for doubt as to the precise moment of death. However, when the moment of death is certain and obvious – such as upon decapitation – there is no need for

---

be-Sifrut ha-Talmudit ve-ha-Rabbanit li-Khevod Professor Hayyim Zalman Dimitrovski (Jerusalem: Magnes, 2000): 439-53.
50 *Magen Avraham, OH* 330, sec. 11.

a "short waiting period," and the bystander therefore acted appropriately in trying to save the baby's life.[51]

The same rule, some might argue, would be true today as well – especially for those defining death as the lack of a heartbeat – as advanced monitoring equipment can detect cardiac or respiratory activity (or lack thereof) with a high degree of certainty. There is no need for a "short waiting period" if we can absolutely determine that such functioning has ceased. The only concern is whether modern technology can establish that the lack of a heartbeat is irreversible – something that currently is not always possible.

Regardless of the criteria used – be they respiratory or cardiac – Rama's hesitancy to precisely identify the moment of death should be of little concern nowadays, as long as the assessment that is made relies upon accurate and reliable methods and data.

Shulhan Arukh's Codification

Largely borrowing from Rambam's formulation, *Shulhan Arukh* codifies this *halakhah* slightly differently:

(3) A person upon whom an avalanche falls [and it is] questionable whether he is alive or dead (*safek hai safek meit*), or [even] whether he is [buried] there or not, and even if he is [buried] there, [it is] questionable whether [the victim] is a Gentile or a Jew – we must [initiate] recovery efforts on his behalf (*mefak'hin alav*), despite [all of] these doubts (*af al pi she-yesh bo kamah sefeikot*).

(4) Even if [the rescuers] found him crushed (*merutzatz*) [in a manner in which] he can only live for a short while (*she-eino yakhol lihyot ela lefi sha'ah*), we must [initiate] recovery efforts (*mefak'hin*) and check until his *hotem*; if [the rescuers] do not sense [perceive] life (*hiyyut*) in his *hotem*, then he is certainly dead, and it does not

---

51 *Responsa Shevut Yaakov* 1:13.

matter whether [the rescuers] encountered [the victim's] head first or his feet first.⁵²

In his codification, *Shulhan Arukh* includes the other questionable issues cited by the Talmud, yet mysteriously omits the concern that prompted Rambam's formulation of the "short waiting period."⁵³ Aiming to preempt any possible questions, *Shulhan Arukh* is explicit that while doubts about the victim's status may be present, the permissive ruling is unchanged and recovery efforts are mandated. The general conclusion of both Rambam and *Shulhan Arukh* is that questions of potential "quantity of life" are irrelevant when it comes to life-saving; regardless of how long a person will live, if he is alive, he must be saved on Shabbat. This is part of a much broader discussion regarding how far one must go to save a life, and will only be touched upon here.

Following the lead of Rambam, *Shulhan Arukh* also makes no mention of Rashi's interpretation, leaving *Shulhan Arukh* open to the same interpretive possibilities as described above for Rambam. This lack of inclusion is only significant if one assumes that without Rashi's comments, Talmud *Yoma* clearly argues in favor of endorsing cessation of respiration as the absolute **criterion** for death and that it is Rashi who understands the Talmud differently. According to this approach, citing the Talmud simply, without comment, is tantamount to disagreeing with Rashi's interpretation. The ramifications of this conclusion are far reaching, as while Rashi's comments are ostensibly intended to interpret and elucidate the Talmudic discussion, Rambam and *Shulhan Arukh* are codifications of laws, meaning that their conclusions and interpretations should be understood as normative. This approach, however, is far from certain and fraught with difficulty.⁵⁴

---

52 *OH* 329:3-4.
53 Rambam's omission of these additional doubts does not appear significant, given the broader context of the chapter in *Hilkhot Shabbat* in which he codifies this ruling, in which he does discuss other cases of doubt.
54 This line of thought broaches the larger issue of Rashi's role in the halakhic process: Did he intend for his comments to be understood as normative rulings when they lend themselves as such? Or did he instead attempt to provide the clearest and most convincing explanation for a given Talmudic discussion, even when that approach is ultimately

It is important to emphasize that none of the classical commentators actually disagree with Rashi. While this Talmudic discussion is frequently cited within that halakhic literature, no one, from the early (*Rishonim*) through the later (*Aharonim*) authorities offers an alternate interpretation. Additionally, neither Rambam nor *Shulhan Arukh*, in codifying these rulings, explicitly argue with Rashi, leading to the conclusion that Rashi's approach is and has always been normatively accepted. Accordingly, Rambam and *Shulhan Arukh*, even in omitting explicit mention of Rashi's interpretation, understood Talmud *Yoma* as debating the most appropriate **tests** to determine death, with universal agreement that the **criteria** for death must at least include a lack of heartbeat.

Conclusion

As one of the most explicit discussions about determining death, Talmud *Yoma* frames the discussion for almost all halakhic analyses of "brain death." Reading this discussion through the lens of the tripartite bioethical differentiation of definitions, criteria, and tests helps explain the various approaches taken by different halakhists, as well as places the discussion within the broader bioethical context.

Explaining the Talmudic debate as pertaining to the proper **criteria** for death, as R. Moshe Tendler advocates, would seemingly allow for a more amenable position regarding accepting "brain death" as a halakhically significant determination of death. Accordingly, it is the ICSR that "brain dead" patients experience that renders them dead. However, reading this discussion as debating the appropriate **tests** for determining cardiac death, as R. Bleich suggests, precludes this conclusion, since "brain

---

not taken as normative? This issue was addressed as early as the *Shulhan Arukh* himself (*Beit Yosef*, OH 10, EH 157), although perhaps limiting its applications to certain circumstances. In Sephardic circles in particular, the question of Rashi's role has taken on additional importance given the Sephardic tendency to resolve questions of Halakhah by deferring to established decision-making protocols (*kelalei ha-pesak*). Hida (*Mahazik Berakhah*, YD 12.1) collects and summarizes much of this literature. For more modern sources since the time of *Hida*, see *Responsa Yehaveh Da'at*, vol. 5, p. 309. This topic is further discussed in chapter 17 below.

dead" patients' hearts continue to beat, a certain sign of continued life according to this approach. Complicating the matter further is how the discussion in Talmud *Yoma* relates to other determination of death discussions in Halakhah, which will be discussed in the next two chapters.

CHAPTER 6:

Mishnah Ohalot

The first chapter of Mishnah *Ohalot* identifies the various people, objects, and substances that engender and transmit ritual impurity (*tum'ah*). The prime objective of the discussion is to identify, analyze, and understand the spread of *tum'at meit* specifically – the ritual impurity engendered by a human corpse – and its particular ability to spread in covered spaces (*"ohalot"*). Interestingly, the Mishnah devotes only one subsection to identifying the moment at which these laws become relevant, stating quite plainly that "a person does not engender *tum'ah* until his spirit [*nafsho*] departs."

> A person does not engender impurity (*tum'ah*) until his spirit departs. Even one who is *meguyyad* or even a *goses* [moribund] may [still be considered alive and as such] establish levirate marriage [*zokek li-yibbum*] or exempt another from a leviratic marriage relationship [*poter min ha-yibbum*] and entitle or deprive [his mother or wife] to eat priestly tithes [*terumah*].
>
> So, too, cattle and wild animals do not engender *tum'ah* until their souls depart.
>
> If their heads were severed [*hutzu rasheihem*], they engender *tum'ah* even though they may be convulsing [*mefarkesin*], such as the tail

of a lizard [twitches after it has been severed]. (Mishnah, *Ohalot* 1:6)

The conclusion of the first part of the *mishnah* is that no matter how close a person may be to death, until that ultimate point is reached, he is considered fully alive for all halakhic matters. Since the dying man is alive, if his brother died childless and his widow must therefore perform *yibbum* (levirate marriage), she cannot marry another man until the dying man first performs *halitzah*, thereby freeing her. Similarly, the fact that he is still alive exempts his mother from *yibbum* or *halitzah* with his paternal uncle, as his father did not die childless. No matter how close to death a person may be, as long as he is still alive, his wife is not considered widowed, nor his mother childless; they may continue to eat *terumah* if he is a *kohen*, even though they themselves are not daughters of *kohanim* and are forbidden to eat *terumah* if their husband/son is no longer alive.

The Meguyyad and the Goses

The *mishnah* provides two examples of people who are close to death, but who are nevertheless certainly considered among the living – "*meguyyad*" and "*goses*." In interpreting *meguyyad*, Rashi and Rosh refer to the Biblical verse, "*godu ilana*" ("cut down the tree"),[1] and Rosh therefore explains that the term refers specifically to one whose veins (*veridim*) are cut.[2] Bartenura interprets simply as "cut" ("*mehutakh*"), referencing the same Biblical verse,[3] and Rambam similarly interprets the term as "cut or stabbed."[4] *Tiferet Yisrael* sums up his discussion by noting that regardless of how one interprets *meguyyad*, the intention is that while such a person will certainly not live (*vaday lo yihyeh*), he still maintains mental facul-

---

1 *Daniel* 1:4.
2 Rashi, *Ohalot* 1:6; Rosh, ad loc. Interestingly, *Tiferet Yisrael* (*Bo'az* 1:30) interprets the term to mean "sectioned in the transverse or axial plane," and suggests that this is what Rambam (*Hilkhot Tum'at Meit* 1:15) refers to in describing one whose abdomen was severed (*nehlak bitno*).
3 R. Ovadia of Bartenura, *Ohalot* 1:6.
4 *Commentary to the Mishnah*, ad loc.

ties/consciousness (*ba'alei sekhel*), and is therefore considered alive.[5] (The ramifications of considering the patient's mental status as an indicator of continued life are discussed in chapter 17.)

Goses is a more widely used term in Talmudic and halakhic literature and describes a moribund person, whose death is soon to come; the manner and proximate cause of the death are not at issue as they are with a *meguyyad*. While the term broadly describes one who is certainly "about to die," this *mishnah* does not provide an upper limit for that window, stating simply that a *goses* is considered alive. Based on other Talmudic discussions, some have defined a *goses* as one who will certainly die within 72 hours despite all resuscitative efforts, while others allow for a more flexible definition predicated upon a physician's clinical judgment.[6]

For those arguing against the halakhic acceptance of "brain death," determining whether or not the patient is a *goses* is of great significance. Sometimes, the clinical impression of the medical team is that despite all efforts, the "brain dead" patient will almost certainly suffer cardiac arrest in the very near future, while sometimes, the assessment is that with continued care, the patient would most likely remain stable for a longer period.[7] Frequently, the assessment is mixed with an uncertain prognosis, leaving the patient's status as a possible or questionable (*safek*) *goses*; it is unclear if his "death" is impending. Practically, this is important, as Halakhah proscribes any unnecessary movement or other intervention for a *goses*, including routine care that is not expected to improve the patient's current state.[8] Thus, while it might be permitted to move a "brain dead" patient who may remain stable for some time, it would be prohibited to move a "brain dead" patient whose death is imminent. Even for those accepting of "brain death" as halakhically meaningful, this prohibition would seemingly forbid diagnostic imaging aimed at establishing a diagnosis of "brain death" if it necessitates any movement of the patient's body.

---

[5] *Yakhin* 1:31.

[6] For a more elaborate discussion of various definitions for *goses* and their practical consequences, see D. Shabtai, "End of Life Therapies," *Journal of Halacha and Contemporary Society* 56 (2008): 22-48.

[7] Cf. D.A. Shewmon, "Chronic 'brain death' Meta-analysis and conceptual consequences," *Neurology* 51 (1998): 1538-45.

[8] *Shulhan Arukh, YD* 339:1; cf. *Nishmat Avraham, YD*, 2nd ed., 451.

Scope of Hutzu Rasheihem

After qualifying that a *meguyyad* and a *goses* are considered alive and therefore do not engender *tum'ah*, the *mishnah* elaborates that similar rules apply to the ritual defilement of animals (*tum'at neveilah*) as well. The *mishnah* concludes that if "*hutzu rasheihem*," "**their** heads were severed," they engender *tum'ah* even if they are still convulsing after death. Although conjugated in the plural, it is somewhat unclear to whom the term "*hutzu rasheihem*" applies. Does it modify the statement that immediately preceded it, limiting its application to animals? Or does it mean to include the first section as well, broadening its scope to include humans?

Tosafot, adopting the first approach, limits the applicability of the *mishnah*'s conclusion to cattle.[9] Rambam, however, adopts the second approach in interpreting the *mishnah*, applying its criteria to humans and animals; he codifies this ruling several times, once when discussing people,[10] a second time regarding animals,[11] and a third with regard to *sheratzim*.[12] Similarly, *Ba'al ha-Ma'or* explicitly adopts the second approach, citing the *mishnah*'s applicability to both humans and animals.[13] Thus, the *mishnah* teaches that decapitation of a human being is equivalent to death.

Rashi, commenting on the *mishnah* as cited in *Hullin* 21a, opts for a third option, limiting its application to only the eight swarming creatures (*sheratzim*) delineated by the Torah as having special rules regarding

---

9 *Tosafot, Hullin* 21a, s.v. *hutzu rasheihem*. Curiously, *Tosafot* include birds within the *mishnah*'s scope as well, although the *mishnah* itself makes no such mention. *Tosafot* may have simply assumed that what is true of cattle is certainly true of birds as well, although they explicitly exclude *sheratzim* without indicating why birds should be any different. It is possible that *Tosafot* took a clue from the Talmud's continuing discussion of possibly comparing the case of *hutzu rasheihem* to that of the technique used to sacrifice a bird as an *olah* offering (*havdalat olat ha-of*), which did not necessarily require completely severing the bird's head from its body. Since the Talmud posits a possible parallel between the two cases, *Tosafot* assumed that what is true of one is true of the other.
10 *Hilkhot Tum'at Meit* 1:14.
11 *Hilkhot She'ar Avot ha-Tum'ah* 2:1.
12 Ibid. 4:14.
13 *Ba'al ha-Ma'or, Hullin* 5a (Rif pagination)

ritual impurity.[14] *Ma'aseh Rokeah* explains that Rashi learned this limitation from the example brought by the *mishnah*. In its description, the *mishnah* compares post-decapitation movements to those of a severed tail of a lizard, which may continue to move even after being separated from the lizard's body, and Rashi therefore concludes that the *mishnah* refers only to animals comparable to the lizard.[15] However, it is certainly strange for the *mishnah* to employ the phrase "*hutzu rasheiheim*" – "**their heads were severed**" – to refer to *sheratzim* when no prior mention of that particular type of animal had previously been made.

Rashba attempts to defend Rashi's position in light of the context in which this *mishnah* is cited in *Hullin*.[16] The Talmud records Shemuel's claim that a person whose spinal column (perhaps cord) and the majority of its accompanying flesh were broken (*nishberah mafreket ve-rov basar imah*) is considered dead even though his trachea and esophagus (*simanim*) remain intact. These lax criteria for death seem to be at odds with those of the *mishnah* in *Ohalot*, which demands complete decapitation; why, then, doesn't the Talmud cite it immediately as proof against Shemuel's claim?[17] While Rashba ultimately rejects Rashi's approach, he suggests that Rashi interpreted the *mishnah* as limited to *sheratzim* alone so as to avoid the problem of the apparent contradiction between Shmuel's position and that of *Ohalot*.[18]

Extent of Hatazat ha-Rosh

In the context of its discussion of neck injuries and their relevance in determining an animal's suitability for consumption, the Talmudic

---

14 Rashi, *Hullin* 21a, s.v. *hutzu*.
15 *Hilkhot She'ar Avot ha-Tum'ah* 4:14.
16 Rashba, *Hullin* 21a, s.v. *amar leih*.
17 In fact, *Tosafot* (*Hullin* 21a, s.v. *hutzu mamash*) assume that the *mishnah* is at odds with Ze'iri (*Hullin* 20b), who applies Shemuel's ruling to animals.
18 Accordingly, Rashi may argue that *sheratzim* have inherently more *hiyyut* (loosely translated as "life force") than humans, and are therefore considered to be living even when suffering injuries that would render a human dead. Therefore, while a person is considered dead when only the "spinal cord and most of its accompanying flesh" is severed, a *sheretz* would be considered alive in such circumstances until its head was completely separated from its body.

discussion in *Hullin* addresses Mishnah *Ohalot* directly. The Talmud records a debate as to the precise definition of *"hutzu,"* with Reish Lakish arguing that it refers to complete decapitation (*hutzu mamash*) and R. Asi in the name of R. Mani claiming that it implies something less than complete decapitation, similar to *havdalat olat ha-of* (the manner of slaughtering a bird *olah* offering). The Talmud clarifies that the latter refers to the severing of the majority of the diameter of the *simanim*, leaving the rest of the neck intact.[19] Accordingly, the *mishnah* describing *"hutzu rasheihem"* is inexorably linked to the Talmudic discussion in *Hullin*, which will be analyzed separately in the following chapter due to its complexity.

Pirkus

The *mishnah* notes that some bodily movements are possible even after decapitation, describing them as *"pirkus,"* and that these movements do not indicate life. As most people have never witnessed an actual decapitation, the *mishnah* compares post-decapitation movements to a more commonly observed phenomenon – that of a lizard's tail continuing to wriggle even after being severed from the lizard's body. These continued movements result from residual electrical impulses in the tail's nervous tissue and are meaningless inasmuch as they do not indicate anything about the life status of the lizard itself. Rashi explains that although the

---

19 Normal *melikah* – the technique of killing birds fit for sacrifice – is similar to *shehitah* in many ways, albeit with some differences. While a *hatat ha-of* (bird sin-offering) requires severing most of only one of the two *simanim* – parallel to *shehitah* – for certain technical reasons, an *olat ha-of* (bird burnt-offering) must have both *simanim* severed. In a previous debate, R. Elazar b. R. Shimon and the Rabbis disagree regarding the specific extent that an *olat ha-of*'s two *simanim* must be severed, with R. Elazar b. R. Shimon concluding that only most of the diameter of the trachea and esophagus must be cut, while the rest of the head should remain intact. The Talmud notes that R. Asi refers to R. Elazar's opinion in describing *hutzu* as parallel to *havdalat olat ha-of*.

The Talmud further explains that both R. Elazar b. R. Shimon and the Rabbis agree that the spinal column/cord must be severed prior to severing one or both of the *simanim* during *havdalat olat ho-of*. Therefore, Reish Lakish's description of *hutzu mamash* as complete decapitation is in fact not very different from the Rabbis' perspective on *havdalat olat ha-of*, according to which everything but the bird's skin is severed.

lizard's tail may move, this does not indicate continued life (*ein zeh hiyyut*) since the tail is completely separated from the lizard's body.[20] Similarly, any bodily movements after decapitation are meaningless. The unstated assumption is that under normal circumstances, movement *is* indicative of life.

Rambam seems to adopt this notion, agreeing that movement ordinarily indicates continued life; he therefore describes *pirkus* as specifically occurring post-mortem. Although not using the modern scientific explanation regarding residual electrical impulses, he closely approximates that explanation, reporting that such movements occur in "some living creatures, when the 'moving force' (*ko'ah ha-meini'a*) that spreads throughout the limbs does not originate in one source (*mi-yesod u-motza ehad*), but rather is dispersed (*muflag*) throughout the body."[21] Adopting this principle, *Tiferet Yisrael* clarifies that it is these non-centralized forces that stimulate the lizard's tail to move even after it has been completely severed from the body. Because the source of the tail's movement is not "from a single source," it does not indicate the presence of life.[22]

R. Moshe D. Tendler argues that, with this explanation, Rambam is attempting to describe "organismal versus organ death;" if there "is no longer an integrated organism with a central source of motion, any organ which shows *pirchus* [*sic*] or trembling is halakhically dead."[23] He describes Rambam's extended explanation as "accurately describing the difference between the localized response of a muscle group to stimulus with [*sic*] the functioning of a central nervous system that integrates all parts of the body."[24] R. Tendler argues that it is precisely neurologically "integrated motion" – controlled exclusively by the brain and clearly absent in a decapitated person – that defines life. Since, he contends,

---

20 Rashi, *Hullin* 21a, s.v. *she-mefarkeset*.
21 *Commentary on the Mishnah*, ad loc.
22 *Yakhin* 1:40.
23 M.D. Tendler, "Halakhic Death Means Brain Death," *Jewish Review* (January-February 1990), 7.
24 Idem., *Responsa of Rav Moshe Feinstein: Care of the Critically Ill* (Hoboken, NJ: Ktav Publishing House, 1996), 70.

"brain dead" patients lack the vital ability for "integrated motion," they are, in fact, dead.

There are two major problems with R. Tendler's analysis, the first medical/factual and the second literary/halakhic. Writing in 1990, R. Tendler records that 48 hours after diagnosing "brain death," "the brain begins to lyse (liquefy)… If you turn the body upside down, the brain would flow out through a hole in the head."[25] While this vivid depiction may have been popular in 1990, it is certainly not true today, as described in chapters 2-3. For a variety of possible reasons, these results are simply no longer observed.[26] Today, most non-pathologists would have a very difficult time differentiating a brain from a "brain dead" patient from a postmortem specimen of a patient declared dead by cardiopulmonary criteria. Decisions and analysis based on these earlier findings must be updated so as to incorporate the current data.

Regardless, the President's Council on Bioethics reported that those advocating "brain death" criteria as determinant of death erred "in focusing on the **loss of somatic integration** as the critical sign" [emphasis added]. The Council claims that "even in a patient with total brain failure [the Council's preferred term for the more popular "brain death"], some of the body's parts continue to work together in an integrated way for some time."[27] While R. Tendler does not precisely elucidate what he means by "integrated function," it should seemingly include fighting infection, healing wounds, and maintaining temperature – precisely those functions that the President's Council cites as evidence for "integration" that continues in "brain dead" patients. Thus, even if we accept R. Tendler's reading of Rambam that lack of neurologically integrated functioning indicates death, "brain dead" patients do not appear to qualify.

From a literary perspective, it is also unclear that Rambam had in mind the theory ascribed to him by R. Tendler. Rambam appears to

---

25 "Halakhic Death," 6.
26 Cf. E.F.M. Wijdicks, E.A. Pfeifer, "Neuropathology of brain death in the modern transplant era," *Neurology* 70 (2008): 1234-7.
27 *Controversies in the Determination of Death: A White Paper by the President's Council on Bioethics* (2008), 59-60.

differentiate between bodily movements that indicate life and those that do not. He explains that when the source of the movement is "singular" – meaning the source of this specific movement is the same as all other movements – then it is indicative of continued life. However, when a movement is stimulated by a non-central force, the fact that an organ responds to such a stimulus **does not indicate** anything about the continued life of the person in question. Thus, while Rambam claimed that integrated motion is certainly indicative of a living being, he never claimed that it was the very **definition** of what it means to be alive. In describing a means to practically determine whether a given movement is indicative of continued life, Rambam did not comment as to how that continued life was to be measured or defined.[28]

"Physiological Decapitation"

Mishnah *Ohalot* appears to provide an additional method of determining if death has occurred; while Talmud *Yoma* describes cardiac and respiratory criteria or tests, the *mishnah* qualifies that decapitation is also tantamount to death. As we will see, halakhic authorities disagree whether these are actually two disparate sets of criteria or if they reflect one unified definition of death.

According to R. Tendler, this *mishnah* is proof that Halakhah takes special cognizance of the brain in determining death criteria, even in the face of continued *pirkus*. Presumably, in the *mishnah*'s case, the victim's heart continued to beat for at least several moments after decapitation, yet the *mishnah* describes this person as dead immediately upon the severance of his head. While the *mishnah* describes a case in which the brain is physically separated from the body, R. Tendler argues that this ruling can be extended to a person with a malfunctioning, although still attached, brain. He cites the discussion in *Hullin* 21a as proof that decapitation as death need not necessarily require completely severing the head from the body.

R. Tendler coined the term "physiological decapitation" to describe "brain dead" patients, arguing that this state ensues when the brain is

---

28 Cf. R. H. Schachter, *Be-Ikvei ha-Tzon* 36:12 for a similar rebuttal of this argument.

no longer perfused with oxygenated blood, even if it is still physically attached to the body. In other areas of Halakhah, organs are sometimes considered detached even though they are still physically connected to the body. Examples include certain aspects of the prohibition of eating live flesh (*ever min ha-hai*)[29] as well as the status of laying *tefillin* upon a gangrenous arm.[30] R. Tendler argues that "[b]y analogy, the cerebral blood flow studies demonstrate the very same thing with respect to the brain: that the brain is halakhically detached even though it is anatomically connected, and this is what is meant by 'physiological decapitation.'"[31] R. Tendler elaborates on this innovative diagnosis, claiming that the "complete destruction of the brain, which includes loss of all integrative, regulatory, and other functions of the brain, can be considered physiological decapitation and thus a determinant *per se* of death of the person."[32] Similarly, "[i]f it can be definitely demonstrated that all brain functions including brainstem function have ceased, the patient is legally dead in Jewish law because he is equated with a decapitated individuals [*sic*] whose heart may still be beating."[33]

In embracing this theory, R. Tendler posits that "physiological decapitation" is in fact the **decisive** and **only** definitive determination of death in Jewish law; all other suggested definitions, be they respiratory or cardiac, are ultimately merely **indicators** that "physiological decapitation" has occurred. "The classic 'respiratory and circulatory death' is in reality brain death. Irreversible respiratory arrest is indicative of brain death."[34] The same is true of cardiac arrest, "because this results in a failure to perfuse the brain, which produces total brain destruction. Thus, cessation of heart action is a cause of death rather than a component of its definition."[35]

---

29 *Shulhan Arukh*, YD 62:4.
30 *Responsa Iggerot Mosheh*, OH 1:8.
31 "Halakhic Death," 7.
32 F.J. Veith, J.M. Fein, M.D. Tendler, et al., "Brain death: A status report of medical and ethical considerations," *Journal of the American Medical Association* 238 (1977): 1653.
33 F. Rosner, M.D. Tendler, "Definition of Death in Judaism," *Journal of Halacha and Contemporary Society* 17 (1989): 25.
34 "Definition," 27.
35 "Brain death," 1654.

In other contexts, while trumpeting irreversible cessation of spontaneous respiration (ICSR) as the prime halakhic indication of death, R. Tendler refers to the concept of "physiological decapitation," although he does not address the relationship between the two notions. Even in those contexts, however, R. Tendler notes the difficulty in relying on evaluation of respiratory ability alone; by strict respiratory criteria, a person choking on a sandwich or a patient with phrenic nerve paralysis should be defined as dead even though such a patient may be "running, waving his hands, [and] making attempts to speak."[36] Even when emphasizing the ability to breathe spontaneously, R. Tendler notes that it is ultimately "brain death" that actually determines death.

R. Tendler's thesis faces several challenges of consistency, medical accuracy, and hermeneutic validity. In his many publications on the notion of "physiological decapitation," R. Tendler alternates between focusing on brain "dysfunction" and the brain's "death" – understood as the lysis, apoptosis, or necrosis of brain cells. In his usage, "dysfunction" appears to encompass failure of "integrative, regulatory, and other" functions, while "death" seemingly refers to the complete lack of cerebral perfusion – but these are far from rigorous definitions. Furthermore, as discussed earlier, even patients diagnosed as "brain dead" maintain important regulatory and integrative homeostatic brain functioning – raising difficult questions for R. Tendler's functional definition.

Moreover, deriving a functional definition of "brain death" from the *mishnah* is quite novel, as it ascribes intricate and intimate knowledge of cerebral and neural networks to the Talmudic sages. The modern scientific understanding of the brain as the prime integrator and regulator of bodily functions, as well as the seat of thought, emotion, and memory, is, in fact, modern – it was unknown in ancient times. It was for this reason that determinations of life and death, regardless of the details, have always been predicated upon clinically observable phenomena, not the brain's ability to function in a specific regard.[37] To claim that the Talmudic sages equated

---

36 *Responsa of Rav Moshe Feinstein*, 73. This problem with ICSR is further discussed in chapter 17.
37 *Responsa Iggerot Mosheh*, YD 2:146.

the cessation of brain function with decapitation is to claim that they had a greater understanding of that function than any of their contemporaries.

Additionally, R. Tendler's reliance on the *mishnah* as the source for his thesis can be challenged. While the *mishnah* does not fully describe the actual decapitation that is equivalent to death, the discussion in Talmud *Hullin* 21a clarifies that for healthy people, decapitation as death must entail the severance of the spinal cord and most of the accompanying musculature. Indeed, in citing the opinions of Reish Lakish and R. Asi, the Talmud probes precisely this point – to what extent the decapitation must be complete – with Rambam siding with the position of *"hutzu mamash."*[38] Regarding birds, the Talmud extends these criteria to require severing of the majority of one or both *simanim* as well. Thus, the Talmud clearly views the **actual separation** of the head from the body as the determinant of death, potentially eliminating the absence of cerebral functioning as a possible explanation of this *mishnah*.

Importantly, R. Tendler's assertion that the Talmud's intent in referring to decapitation is to specify the severance of the brain, and not the other organs of the face and head, is accepted by others, including R. Shelomoh Zalman Auerbach.[39] Although the *mishnah* and subsequent Talmudic discussion mention severing the head – seemingly completely – R. Auerbach assumes as a basic premise that the intent was disconnecting the brain from the rest of the body. R. Auerbach therefore allows for R. Tendler's comparison of "brain death" to Mishnah *Ohalot*'s case of decapitation – but only along with its accompanying limitations. In physical decapitation, the head is completely separated from the body; the halakhic equivalent, argues R. Auerbach, is the death of each and every cell of the brain. Unlike R. Tendler, R. Auerbach insists that only death of the **entire** brain qualifies as "physiological decapitation," not the cessation of "integrated functioning." By limiting his parallel between the two notions to structure and not function and rigorously defining the necessary criteria, R. Auerbach escapes the critiques of R. Tendler's thesis outlined in the past few paragraphs. His opinion will be analyzed and dealt with at length in chapter 16.

---

38 *Hilkhot Tum'at Meit* 1:14.
39 Quoted in *Mishnat Hayyei Sha'ah*, 49.

Analyzing this *mishnah* differently, R. J.D. Bleich rejects any comparison between a "brain dead" patient and a decapitation victim. "Brain dead" patients' brains remain intact, although largely non-functional, a reality vastly different from the complete absence of the brain resulting from decapitation. Were the brain to be completely lysed (liquefied), R. Bleich argues, perhaps a comparison could be suggested, but as explained in detail in chapter 2, this is simply not the case in clinically diagnosed "brain death." Moreover, equating the two circumstances not only is not necessarily logically compelling, but also runs counter to established halakhic principles. R. Bleich explains:

> For halakhic purposes, dysfunction of an organ is not the equivalent of its destruction or excision. A male whose testes have been removed is forbidden to cohabit with a Jewess of legitimate birth; a person whose testes remain intact but have been rendered dysfunctional suffers no such liability. Similarly, an animal whose liver has been removed is a *treifah* and its meat is forbidden; the meat of an animal whose liver performs no physiological function is permissible. Excision is defined as removal, either as a result of trauma or surgical procedure. Alternatively, it is defined as degeneration of tissue either through necrosis to the degree that it becomes "tissue which crumbles in the finger" (*basar she-nifrakh be-ziporen*) or through "decay" to the degree that it becomes "tissue which a physician scrapes away" (*basar she-ha-rofeh gorero*), e.g., gangrenous tissue. The brain tissue of a patient pronounced dead on the basis of neurological criteria does not match, or even approximate, those levels of degeneration.[40]

Were it possible to more accurately parallel the *mishnah*'s description of a missing brain, then the comparison to "brain death" might be valid, but clinical medicine does not appear to point to closer parallels in the near future.

---

40 J.D. Bleich, "Of Cerebral, Respiratory and Cardiac Death," *Contemporary Halakhic Problems, vol. IV* (Hoboken, NJ: Ktav, 1995): 322-3.

"Vital Motion"

After fundamentally rejecting any comparison between "brain death" and decapitation, R. Bleich suggests a different approach to determining death in Halakhah that clearly excludes recognizing "brain death" as death.[41] R. Bleich capitalizes upon the *mishnah*'s unstated assumption that motion is always a sign of life, positing that the ultimate (and only) indication of life is "vital motion" and that its irreversible cessation is therefore determinant of death. R. Bleich argues that the *mishnah* takes this contention so seriously that it considers the possibility that even the movements of the severed tail of a lizard might be signs of life; it is only because these movements are considered *pirkus* – meaning non-vital – that they do not qualify.

"Vital motion," in R. Bleich's view, implies any clinically observable or perceivable movement that promotes the continued viability or health of an organism. The motion of the lizard's severed tail does not provide any support to the lizard proper, identified by the *mishnah* as the hemi-section containing the head. Similarly, a heart removed from a person that continues to beat when placed in appropriate electrolyte medium does not promote the health or viability of its former owner in any way. Importantly, however, while the heart is still in its proper location – regardless of whether its continued importance lies in its status within the body of a living person or in its intrinsic ability for automaticity – its beating constitutes "vital motion," as it fulfills its role as the primary circulatory pump of oxygenated blood. Since all "brain dead" patients continue to express "vital motion" in the form of a heartbeat, they certainly qualify as living.

"Vital motion" indicates life as long as the motion not only promotes the continued viability of the person, but is also "produced" by that person. This caveat excludes artificial or external causes for bodily motion that may mimic "vital" motion. If an observer were to lift up and wave the hand of a corpse, no one would contend that the recently deceased person is alive because he is waving; the same is true of artificially induced

---

41 *Bi-Netivot ha-Halakhah* 3 (henceforth, *BNhH*), 109, 119, 122; "Of Cerebral, Respiratory, and Cardiac Death," 316-50.

cardiac and respiratory motion. If a patient were to be theoretically sustained on a continuous heart-lung machine but otherwise completely lack any other independent, spontaneous motion, he would not be considered possessing "vital motion" despite continued circulation and blood pressure, as long as no other "vital motion" exists.[42]

Given his rejection of the comparison between "brain death" and decapitation, how does R. Bleich explain the *mishnah* itself, which posits decapitation as death even in the face of a continued heartbeat? Indeed, the *mishnah* seems to prove that a heartbeat is **not** indicative of life, while R. Bleich claims that it is one form of "vital motion."

R. Bleich answers this challenge on two fronts. First, he acknowledges the possibility that there are two tracks to determine death – either the irreversible cessation of "vital motion" (including heartbeat) or complete and actual decapitation. Under ordinary circumstances, the lack of "vital motion" determines death, but decapitation is a *sui generis* definition – meaning that it applies even in situations of continued "vital motion."[43] According to this approach, decapitation qualifies as death by definition; no matter what else may be occurring in a body, the person is dead. This fits in squarely with the *mishnah*, which identifies the decapitation victim as dead despite continued "vital motion" in the form of a heartbeat.

On a more fundamental level, however, R. Bleich argues that decapitation as death even in the face of continued cardiac function need not be understood as a novel definition of death, but rather as an application of the "vital motion" principle. This alternate approach allows for a single, universal determination of death that incorporates both sets of criteria. While R. Bleich's opposition to halakhically recognizing "brain death" is independent of accepting this idea, it provides a useful and interesting model.

R. Bleich explains that this *mishnah* precludes the possibility of accepting **strict** cardiac criteria for death, as it defines the person as dead

---

42 Referring to one of the motifs of any determination of death discussion, R. Bleich relies on the concept of irreversibility, arguing that a person is dead only when suffering from an irreversible loss of "vital motion." Thus, during open-heart surgery, when these technologies are routinely employed, the patient is considered still alive since his condition is (hopefully) reversible.
43 "Of Cerebral, Respiratory and Cardiac Death," 318.

even though his heart may continue beating. Normally, however, irreversible cardiac arrest is tantamount to death, as it represents the patient's last efforts at "vital motion." In that case, R. Bleich explains, it is not the "death" of the heart *per se* that defines the individual's death, but rather the cessation of all "vital motion" – including the pumping action of the heart. The heart is only one of many examples of "vital motion," and a person may thus be deemed alive if other "vital motions" persist after the heart fails. Therefore, if a patient's heart is removed and replaced with an "artificial heart," he is not considered dead even though he will forever lack any intrinsic cardiac activity and his entire circulatory system is artificially generated. Rather, assuming he retains the capacity for "vital motion" in other aspects of life – breathing, walking, talking – he is deemed alive regardless of his cardiac function.

R. Bleich explains that decapitation is death precisely because once the head is severed, the only organ that continues to maintain any motion at all – the heart – can no longer be described as fulfilling a "vital" purpose. Upon traumatic decapitation, the victim's circulation – the essential goal of the heart's motion – is completely ineffective, since it no longer circulates oxygenated blood throughout the body. With a gaping hole just inches above the heart, effective circulation is impossible since the blood is actually being pumped out of – instead of through – the body. Even though the heart muscle may still be contracting, this motion cannot be considered "vital" since it is not promoting any productive purpose.

There are some theoretical (and some not-so-theoretical) practical ramifications of the idea that decapitation only qualifies as death when it causes the cessation of all "vital motion." If circulation could somehow be maintained so that, despite lacking a head (or brain), blood continues to flow effectively throughout the body – meaning that the heartbeat still qualifies as "vital motion" – R. Bleich would describe such a patient as alive. This position has important ramifications for the famous "sheep experiment" performed at R. Auerbach's behest, described in detail in chapter 16.[44]

---

44 The parallel debate in the world of secular bioethics was described in chapter 4.

Those who posit strict cardiac criteria for death rarely analyze their position from this perspective. It is likely, however, that in the final analysis, they would agree with and adopt R. Bleich's theory, arguing that it is not cardiac function *per se* that defines life, but rather that the heartbeat is only an example of continued "vital motion." Proponents of strict respiratory criteria for death, however, cannot accept R. Bleich's thesis without abandoning their own; if the lack of heartbeat is irrelevant, "vital motion" cannot be the determining factor. Thus, they explain decapitation as death precisely because the person has irreversibly lost the capacity for spontaneous respiration. While they do not relate directly to the *mishnah*'s phrase, "*af al pi she-mefarkesin*" (and to R. Bleich's point as to why such language is necessary), proponents of such a theory might argue that the *mishnah* adopted a rhetorical or literary flourish – something not unheard of in Mishnaic language – that was not intended as halakhically important. While this is not necessarily the clearest reading of the *mishnah*, the conviction that respiratory criteria are the sole determinants of death (based on other sources) may force this reading.

Relating the Discussions

How does Mishnah *Ohalot* relate to Talmud *Yoma*'s discussion of determining death?

R. Tendler claims that the underlying thesis of both discussions is that when the brain no longer controls and integrates the body's function, a person is dead. While Mishnah *Ohalot* more explicitly describes this notion in its analysis of decapitation, R. Tendler argues that the same is true of Talmud *Yoma*. The conclusion that death is determined by ICSR, according to R. Tendler, is simply an indication of brainstem dysfunction, and therefore death. Relying on respiratory or even cardiac criteria was merely pre-modern man's way of approximating "brain death" as best he could.

While open to a two-track definition of death, R. Bleich argues that a single uniform definition of halakhic death more elegantly explains and elucidates both sources. In his view, both Mishnah *Ohalot* and Talmud *Yoma* represent determinations of death as irreversible cessation of "vital motion," not novel divergent definitions of death. While defining death somewhat differently, R. Hershel Schachter also adopts R. Bleich's approach in understanding Mishnah *Ohalot*, arguing that circulation is no longer halakhically meaningful after decapitation has effectively caused the person's blood to spill uncontrollably and irreversibly from the gaping gash in his neck.[45]

On the other hand, some opt for a dual definition of halakhic death. R. Auerbach accepts both cessation of cardiac activity (likely interpreted as per R. Bleich's theory) as well as decapitation – even in the face of persistent cardiac function – as determinants of death.[46] He even accepts the parallel between "brain death" – understood as the death of each and every brain cell – and decapitation, although practically, he has significant hesitations about implementing this concept. While a unitary definition of death may be more logically appealing, there does not seem to be any major philosophical problem with positing more than one definition of death. If death ultimately refers to the soul's departure from the body – a metaphysical notion – it can have more than one physical manifestation.[47]

How one relates these two discussions together has important implications for understanding R. Auerbach's famous "sheep experiment" (discussed in chapter 16) and its attendant applications for understanding "brain death" more generally. This *mishnah* forms one of the basic texts of this discussion, relating directly to the role of the head and/or brain in determining death, as well as its relationship to continuing physiological functions. Navigating these sources by suggesting either a unitary or dual definition of death, each halakhist blazed their own trail in adapting the halakhic criteria to meet a modern challenge.

---

45 *Be-Ikvei ha-Tzon*, no. 36.
46 Consistent with this approach, he describes a surgically decapitated sheep as dead even though its circulation was artificially maintained for close to three hours. This is discussed at length in chapter 16.
47 While positing decapitation as a halakhic definition of death without offering much in the way of rationale, R. Yisrael Ya'akov Fisher (*Responsa Even Yisrael* 9:15) argues that without a head, a person can longer halakhically qualify as a human being. Therefore, potentially continuing biological functions are of no relevance in determining death, since death is identified with the loss of identity as a person.

CHAPTER 7:

Talmud Hullin

Ze'iri said: If the spinal column of an animal was broken [severed] together with the majority of its accompanying flesh (*nishberah mafreket ve-rov basar imah*), the animal is rendered a *neveilah*... R. Yehudah said in the name of Shemuel: If [regarding a human being] the spinal column and the majority of its accompanying flesh was broken, the body immediately defiles [people and vessels that are] in the same tent. And if you will ask: But was not the death of Eli a case where the spinal column was broken without the majority of its accompanying flesh? [I would reply that] the case of old age (*ziknah*) is different, as it is written: "And it came to pass when he mentioned the ark of God, he [Eli] fell off his seat backward next to the gate, and his neck (*mafrakto*) broke and he died, for he was elderly and heavy" (*I Shemuel* 4:18).

R. Shemuel bar Nahmani said in the name of R. Yohanan: If one ripped up (*kar'o*) a human being as one does a fish, the body immediately defiles [people and vessels that are] in the tent. R. Shemuel bar Yitzhak added: Provided [he was ripped up] along the back. Shemuel said: If one split an animal into two, it is immediately rendered a *neveilah*...

We have learned elsewhere: If their heads were severed (*hutzu rasheihem*), they engender *tum'ah* even though they may be convulsing (*mefarkesin*), such as the tail of a lizard [twitches after it has been severed]. What is meant by "were severed"? Reish Lakish said: [It means] actually cut off (*hutzu mamash*); R. Asi said in the name of R. Mani: [It means severed in the same way] as the head of the burnt-offering of a bird [*olat ha-of*] is severed. (Talmud *Hullin* 20b-21a)

Talmud *Hullin* 20b-21a discusses the technical specifications of *melikah*, the ritual slaughter of sacrificial birds, comparing and contrasting it to the more familiar *shehitah* of larger animals. *Melikah* is done with the hands (without a knife), severing the bird's neck from behind. In this context, the Talmud discusses other types of injuries, identifying some as life-limiting and others as life-ending. It is within this context that the Talmud cites Mishnah *Ohalot* 1:6.

In analyzing *melikah*, the Talmud quotes Ze'iri's claim that an animal whose spinal column and the majority of its accompanying flesh were severed (*nishberah mafreket ve-rov basar imah*) is considered a *neveilah*, an animal that died through means other than kosher *shehitah*, and is subject to various rules of ritual defilement (*tum'at neveilah*). While *shehitah* of large animals requires severing the majority of the diameter of both the trachea and esophagus (the "*simanim*"), Ze'iri's novelty is that an animal is considered dead upon severing the *mafreket ve-rov basar imah* alone – the posterior portion of the neck – even if the *simanim* remain intact.

Shemuel expands this idea to include humans, arguing that a person whose *mafreket ve-rov basar imah* were severed engenders ritual defilement of a corpse (*tum'at meit*) – meaning that such a person is dead. The Talmud, however, does not relate this notion to the "standard" definitions of death, such as those discussed in Talmud *Yoma* 85a. It also does not address the victim's functional status post-injury – prompting the question of whether the victim continues to breathe (highly unlikely) or maintain a heartbeat (probable, at least for a short while) after suffering this trauma, and whether or not it even matters.

This omission can be broadly understood in one of three ways.

First, one can argue that there is no discussion of other functional parameters in this context because they are irrelevant. *Shevirat ha-mafreket ve-rov basar imah* serves as one of multiple, unrelated definitions of death. It is an independent indication of death, regardless of whether or not the victim continues breathing or his heart continues beating. According to this approach, there are several definitions of death that do not necessarily relate to each other physiologically.

Arguing for a novel definition of death, however, is quite challenging, as along with *nishberah mafreket ve-rov basar imah*, the Talmud presents additional severe injuries that are also considered life-terminating. These include traumas such as slicing a person vertically along the spinal column in the same way in which one opens a fish (*kar'o ke-dag… u-migabo*) and transecting a person axially through the abdomen, thereby separating the torso from the legs (*asa'ah gistera*).[1] According to this approach, the Talmud is positing three new definitions/criteria for death without providing any sources or explanations for why these injuries should qualify as such.

Furthermore, from a physiological perspective, the injuries described by the Talmud do not neatly parallel a medically coherent definition of death, even while they all involve massive spinal cord trauma, that may likely lead to spinal and/or neurogenic shock. Spinal shock refers to the temporary loss of spinal reflex activity below a total or near-total spinal cord transection; whether or not these symptoms improve or become worse depend on many factors.[2] Neurogenic shock results from lesions of the cervical and thoracic (back of neck and chest) spinal cord that disrupt the descending sympathetic pathways, leading to peripheral vasodilation ("expansion" of veins, causing pooling of blood in peripheral spaces and a

---

1 While the Talmud cites the former trauma specifically in reference to a person, claiming that a human corpse engenders ritual impurity after such an injury, the Talmud mentions the latter example only with regard to an animal, describing an animal suffering from such an injury as a *neveilah*. Nonetheless, in line with the frequent comparisons within this Talmudic discussion, Rambam (*Hilkhot Tum'at Meit* 1:15) describes both injuries as equally applicable to both humans and animals.

2 B. Euerle, T.M. Scalea, "Neurogenic shock" in J.E. Tintinalli, G.D. Kelen, S. Stapczynski, et al. (eds.), *Tintinalli's Emergency Medicine*, 6th edition (New York: McGraw-Hill Professional, 2004), ch. 35.

lack of effective end organ perfusion), hypotension (low blood pressure), and, if injured above the T3 vertebra, bradycardia (slow heartbeat) as well.[3] With such life threatening injuries, these patients are best vigilantly and carefully monitored in an intensive care setting. Survival rates are poor, with the likelihood of recovering from a complete transection of the spinal cord (as seemingly indicated by *shevirat ha-mafreket*) at 15.5% for cervical injuries and 7% for thoracic injuries, and even then, with no recoverable motor or sensory function below the lesion.[4] Less extensive injuries resulting in incomplete separation of the spinal cord have higher chances of recovery. Even though suffering horrible trauma and with the odds stacked against them, these patients are most certainly not dead. While they may be dying, they are still alive according to all definitions, with specific therapies aimed at increasing the chances of meaningful recovery. Thus, from a medical perspective, these injuries in themselves do not appear to qualify as definitive of death.

A more plausible explanation is that these injuries fall under the gamut of the already established and accepted definitions/criteria for death and do not represent completely novel notions. It is possible that these injuries induce or even occur simultaneously with irreversible respiratory and/or cardiac arrest (certainly in the pre-modern era), thus meeting criteria for death under well-established guidelines. From a practical perspective, however, this is somewhat speculative, at least as far as cardiac function is concerned, as the heartbeat may continue after a person suffers such injuries. Alternatively, one could argue that these injuries may induce or occur simultaneously with the irreversible cessation of "vital motion." Since all the injuries described result in gaping wounds that allow for the quick and massive spillage of blood, this relegates any post-injury motion or movement, including the heartbeat, to the realm of *pirkus* and therefore, by definition, not "vital."

According to this approach – which is articulated by R. Bleich – the injuries described in Talmud *Hullin* do not add much to our understanding

---

3 G.S.F. Ling, "Traumatic brain injury and spinal cord injury" in L. Goldman, D. Ausiello (eds.), *Cecil Medicine*, 23rd edition (Philadelphia: Saunders Elsevier, 2008), ch. 422.
4 Ibid.

of the moment of death; it is the physiological ramifications of these injuries, not the injuries themselves, that determine that death has occurred. If, for some reason, such an injury or something parallel to it would not cause or induce the immediate irreversible cessation of "vital motion," the trauma victim would certainly not be considered dead until such time that "vital motion" irreversibly ceased.

Possible Parallel to Decapitation

A third possible explanation is that these injuries are equivalent to, or at least parallel to, decapitation, as described in Mishnah *Ohalot*. R. Tendler advocates strongly for this last approach, arguing that it supports his notion of "brain death" as "physiological decapitation."[5] R. Tendler claims that "brain death" is meaningful because it indicates that the brain no longer directs the integrated functioning of the person. He explains that this is what happens in *shevirat ha-mafreket ve-rov basar imah*; bisecting the spinal cord both prevents any neurological input from reaching the brain as well as inhibits the brain from controlling other organs. R. Tendler argues that even though the brain is still technically "alive" after *shevirat ha-mafreket* (as defined by continuing biological functioning), since it no longer plays an integrative or regulatory role, it is considered as if it were absent entirely.

R. Tendler posits that whenever the brain irreversibly ceases integrating and regulating the body – such as when the spinal cord is severed and in "brain death" – it is parallel to the notion of decapitation, and hence qualifies as death. Indeed, Talmud *Hullin*'s description may actually be a better support for "brain death" than that of Mishnah *Ohalot*. While the comparison between "brain death" and decapitation as death is incomplete, since the brain, or parts thereof, can continue functioning even after a patient is diagnosed as "brain dead," *shevirat ha-mafreket* does not require the "death" or absence (physiological, virtual, or otherwise) of the brain – only the failure of the brain to communicate with the body.

R. Tendler's argument is predicated on the assumption that *shevirat ha-mafreket* (literally, the shattering of the spinal column) includes

---

5 "Halakhic Death Means Brain Death," *Jewish Review* (January-February 1990), 7.

severing the spinal cord, the main neurological channel for input to and output from the brain. Accordingly, *shevirat ha-mafreket* more generally describes breaking the connection between the brain and the body, thereby limiting the brain's ability to control, regulate, and integrate the body's continued biological activity.

This assertion, however, is subject to serious disagreement. While *Tosafot* indeed assume that *shevirat ha-mafreket* includes severing the spinal cord,[6] several later halakhists dispute this point. *Hakham Tzvi*[7] argues that the early decisors who simply cite *nishberah mafreket ve-rov basar imah* as an indication of death without elaboration (such as Rambam[8]) claim that the status of the spinal cord is irrelevant, since otherwise, it would have been incumbent upon them to mention it. This is even more evident in the case of decisors who were clearly familiar with *Tosafot*'s position, such as *Tur*.[9] Others, however, disagree with *Hakham Tzvi*'s conclusion, arguing that *shevirat ha-mafreket ve-rov basar imah* only renders an animal dead when severing the spinal cord. *Taz* uncharacteristically cites and agrees with a responsum by his brother, R. Isaac ha-Levi, that argues this point,[10] and R. Yonatan Eyebeschutz similarly agrees with this approach.[11] (While the halakhic discussion pertains to animals, the Talmudic discussion compares animals to humans; therefore, while perhaps unstated, this dispute is relevant to people as well.)

For R. Tendler, *shevirat ha-mafreket* must include severing the spinal cord in order for the injury to be neurologically meaningful, and he thus adopts *Taz*'s position as a basic premise. According to *Hakham Tzvi*'s approach, however, the injury actually spares the spinal cord; the reason *shevirat ha-mafreket* is identified with death must have nothing to do with the brain's neurological control of the body. Thus, while R. Tendler implicitly assumes *Taz*'s approach to be correct, it is certainly

---

6 *Tosafot, Hullin* 32b, s.v. *ve-lihshov*.
7 *Responsa Hakham Tzvi*, 28.
8 *Hilkhot Shehitah* 3:19.
9 *Tur, YD* 27.
10 *Taz, YD* 27 (end).
11 *Peleiti, YD* 27.

not unambiguously so, calling into question his conclusion regarding the implication of *shevirat ha-mafreket*.

The significance of the *rov basar* severed along with the *mafreket* is similarly vague, as it is not specifically expounded upon by the Talmud. With the literal definition of *basar* being "flesh" (muscle), it seems to refer to the thickness of the neck muscles surrounding the vertebral column. It remains unclear, however, what, if any, the intended physiological parallel or consequence of the severance of this muscle is.

R. Shelomoh Amar, the Sephardic Chief Rabbi of Israel, suggests that severing the *rov basar* stops blood flow to the brain, likely by cutting the vertebral arteries, located bilaterally between the vertebral bones and the neck muscles.[12] Since the brain is no longer perfused in such a situation, the victim is no longer considered alive. However, severance of the vertebral arteries would not necessarily completely stop all blood flow to the brain, as the carotid arteries, the main suppliers of blood to the head, are located in the anterior portion of the neck and would remain intact. If *shevirat ha-mafreket* is identified as death because it prevents the proper functioning of the brain, as R. Amar and R. Tendler argue, limiting cerebral blood flow without completely occluding it would not accomplish this.

Since R. Bleich is not concerned with creating a parallel between *shevirat ha-mafreket* and decapitation or with describing either as indication of the brain's failure to control the body, the precise definition of *shevirat ha-mafreket* and *rov basar* is largely irrelevant. In his view, the grievous injury to the spinal column/cord, like decapitation, is only meaningful when it indicates that "vital motion" has ceased, not as a definition of death in and of itself. According to R. Tendler's position, however, the Talmud's intent in describing these injuries is crucial, as they are essentially advancing "brain death" criteria. His conclusion, however, that *shevirat ha-mafreket ve-rov basar imah* indicates the cessation of neurological control is far from necessarily conclusive.

---

12 Lecture delivered at Yeshivat Hazon Ovadiah, March 2008.

Mafreket and Rov Basar

Regardless of the precise physiological correlate, the Talmud is relatively clear that severing the *mafreket* but not *rov basar* or vice versa does not render a person or an animal immediately dead; both must be severed. Nevertheless, the Talmud notes an exception. Citing the story of Eli the prophet, whom Scripture specifically notes was "dead" after injuring only his *mafreket* but not any *basar*, the Talmud explains that this is entirely possible in the case of an elderly person (*ziknah shani*). The Talmud offers little in the way of explanation of why this should be so or who qualifies as "elderly."[13]

R. Yehudah Asad offers a possible explanation, arguing that the real determinant of death in all of the injuries described by the Talmud is the severing of the spinal cord **alone**; severing the *rov basar* of a healthy person is necessary only as **proof** that the spinal cord has been severed. In an elderly, more generally weakened person, R. Asad argues, the cord is broken by even a lesser injury, which does not sever *rov basar*.[14]

Proponents of "brain death" could argue that R. Asad's position supports their contention that severance of the *mafreket* constitutes death because the brain is no longer connected to the body via the spinal cord; once there is no communication between the brain and the body, as in "brain death," the person is dead.

This approach is subject to challenge, however. Aside from the disagreement as to whether severing the spinal cord is even relevant to this discussion, as we noted above, almost all commentators argue that severing the *mafreket* alone without *rov basar*, while traumatic and likely life-limiting, is most definitely not definitive of death. Severance of *rov basar* is more than proof of severance of the *mafreket*, it is a necessary prerequisite of death.

Additionally, neither the Talmud nor R. Asad make any mention of the precise spot at which the *mafreket* was broken. The phrenic nerve

---

13 See *She'iltot de-Rav Ahai Gaon* 103 for an alternate understanding of the Talmudic discussion, arguing that the entire ruling is derived from the *ziknah* exception. *Netziv*, in his *Ha'amek She'eilah* commentary (ad loc.), argues that this approach stems from an alternate text of the Talmudic discussion. *Yam shel Shelomoh* (Hullin 1:44) comments that while the overall Talmudic discussion refers to both people and animals, the notion of *ziknah* as an exception to the rule is limited to humans.

14 *Responsa Yehudah Ya'aleh*, YD 70.

controlling the diaphragm emerges from the spinal cord high in the neck, from cervical vertebra 3-5. An injury of *shevirat ha-mafreket ve-rov basar imah* can thus potentially spare the phrenic nerve (if severed below that point) and allow for continued respiration. If, as R. Asad argues, severance of the spinal cord alone determines death, regardless of where, he would accordingly be left in the somewhat uncomfortable position of declaring dead a spontaneously breathing trauma victim, raising the specter of the "Christopher Reeve problem" (discussed more extensively in chapter 14).

To avoid this difficulty, proponents of "brain death" would have to argue that *shevirat ha-mafreket* is not a **definition**, but rather only an **indication** (or proof) of death, applicable in some – but not all – circumstances. A person suffering from *shevirat ha-mafreket ve-rov basar imah* can generally be described as dead, assuming that victims suffering from this type of injury **also** fulfill the "standard" criteria for death. It is not the severing of the *mafreket*, spinal cord, or the *rov basar per se* that constitutes death, but rather the standard criteria of death that normally accompany these injuries. Thus, while *shevirat ha-mafreket* indeed indicates death under ordinary circumstances, when the trauma victim continues to display signs of life – such as breathing – the necessary assumption is challenged and the conclusion cannot be drawn.

This is, however, effectively a restatement of R. Bleich's opinion. As noted above, proponents of "brain death" cannot accept his notion of "vital motion" without abandoning their support for "brain death," and they are thus left with somewhat of a conundrum. This approach effectively leaves undefined precisely which movements or functions qualify as sufficient signs of life to reject an automatic presumption of death upon severance of the spinal cord. Even if a patient suffers a trauma high in the spinal cord, superior to the emergence of the phrenic nerve, and is therefore unable to breathe on his own, he could still (at least theoretically) have conscious control over his facial muscles if properly medically supported. Intuitively, conscious voluntary motion strongly argues in favor of viewing this person as alive. Even more intriguing is the question of hypothalamic function. As long as the hypothalamus communicates with the rest of the body through a blood supply, it still exerts important regulatory endocrine control. Even if the spinal cord is severed, blood can still reach the brain through both the vertebral and carotid arteries, allowing the hypothalamus to continue to regulate various metabolic processes. Can such a person be considered dead? More importantly, since "brain dead" patients' hearts continue to beat, one would need to argue that a continued heartbeat is not a sign of life in order to use R. Asad's position as a defense of "brain death."

In fact, in originally articulating an argument against recognizing neurological determinations of death (before reversing his opinion later on), R. Tendler explicitly rejects this notion. He initially agrees with R. Asad that the *rov basar* represents the extent of the injury; that a minor injury (without *rov basar*) does not cause death, while a more serious injury (that also severs *rov basar*) does cause death.[15] Since an older person is generally weaker than his younger counterparts, even a more minor injury (without *rov basar*) can cause death. R. Tendler himself is troubled by this distinction, since the Talmud provides no measure by which to distinguish between major and minor injuries, nor of how to gauge who is considered elderly. However, instead of adopting R. Asad's distinction, R. Tendler chooses to leave this distinction somewhat vague, arguing that the extent of the injury has nothing to do with severing the connection between the brain and the body.[16] Simply severing the connection between the brain and the body (*nifsad ha-hibbur bein ha-mo'ah li-she'ar ha-guf*), he explicitly argues, is insufficient to determine death without some other contributing factor (be it severing *rov basar* or entailing a "major" injury).

In later reversing his opinion to recognizing and even becoming one of the staunchest advocates of "brain death" as death, R. Tendler clearly reads this Talmudic passage differently, as discussed previously. However, his original interpretation is still at least equally as valid; there does not appear to be a compelling reason to choose his latter approach over the former.

Although he subsequently rejects this approach, R. Yaakov Sasson initially defends the comparison to "brain death" by limiting the notion

---

15 M. Tendler, "Determining Death in Halakhah: Defining 'Life and Death' in Science" (Hebrew), *Be'er Yitzhak* (5732): 10, n.6.
16 Ibid., 11, n.4.

of *shevirat ha-mafreket* as death to people who are lying completely motionless.[17] Thus, *shevirat ha-mafreket* only indicates death when there is no evidence to the contrary. If the person is not lying motionless, but rather shows continued signs of life, he is most certainly alive, regardless of whether or not his spinal cord is intact.[18] Furthermore, R. Sasson argues that the brain's continued exertion of control over the body is a certain sign of continued life. Therefore, as long as the carotid arteries perfuse the brain and it can continue to function, the person is alive. The severance of the spinal cord only indicates death when **all** cerebral blood flow is interrupted – his understanding of the implication of the severance of *rov basar*.

R. Sasson argues that severing both *mafreket* and *rov basar* are necessary in order to more accurately parallel Mishnah *Ohalot*'s description of decapitation as death. If a person's spinal cord has been severed and cerebral blood flow has ceased, his brain is completely irrelevant, devoid of consciousness and without any control over the body – parallel to actual decapitation. *Nishberah mafreket ve-rov basar imah* – severance of the spinal cord and complete lack of cerebral perfusion, accompanied by lack of motion and no signs of life – is comparable to "brain death," in which the brain no longer exerts any influence over the body, and both, in turn, are comparable to decapitation. Consistent with his general approach, R. Sasson assumes that such a person can no longer breathe on his own, as spontaneous respiration would certainly qualify as an indication of life despite the severe injuries.

However, R. Sasson's technical description of "brain death" is problematic, as he incorrectly assumes that when used medically, the term refers to the complete destruction and death of each and every brain cell.[19] He accords halakhic relevance only to this specific scenario, comparing a case of the death of each and every cell of the brain to Mishnah *Ohalot*'s description of decapitation as death.

---

17 *Ruah Ya'akov*, sec. 37; he borrows this concept from Rashi, *Yoma* 85a, s.v. *hakhi garsinan*.

18 This explanation leads to difficulty in explaining Mishnah *Ohalot*'s rejection of *pirkus* after decapitation as indication of life. R. Sasson must therefore classify types of movements that qualify as *pirkus* and distinguish them from those movements that indicate continued life.

19 See *Ruah Ya'akov*, sec. 55.

Furthermore, R. Sasson's argument that death of each and every brain cell indicates death does not follow from his understanding that lack of cerebral perfusion constitutes death. When cerebral perfusion is abruptly stopped, the brain cells are not quite dead just yet. Without any oxygen or glucose delivery system, the brain cells will most certainly die in short order (faster, in fact, than most other body cells deprived of these nutrients), but they will most definitely survive for some short time after the injury. Nonetheless, the Talmud categorizes *shevirat ha-mafreket ve-rov basar imah* as determinant, and not merely predictive, of death.

Moreover, this approach leads to a rather forced reading of the Talmud. R. Sasson must explain that when the Talmud describes a person suffering *shevirat ha-mafreket ve-rov basar imah* as immediately dead, it was specifically referring to the limited case in which the brain was completely non-perfused; all of the arteries, including the carotids, fail to perfuse the brain. As noted above, there is no indication in the Talmud that the carotids are effected in any way by the severance of the *mafreket*, leaving R. Sasson's claim speculative at best.

An Additional Challenge – Severing the Meninges

An additional difficulty is raised by a Talmudic statement in another context. In discussing various *tereifot* of the spinal column (life-limiting injuries that render an animal unfit for consumption even after proper *shehitah*), Talmud *Hullin* 45b indicates that an animal with a severed spinal cord is considered **alive**. The Talmud writes that if the meninges (membranes) surrounding the spinal cord are intact, the animal is not a *tereifah* even if the neurological tissue (*mo'ah*) – the actual cord – is completely severed. An animal is only rendered a *tereifah* when a majority of the diameter of the meninges is cut. *Shulhan Arukh* follows this approach and describes an animal with intact spinal meninges but a severed cord as kosher,[20] with *Shakh* citing the Talmudic explanation that the status of the neurological tissue makes no difference in this determination (*de-pesikat ha-mo'ah lo ma'aleh ve-lo morid*).[21]

---

20 *Shulchan Arukh*, YD 32:1.
21 *Shakh*, YD 32:2.

While it may be difficult to picture an animal with a severed spinal cord but intact spinal meninges, and it is uncertain why the Talmud accords greater significance to the spinal cord meninges than to the cord itself,[22] the implication of this passage is quite clear. Even when the brain no longer exerts regulatory control over the body, as the spinal cord that transmits neurological signals is severed, the animal is still rendered kosher – meaning that prior to *shehitah* the animal is considered alive (and not even a *treifah*) despite this injury.

This ruling is somewhat more understandable according to *Hakham Tzvi*, who understands that *shevirat ha-mafreket ve-rov basar imah* does not require the severance of the spinal cord. Accordingly, it is possible to argue that an animal is considered alive even when its spinal cord is severed. According to R. Tendler's approach, however, the animal should be considered dead upon severance of the spinal cord – his definition of *shevirat ha-mafreket* – and therefore forbidden for consumption as a *neveilah*, since the animal died through non-*shehitah* means.[23] R. Asad's approach

---

22 R. Yisroel Belsky (cited in Y.D. Lach, *Chullin Illuminated* [New York: Hamesivta Publications, 2003], 157, sec. 3.35) suggests that severing the cord causes paralysis, but not necessarily death: "While paralysis at the upper extremity of the cord is at times fatal, this is not *treifah*, for it results in *immediate* death, rendering the animal a *nevailah*. However, if the protective membrane that envelops the spinal cord is cut open at any point, the exposed white/gray matter will not only split, but most likely will become subject to infectious decay… [and] eventual death can also be expected, as the infection travels up the cord… This is a *treifah* injury, an injury leading to eventual death."

While this interpretation is certainly plausible, the fact that *Shulhan Arukh* describes an animal with a severed cord but intact membranes as *"kasher"* indicates that it is fit for consumption and not a *nevailah*. All opinions would certainly agree that the animal is a *nevilah* when such an injury does, in fact, so completely devastate the animal that it dies from the effects of the injury. Nevertheless, describing the animal as kosher means that at least in some circumstances, the animal is considered alive even after suffering a severed cord and that proper *shehitah* permits its consumption. Furthermore, Halakhah makes no distinctions as to where the injury occurs in the length of the spinal cord. Ultimately, then, even R. Belsky must agree that were the animal to show signs of life, regardless of where the injury occurred, it is considered alive and cannot be considered a *neveilah*.

23 Although *Taz* requires that *shevirat ha-mafreket* includes severing the spinal cord to qualify as death, he argues that this is true based on Talmudic sources, not because the injury necessarily causes the loss of the brain's neurological control over the body

further highlights this problem, as he insists that *shevirat ha-mafreket* constitutes death precisely because it includes severing the spinal cord itself.

The opinions that define *shevirat ha-mafreket* as the severance of the spinal cord might slightly reformulate their position to argue that *shevirat ha-mafreket* constitutes death because it entails severing the spinal cord and its meninges, since severing the cord alone is not necessarily identified with death. But if *shevirat ha-mafreket* signifies the disjunction of the brain and the body, why should severance of the meninges be necessary, as they play no role in the transmission of neurological impulses from the brain?

Neither the *Shulhan Arukh* nor most classical commentators relate these different rulings to each other. The two cases are also not necessarily analogous, as *shevirat ha-mafreket* entails a physical injury, while an infection may cause separation in the spinal meninges. Regardless of how one relates these discussions, however, it is clear that at least in some circumstances, Halakhah recognizes an animal as alive even when its brain no longer exerts control over its body. Since Halakhah posits situations in which (according to R. Asad's approach) severing the neurological control between the brain and body constitutes death (*shevirat ha-mafreket*) and others where it does not, extending the notion to "brain death" remains speculative at best.

The Extent of Decapitation

As we have seen above, interpreting the Talmudic passage as equating *nishberah mafreket ve-rov basar imah* as implying the complete cessation of neurological control of the body, and therefore equivalent to "brain death," encounters many interpretive obstacles. A further challenge is

---

(as R. Tendler does). He therefore can accept multiple scenarios that qualify as death, each with their own specific requirements. For *Taz*, the fact that *shevirat ha-mafreket ve-rov basar imah* determines death only when the spinal cord is severed and that when the spinal meninges are intact the animal is deemed kosher even when the neurological components of the cord are disintegrated does not pose a contradiction. It is only because R. Tendler suggests that *shevirat ha-mafreket* represents some other definition of death that forces the contradiction.

presented by the continuation of the passage, in which the Talmud cites Mishnah *Ohalot*'s description of decapitation as death. Is the Talmud's description of *nishberah mafreket ve-rov basar imah* as defining, or at least indicating, death indeed equivalent to the *mishnah*'s description of *hutzu rasheihem*, as proponents of "brain death" argue?

The relationship between these two injuries is, in fact, a point of serious contention.[24] *Tosafot* note that Shemuel and Ze'iri's description of *nishberah mafreket ve-rov basar imah* as death is certainly at odds with Reish Lakish's later explanation of Mishnah *Ohalot*'s *hutzu rasheihem* as *hutzu mamash*, actual complete decapitation.[25] Ramban

---

24 As we noted in the previous chapter, Rashi, commenting on Talmud *Hullin* 21a, notes that *hutzu rasheihem* of Mishnah *Ohalot* refers exclusively to *sheratzim*, implying that the previously cited criteria of *nishberah mafreket ve-rov basar imah* is sufficient for humans; Reish Lakish's more extensive *hutzu mamash* is not necessary. This point is clarified by Rashba (*Hullin* 21a, s.v. *amar leih*), who argues that *sheratzim* are unlike other living creatures. Since they are inherently more resilient (*nafish hiyyuteih*, lit., with excess life-force), they are not considered dead through *shevirat ha-mafreket ve-rov basar imah* alone, but also must suffer from complete *hatazat ha-rosh*. According to Rashi's interpretation, Mishnah *Ohalot* is irrelevant to the discussion of human death.

Interestingly, in defining the death of *sheratzim* (small swarming creatures), Rambam (*Hilkhot She'ar Avot ha-Tum'ah* 4:13) only cites *hutzu rasheihem*, omitting any mention of *nishberah ha-mafreket*. He adds that *hatazat ha-rosh* qualifies as death even if the skin of the neck remains intact (*af al pi she-adayyin ha-rosh me'ureh be-or ha-guf*) – a caveat that he does not mention regarding humans or larger animals. R. Te'omim (n.32 below) adopts Rashba's interpretation to explain why Rambam omitted any reference to *shevirat ha-mafreket* of *sheratzim*, while nonetheless including *hatazat ha-rosh* as a death-defining injury.

Coming from a different perspective, R. Asad (n.14 above) argues that the rules of *sheratzim* are parallel to the exceptional status of *ziknah* by humans. While Rashba argues that *sheratzim* are more resilient and therefore demand more complete *hatazat ha-rosh*, R. Asad claims just the opposite; for some undescribed physiological reason, *sheratzim* are more easily killed, just like the elderly. As we noted above, R. Asad advocates for determining death based on the severance of the spinal cord alone, with *rov basar* normally necessary simply as a means to indicate and ensure that it had occurred. The elderly are more susceptible to severing their spinal cords even when not injuring their *rov basar*, as are *sheratzim*, and the more stringent criteria of *nishberah mafreket ve-rov basar imah* are therefore not required.

25 *Tosafot*, *Hullin* 21a, s.v. *hutzu mamash*. This *Tosafot* perforce assumes that Mishnah *Ohalot*'s *hutzu rasheihem* refers to humans as well, disagreeing with the previous *Tosafot*'s

also perceives a conflict between the two descriptions, but instead of portraying them as disagreeing, he uses one to modify the other. He comments that the Halakhah follows Shemuel and Ze'iri, and Mishnah *Ohalot*'s *hutzu rasheihem* should therefore be interpreted not as describing complete decapitation, but rather only *nishberah mafreket ve-rov basar imah*.[26] *Tiferet Yisrael*, although interpreting the Talmud differently than Ramban, reaches the same halakhic conclusion.[27]

These commentators either argue that there is a disagreement between the two descriptions and that only one is accepted as halakhically valid, or that they are, in fact, one and the same. This interpretation would certainly support R. Tendler's equation between *nishberah mafreket ve-rov basar imah* and decapitation.

Rambam, however, in delineating various death-defining injuries for both humans and animals, lists both *hatazat ha-rosh* as well as *shevirat ha-mafreket ve-rov basar imah*, seemingly indicating that they represent different injuries and that both are halakhically meaningful.[28] *Maggid Mishnah* explains that from Rambam's formulation, it is clear that *hatazat ha-rosh* refers to severing the *simanim* as well as the neck (while not discussing the specific extent of the particular spinal injury).[29] Accordingly, many commentators question why Rambam cites both injuries as defining death, as *hatazat ha-rosh* must already include *shevirat ha-mafreket*. What does including *hatazat ha-rosh* in this list of death-defining injuries add?

Many later authorities distinguish between the two types of injuries so that one would not necessarily be subsumed under the other. R. Yonatan Eyebeschutz claims that *hatazat ha-rosh* describes an injury severing the *simanim* (and possibly *rov basar*), but not the spinal cord itself – essentially the front of the neck – while *shevirat ha-mafreket ve-rov basar imah* refers to severing the spinal cord along with *rov basar* without affecting the *simanim* – the back of the neck. Both constitute death-defining

---

(s.v. *hutzu rasheihem*) limitation to cattle and birds.
26 Ramban, *Hullin* 20b, s.v. *ha de-amar*.
27 *Ohalot* 1:6, *Bo'az* 13.
28 *Hilkhot Tum'at Met* 1:15; *Hilkhot She'ar Avot ha-Tum'ah* 2:1.
29 *Maggid Mishneh*, *Hilkhot Tum'at Met* 1:15.

injuries, but only when all of their respective criteria are met.[30] R. Yosef Te'omim[31] and R. David Pardo[32] take a different approach, contending that *hatazat ha-rosh* includes severing the *simanim* and spinal cord, but not *rov basar*, while *shevirat ha-mafreket ve-rov basar imah* refers specifically to severing the spinal cord along with *rov basar*.[33]

While each of these positions clearly focuses on the importance of severing the spinal cord, each assigns it to a different type of injury, raising the important question of what definitions of death these injuries represent. If, as R. Tendler argues, severance of the spinal cord is significant because it means that the brain no longer exerts neurological control over the rest of the body, why should it matter whether or not the esophagus and trachea are intact? If *hatazat ha-rosh* does not involve severance of the cord, why should it constitute death, and if it does, what does the

---

30 *Kereiti u-Pleiti* 27:2, s.v. *ve-hineh yesh li*.

31 *Rosh Yosef*, *Hullin* 21a.

32 Commentary to *Sifrei de-Bei Rav*, *Hukkat*, s.v. *asher*. R. Pardo draws support for his contention that *hatazat ha-rosh* refers specifically to severing the *simanim* and the spinal cord, but not the *rov basar*, from Rambam's specific formulation regarding *sheratzim* (n.28 above). Although Rambam describes *hatazat ha-rosh* of *sheratzim* as death-defining even "if the skin of the neck remains intact," this caveat is applicable to all cases of *hatazat ha-rosh*, including human and large animal trauma victims. R. Pardo contends that the intact skin of the neck represents undamaged *rov basar*; nevertheless, this injury qualifies as death per *hatazat ha-rosh* criteria, even though failing *nishberah mafreket* criteria due to the obvious lack of *rov basar imah*.

33 *Tiferet Ya'akov* (*Hullin* 21a) attempts to resolve the discrepancy differently, arguing that *hatazat ha-rosh* refers to a decapitation high in the neck, above the *mafreket*, and demands a more complete decapitation than simply *mafreket ve-rov basar*, which is relevant to injuries lower down on the neck. While this technically resolves the difficulty, this approach invites far more problems than it solves. Where precisely does *Tiferet Ya'akov* contend that the injury occurs? The first cervical vertebrae lies right below the base of the skull; if the *mafreket* is identified with the vertebral column, according to *Tiferet Ya'akov*, a *hatazat rosh* injury occurs through the skull and the base of the brain itself. From a physiological standpoint, it is rather difficult to understand why severing the spinal cord alone together with *rov basar* (whatever that may be) qualifies as death, but cutting through the brain itself does not qualify as death unless it is severed completely! Moreover, Talmud *Hullin* 21a is quite clear that Reish Lakish's expansive interpretation of *hutzu mamash* certainly entails severing the *simanim* as well. It is hard to imagine how an injury above the vertebra and through the brain itself, as *Tiferet Ya'akov* essentially defines *hatazat rosh*, could also sever the *simanim*.

severance of the *simanim* add to the severance of the cord described by *shevirat ha-mafreket*? The question is important also as regards the *rov basar*, especially given the difficulty in identifying its anatomical or physiological correlate. Why should the severance of the *rov basar* affect one's status if all that matters is whether or not the brain is still connected to the body? These questions lead to great difficulty in drawing any conclusive parallels between these injuries and "brain death."

The same difficulty results from the alternative position that each of these injuries represents a unique definition of death, with no common underlying rationale. If this is true, each death-defining injury must meet strict criteria as a unique definition of death, which would limit any extrapolation to anything other than precisely parallel circumstances. "Brain death" especially would not qualify, as the comparison is far from complete.

Neveilah me-Hayyim

This discussion is complicated further by Rambam's formulation of the relevant *halakhot* in various contexts. In *Hilkhot Shehitah*, in detailing various pathologies that invalidate an animal for human consumption, Rambam writes:

> And so too, if it broke its neck and the majority of the accompanying flesh (*nishberah mafreket ve-rov basar imah*), or it was split open through its back like of a fish, or the majority [of the diameter] of the trachea was severed, or it sustained a penetrating wound to its esophagus of any size (*nekuvat ha-veshet be-kol shehu*) in a location appropriate for *shehitah*, [an animal that sustained any of these injuries] is [considered to be] a "living carcass" (*neveilah me-hayyim*), and *shehitah* does not help [such an animal].[34]

While "*neveilah me-hayyim*" is certainly an interesting formulation and its precise meaning is highly debated, Rambam's clear intent is to differentiate such an animal from a *tereifah*. A *tereifah* is an animal with particular injuries that are considered to be life-limiting, often described

---

34 *Hilkhot Shehitah* 3:19.

as surviving no longer than twelve months; even if the animal is inherently kosher and proper *shehitah* were performed on it, it would be forbidden for consumption. A *neveilah* usually refers to an animal that died through any manner other than valid *shehitah*, which is forbidden to eat and engenders *tum'at neveilah*. Rambam's novel term, *neveilah me-hayyim*, invokes language referring to both the living and the dead. What does it mean?

Furthermore, while Rambam terms all of the injuries that he lists here as *neveilah me-hayyim*, from a physiological perspective, the underlying theme of the group is unclear; they certainly do not all qualify as death-defining. It is difficult to compare the case of *nishberah mafreket ve-rov basar imah* – in which the animal is almost certainly immobilized, likely in shock, and possibly suffering from cardiac arrest – to one of *nekuvat ha-veshet be-kol shehu* – in which the animal may have some difficulty swallowing, but does not even ostensibly appear to be dying. Nonetheless, some argue that Rambam's intent is that an animal suffering from such injuries already engenders *tum'at neveilah*, even though it seems to still be alive by all accounts; it has (*tum'at*) *neveilah* (even though it is) *me-hayyim*.[35]

This position presents a difficult challenge, since *tum'at neveilah* usually applies exclusively to dead animals, to the extent that an animal with both *simanim* severed but that is still moving/convulsing does not engender *tum'at neveilah* until it lies still.[36] This difficulty led many commentators to offer an alternate approach, distinguishing between the prohibition to eat a *neveilah* and the *tum'ah* that a *neveilah* engenders. Once suffering these injuries, an animal is prohibited for consumption on account of qualifying as a *neveilah*, but the *tum'at neveilah* does not devolve upon the animal until it actually dies; it is (forbidden as) *neveilah* (even though it is) *me-hayyim*.[37]

---

35 *Shulhan Arukh*, YD 33:3 according to *Shakh* 33:4 and Rambam according to *Kesef Mishnah, Hilkhot Shehitah* 10:9 and *Arukh ha-Shulhan*, YD 33:8.
36 *Tum'at okhelim*, however, a lesser form of *tum'ah*, does exist at this time
37 *Arukh ha-Shulhan*, YD 29:2, 33:8; *Rosh Yosef, Hullin* 22b, s.v. *ha-Ra"m*; *Kereiti u-Peleiti* 33:2.

Focusing on the latter part of Rambam's formulation, *Arukh ha-Shulhan* entertains an additional approach, claiming that Rambam never intended to describe a living animal as a *neveilah*, neither for purposes of prohibited consumption nor for issues of *tum'ah*. Rather, Rambam describes injuries that, although not necessarily death-defining, automatically qualify such an animal as engendering *tum'at neveilah* even upon proper *shehitah*. After *shehitah*, one cannot be sure that the animal's death was a direct result of the *shehitah* alone and not also of its prior injury, thus prohibiting human consumption and engendering *tum'at neveilah* after its death.[38] This approach is also somewhat speculative, however, since Rambam's formulation would seem to indicate that the animal's status as a *neveilah* is certain in these cases and not dependent upon possible or questionable reasons for the animal's death.

Given that Rambam seems to mean that an animal with these injuries – including *nishberah ha-mafreket* – is not necessarily dead, the Vaad Halacha of the Rabbinical Council of America questions whether *shevirat ha-mafreket* in any form can be employed as supportive of possible halakhic recognition of "brain death."[39] This challenge, argues the Vaad Halacha, is further supported by Rambam's similarly ambiguous formulation in *Hilkhot She'ar Avot ha-Tum'ah*, where he writes:

> If he split the animal in two or he removed its thigh/leg and the accompanying cavity (*she-nitlah yerekh ve-halal shelah*), such an animal is a *neveilah* and engenders *tum'ah* through both direct and indirect contact (*be-maga u-ve-masa*), even though it is still alive (*af al pi she-adayyin ba-hayyim*). So too, if he split the animal along its back (*kar'ah mi-gabbah*) or severed its spine and the majority of its accompanying flesh (*nishberah mafreket ve-rov basar imah*), such an animal is also like a *neveilah* for all matters.[40]

---

38 *Arukh ha-Shulhan*, ibid.
39 Vaad Halacha of the Rabbinical Council of America, "Halachic Issues in the Determination of Death in Organ Transplantation – Including an Evaluation of the Neurological 'Brain Death' Standard, Sivan 5770 – June 2010," 35.
40 *Hilkhot She'ar Avot ha-Tum'ah* 2:1.

Here, too, Rambam writes that an animal suffering from *shevirat ha-mafreket ve-rov basar immah* "has the status of *neveilah* even though it is still alive."[41]

Regardless of Rambam's intent in classifying an animal in which *nishberah ha-mafreket* as a *neveilah me-hayyim*, and whether his formulation in *Hilkhot She'ar Avot ha-Tum'ah* verifies that he considers such an animal alive, these *halakhot* actually have little bearing on the discussion. When it comes to humans, Rambam is quite clear that *shevirat ha-mafreket* qualifies as death. In the context of the laws of *tum'at meit*, Rambam notes that "a corpse does not engender *tum'ah* until its soul departs (*ad she-tetze nafsho*)," and, with that in mind, notes that if *"nishberah mafrakto ve-rov basar imah*… such a person engenders *tum'ah*… even though he may still be moving/convulsing in one/some of his limbs (*af al pi she-adayyin merafref be-ehad me-eivarav*)."[42] If a person in whom *nishberah mafrakto* engenders *tum'ah*, he must be dead. While it may be possible to distinguish between the prohibition of eating *neveilah* and the *tum'ah* engendered by a *neveilah* – thereby defining a class of *neveilah me-hayyim* – making this distinction regarding humans, thus allowing for *tum'at meit* even during the person's lifetime, is far more speculative.[43] Rambam's specific formulation in the opening of this *halakhah* explicitly creates a dependency between the two notions, not allowing for one without the other.

Thus, the Va'ad Halacha's objections to the equation between *shevirat ha-mafreket* and "brain death" based on Rambam's formulations in *Hilkhot Shehitah* and *She'ar Avot ha-Tumah* are not entirely clear, and even granting the Va'ad Halacha's hesitancies, they appear limited in scope to animals alone. Regarding humans, Rambam's specific formulation leaves no room for doubt that *shevirat ha-mafreket* is an indication of death. As noted by the Va'ad Halacha, even their conclusions from these discussions are far from obvious or necessarily correct, thus adding additional layers of ambiguity to an already vague term, further complicating any parallel drawn between *shevirat ha-mafreket* and a medical diagnosis of "brain death."

---

41 "Halachic Issues," 35.
42 *Hilkhot Tum'at Meit* 1:15.
43 Cf. Rif, *Hilkhot Tum'ah* 2b; Rosh, *Hilkhot Tum'ah*, sec. 9.

Conclusion

After an examination of the sources, one is left wondering whether "brain death" is indeed parallel to any of the injuries described, and even if it is, whether it is legitimate to determine questions of life and death based on such questionable comparisons. The main difficulty is in identifying the physiological correlates to the specific injuries mentioned in the Talmud and how they relate to the sources in Talmud *Yoma* and Mishnah *Ohalot*.

R. Bleich, consistent with his general approach, argues that all of these injuries cause or induce an immediate irreversible cessation of "vital motion;" these injuries are not unique definitions of death, but rather applications of what R. Bleich argues is the single halakhically valid definition of death. In listing these specific injuries, the Talmud was merely describing the majority of such cases, in which cessation of "vital motion" immediately ensues.[44] If such an injury does not cause or induce the immediate irreversible cessation of "vital motion," the trauma victim would certainly not be considered dead. Accordingly, if one considers a continued heartbeat as qualifying as "vital motion," as R. Bleich does, there is no room for any parallel between any of these injuries and "brain death." R. Bleich's approach is analyzed and discussed in further detail in chapter 17.

Conversely, R. Tendler relies heavily on this discussion as supportive of his general approach.[45] Focusing on the lack of communication between the brain and the body resulting from completely severing the spinal cord as the reason for identifying *shevirat ha-mafreket* as death, R. Tendler argues that the same is true of "brain death," in which the brain no longer exerts its control over the bodily organs.

This suggestion presents two different sets of difficulties. The first is that it is simply not completely factually accurate – even the brains of "brain dead" patients can and do exert some level of control, by secreting anti-diuretic hormone (arginine vasopressin) to control blood pressure and maintaining thermal homeostasis in many patients. Second, it is not at all clear that Talmud *Hullin*'s focus is solely on the lack of neurological

---

44 *Bi-Netivot ha-Halakhah* 3, 138.
45 "Halakhic Death," 7.

communication between the brain and the body. While according to R. Asad, it is the severing of the spinal cord that is the ultimate determinant of death (and all other "required" criteria merely ensure the complete severance of the cord), he is alone in advocating this approach. All other commentators and halakhic decisors do not allow a determination of death based on severing the spinal cord alone without the concomitant severing of at least the *rov basar* or the *simanim*. Few, if any, other than R. Asad, explain the Talmud's exception for *ziknah* in the example of Eli the prophet at all – effectively limiting drawing any conclusions and parallels from that specific case. Conclusions and derivations from that case are by definition completely novel and appear insufficiently compelling to determine matters of life, death, and potential murder. Moreover, in different circumstances, Halakhah describes an animal with a severed spinal cord as alive – despite the fact that the brain no longer exerts any neurological control over the body.

In describing various death-defining injuries, Talmud *Hullin* compares and contrasts these with Mishnah *Ohalot*'s description of decapitation as death. Although never clearly arriving at a comprehensive definition of death, various comparisons can be drawn between the several cases. As incomplete parallels, however, the conclusion to be derived from here is a matter of serious debate.

CHAPTER 8:

Hakham Tzvi

A series of famous responsa of R. Tzvi Ashkenazi (1656-1718) in his *Responsa Hakham Tzvi* have become basic texts for studying "brain death" in Halakhah.[1] Although ostensibly unrelated to the specific question of determining the moment of death, as they analyze a practical question about *tereifot* (animals suffering from life-limiting injuries rendering them unfit for kosher consumption), many have looked to *Hakham Tzvi*'s discussion of the role and function of the heart for clues in halakhically analyzing the notion of "brain death." Only some aspects of these lengthy responsa are truly relevant to the issue at hand; *Hakham Tzvi* devotes significant effort and energies to other areas of Halakhah more specifically related to his particular issue than to ours (largely related to questions of *tereifot* and trustworthiness/believability). The following discussion and analysis will highlight the more salient and relevant aspects, while noting, but largely not dealing with, some of the tangential topics.

Hakham Tzvi describes a case in which a young woman was preparing a chicken carcass after *shehitah* and could not find the chicken's heart. The girl's mother suggested that her daughter inadvertently tossed the heart to a nearby cat without paying much attention to what she was doing, but the girl protested that she was careful to give only the chicken's spleen to the cat, not the heart. The girl also reported that all of the

---

[1] *Responsa Hakham Tzvi*, 74, 76-78.

chicken's other organs appeared healthy, without any signs of disease, and that prior to *shehitah*, the chicken acted no differently than any of the others in the coop. Based on *Shulhan Arukh*'s ruling that an animal without a heart (lit., whose heart was removed) is considered a *tereifah* and therefore forbidden for consumption even after valid *shehitah*,[2] the students in the local *yeshivah* collectively argued that the girl's chicken should not be eaten.

In responsum no. 74, *Hakham Tzvi* strongly argues against the conclusion of these students, stating quite emphatically that "it is clear to anyone with intelligence in his heart and a brain in his head" that it is simply impossible for any living being to exist and function normally without a heart. Since the chicken was inarguably healthy prior to *shehitah* and, based on postmortem inspection, was clearly not suffering from some type of organ-disintegrating illness, logic dictates that this chicken most certainly had a heart while alive, which, despite the girl's protestation to the contrary, was lost upon opening the carcass. *Hakham Tzvi* is so convinced of this principle that he feels that no other proof is really necessary, but to bolster his point further and show that the Torah agrees with that which is logically mandated, *Hakham Tzvi* cites several proofs.

In *Hilkhot Shehitah*, Rambam lists 70 types of *tereifot*, but *Kesef Mishnah*[3] notes that Rambam seemingly omits certain *tereifot* that he should have included according to his rulings elsewhere. Previously, Rambam rules that a puncture (*nikav*) in any one of ten specific organs, including the heart, renders the animal a *tereifah*;[4] later, he extends this notion, arguing that just as a puncture wound in any of these organs renders an animal a *tereifah*, so does the removal of any of these organs (*nital*).[5] Yet Rambam does not include the case of a missing heart (*nital ha-lev*), brain, esophagus, or trachea in his list of 70 *tereifot*. *Kesef Mishnah* explains that Rambam listed only those *tereifot* with which an animal can possibly survive, even if only for a short while, omitting all cases

---

2 *Shulhan Arukh, YD* 40:5.
3 *Kesef Mishnah, Hilkhot Shehitah* 10, note 8.
4 *Hilkhot Shehitah* 6:1.
5 Ibid. 6:20.

that would have otherwise been labeled as *tereifot* but are completely incompatible with life – such as the removal of a heart or trachea, which would render the animal dead. An animal suffering such an injury should be more accurately labeled as a *neveilah*, an animal that died of causes other than *shehitah*, and not a *tereifah*, an animal that will ultimately die as a result of its injury. *Kesef Mishnah* argues that Rambam purposely left these injuries off of this list, which is limited to actual *tereifot*.[6] Accordingly, Rambam maintains that a chicken without a heart simply cannot live.

Demonstrating his profound breadth of knowledge, *Hakham Tzvi* finds further support for this position in the *Zohar*, which tangentially comments that all of the organs are maintained through the force and "power" of the heart and could not survive for even a moment without it.[7] *Hakham Tzvi* notes that while he generally does not derive halakhic rulings from the *Zohar*, in this case, the *Zohar* merely supports that which is eminently obvious and it is not contradicted by anything else found in the Talmud.

The series of responsa contain a letter of support (no. 76) from R. Naftali ha-Kohen of Frankfort-am-Main regarding several of *Hakham Tzvi*'s recorded opinions, including this issue. R. Naftali ha-Kohen writes that he himself arrived at the very same conclusion when presented with a similar case, enlisting the support of two local rabbinic decisors, R. Wolf Levy and R. Zusman. R. Naftali ha-Kohen reports that while he normally decides halakhic matters independently, he deviated from his norm in this case because he was somewhat hesitant as to the conclusion argued by *Hakham Tzvi*. He reports that R. Wolf Levy had in his possession an heirloom copy of *Shulhan Arukh* with a note in the margin relating that the famed Maharal (R. Judah Lowe) of Prague ruled similarly in such a case. Maharal maintained that it is simply impossible to conceive of any living creature surviving for even a moment without a heart, claiming that it must have simply gotten lost post-*shehitah*.

---

6 Rambam similarly omitted cases of animals born without organs in cases in which such a situation is incompatible with life, even though he ruled earlier that in an animal born with these organs, a puncture wound in one of them renders the animal a *tereifah*.
7 *Zohar, Pinhas* 321b.

The next responsum (no. 77) in the collection is *Hakham Tzvi*'s lengthy and detailed response to R. David Oppenheim's critique[8] of *Hakham Tzvi*'s original published position on this matter (published in *Responsa Hakham Tzvi* as no. 75). Furthering the debate, R. Oppenheim[9] responded to *Hakham Tzvi*'s very response; no further reply by *Hakham Tzvi* was offered, or at least not recorded. As many of the issues debated relate more narrowly to the chicken in question and not the broader question of the function of the heart, the following discussion will be arranged topically rather than chronologically, highlighting the more salient features of the debate.

Neveilah or Tereifah?

R. Oppenheim begins his critique[10] by questioning *Hakham Tzvi*'s proof from *Kesef Mishnah*'s conclusion that an animal without a heart is, by definition, a *neveilah*. He notes that *Kesef Mishnah* and *Shulhan Arukh* were written by the same author – R. Yosef Karo – and that his conclusions are different in each. Given his different conclusion in *Kesef Mishnah*, it is clear that his ruling in *Shulhan Arukh*, in which he clearly identifies an animal with a missing heart as a *tereifah* and **not** a *neveilah*, was purposeful. While *Hakham Tzvi* relies heavily on the position of *Kesef Mishnah*, R. Oppenheim notes that when it came to practically deciding matters of Halakhah, R. Karo ruled in accordance with the majority of medieval commentators – including *Tosafot*,[11] Rashba,[12] Ran,[13] and Rosh[14] – who concluded that such an animal is halakhically described as a *tereifah*. This position allows for the possibility of an animal, although suffering a life-limiting injury, living for at least a short while without a heart.[15]

---

8 *Responsa Nishal David* (henceforth *ND*), YD 1:2.
9 Ibid. 3:3.
10 Ibid. 1:2.
11 *Tosafot, Hullin* 42a, s.v. *nikav*.
12 Rashba, *Hullin* 42a, s.v. *kol hani*; *Torat ha-Bayit* 2:3 (30b in the standard edition).
13 Ran, *Hullin* 8b (Rif pagination), s.v. *elu*.
14 Rosh, *Hullin* 3:1.
15 The assumption of this position is that a heartbeat is not a necessary condition for life. As such, it is hard to assess this position from a medical standpoint, as the terms by which life is defined are unclear.

R. Oppenheim argues that even if *Kesef Mishnah*'s opinion were to be taken independently of his ruling in *Shulhan Arukh*, it would be improper to decide a matter of practical Halakhah based on a single opinion despite significant opposition from other authorities.

Hakham Tzvi attempts to defend his position by demonstrating that many of the commentators whom R. Oppenheim cites did not really endorse this approach, but rather only used it as a means of resolving certain questions. R. Oppenheim, however, shows that these commentators advocate the same position even in other contexts, bolstering R. Oppenheim's original contention.[16]

Some later decisors understood Rambam and *Kesef Mishnah* differently than both *Hakham Tzvi* and R. Oppenheim. R. Yosef Teomim (1727-1792) comments that Rambam's position as presented by *Kesef Mishnah* need not be understood in such stark terms. *Kesef Mishnah* was not arguing that an animal lacking a heart is not a *tereifah*, but rather that one must adopt the stringencies of both *neveilot* and *tereifot* in such a case.[17] Responding to *Hakham Tzvi*'s overall position, R. Yonatan Eyebeschutz (1690-1764) takes a parallel, but slightly different approach.[18] He notes that Rambam never writes explicitly that an animal without a heart (or whose heart was removed) should be considered a *neveilah*; *Kesef Mishnah* derived this conclusion only by piecing together different parts of Rambam's rulings, noting the lack of Rambam's explicit mention to the contrary. R. Eyebeschutz maintains that Rambam was deliberately vague on the matter, hesitant to arrive at a halakhic conclusion due to two contradicting assessments. Based on his medical background, Rambam was keenly aware that no living creature could survive for even a short while without a circulatory system, but on the other hand, he was also cognizant that several Talmudic passages seem to indicate that an animal with a missing (or removed) heart is deemed a *tereifah*, and not a *neveilah*.

---

16 R. Yaakov of Karlin (*Mishkenot Ya'akov*, no. 10), citing *Yerushalmi Avodah Zarah* (1:9), is similarly supportive of the notion that the removal of an animal's heart renders the animal a *tereifah*

17 *Peri Megadim, Mishbetzot Zahav*, YD 40:1.

18 *Kereiti u-Peleiti* 40:4.

Highly speculative and certainly novel, R. Eyebeschutz's approach leads to more questions than it answers – not only regarding this matter, but in terms of understanding Rambam's rulings in general, the ramifications of which are beyond the scope of this analysis. The relevant point here is that some later decisors understood Rambam and *Kesef Mishnah* differently than both *Hakham Tzvi* and R. Oppenheim, even though these alternatives seem somewhat forced in the very text that they attempt to explicate.

Can a Living Being Survive Without a Heart?

In what appears to be a question of medical/veterinary reality, *Hakham Tzvi* and R. Oppenheim debate the question of whether a chicken could actually live without a functioning circulatory system. Throughout his lengthy analysis, *Hakham Tzvi* makes repeated mention that in his opinion, it is blatantly obvious and eminently logical that the absence of a heart is simply incompatible with life, frequently describing this notion as a "primary principle" (*muskal rishon*). R. Oppenheim strongly disagrees, noting that all the authorities who describe an animal with such a condition as a *tereifah* must, by definition, assume that such an animal could live for at least a short time; if not, the animal would qualify as a *neveilah*, not a *tereifah*. He reports that many of the great halakhic decisors before his time deemed animals found without hearts to be *tereifot*, specifically noting the ruling of R. Yisrael of Raburk. R. Oppenheim questions the authenticity of R. Naftali ha-Kohen's citation of Maharal of Prague ruling differently, noting the lack of any mention of such a ruling by Maharal in any other source and the unknown identity of the author of the marginal note in which the story was recorded.[19]

Arguing from a more Talmudic perspective, R. Oppenheim[20] cites the famous notes of R. Tzvi Shohet to R. Yaakov Weil's *Sefer Shehitot u-Bedikot*,[21] which record an incident in which, upon post-*shehitah* inspection,

---

19 *ND* 3:3.
20 Ibid. 1:2.
21 Referred to by R. Oppenheim as *Shehitot ha-Ra"tz*; cited towards the end of *Gevul Binyamin*'s (R. Binyamin Wolf) commentary to R. Weil's compendium.

a cow was found to have two hearts – one in its "normal" location and a second slightly above it, filled half with blood and half with pus. R. Shohet reports that he deemed the animal a *tereifah* and was supported in his decision by R. Shelomoh Klipara, an "expert doctor" from Krakow. Employing the Talmudic precept that "all additional [or duplicative] organs are halakhically considered as [if they are both] missing" (*kol yeter ke-natul dami*),[22] R. Oppenheimer argues that the Talmudic parallel should be interpreted literally – a cow with two hearts is comparable to a cow without any at all. Just as a cow could survive with two hearts (as it was deemed a *tereifah*), it could similarly survive without any. He cites numerous Talmudic precedents for interpreting such similes in a precise fashion, and not as loose and possibly allegorical comparisons.[23]

Hakham Tzvi strongly disagrees, arguing that such similes are frequently employed imprecisely; this comparison was certainly not meant to equate two notions or ideas in every aspect. Regardless of one's general approach to such similes, however, *Hakham Tzvi* argues that given the options, this specific simile – comparing additional or duplicated organs to the complete lack thereof – must certainly be understood as incomplete or imprecise. He references the Talmudic case of a firstborn child born with two heads, with the question raised as to the appropriate sum incumbent upon the father to pay a *kohen* to adequately fulfill the mitzvah of redeeming the firstborn.[24] *Hakham Tzvi* notes that R. Oppenheim's logic would dictate arguing that since "all additional [or duplicated] organs are halakhically considered as [if they are both] missing," just as it is possible for a child live with two heads, it must be possible to live with no head at all! This is a claim that *Hakham Tzvi* assumes R. Oppenheim is unwilling to concede.

Responding to *Hakham Tzvi*, R. Oppenheim notes[25] that this is indeed a difficult Talmudic passage. It is so difficult, in fact, that *Tosafot* claim that such a two-headed being is simply non-existent in our world, leaving the Talmud's report of a child being born in such a manner

---

22 *Hullin* 58b.
23 *ND* 3:3.
24 Talmud *Menahot* 37a.
25 *ND* 3:3.

unexplained.[26] Building upon *Tosafot*'s claim, R. Oppenheim suggests that despite what may seem scientifically impossible, God, the "source of all life," can and does do that which appears otherwise inexplicable – thus defending several Midrashic sources describing such a living creature.[27] Leaving this difficulty unanswered, R. Oppenheim feels that it is insufficiently compelling to permit an animal that would otherwise be deemed a likely Torah prohibition (*safek de'oraita*).

The Role of the Heart in Sustaining Life

In searching for scientific support for his position, R. Oppenheim[28] quotes *Sefer Sha'ar ha-Shamayyim*, a work by R. Gershon b. Shelomoh (father of Gersonides) dealing with what the 5561 (1801) Rodelheim edition describes as "*physica, astronomia, et metaphisica.*" In the midst of describing the "nature" and function of the heart, R. Oppenheim quotes *Sha'ar ha-Shamayyim*'s claim that all motion stems from and depends upon the brain, and not the heart.[29] Supporting this claim with empirical proof, *Sha'ar ha-Shamayyim* cites an experiment recorded by Galen in which he removed the heart of a monkey and the monkey continued to move (*hitno'e'a*) for 12 hours. Galen notes that this supports the "common" observation of bird and fowl hunters, who remove the hearts of their catch to feed to other birds while the caught bird continues to flap around (*ve-ye'ofefu*) for a long while (*zeman merubeh*) – "proving" that the source of living motion must be the brain and not the heart. *Sha'ar ha-Shamayyim* continues to cite from a "reliable member of our nation" (*ehat me-umoteinu ha-ne'emanim*) who witnessed a chicken that continued to jump up and down for some time after its heart was removed, further bolstering his original contention.

Relating to R. Oppenheim's proof from *Sha'ar ha-Shamayyim*, *Hakham Tzvi* (having clearly never seen the actual text) observes that

---

26 *Tosafot, Menahot* 37a, s.v. *o kum gali.*
27 ND 1:2. In an attempt to provide some coherence to the Talmudic description of such a child, R. Oppenheim alternatively suggests that it refers to conjoined twins, which he considers to be two separate beings, although he finds some difficulty with this approach based on Rashi's comments.
28 Ibid.
29 *Sha'ar ha-Shamayyim*, sec. 9, s.v. *ha-lev.*

this approach is consistent with that of Galen, which is clearly opposed to the "well-known" contrary position of Aristotle, with whom Rambam appears to concur.[30] Had *Hakham Tzvi* actually seen the text of *Sha'ar ha-Shamayyim*, he would have noted that *Sha'ar ha-Shamayyim* makes this distinction quite clear. While R. Oppenheim only quotes a small segment from this work, the discussion there is far more elaborate, recording Aristotle's contention that human movement actually stems from and depends upon the heart and including supporting empirical evidence for this view as well. *Sha'ar ha-Shamayyim* "concludes" that the truth, in all likelihood, includes some elements of both positions, arguing that both organs are vital and that, when necessary, they can supplant each other's vital functions. Thus, R. Oppenheim's citations from *Sha'ar ha-Shamayyim* hardly reflect the author's actual conclusions, and certainly do not reflect a medical consensus, as *Hakham Tzvi* notes.

Hakham Tzvi goes on to refute the proofs cited by *Sha'ar ha-Shamayyim* for Galen's view, explaining that any movements occurring post-heart removal are considered *pirkus* and not living, voluntary motion, as per Mishnah *Ohalot* 1:6 (discussed in chapter 6). The *mishnah* is clear that movements in and of themselves are not necessarily indicative of life; thus, even in the dichotomous world of *Sha'ar ha-Shamayyim*, the fact that a given animal continued to move after its heart or head was removed does not necessarily support either Aristotle or Galen.

Responding to this point, R. Oppenheim[31] claims that it represents an incomplete and incorrect understanding of *pirkus*. According to Rambam, he insists, *pirkus* represents involuntary, short-lived, spasmodic movements, uncontrolled and uncoordinated, stemming specifically from the last vestiges of energy in various muscles (what might currently be termed electrical potential).[32] *Sha'ar ha-Shamayyim*, however, specifically describes coordinated and seemingly voluntary motion. Jumping or flapping wings, which may appear to be simple movements, actually require the synchronized effort of many muscle groups and cannot be accomplished by arbitrary convulsive forces in random muscles. Such movements, argues

---

30 *Guide for the Perplexed* 1:39, 72.
31 *ND* 3:3.
32 Rambam, *Commentary on the Mishnah*, *Ohalot* 1:6.

R. Oppenheim, cannot correctly be termed *pirkus*; thus, contrary to *Hakham Tzvi*'s claim, they are in fact indicative of continued life.

The Mystical Approach

As we noted above, in first addressing the issue, *Hakham Tzvi* chooses to find support for his "primary principle" from the words of the *Zohar*. In his response to R. Oppenheim's original critique, *Hakham Tzvi* continues to bolster his position by citing additional sources from the *Zohar*. Aware of this rather unorthodox approach, especially among Ashkenazi halakhic decisors, *Hakham Tzvi* defends this practice from the outset. In his first piece, he explains that he is not attempting to derive halakhic principles or decisions from kabbalistic texts, but rather only to find textual support for that which he already knows to be true.[33]

Quoting from the full breadth of the *Zohar*,[34] *Hakham Tzvi* focuses on its insistence of the importance of the heart in sustaining life, reporting that in a dying individual, the very last organ to fail is the heart, at which time a person may be declared dead. Continuing on the mystical motif, *Hakham Tzvi* cites the famed Arizal (R. Isaac Luria) as arguing that human death should be determined only upon the death (or irreversible failure) of the heart, the last bodily organ to fail.[35]

In response to the *Zohar*'s claim that life could not continue for even a moment without a functional heart,[36] R. Oppenheimer suggests[37] that the *Zohar*'s focus on the heart is limited to humans, whose intellect resides therein (as per the understanding of Aristotle and Rambam), and thus plays

---

33 *Hakham Tzvi* seems to be aware that the relationship between the *Zohar* and normative Halakhah has historically been somewhat tumultuous, especially when the more esoteric approach appears to contradict the plain meaning of the Talmud. These issues have been extensively discussed, mostly among Sephardic decisors, and will not be further analyzed in this context. For example, see *Sefer Yabi'a Omer, Helek ha-Maftehot*, p. 297, for more than 30 instances of discussion on the relationship between the Talmud and the *Zohar* in *Responsa Yabi'a Omer*.
34 *Va-Yakhel* 198b; *Naso* 126b; *Shelah* 161a; *Pinhas* 221b.
35 R. Isaac Luria, cited by Maharit, *Tzofnat Pa'ane'ah, Beha'alotekha, derush* 2.
36 *Zohar, Pinhas* 221b.
37 *ND* 1:2.

a more prominent role in sustaining life than in animals, who lack intellect. According to this reading of the *Zohar*, the passage is relevant for issues of "brain death" in Halakhah, but its relevance to the case of the chicken at hand is mitigated. Continuing to demonstrate his vast knowledge, *Hakham Tzvi* notes that the *Zohar* quotes this particular passage in the name of R. Eliezer, who, in a different context, states specifically that the human intellect resides within the brain.[38] Thus, *Hakham Tzvi* concludes, the primacy of the heart in sustaining life and its failure as determinant of death is accepted even according to the opinion that the intellect does not reside therein.[39]

Given the esoteric nature of the *Zohar*, *Hakham Tzvi* questions whether it is perhaps more appropriate to understand these passages allegorically. He concludes that at least in these few cases, nothing compels a non-literal reading, and absent such an impetus, it is improper to understand these passages in any way other than at their face value. R. Oppenheim disagrees, noting that unlike Scripture, where a non-literal interpretation is offered only as a last resort when the plain meaning of a text simply cannot bear an exact explanation, the *Zohar*, with its multiple and varied levels of meaning and its myriad mystical connotations, frequently employs metaphors and allegories and should be understood in such a light.[40] R. Oppenheim further argues that the testimony of several

---

38 *Midrash Mishlei* (Buber) 1:1, s.v. *ve-ha-hokhmah*.
39 *Zohar Pinhas* relates a story in the name of R. Eliezer, who was approached by a gentile scholar with three theological questions. This scholar was particularly spiteful and asserted that he would not even wait for a response, as he was so certain of his own position. R. Eliezer "raised his eyes at him" and transformed the scholar into a pile of bones. The *Zohar* reports that R. Eliezer was so bothered by this scholar's questions that he began weeping, until Eliyahu the prophet appeared to him and reported that these questions were already analyzed and answered by the heavenly tribunal (*metivta de-raki'a*). It is in the course of answering the second question that the relevant point is made. While it is not specifically R. Eliezer who makes this assertion, the *Zohar* does not make mention of any hesitation on R. Eliezer's part in accepting it as true (although one may wonder whether he had the temerity to argue with the *metivta de-raki'a*!).
40 *ND* 3:3. Specifically regarding the passage from *Zohar Pinhas*, R. Oppenheim (*ND* 1:2) notes that the *Zohar* never explicitly states that a person will certainly die without a heart, but rather uses a more elaborate formulation, stating that a person "cannot exist or survive" without one (*lo yakhlu le-meikam*). He believes that this language is similar to that of *Yehoshua* (2:11), "We heard and our hearts melted, no spirit remained in any man

halakhic decisors describing chickens and other animals lacking a heart as *tereifot* forces an allegorical explanation, as a literal translation of the *Zohar* is contradicted by empirical evidence.[41]

Talmudic Support

In the course of citing supporting evidence for his view, R. Oppenheim quotes Talmud *Yoma* 85a with Rashi's comments.[42] He focuses on the Talmud's conclusion that according to all opinions, the crux of the "life-force" is found in the nose (*ikar hiyyuteih be-appeih*), concluding that

---

(*ve-lo kamah od ru'ah be-ish*) because of you" – referring to the fear of the Jericho residents from the Israelites after hearing about the Israeli military triumphs in the desert. The meaning in *Yehoshua* is clearly non-literal, as the fearful residents were most certainly alive at the time. So too, argues R. Oppenheim, many of these passages must be understood in a similar light; the focus on the heart represents something allegorical and does not necessarily refer to the muscular circulatory pump of the body.

41 ND 3:3. Interestingly, *Ru'ah Ya'akov* (sec. 75) cites an older and similar discussion about another difficult passage in the *Zohar* about the heart. The *Zohar* (*Mishpatim* 107b) quotes King David as describing the heart as having two chambers, one filled with blood and another with spirit (*ru'ah*), with the "evil inclination" (*yetzer ha-ra*) residing in the former. R. Menahem Azaryah of Pano, in detailing the technical aspects of cardiac anatomy (*Responsa Rama mi-Pano*, 92), quotes this idea without providing the source and explains it to be physiologically accurate. He explains that while post-mortem inspection consistently reveals "both" chambers filled with blood, upon death, blood enters the spirit-filled chamber, perhaps because the spirit has left, resulting in a "vacuum" (as per Talmud *Keritot* 22a). Current anatomical science differs significantly with this description both as regard to the number of heart chambers and to their contents. Normal human hearts have four chambers, although the two ventricles are significantly larger and more muscular than their atrial counterparts, perhaps allowing for some leeway for the *Zohar*'s interpretation. Additionally, all the chambers are filled with blood; air does not enter any of them at any point during life. Aware of these difficulties, *Ru'ah Ya'akov* suggests a novel interpretation, suggesting that the *Zohar*'s description of "blood" refers specifically to the deoxygenated blood of the right atrium and ventricle, while the "spirit" refers to the oxygenated blood of the left atrium and ventricle. This innovative reading blends an allegorical interpretation of the *Zohar* with a somewhat rationalist explanation, begging the question of whether such an approach is necessary or whether a completely allegorical interpretation is warranted – foreshadowing the very issue debated by *Hakham Tzvi* and R. Oppenheim some years later.

42 ND 1:2.

according to all opinions, one determines death only upon a negative respiratory exam. R. Oppenheim maintains that this supports the notion that living without a heart is possible, since the mainstay of life (*ikkar hiyyuta*) is respiration dependent.

Building upon Talmud *Yoma*'s conclusion and providing a close reading of Rashi's comments, *Hakham Tzvi* arrives at the diametrically opposite conclusion. He quotes Rashi's entire comment – "Sometimes life (*hiyyut*) is not perceptible in the heart, but is noticeable in *hotmo* (*de-zimnin de-ein hiyyut nikkar be-libbo ve-nikkar be-hotmo*)." *Hakham Tzvi* interprets this to mean that in actuality, the determinant of death is the (irreversible) cessation of heartbeat. However, since the heart is "hidden" beneath the chest wall, a heartbeat cannot always be palpated when the heart is functioning sub-optimally due to damage or disease, even though it continues to pump blood throughout the body. Since checking for respiration is practically simpler than assessing a heartbeat, *Hakham Tzvi* interprets Rashi as concluding that the respiratory exam is the most effective and accurate method for determining (irreversible) **cardiac** cessation – that is, death. In effect, *Hakham Tzvi* explains that the Talmud is debating the most appropriate **tests** to ascertain whether or not the heart is beating, assuming all along that cardiac criteria determine death (see chapter 5).

Justifying the Talmud's conclusion, *Hakham Tzvi* cites numerous sources that indicate that cardiac activity is completely dependent upon respiration; indeed, respiration derives from and sustains cardiac activity (*mimenu u-le-tzorkho hi ha-neshimah*). He quotes R. Abraham ibn Ezra, who explains that exhalation allows for the "heat" produced by the vigorous work of the heart to dissipate, while inhalation introduces colder air to the cardiac system to "cool" off the heart while it performs its powerful, never-ending work.[43] *Hakham Tzvi* cites numerous sources supporting this ancient understanding of physiology, such as R. Yehudah ha-Levi,[44] R. Gershon b. Shelomoh,[45] R. Meir Aldebi,[46] and R. Sa'adyah

---

43 Ibn Ezra, *Bereishit* 2:7.
44 *Kuzari* 2:26, 4:25.
45 *Sha'ar ha-Shamayyim*, sec. 9.
46 *Sefer Shevilei Emunah*, *netiv* 4.

Gaon,[47] explaining that Rashi operated under similar physiological assumptions. Rashi assumed that the heart could not continue to beat without functional respiration and concluded that the irreversible cessation of respiration is therefore equivalent to and evidence for completely irreversible cardiac failure.

Leaving the question of the accuracy of these scientific premises aside for a moment (as they will be discussed below), *Hakham Tzvi*'s reading of Rashi appears far more compelling than that of R. Oppenheim. Rashi's reading of Talmud *Yoma* supports *Hakham Tzvi*'s claim that the presence or absence of cardiac function is the criteria necessary to determine death.

Alternative Explanations

Relating specifically to the matter of the chicken at hand, R. Yonatan Eyebeschutz takes issue with *Hakham Tzvi*'s conclusion.[48] Quoting the numerous authorities who argue that a chicken found without a heart is a *tereifah* and not a *neveilah*, R. Eyebeschutz is unwilling to accept *Hakham Tzvi*'s "primary principle" that it is impossible for a living creature to exist without a heart. However, acutely aware of the importance of the circulatory system in maintaining life, R. Eyebeschutz proposes a "compromise" attempting to satisfy all positions. He suggests that while an animal must maintain circulation in order to live, the "source" of the circulatory pump need not necessarily take the specific structural form of a heart. R. Eyebeschutz suggests that in some disease states, the heart may suffer irreparable damage and some other organ or muscle tissue then takes on the role of circulation. Thus, circulation can be maintained even when the actual muscle tissue of the heart is severely damaged and has even possibly completely disintegrated. He therefore argues that it is possible that the chicken that *Hakham Tzvi* was asked about was indeed outwardly healthy before *shehitah* and that the girl in question was still correct in stating that she did not find its heart. She was referring to a heart of the normal size and shape, which she expected to find in its normal location, and this, in fact, was missing from this chicken. The

---

47 *Sefer Emunot ve-De'ot* 6:1.
48 *Kereiti u-Peleiti* 40:4.

chicken survived through an alternate circulatory pump that was not identifiable to the young girl upon casual visual inspection.

Taking this idea one step farther, R. Eyebeschutz suggests that stories in the halakhic literature of chickens found without hearts and deemed to be *tereifot* refer specifically to this reality – the heart proper no longer exists, and some other organ substitutes for its role as the circulatory pump of the body. Taking his argument very seriously, R. Eyebeschutz performed his own research, querying local doctors, who, according to his report, agreed that his suggestion was indeed rather plausible and certainly likely.

Others offer similar suggestions in commenting on *Hakham Tzvi*'s position. *Hakham Tzvi* records the letter of his brother-in-law, R. Meir Prostitz,[49] suggesting that perhaps the chicken suffered from a strange disease that caused the heart to disintegrate or diminish in size so significantly that the young girl was completely oblivious to its presence and discarded it unknowingly. R. Mordechai Ziskind, taking a rather dismissive approach to *Hakham Tzvi*'s position, makes a similar suggestion, arguing quite forcefully that the heart likely suffered from a disintegrating disease process, disappearing only moments before *shehitah*. He is thus able to maintain both the premise that life is not sustainable without a heart and that an animal found in such a manner is indeed a *tereifah*.[50]

Even if we assume the science to be correct and that this general approach is possible, the likelihood of this taking place in such a precise timeframe makes the story seem overly coincidental according to Maharam Ziskind. R. Avraham Yishayah Karelitz (*Hazon Ish*; 1878-1953) further argues that from a purely halakhic perspective, R. Eyebeschutz's suggestion is problematic.[51] He claims that Halakhah does not provide a rigorous definition for a particular cardiac structure; regardless of where it is located, any tissue that acts as the body's circulatory pump is halakhically defined as a heart. An animal found to have this particular anatomy cannot be considered to be missing a heart, since

---

49 Recorded as *Responsa Hakham Tzvi*, 78.
50 *Responsa Maharam Ziskind*, 33.
51 *Hazon Ish*, YD 4:14.

it does (and, R. Eyebuschutz argues, must) have a functional circulatory pump. *Hazon Ish* explains that while Halakhah recognizes the case of a missing heart as one of *tereifah*, as per *Shulhan Arukh*'s ruling, it makes no comment as to the status of a disfigured or misplaced heart (*lev she-nishtaneh mar'ito*). Thus, a chicken meeting R. Eyebeschutz's description is completely kosher and not a *tereifah* at all.

R. Abraham Danzig (1748-1820) notes[52] that elsewhere, R. Eyebeschutz cautions[53] against hastily pronouncing a chicken to be completely lacking a spleen (and hence a *tereifah*), as it sometimes can be found in abnormal positions or be irregular in appearance, rendering the animal kosher. R. Danzig notes that the same logic should be true of the heart – when Halakhah does not specify otherwise, a functional circulatory pump halakhically qualifies as a heart, regardless of whether nor not is appears to be "normal," rendering an animal containing such an organ to be kosher and not a *tereifah*. Thus, given R. Eyebeschutz's position regarding the spleen, he should certainly accept *Hazon Ish*'s point regarding the heart.

Most of the rest of the discussion between *Hakham Tzvi* and R. Oppenheim relates more specifically to the chicken in question and the testimony/believability of the young girl who inspected it; while fascinating, this is unrelated to the issue at hand.

Where To Go From Here?

Many, and perhaps even most, contemporary discussions of "brain death" in Halakhah quote from or at least relate to these responsa of *Hakham Tzvi*, although often omitting any mention of R. Oppenheim's position. The first focus is most often on *Hakham Tzvi*'s insistence that life is maintained by the heart, with death seemingly only defined upon the "death" of the heart, or at least the irreversible cessation of its activity. The second focus is *Hakham Tzvi*'s interpretation of Rashi, arguing for determining death only by the (irreversible) cessation of cardiac activity.

---

52 *Binat Adam, sha'ar issur ve-heter* 11.
53 *Kereiti u-Peleiti* 42:6.

Modern science certainly supports *Hakham Tzvi*'s contention that it is impossible for a living creature to exist without a heart; indeed, R. Oppenheim's position has been largely ignored largely due to the fact that it is scientifically untenable. Moreover, modern medicine has remarkably actualized R. Eyebeschutz's description of physiology with the advent of the cardiac bypass machine and ventricular assist devices, which externally support circulation when the heart's innate ability to do so has been halted (although no natural means of doing so has ever been reported).

Given the medical consensus and our modern scientific knowledge, it is indeed challenging to understanding the position of the decisors who declare an animal found without a heart to be a *tereifah*. One could suggest, based on R. Moshe Feinstein's explanation,[54] that the laws of *tereifot* regarding animals need not correspond to modern veterinary science. The Talmudic assumption is that *tereifot* are life-limiting conditions, rendering the animal unfit for kosher consumption. This remains true, argues R. Feinstein, regardless of whether these very same conditions are currently treatable by veterinary science; once an animal was declared a *tereifah*, it remains a *tereifah*. *Hazon Ish*[55] arrives at the same conclusion, although coming from a different perspective, claiming that the conditions rendering an animal a *tereifah* were determined during the specific time-period of the giving of the Torah, and are thus not amenable to change. Nevertheless, explaining how it was possible for a living creature to exist without a heart in the ancient world while this is no longer possible today certainly stretches the limits of the scientific imagination. Barring accepting this position as simply true by definition – perhaps falling within the rubric of *Halakhah le-Mosheh mi-Sinai* (an oral Mosaic tradition) – it is truly intellectually difficult to argue that an animal could live in such a state, even for mere moments. Along the same lines, there does not appear to be any disease or other condition known to cause heart disintegration while allowing for another organ to take on the role as the central circulatory pump – rendering the suggestions of R. Eyebeschutz and R. Ziskind practically irrelevant.

---

54 *Responsa Iggerot Mosheh*, HM 2:74:4.
55 *Hazon Ish*, YD 5:3.

Regarding the specific question of *tereifah* vs. *neveilah*, even R. Oppenheim seems willing to concede that as regards humans, it is certainly not possible to live without a heart – limiting the disagreement to the realm of *tereifot* in animals alone, and thus irrelevant to understanding the halakhic approach to "brain death." Moreover, R. Shaul Nathanson (1808-1875) notes that the disagreement between *Hakham Tzvi* and R. Oppenheim only regards whether or not it is possible for a living being to be born without a heart and live; both *Hakham Tzvi* and his detractors agree that a "normal" person or animal, meaning one born with a heart, can only be determined to be dead once his heart has (irreversibly) stopped.[56]

Seemingly more relevant is the debate as to the proper understanding of Talmud *Yoma* and Rashi's comments thereupon in particular. While *Hakham Tzvi*'s reading of Rashi appears more accurate both in terms of the text and Rashi's likely intent, the physiological basis for this approach, as elucidated by *Hakham Tzvi*, presents substantial difficulty. Although the conception was popular in the ancient world, modern science has definitively shown that respiration is not a "cardiac ventilation system" allowing for cooling of the hard-working muscle and dissipation of heat. Respiration allows for gas exchange in the lungs, promoting the absorption of oxygen into the blood cells and the removal of carbon dioxide – a difference of molecular composition, not one of heat. More importantly, the inhaled and exhaled air never touches the heart muscle, as the gas exchange takes place between the pulmonary vasculature and the lung alveoli. The two systems are certainly intricately connected, with the right ventricle of the heart pumping deoxygenated blood into the pulmonary artery for the purpose of gas exchange and the left atrium of the heart receiving the newly oxygenated blood from the pulmonary vein. Nevertheless, it is possible for the heart to continue beating even in the absence of breathing; while interrelated, heartbeat is not dependent on respiration. Thus, Rashi's assumption as explained by *Hakham Tzvi* does not appear to be correct; lack of respiration is not inherently an indication of cardiac failure.

Although anatomically incorrect, however, *Hakham Tzvi*'s assumption is likely historically accurate. In general, patients who were unable to

---

56 *Yad Sha'ul*, YD 394:3.

breathe for a significant period of time also lacked a heartbeat. Brainstem specific lesions, which would lead to cessation of respiration but not of the heartbeat, are quite rare. In the modern world, they frequently develop in the course of treating brain trauma in a ventilated patient – one who would have been dead long ago without the aid of modern medicine.

Given this situation, what relevance does or should *Hakham Tzvi*'s analysis have to the modern halakhic understanding of "brain death"? Dr. Avraham Steinberg argues that since the scientific basis for *Hakham Tzvi*'s comments has been shown to be inaccurate, his conclusions must also be dismissed.[57] Dr. Steinberg argues that ignoring the truth of medical reality is simply not an acceptable halakhic option, even if doing so requires contradicting or disagreeing with the conclusions of earlier decisors. Moreover, the bulk of *Hakham Tzvi*'s argument relates specifically to issues of *tereifot* and believability, only tangentially relating to Talmud *Yoma*'s discussion and even only then in response to R. Oppenheim's citation of Rashi's comments there in his critique of *Hakham Tzvi*'s original responsum. If we dismiss Rashi's comments as inconsistent with reality, we are left, Dr. Steinberg argues, with the simple reading of the Talmudic discussion, which seemingly discusses the **criteria** for death and **not tests** aimed at determining whether some other, unnamed criteria have been met, thus supporting a strictly respiratory standard – *"kol asher nishmat ru'ah hayyim be-appav."* Rendering *Hakham Tzvi*'s argument irrelevant, Dr. Steinberg concludes that the straightforward reading of Talmud *Yoma* argues in favor of defining death as the irreversible cessation of spontaneous respiration, consistent with a rigorous modern diagnosis of "brain death."[58]

R. J. David Bleich takes serious issue with this approach, advocating for a more cardiac-based criterion for death.[59] He explains that while *Hakham Tzvi*'s explanation of Rashi's position is certainly not in

---

57 A. Steinberg, "Determining the Moment of Death and Heart Transplants" (Hebrew) in *Kevi'at Rega ha-Mavet*, 2nd edition, M. Halperin (ed.) (Jerusalem: Schlesinger Institute, 2007), 48-50.

58 Nonetheless, Dr. Steinberg would likely agree with *Hakham Tzvi*'s conclusion that since it is impossible for an animal to live without a heart, the chicken under discussion most certainly had one and it was mistakenly misplaced.

59 *Bi-Netivot ha-Halakhah* 3, 134.

accordance with modern science, that does not necessarily imply that Rashi's position should be ignored entirely. Rashi himself does not provide a rationale for his comments; it is possible that, while intriguing, *Hakham Tzvi*'s explanation missed its mark. Moreover, R. Bleich argues, *Hakham Tzvi* explains only why Rashi presents respiration as an effective **test** to determine whether the heart has completely (and irreversibly) stopped. On this point, ancient physiology may have led Rashi astray, leading him to assume that cardiac function could be effectively, accurately, and absolutely ascertained through respiration. But Rashi's comments regarding the **criteria** for death are independent of the reliability of his analysis of the **tests** – Rashi is clear that death is determined only upon the (irreversible) cessation of heart function. Arguing for a modern understanding of physiology only disrupts this specific link in the chain – the **test** (respiration) is not necessarily indicative of the **criteria** (heartbeat) – but the criteria for death is not a matter for science to discover or diagnose. While scientific progress may clarify how the body works or which tests best measure cardiac function, what death means remains unchanged with more advanced understandings of science, physiology, or anatomy. Thus, R. Bleich finds support for his position in *Hakham Tzvi*'s reliance on Rashi's comments as representing a valid interpretation of the Talmud specifically as regards the **criteria** for death, even though it presents a **test** that is now known to be outdated and incorrect for its most accurate diagnosis.

Conclusion

Analyzing the arcane and often foreign world of *tereifot*, *Hakham Tzvi* introduces many factors and topics relevant to understanding the role of the heart within the context of a living being, and specifically its role in determining death. Spanning the breadth of halakhic literature, *Hakham Tzvi* fought adamantly to defend his position, culling from Talmudic, scientific, and mystical sources. While often unmentioned in contemporary halakhic literature, R. Oppenheim's critique and response to *Hakham Tzvi*'s original and subsequent positions shed important light on the debate. R. Oppenheim's position, however, appears to have taken a back seat to *Hakham Tzvi*'s position, unable to claim even a citation in the course of almost any serious discussion of the halakhic understanding of the moment of death.

Given the apparent historical acceptance of *Hakham Tzvi*'s approach, the question of advances in scientific, physiological, and anatomical understanding looms large. While an often cited source in many such halakhic discussions, *Hakham Tzvi*'s full position, especially within the context of the larger responsum, is frequently lacking. Nonetheless, even when trying to understand the various positions more fully, no clear cut conclusion is readily evident. This is complicated even further by *Hakham Tzvi*'s reliance on physiological principles now known to be inaccurate, leading to serious methodological questions as to the proper way to relate to his position in general and many of his points in particular. With each side adopting different perspectives on this matter, Dr. Steinberg and R. Bleich arrive at radically different conclusions – each citing *Hakham Tzvi*'s position to prove their point.

CHAPTER 9:

Hatam Sofer

Background

In 1772, the Duke of Mecklenburg-Schwerin (Germany) promulgated an edict that required delaying all burials in his jurisdiction for three days after presuming that a person had died. In those 72 hours, signs of organic tissue decomposition following death should become obvious, adding certainty to an otherwise nebulous determination. This edict was followed by numerous others in many locales after a rash of "premature burials" were discovered, with the press describing numerous instances of the "supposedly newly-dead" rising from their caskets.[1] This and similar edicts caused great problems for the Jewish community, which insisted on as speedy a burial as possible after death.

In 1837, R. Moshe Sofer (popularly known by the title of his works, *Hatam Sofer*) penned a responsum dealing with this question and, among other important points, analyzing and detailing the definition of death in Halakhah. While *Hatam Sofer* does not identify the questioner, we now know that it was R. Tzvi Hirsch Chajes (commonly known as Maharitz Hiyyut), who then penned a response to *Hatam Sofer*'s letter in

---

1 See V. Tebb Hadwen, *Premature Burial and How It May be Prevented* (London: Swan Sonnenschein and Co., 1905), 179ff, "Danger of Jewish Custom."

his *Darkei Hora'ah*.[2] R. Chajes asked about a related governmental regulation requiring a qualified physician to declare a person dead prior to burial. Although common practice in modern society, this was certainly not the norm in years past. Death was usually "determined" by those at the bedside – in the Jewish tradition, often by the *hevrah kadisha*. The specific question that *Hatam Sofer* was asked was whether a physician who is a *kohen* may examine a patient to declare him dead, thereby enabling burial. As male *kohanim* are prohibited from coming in contact with or even entering the same room as a corpse, determining the moment of death is of prime importance in resolving this issue.

The responsum effectively contains two sections. The first, shorter, and more famous section deals with demarcating death, while the second section is a longer treatise addressing the question of a *kohen* physician visiting a patient to make this determination. Although often neglected, this latter segment contains fascinating insights, novel interpretations, and historical nostalgia surrounding the vexing questions of *tum'at kohanim* (defiling the priestly status).

This important responsum is frequently cited in the modern literature on "brain death." In fact, there are few authors who do not reference, cite, and ultimately base their interpretation on this particular responsum. The following analysis of the first section will be thematic in nature and does not necessary represent the sequential chronology of the actual responsum.

Delaying Burial – Moses Mendelssohn's Argument

In addressing the question, *Hatam Sofer* begins by noting the history of the burial controversy, the pertinent players, and a few relevant sources.

---

2 *Darkei Hora'ah*, responsa section, no. 3. Notably, R. Chajes's response is limited to criticizing *Hatam Sofer*'s tone and arguing as to the possible prohibitions regarding delaying burial. While *Hatam Sofer* maintains that there is both a positive commandment demanding speedy burial as well as a prohibition against delay, R. Chajes is more hesitant regarding the positive commandment. R. Chajes does not respond to the bulk of *Hatam Sofer*'s more substantive points regarding determining death.

Hatam Sofer cites Moses Mendelssohn, whom he refers to as "Rav M.D.,"[3] who argued in favor of following the government edict regarding waiting before burial, despite the apparent variance with Jewish tradition. He insisted that doctors in his time did not have a complete enough understanding of the transition between life and death to accurately identify the moment at which death occurred. Therefore, Mendelssohn argued, the only objective measure of death is bodily decomposition. Although in all likelihood a person has certainly died prior to tissue decomposition (and certainly before an observer begins noticing it), Mendelssohn felt that no earlier assessment of the moment of death was accurate enough to be practically actionable. He argued that these were not merely his instinctive feelings, but rather that Talmudic sources support his view.

Hatam Sofer identifies two of these sources, noting that R. Yaakov Emden had already rather forcefully rejected all of them, albeit without actually reporting R. Emden's logic. While each source is interesting in its own right, only the second source is of current relevance.

Masekhet Semahot[4] describes an age-old custom of visiting the graves of the recently deceased during the first three days after burial (in a burial crypt). It relates that mourners once found the recently buried person to actually be alive, and he subsequently went on to live another 25 years, fathering a number of children. The concern raised is that the practice of visiting the graves might constitute *darkei ha-Emori*, as it is similar to the "gentile custom" of visiting the dead. *Masekhet Semahot* concludes that this concern is alleviated by the anecdotal evidence that such a visit can sometimes be lifesaving.

Mendelssohn argued that while the Torah mandates a speedy burial following death and forbids unnecessarily postponing burial, Halakhah allows such procrastination when the intended purpose is for the honor of the deceased (*kavod ha-meit*) – for example, when the deceased's children are en route to the funeral and will arrive shortly. Basing himself on this passage from *Semahot*, Mendelssohn argued that if Halakhah permits

---

3 This is the eponym by which *Hatam Sofer* refers to Mendelssohn in various contexts. See M. Hildesheimer, "The Attitude of the Hatam Sofer toward Moses Mendelssohn," *Proceedings of the American Academy for Jewish Research* 60 (1994): 144.
4 *Masekhet Semahot* 8:1.

delaying burial for reasons of honor and proper respect for the deceased, given the current medical climate at the time and the precedent set by *Masekhet Semahot*, it should similarly permit, if not demand, delaying burial for purposes of possibly saving lives.

Burial vs. Pikuah Nefesh

Hatam Sofer begins by indirectly responding to this last argument. At first glance, it indeed appears quite convincing. Are not almost all *halakhot* set aside for matters of *pikuah nefesh*? Why should the command demanding immediate burial be any different?

Hatam Sofer begins by noting the Torah's requirement for a speedy burial. The Halakhah[5] derives this requirement from the Torah's description of punitive hanging, "You shall certainly bury him on that very day and not allow his corpse to remain ... overnight."[6] *Hatam Sofer*'s thesis is that the Torah must have objectively defined the moment of death (*shi'ur mittah*) when it demanded immediate burial and forbade its postponement; otherwise, the requirement for immediate burial is devoid of meaning. The Torah could not have demanded speedy burial upon death without providing some means of evaluating when death occurs.

Hatam Sofer notes that while there is no explicit mention of such a moment in the Torah, Talmud *Yoma* delineates such criteria. He offers three possible sources for this determination:

1. It is possible that the Talmudic sages possessed an oral tradition dating back to the "original naturalists" (*ba'alei teva'im ha-rishonim*; lit., the first masters of nature) in identifying the moment of death. The dispute at the time (as recorded in Talmud *Yoma*) stemmed from a "glitch" in the transmission of this oral tradition, so that it effectively became lost. *Hatam Sofer* cites Talmudic evidence as precedent for relying on these scientists.[7]

---

5 Talmud *Sanhedrin* 46a; *Shulhan Arukh*, YD 357:1-2.
6 *Devarim* 21:22-23.
7 Talmud *Shabbat* 85a. The Talmud there identifies the various distances required between certain trees so as not to violate the prohibition of *kilayim* (forbidden mixing of

species), specifically relating the area of land that provides "nourishment" for that tree. The Talmud hermeneutically interprets the verse, "These are the descendants of *Se'ir* the Horite, the inhabitants of the land" (*Eileh benei Se'ir ha-Hori yoshevei ha-aretz*) (*Bereishit* 36:20), as identifying certain people who were "experts in the inhabitance of land" (*beki'im bi-yeshuvah shel aretz*). It then exegetically interprets the verse, "You shall not encroach on the border [landmark] of your neighbor, that those of old have set" (*Lo tasig gevul re'akha asher gavlu rishonim*) (*Devarim* 19:14) as permitting (or possibly demanding) reliance on these experts.

A simple reading of this text may suggest that the Talmud limited relying on such experts to specific agricultural matters. The proof-text's delineation of "*asher gavlu rishonim*" refers specifically to the notion of *gevul* – boundaries – and is likely the reason that the Talmud chose this text permitting (or possibly requiring) reliance on gentile sages in this matter. *Hatam Sofer*, however, clearly understood the conclusion as permitting/requiring reliance on secular knowledge more expansively, at least as regards differentiating life from death.

Others have actually used this very same Talmudic passage to **limit** relying on outside or foreign experts. R. Abraham Isaac Kook (*Responsa Da'at Kohen*, YD 19) focuses on the Talmud's additional explanation of the term *Hori* as referring to the senses of smell and taste. R. Kook argues that reliance on outside experts is valid only in empirical matters, such as those that can be smelled or tasted. This is somewhat parallel to the discussion in Talmud *Niddah* 22b, where the Sages consulted with doctors and also performed an experimental test to identify the source of a certain type of blood. Some argue that the Sages needed to perform the experiment because the physicians merely asserted their professional opinion without any empirical evidence for their claim – similar to R. Kook's position. As a result, R. Kook is only willing to rely on a physician's testimony with regard to a matter of *niddah* when the physician reported that he had seen or had not seen blood – a matter of factual verification. The doctor's expert opinion, best guess, or estimates based on his experience, R. Kook argues, are of no import in establishing Halakhah.

R. Kook recognizes that Halakhah sometimes allows for less demanding criteria than absolute fact, such as when the question at hand is one of "establishing" doubt. For example, one is permitted to violate Shabbat or eat on Yom Kippur in cases of even questionable danger to life. In such instances, argues R. Kook, expert opinion is certainly sought and relied upon, as even doubtful danger requires overriding the standard prohibitions. However, R. Kook would not allow reliance on outside experts in determining the moment of death – something that must be ascertained absolutely and is not merely a question of determining whether a doubt exists. Given the lack of any evidence that R. Kook disagreed with *Hatam Sofer*'s conclusion, however, it is likely that R. Kook relies on one of the two following options as sources for the Talmud's determination of death.

Determining death however, is not necessarily a question of determining fact, although correct facts are invaluable in arriving at a proper conclusion. Whether or not *Hatam Sofer* could agree with R. Kook and still make the same argument is indeed

2. A second possibility is that Moses received such a tradition from God himself, known as a *Halakhah le-Moshe mi-Sinai* (an orally recorded revelation from Sinai).
3. Alternatively, the Talmudic sages based their criteria or tests upon the verse, "All that has the breath of life in its nose" (*kol asher ru'ah hayyim be-appo*), therefore insisting that determining or testing for life and death rely on respiration alone.[8]

Although he insists that Halakhah must provide an objective evaluation of death, *Hatam Sofer* nevertheless appears to be bothered by Mendelssohn's question (without admitting so openly). Are we entirely free to ignore contemporary physicians' hesitations and ambivalence in determining death? Is their hesitancy so irrelevant that it cannot even create some sense of doubt (*safek*), especially with regard to life saving measures (*pikuah nefesh*)? Even possible or questionable doubts are relevant when it comes to issues of *pikuah nefesh*, as per the dictum, "We do not follow probability in matters of *pikuah nefesh*" (*ein holkhin be-pikuah nefesh ahar ha-rov*).[9] Furthermore, even if we are hard-pressed to take these physicians at their word, should Halakhah not take cognizance of the story in *Masekhet Semahot*, which similarly seems to impart doubt as to the precise moment of death?

In dealing with these issues, *Hatam Sofer* both explains why the contemporary medical controversy is irrelevant as regards Halakhah as well as finds supporting evidence that Halakhah has already taken these questions into consideration when establishing its guidelines.

Hatam Sofer maintains that the story in the passage in *Semahot* is significant only in that it is an extreme outlier – representing a case that happens, in his estimate, less than once every 1,000 years. Indeed, was the concern significant, Halakhah should have demanded posting guards

---

a fascinating question. For further discussion of the issue of the physician's role in the halakhic process, see A. Steinberg, *Entzyklopedia Hilkhatit Refu'it* (Jerusalem: Schlesinger Institute, 2006), vol. 5, s.v. *ne'emanut ha-rofei*, col. 1-33.

8 While this is not an actual verse, it is likely that *Hatam Sofer* intended to refer to the more familiar *"kol asher nishmat ru'ah hayyim be-appav"* from *Bereishit* 7:22.

9 Talmud *Yoma* 84b.

by each freshly buried corpse in case the decision to bury was made in undue haste. The once a day visitation condoned by *Masekhet Semahot* is certainly insufficient to accurately make a life and death determination. He therefore argues that such a miniscule incidence must be considered halakhically meaningless and irrelevant, not even approaching the criteria of *mi'uta de-mi'uta* (a minority of a minority). Such rare and infrequent occurrences are considered miraculous events (*ma'aseh nisim*) and outside the framework of the natural world, not reaching the threshold for even *pikuah nefesh* activities. It is true, admits *Hatam Sofer*, that such events have happened in world history and may possibly happen again; nonetheless, we live our halakhic lives oblivious to them, precisely because of their rarity. The mitzvah of rapid burial therefore must take place immediately after death, in spite of both *Masekhet Semahot* and the then-current medical controversy.

Rambam – Waiting to Remove Doubt

Hatam Sofer cites proof for his thesis from a cross-sectional analysis of several rulings of Rambam. When Rambam codifies the proper procedures and etiquette to be taken with the dying and recently deceased,[10] he cites Talmud *Shabbat*'s declaration that "One who closes the eyes with the departure of the soul (*im yetziat ha-nefesh*) is [considered to be] a murderer."[11] Rambam then adds to the text of the Talmud, writing, "But rather one should wait a short while (*yishheh me'at*)" to ensure that the person in question did not merely faint and only appears to be dead (*shema nitalef*).

Talmud *Shabbat* explains that a dying person is comparable to a flickering candle – although it is going out on its own, if a person were to place his finger on the wick, it would extinguish immediately. Similarly, although the person is clearly dying, as long as he is still alive, even slight movements may hasten his death even by mere moments.[12] Presumably, after Rambam's "short while" has passed, an observer can be certain that

---

10 *Hilkhot Avel* 4:5.
11 *Shabbat* 151a, based on *Semahot* 1:8.
12 See Rashi, *Me'iri* ad loc.

the patient has in fact died and that the soul has completed its departure. Interestingly, however, nowhere in these *halakhot* does Rambam identify, or even hint at, how to determine the moment of death. We are left not only wondering how "short" this interval must be, but also when it begins.

Hatam Sofer argues that Rambam omitted these details because he relied on the reader referencing his discussion of the laws of Shabbat. There, Rambam states simply that "If they [uncovered a victim sufficiently and] exposed his nose but could not find any respiration – they must [cease their rescuing efforts] and leave the victim in his place, as he has already died [and it is forbidden to prepare the dead for burial on Shabbat]."[13] *Hatam Sofer* notes that Rambam identifies a victim as dead by the inability to breathe alone, as per Talmud *Yoma*, certainly not requiring any evidence of tissue decomposition, which may take additional hours or even days to become visible. *Hatam Sofer* combines these two *halakhot* and explains that Rambam's "short" interval should be calculated from the moment that the victim can no longer breathe and should last as long as necessary to assure that the victim has not "merely" fainted (or presumably experienced any other reversible condition). *Hatam Sofer* is quite emphatic, arguing, "This is a universal rule for all deaths – it is the received determination for the moment of death (*shiur ha-mekubbal be-yadeinu*) ever since we became a holy nation, and all the 'winds of the world,' despite their strength, cannot alter our holy Torah's determination."

Hatam Sofer maintains that this is a universal determination that is not limited to the specific case of avalanche victims discussed in Talmud *Yoma*.[14] He argues that the Talmud highlighted these rulings specifically in the context of an avalanche victim, where there is an increased likelihood of the victim merely appearing dead due to non-lethal injury or shock; **even** in such circumstances, the same principles hold true. Although there may be more room for error in these instances, the Talmud is adamant, argues *Hatam Sofer*, that we are never required to – and are likely forbidden to – wait for visible signs of tissue decomposition before determining death. Indeed, whenever a patient appears

---

13 *Hilkhot Shabbat* 2:18-19.
14 R. Chajes had apparently assumed otherwise in his question.

to be dead, similar to an avalanche victim, we are guided by these standards.[15]

Guide for the Perplexed

Before summarizing his position, *Hatam Sofer* analyzes a difficult passage from Rambam's *Guide for the Perplexed*. Rambam relates to the Biblical story of the Tzarfatit woman, whose son became ill to the point that "there was no breath left in him" (*lo notrah bo neshamah*) and was then revived by the prophet Eliyahu:

> The [Bible's use of the] term *"mavet"* signifies death as well as severe illness, as in "[Upon hearing the news,] his [Naval's] heart died within him (*va-yamot libbo be-kirbo*), and he became as a stone" (*I Shemuel* 25:37) – that is, his illness was severe [but he did not die at this time]. For this reason, by the son of the Tzarfatit, the verse states, "And his sickness was so severe, that there was no breath left in him" (*I Melakhim* 17:17). For had the verse stated *"va-yamot,"* it may have implied that he was very ill, near death, similar to Naval when he heard what had taken place.
>
> Some of the Andalusian authors say that his breath was suspended so that it could not be perceived, as occurs sometimes in apoplexy or with asphyxia deriving from the womb,[16] where it cannot be ascertained whether he is alive or dead; this doubt may linger for [even] a day or two.[17]

---

15 *Hatam Sofer* would accordingly have no difficulty identifying a choking victim as alive even when no longer able to breathe since the rule only applies to those who appear to be dead, like an avalanche victim. Someone whose arms are flailing and signaling for help is decidedly not comparable to a motionless victim of a building collapse.

16 The translation of these two terms follows Pines' version, *The Guide of the Perplexed*, vol. 1, trans. S. Pines (Chicago: University of Chicago Press, 1963), 92. R. Kapih's translation reads *"ha-me'ulafim u-be-hehanek ha-rehem,"* the first term referring to fainting and the second describing a female specific disease, which he cites some as describing as *"histiriah."*

17 *Guide of the Perplexed* 1:42.

This passage raises almost as many questions as it attempts to answer, with the classical commentators to the *Guide* offering a wide variety of interpretations. Rambam maintains that while Naval did not actually die, although his "heart died within him," the son of the Tzarfatit woman did die – "there was no breath left in him" – and was brought back to life by Eliyahu. The Andalusian scholars whom he cites disagree – but regarding which point? Furthermore, according to Rambam's linguistic analysis, how are we to interpret the story of the son of the Shunamit, a similar biblical story in which Elisha, Eliyahu's disciple, resuscitates a young child? The language describing that story differs significantly, employing the vague term *"va-yamot."*[18] The implication from the *Guide* seems to be that, unlike the son of the Tzarfatit, the Shunamit's son did not actually die, but was rather severely ill, like Naval – greatly mitigating the miraculous nature of Elisha's intervention.[19]

Talmud *Niddah* 70b complicates the matter even further. The Talmud questions whether or not the son of the Shunamit engendered *tum'at meit* (ritual defilement of a corpse) and offers a cryptic resolution, stating that a dead person engenders *tum'at meit* while a living person does not. Rashi and Me'iri claim that the Talmud specifically refers to the child's status after he was resurrected; beforehand, he was dead, and therefore clearly engendered *tum'ah*.[20] Other commentators wonder why the Talmud asked only about the Shunamit's son when a similar and historically earlier story happened to the son of the Tzarfatit. The implication of both the Talmud and the commentators is that both boys were dead – seemingly contradicting Rambam's thesis.

The second question stems from Daniel's description of receiving revelation, in which he describes, "There remained no strength in me, nor did any breath remain within me" (*u-neshamah lo nish'arah bi*).[21] This formulation is parallel to the Bible's description of the son of the Tzarfatit (*lo notrah bo neshamah*). In Daniel's case, however, it is clear that he was still alive despite being described as no longer breathing, while according to the *Guide*, the same phrase describes the demise of the Tzarfatit's son.

---

18 *II Melakhim* 4:20.
19 Cf. R. Moses Narboni's commentary to the *Guide* 1:42.
20 Rashi, *Meiri*, Talmud *Niddah* 70b.
21 *Daniel* 10:17.

The classical commentators to the *Guide* offer divergent explanations, ranging from R. Joseph ibn Caspi's claim that neither child actually died[22] to R. Yitzhak Abravanel's explanation that both children died.[23] *Hatam Sofer* explains this passage in his own way, taking Rambam's definitions and their implications at face value – meaning that, according to Rambam, while the son of the Tzarfatit died, the Shunamit's son did not. He explains that the Andalusian scholars take the opposite approach, assuming that the term *mavet* indicates actual death – implying that while the Shunamit's son died (as the verse states *va-yamot*), the son of the Tzarfatit did not. *Hatam Sofer* argues that even the Andalusians, however, would admit that Naval remained alive, even though he is described by the term *va-yamot*, since the verse elaborates, "*Va-yamot libbo be-kirbo*" ("And his heart died within him"), deviating from the standard description of death simply as *va-yamot*. *Hatam Sofer* concludes by noting that, contrary to Rambam, the traditional interpretation of *Hazal* is that both boys died natural "complete" deaths and required miraculous prophetic intervention for their resurrection.

What in fact happened to those who did not die, whether the son of the Shunamit, the son of the Tzarfatit, or Naval? *Hatam Sofer* postulates that the "death of Naval's heart" (*va-yamot libbo*) refers to the cessation of a pulse; despite this, Naval did not die according to all opinions.[24] In contrast, while the son of the Tzarfatit was not breathing, he still maintained a pulse – and was deemed alive by the Andalusian scholars. According to *Hazal*'s approach, both boys died – with the cessation of both respiration and heartbeat – and were later resurrected by the respective prophets.

---

22 *Maskiyot Kesef*, *Guide* 1:42.
23 *Commentary to the Guide*, ad loc. Cf. R. Hasdai Crescas and Narboni's commentaries ad loc. for additional interpretations.
24 *Hatam Sofer* cites the parallel notion in Ramban's interpretation of the description of Yaakov's reaction to the revelation that Yosef was still alive (*Bereishit* 45:26): "And his heart fainted (*va-yafag libbo*) because he did not believe them." Ramban explains (*Commentary to the Torah*, ad loc.) that Yaakov's heart stopped beating, he stopped breathing (*nitbatel libbo u-paskah neshimato*), and he appeared to be dead. This perhaps lends greater meaning to the subsequent description of Yaakov's spirit as "revived" (*va-tehi ru'ah Ya'akov*).

According to the simplest reading of this section of the responsum, under certain physiological conditions, *Hatam Sofer* argues that it is possible to continue breathing despite lacking a heartbeat (like Naval, according to all opinions) and that it is similarly possible to maintain a heartbeat even when no longer breathing (like the Tzarfatit's son, according to the Andalusian scholars). The rarity of these situations is irrelevant; the importance for *Hatam Sofer* lies only in the fact that they are possible.[25] Medically, this explanation is hard to defend, as the circulatory and respiratory systems are intimately intertwined and interdependent. While it is certainly possible for the heart to continue to beat even without concomitant respiration (such as in a choking victim), without medical intervention, this state would certainly last only a short time – certainly not long enough for the Tzarfatit woman to travel to the prophet, beg him to help her, have the prophet send his messenger to the boy and report back to him, and have the prophet himself travel to the boy to assess the situation and subsequently revive him, as described in the Bible.

A more likely interpretation is that *Hatam Sofer* intended only to describe clinically observable phenomenon. Although the pulses of the Tzarfatit's son were still palpable, he did not **appear** to be breathing. Similarly, while Naval's respiratory efforts were visible to an observer, his pulses could not be **felt**, although his heart most certainly continued beating. *Hatam Sofer* thus parallels these phenomena to that which occurs during certain disease states, such as *"shlag," "hinuk ha-rehem,"* and cholera, in which the carotid or temporal pulses may be **felt**, but respirations may not be **perceivable** (*she-lo nirgash bo ela dofek… aval neshimah leika*). *Hatam Sofer* is not interested in identifying rare physiological states (although such possibilities would be important in creating an instance of doubt), but rather with describing empirical phenomena. It is clinically perceivable evidence of respiration and cardiac activity that are of prime importance for *Hatam Sofer*'s definition of death; if one or the other is present, the person cannot be considered dead.

Interestingly, the question of reversibility does not play a role in *Hatam Sofer*'s analysis. Since both boys ultimately lived, one could argue

---

25 R. Moshe Feinstein (*Responsa Iggerot Mosheh*, YD 2:146) identifies with this interpretation and employs it in interpreting the passage in Talmud *Yoma*.

that regardless of their precise symptoms, they could not be determinant of death since they were eventually reversed. While this observation is accurate, the conclusion is not, and this is likely why *Hatam Sofer* did not address this specific point. The notion of reversibility applies to the **natural** course of a disease; a heart that stops temporarily and can be restarted, even only with medical intervention, cannot be considered to have irreversibly stopped beating. However, a disease process that requires prophetic intervention to reverse no longer conforms to the laws of nature and therefore qualifies as irreversible. The distinction applies linguistically as well – doctors **resuscitate** patients, while prophets **resurrect** them.

Conclusion – Or Is It?

Before beginning a lengthy discourse on the intricacies of *tum'at kohanim*, *Hatam Sofer* summarizes his position:

> However, any person who lies [still] as a stone (*munah ke-even domem*), and has no heartbeat [or pulse] (*defikah*), and then ceases to breathe – we must rely on the determination of our Holy Torah that he is dead. His burial should not be delayed and *kohanim* who come into contact with him violate a prohibition…

This concluding passage, in which *Hatam Sofer* ostensibly intends to clarify his position, has led to intense and heated debate as to his true opinion.

Hatam Sofer lists three criteria for determining death with the intention of purposely excluding any mention or requirement of visible tissue decomposition (as argued by those who wished to delay burial). The first requirement of "lying [still] as a stone" is parallel to (and likely borrowed from) Rashi's commentary to Talmud *Yoma* 85a; were the person to be moving about, it would be hard to argue that he has indeed already died. *Hatam Sofer*'s inclusion of cardiac criteria also appears to stem from Rashi's commentary to that Talmudic passage (discussed in chapter 5), noting the importance of cardiovascular function. *Hatam Sofer* saves for last the criteria that he has built up in the preceding sections of this responsum – namely, cessation of respiration.

Many writers note that until this point in the responsum, *Hatam Sofer* does not mention the heartbeat as relevant to the determination of death. Rather, the focus is completely on his understanding of Talmud *Yoma* – that the irreversible cessation of respiration satisfies the criteria for death. Some go so far as to put this line at odds with the previous paragraphs, arguing that there is a blatant contradiction in the words of *Hatam Sofer*; while he initially chose respiratory criteria as the only relevant factor for determining death, in these concluding words, he did an about-face, adding cardiac criteria as well. This reading greatly complicates the discussion in modern literature on the topic. When referencing this responsum without elaboration, does the writer mean to refer to *Hatam Sofer*'s reliance on respiratory criteria alone (as appears from the initial paragraphs) or to the composite picture, including both respiratory and cardiac criteria (as per his conclusion)? This ambiguity is further exaggerated by the dearth of detailed analysis of the bulk of this responsum.

It is important to remember the historical context of this responsum – *Hatam Sofer*'s primary focus is arguing against waiting for visible tissue decomposition before permitting burial. He therefore focuses on the **perceivable** signs of life – namely breathing and a pulse. When they are no longer evident, the Torah declares a person to be dead without waiting for tissue decomposition. This is precisely the point *Hatam Sofer* attempts to drive home throughout this responsum. Even though the very rare possibility of returning to life exists (as described by *Masekhet Semahot*), Halakhah takes no cognizance of such infinitesimally infrequent instances and declares a person dead upon the irreversible cessation of **observable** signs of life.

Hatam Sofer focuses on that which can be observed and measured. Often in dying, pulses are hard to detect, especially in elderly patients. This was certainly the case before the advent of modern medical equipment, such as the stethoscope, which was not widely used until the early to middle 1800's. In most people's experience, the last visible sign of a person's life was respiration; by the time a person had stopped breathing, his pulse was usually no longer palpable, thereby meeting the halakhic definition of death as defined by *Hatam Sofer* in his concluding statement – cessation of both cardiac **and** respiratory function.

Any determination as to the status of a mechanically ventilated "brain dead" patient based on this or any other historical responsum necessitates maneuvering past at least a few logical gaps. It is hard to believe that *Hatam Sofer* could have ever imagined the medical reality of today, in which a patient who can no longer breathe on his own can rely on mechanical means for respiratory support. *Hatam Sofer* was dealing with a far simpler reality, in which uncertainty was limited to identifying facts and clarifying physiological states: Is the patient still breathing? Does he still have a heartbeat? The modern uncertainty, in contrast, revolves around "meta" issues and value judgments: When is a person considered to be dead? How should we describe the status of a ventilated patient's heartbeat – as spontaneous or artificial? While almost all halakhic discussions of "brain death" reference and often heavily invest in understanding this responsum, this limiting caveat is important when attempting to draw parallels from *Hatam Sofer*'s world to ours.

Advocate of Respiratory Criteria?

Some authors, recognizing the ambiguity raised by *Hatam Sofer*'s concluding line, have tried to relieve the apparent contradiction by analyzing the concluding statement very closely. R. Shaul Yisraeli[26] and Dr. Avraham Steinberg[27] argue that *Hatam Sofer* truly insisted on **respiratory criteria alone** as determinant of death. This is the notion that *Hatam Sofer* began his responsum with and that he repeats throughout; the notion of the heart's significance in this discussion only stems from the issues raised in Rambam's *Guide*. Focusing on the chronological parsing of the concluding line, they argue that *Hatam Sofer* meant this sentence to be read extremely precisely: If a person is lying still and has no heartbeat, he is still considered alive, since the criteria for death have not

---

26 Sh. Yisraeli, "Regarding Permitting Heart Transplants Today" (Hebrew) in M. Halperin (ed.), *Kevi'at Rega ha-Mavet* 2nd edition (Jerusalem: Schlesinger Institute, 2007), 307-8.
27 A. Steinberg, "Determining the Moment of Death and Heart Transplants" (Hebrew), ibid., 50-51.

yet been met. However, "if he **then** ceases to breathe," he is then – and only then – considered dead according to the Torah. *Hatam Sofer*, they argue, intended to specifically exclude determining death based solely on cardiac criteria, insisting that even if the heart irreversibly stops functioning, one must wait until respirations have finally ceased before declaring death. The implication, they argue, is clear – were the respiratory function to irreversibly fail earlier in this sequence, the patient would be declared dead at that point, regardless of whether or not he had a heartbeat.

These scholars employ their resolution of the apparent contradiction in the words of *Hatam Sofer* as proof that the cessation of cardiac function is irrelevant to the determination of death. Accordingly, "brain death," in which the heartbeat continues despite irreversible cessation of respiratory function, should certainly be recognized by Halakhah.

This analysis faces difficulties, however. *Hatam Sofer* mentions cardiac criteria several times in his responsum, and in each instance the implied assumption is that the heart must stop beating in order to determine death.

As correctly pointed out by R. Yisraeli, *Hatam Sofer* first discusses the notion of the heartbeat as relevant for determining death in his analysis of the passage from the *Guide*. This reference, however, is not merely made in passing, but rather significantly informs the discussion at hand. According to *Hatam Sofer*'s presentation of the approach of the Andalusian scholars, it is clear that a continued heartbeat **is** sufficient evidence for continued life, even when the person in question no longer appears to be breathing. The son of the Tzarfatit, according to this approach, was no longer breathing (*lo notrah bo neshimah*); nonetheless, *Hatam Sofer* argues, his heartbeat persisted and he was therefore considered alive according to these scholars. While arguing with this particular exegesis, *Hatam Sofer* readily accepts it as possible; he essentially agrees with its approach to determining death even though he disagrees with its conclusion.

Hatam Sofer concludes that discussion by noting that *Hazal*'s traditional understanding is that both boys died and were ultimately prophetically resurrected, explicitly contrasting this approach with that of Rambam and the Andalusian scholars. Accordingly, it seems clear that *Hazal* interpreted the passages to mean that both boys suffered both the cessation of respiration as well as cardiac function and that the cessation of both is necessary to determine death. If one or the other had been present, *Hazal*'s reading of the stories would not differ from either that of Rambam or the Andalusians, as everyone concurs that the presence of either respiration or heartbeat indicates life.

Hatam Sofer mentions the notion of the heartbeat as indicative of life later as well, albeit succinctly, in his analysis of Mishnah *Niddah* 10:4. When describing the "normal" course of events in a dying patient, he claims that a heartbeat alone is indicative of life. In differentiating between the ability of experts to accurately ascertain the moment of death from the difficulties in doing so by the masses, *Hatam Sofer* notes that the members of the *hevra kadisha* look for even the slightest sign of breathing and **heartbeat** ("*hergesh kol shehu bi-neshimah u-defikah*"). While not offering a rigorous definition of the determination of death, he likely felt it unnecessary at this point, having previously analyzed and defended it three paragraphs earlier.

Thus, although *Hatam Sofer* indeed neglects to mention any hint of the importance of cardiac function in his discussion of Talmud *Yoma*, this is possibly because he simply assumed that it was obviously necessary and that his subsequent mentions of heartbeat as important in sustaining life vouched for this necessity – which is why he mentions it in his concluding summary statement. As R. Hayyim David ha-Levi argues, it was simply inconceivable to *Hatam Sofer* to declare dead a person whose heartbeat could still be felt.[28]

A further technical, but important, objection can be raised against R. Yisraeli's and Dr. Steinberg's reading of *Hatam Sofer*'s concluding summary statement. According to their argument, *Hatam Sofer* parsed his words carefully, indicating a particular sequence of death-determining criteria. R. Yisraeli and Dr. Steinberg argue that for *Hatam Sofer*, lying motionless and lacking a heartbeat alone are insufficient determinants of death – such a person may still be alive. They claim that *Hatam Sofer* ordered the criteria in this way to insist on determining death only after respiration has ceased.

---

28 *Responsa Aseh Lekha Rav* 8:64.

This suggestion is problematic, however, since it is impossible to breathe without a heartbeat. Accordingly, *Hatam Sofer* may have parsed his words intentionally simply to exclude a scenario that is not physically possible; if the heart has actually stopped, respiration clearly has as well. Perhaps R. Yisraeli and Dr. Steinberg mean that *Hatam Sofer*'s intent is that a person found without a **perceptible** heartbeat cannot be declared dead because, as *Hakham Tzvi* asserted, it is possible for the heart to be functioning even if its motion is undetectable by a physical exam; under such circumstances, however, breathing is still possible. When such a person is found to no longer be breathing, only then can he be declared dead – that is, only when found without evidence of both cardiac **and** respiratory function. Thus, unless R. Yisraeli and Dr. Steinberg are asserting that *Hatam Sofer* posits the ability to breathe without a heartbeat, their suggestion boils down to proving that *Hatam Sofer* agreed to determine death when no signs of heartbeat **and** breathing are evident. Their intent, however, was to demonstrate that *Hatam Sofer* argued for determining death based on (irreversible) cessation of spontaneous respiration alone, even in the face of continued cardiac activity.

Even granting their reading of *Hatam Sofer*'s concluding summary statement, R. Yisraeli and Dr. Steinberg's conclusion is still problematic. According to their suggested sequence, unresponsiveness and lack of pulse are insufficient to determine death until the patient is also found to be irreversibly unable to breathe. Even if this is correct, there is no indication that were the order to be switched – unresponsiveness, then apena, and only then pulseslessness – *Hatam Sofer* would agree to determine death after apena alone. While possible, evidence for this claim is certainly lacking. At best, *Hatam Sofer* can be interpreted as not necessarily rejecting this notion outright.

What was Hatam Sofer Really Referring To?

In addition to the approach outlined by R. Yisraeli and Dr. Steinberg, there are two other broad approaches to this responsum. The first, represented most extensively by R. J. David Bleich, argues that *Hatam Sofer* must be understood according to the straightforward meaning of his concluding summary statement.[29] *Hatam Sofer* discusses both respiratory and cardiac criteria at different points in this responsum and, importantly, cites both in his concluding summation. The simplest reading of the whole of this responsum, R. Bleich argues, is that *Hatam Sofer* defined death by necessitating the irreversible cessation of **both** cardiac and respiratory function, in addition to complete unresponsiveness. It is precisely when these three elements come together – as clearly delineated in the summary – that death is halakhically determined; they are **all** listed because they are **all** necessary.

R. Moshe Tendler, who later became one of the staunchest advocates of accepting "brain death" as halakhic death, interprets *Hatam Sofer* similarly.[30] In one of his earliest essays on the topic, arguing against neurological criteria for death (prior to reversing his opinion), R. Tendler explains that the overall thrust of *Hatam Sofer*'s responsum cannot be reduced to determining death solely based on respiratory criteria. Rather, as *Hatam Sofer* delineates in his concluding sentiment, there are a combination of physiological parameters that are determinant of death, including both respiration **and** cardiac criteria. While not without some difficulty in explaining each line of the text, the plain reading of the responsum as a whole seems to argue for this interpretation.

Aware of *Hatam Sofer*'s requirement for lack of pulse, yet cognizant of his reticence in discussing its necessity earlier in the responsum, R. Zalman Nehemiah Goldberg opts for a middle position.[31] He maintains that *Hatam Sofer* actually advocates for determining death solely by respiratory criteria. This is, after all, R. Goldberg argues, the simplest interpretation of the discussion in Talmud *Yoma* were it not for Rashi's comments, which *Hatam Sofer* completely neglects in analyzing this Talmudic passage.[32] *Hatam Sofer* invokes the role of cardiac activity, argues R. Goldberg, only during the practical part of his discussion,

---

29 *Bi-Netivot ha-Halakhah* 3, 101, 106, 109, 134-5.
30 M. Tendler, "Determining Death in Halakhah – Defining 'Life and Death' in Science" (Hebrew), *Be'er Yitzhak* (5732): 21.
31 Quoted in *Mishnat Hayyei Sha'ah*, 58.
32 R. Goldberg would seemingly argue that *Hatam Sofer* purposefully ignored Rashi's comments so as not to detract from the focus on respiratory criteria.

in answering the question, "How can we tell that a given person has in fact died?" R. Goldberg argues that pulselessness (the complete absence of heartbeat), while often necessary in making this determination, is not part of the definition. He believes that according to *Hatam Sofer*, the lack of heartbeat is not a **criterion** for death, but only a **test** to determine that the concomitant cessation of respiratory function is indeed irreversible. (Were cardiac activity to persist, it would be practically difficult to ascertain whether or not respirations have irreversibly ceased, given the tools available in Talmudic or even early modern times.) However, the true **definition** of death, according to R. Goldberg, is the irreversible cessation of respiration, even in the face of a continuing heartbeat.[33]

Because of the difficulty in identifying the absence of a physiological parameter, *Hatam Sofer* posits that the absence of cardiac activity acts as a surrogate marker, indicating that a person has irreversibly stopped breathing. Although not fundamental to the actual definition of death, together with the complete lack of movement, the lack of heartbeat verifies the otherwise elusive prognosis that the person will never breathe again.

Although arguing for a slightly different conclusion, R. Moshe Sternbuch interprets this responsum similarly,[34] focusing on the third element of *Hatam Sofer*'s concluding summary statement. Completely neglecting *Hatam Sofer*'s instances of mentioning cardiac activity, R. Sternbuch argues that death should be determined by respiratory criteria alone. This is only true, however, when it is truly irreversible, prompting Rambam's requirement for waiting "a short while" so as to rule out "fainting" and other reversible etiologies for the apnea. It is specifically to confirm the irreversibility of the respiratory failure, argues R. Sternbuch, that *Hatam Sofer* included "lying still as a stone" in his concluding summary. It is not a defining **criterion**, but rather, as R. Goldberg argued, a confirmatory **test** certifying that the respiratory arrest, which actually

---

33 R. Shelomoh Goren ("The Definition of Death in Halakhah," *Shanah be-Shanah* [5734]: 127) also argues that *Hatam Sofer* added cardiac criteria as a means of simplifying the determination. How this works, however, is somewhat unclear. R. Goren assumes that *Hatam Sofer* introduced the notion of cardiac criteria in response to Rambam's claim that a person could be alive even though unable to breathe.

34 *Be'ayot ha-Zeman be-Hashkafat ha-Torah*, 10.

constitutes death, is in fact irreversible. In a later responsum, R. Sternbuch writes explicitly that were Halakhah based on *Hatam Sofer* alone, determining death would most certainly be based solely on the ability or inability to breathe spontaneously.[35]

Concluding Remarks

While this responsum of *Hatam Sofer* is the most oft quoted "source" in halakhic discussions of the determination of death, the implications of this responsum are significantly debated. It is certainly difficult to predict how *Hatam Sofer* would relate to modern medical realities, likely never having imagined the disjunction of cessation of respiration and cessation of heartbeat. Even what can best be described as intuitions or "gut reactions" to this responsum vary wildly. R. Yisraeli claims that, "*Hatam Sofer* never even thought to require that cessation of respiration be accompanied by cardiac asystole as well,"[36] while R. Hayyim David ha-Levi argues, "It is simply inconceivable… that after finding a pulse… if the person is not breathing he is considered dead, while we can see that his heart is still beating."[37] While according to the simple reading of his concluding summary statement, *Hatam Sofer* would seemingly oppose recognizing "brain death" as halakhically meaningful because of the persistent heartbeat, R. Goldberg raises a thought provoking interpretation that may force the very opposite conclusion – cessation of cardiac activity is only a test of respiration, and "brain death" is a certain indication of it.

R. Bleich and others find support for their position from *Hatam Sofer*'s concluding inclusion of cardiac function as a necessary component of any death determination. R. Yisraeli and Dr. Steinberg similarly rely on

---

35 *Teshuvot ve-Hanhagot* 4:267. To avoid misinterpretation, while in *Teshuvot ve-Hanhagot* 3:331, R. Shternbuch argues for a purely respiration-based determination of death, in 4:267 he clarifies that he does not support (and actually condemns) brain death dependent organ donations. Later, however (*Assia* 87-88 (2010): 79-80), he is quoted as supportive of a purely respiratory based criterion for death, although practically he refrains from endorsing or promoting organ donation out of mistrust of the medical establishment.
36 See n.26 above.
37 See n.28 above.

Hatam Sofer's conclusions to bolster their approach, although ultimately, this responsum does not so much support their position as not necessarily contradict it. *Hatam Sofer*'s opinion has thus become firmly entrenched as one of the core principles upon which this entire discussion revolves. All insist that this responsum addresses the fundamental issues relevant for understanding "brain death" in Halakhah, but where its importance lays spans the spectrum from those fiercely advocating for the halakhic recognition of "brain death" to those adamantly opposing neurological determinations of death.

SECTION III:

MODERN OPINIONS ON BRAIN DEATH

CHAPTER 10:

Rabbi Moshe Feinstein – First Responsum

Iggerot Mosheh, Yoreh De'ah 2:174

The preeminent halakhic decisor of American Jewry in the late twentieth century, R. Moshe Feinstein (1895-1986) witnessed the introduction of "brain death" as a medical possibility through its eventual development into a legal definition. Never shying away from adjudicating Halakhah in all realms, R. Feinstein published four separate responsa addressing these issues in the course of over a decade (1968-1984). Because his overall stance is fiercely debated and each responsum forms part of a larger whole, each of the four responsa will be analyzed separately. This will allow for a detailed analysis of each responsum in its own right and a better understanding of the many local issues involved. This will be followed by a more comprehensive analysis (chapter 14) searching for themes, common ideas, and prevalent attitudes permeating these responsa.

While the question of determining death stands on its own as an independent inquiry, in modern times, it has been inextricably linked to the issue of organ transplantation. While not necessarily evident from modern practice, until the early 1980's, post-transplant recipient survival rates were quite miserable, reaching "reasonable" success only late into

R. Feinstein's life. The high risk entailed in the endeavor contributed significantly to R. Feinstein's perspective, and he made his attitudes and biases toward transplants in particular and the medical establishment in general clearly known.

R. Feinstein first addressed the issue of cardiac transplantation in 1968 (19 *Tamuz*, 5728/ July 15, 1968) in a letter to R. Yitzhak Yaakov Weisz, the author of *Responsa Minhat Yitzhak*, then the rabbi of Manchester, England, and later of Jerusalem. For unexplained reasons, although this responsum was penned prior to the next responsum to be discussed, this one is printed later in the second volume of *Iggerot Mosheh, Yoreh De'ah*, but this does not appear to be of much significance.

Although the question posed to R. Feinstein relates to cardiac transplantation, the notion of "brain death" is never explicitly mentioned in this responsum. In fact, there is not even any discussion of cardiac vs. respiratory determinants for death. Nonetheless, R. Feinstein attempts to define and clarify the moment of death through the Talmudic and halakhic sources, navigating the uncertainty that naturally prevails in applying them to modern medical practice.

R. Feinstein divides this lengthy responsum into two distinct sections. The first is a bold declaration of his position, clearly articulating that cardiac transplantation constitutes a double murder – of both the donor and the recipient. The second half is dedicated to reacting to R. Weisz's previously published essay on this very topic.[1] Neither section expressly deals with the medical reality of "brain death" necessary for transplantation; there is no mention of the donor's lack of spontaneous respiration while maintaining a continuous heartbeat. While both sections analyze various Talmudic and halakhic determinants of death, neither discusses practically how these analyses are relevant to the current medical realities.

A Living Donor

The explicit assumption of R. Weisz's question is that the cardiac donor is still alive, albeit not for very long. Since removing the donor's

---

[1] Later published in *Responsa Minhat Yitzhak* 5:7.

heart would instantly cause his death, the question posed was whether it is permissible to end the life of a moribund patient with no hope of recovery so as to (hopefully) extend the life of another patient, whose condition is potentially reversible with a cardiac transplant.[2]

R. Feinstein's opening statement makes his opinion quite clear:

I do not wish to engage in extended proofs, theories or elaborations, since I say that those who engage in extensive discourse on this issue certainly detract from the strength of their opinion (*kol ha-mosif le-falpel u-lehavi re'ayot hu... gore'a*); by doing so, it appears that proofs are necessary and the matter is not simple and clear cut, and [people may] come to be lenient and attempt to argue on these proofs. And even if these [counter] arguments will be weak and vain, people will say that since there is rabbinic disagreement on the matter, it is possible to be lenient, God forbid. Therefore, I am stating [my position] clearly in this responsum, *Halakhah le-ma'aseh*, clearly and emphatically, and it is completely inappropriate to further explore or elaborate (*la-dun u-le-falpel*) on these matters.

The recently developed surgery of cardiac transplantation is actually a double murder. It actively kills the cardiac donor, as he is considered to be alive – not only according to the laws of the Torah, where determination of death is emphasized (*she-nimsar lanu hashivut mittah*), but even according to the physicians, there are those who tell the truth and attest that the donor is still alive prior to the donation, but because of their wickedness, they are not concerned with the donor's life since it is only short-lived (*hayyei*

---

[2] R. Weisz notes that since the moment of death cannot be medically ascertained, the practice of the doctors is to artificially extend a patient's life – when he would have naturally died earlier – so that a transplant can be arranged and the requisite organs removed. What he is referring to medically is hard to determine, and R. Weisz does not give many scientific details. He does not explain the meaning of artificially extending life vs. doing so naturally.

sha'ah), possibly for [only] a few days. Additionally, they actively murder the intended recipient by years and sometimes even decades, since it is known that many cardiac patients [potential recipients] can live long lives. Those who have received cardiac transplants all died in a short time, most within several hours and some within a few days [after surgery]. And even though there is one recipient in Africa who is still alive six months after receiving a transplant, according to what I have heard, the physicians have already decided that he will not live much longer.

It is astonishing that the governments of all of these countries permit the wicked doctors to murder two people for each transplant. Since they have already seen that [the surgery fails] and nobody is actually saved, they should have punished these physicians as absolute murderers. This is [true] despite the procedures only occurring with the recipients' consent, since the recipients have been duped by the evil physicians. Moreover, regardless, consent is meaningless in this manner, since a person is not permitted to kill even himself [let alone give permission to others to do so on his behalf].

This is the responsum that is to be [publically] disseminated, in these words, no less and no more.

Thus, R. Feinstein certainly agrees that the cardiac donor is very much alive; organ harvesting is therefore tantamount to murder of the donor. Furthermore, given the abysmal failure rate of heart transplants, it also constitutes murder of the recipient.

Reversible Decapitation and Determinants of Death

Without explicitly referencing the broader question of definitions as opposed to indications of death, R. Feinstein posits that decapitation certainly qualifies as determinant of death (*"hu be-din meit mamash"*), as per Mishnah *Ohalot* 1:6. He further develops this thesis by noting that even if it were possible to reattach the freshly decapitated head to its body – that is, even if decapitation were reversible – there is certainly no requirement to do so, as it would constitute **resurrection** and not **resuscitation**. The Torah requires only healing the sick, not resurrecting the dead.³ Consequently, violating Shabbat to reattach the head is forbidden, since it does not qualify as saving a life.

R. Feinstein notes that his position puts him at odds with *Tosafot*,⁴ who relate that Eliyahu the prophet (whom the Talmud identifies with Pinhas the high priest) was permitted to resurrect the son of the Tzarfatit even though this necessitated actively defiling the Priestly sanctity (as he was under the same roof as a dead body). *Tosafot* argues that resurrection qualifies as *pikuah nefesh*; for the purpose of saving a life, the prohibition against defiling the Priestly sanctity is suspended.

Firmly maintaining his previously articulated assertion, R. Feinstein is forced to re-interpret *Tosafot*'s claim so as not to be squarely at odds with it. According to R. Feinstein, the notion of *pikuah nefesh* temporarily permitting prohibitions is simply not possible when it comes to the deceased. He therefore reads *Tosafot*'s reliance on the *pikuah nefesh* allowance not as referring to saving the young boy's life (as he was quite dead), but rather to either saving the boy's mother or Eliyahu himself. Perhaps the boy's mother was so distraught at the thought that her sincere devotion to God may have brought about her son's death that her mental state put her life in danger. Alternatively, perhaps Eliyahu became physically or severely psychologically ill at the notion that he may have caused the death of the boy. While these suggestions are certainly not in accord with the plain sense of *Tosafot*'s statement, nor the simple reading of Scripture, it appears that R. Feinstein was so confident of his position that he was willing to tolerate a forced reading of *Tosafot* to this end.⁵

---

3 R. Feinstein references Talmud *Bava Batra* 74b, which discusses a certain precious stone that had the ability to revive the dead that has been hidden from mankind. He writes that even if this stone were to be discovered, there would certainly be no obligation to avail oneself of its properties.
4 *Tosafot, Bava Metzi'a* 114b, s.v. *amar*.
5 It is, in fact, difficult to assume that *Tosafot* viewed Eliyahu's actions completely as *pikuah nefesh*. After all, *pikuah nefesh* is more than a license to temporarily override prohibitions; it is an obligation incumbent upon all who have the ability to save others.

Thus, R. Feinstein posits that decapitation is determinant of death even though it is theoretically reversible. As noted in chapter 3, however, almost all definitions of death, whether halakhic or secular, encompass the notion of irreversibility, regardless of the determination relied upon – be it cardiac, respiratory, or neurological. R. Feinstein's approach is both exceptional and remarkable in apparently disregarding irreversibility as a requisite criterion. In fact, Dr. Abraham S. Abraham wonders why doctors regularly attempt to resuscitate patients who appear clinically dead – with no spontaneous respiration, heartbeat, or other movement – on Shabbat without any Rabbinic censure.[6] According to R. Feinstein's logic, once death is definitely determined, there is no further obligation to heal/resuscitate/resurrect the patient, and therefore no permission to do so if it necessitates violating Shabbat restrictions.

Ignoring the reversibility criterion would mean relating to a pulseless and asystolic (flat-line EKG) patient as dead and to his resuscitation as resurrection; this is not only somewhat counterintuitive, but also contradicts the Talmudic dictum that mortals do not have the ability to resurrect the dead without Divine assistance.[7] As is evident from R. Feinstein's other responsa,[8] he similarly rejects such a notion. Since the patient's heart ultimately starts beating again, it must be that it was never irreversibly stopped; even while he may have appeared to be dead, in reality he was not. How, then, are we to understand R. Feinstein's lack of concern for proof of irreversibility regarding decapitation?

The Uncertain Dying Process

R. Feinstein does not directly address the issue of reversibility, nor explicitly relate to the discussion of definitions vs. indications of death.

If Eliyahu's ability to resurrect the dead is considered *pikuah nefesh*, he should have employed this power more frequently, travelling the world and resurrecting as many corpses as possible! There is no record of Eliyahu doing so, nor of any classical commentator asking why he did not – likely because *Tosafot's* comparison to *pikuah nefesh* was meant as less than absolute.

6 *Nishmat Avraham YD*, 2nd ed., 481.
7 Talmud *Ta'anit* 2a.
8 *Responsa Iggerot Mosheh*, YD 2:146.

Nonetheless, the latter part of this responsum may shed some light on his approach to this issue.

In continuing his analysis, R. Feinstein turns to Rambam's position and specifically addresses what R. Weisz describes as an apparent contradiction between two positions of Rambam. In the first *halakhah*,[9] Rambam quotes the ruling of Mishnah *Shabbat*[10] and *Masekhet Semahot*[11] that compares one who closes the eyes of a dying patient (*im yetziat ha-nefesh*) to a murderer and, adding to the Mishnaic dictum, requires waiting a short while (*yishheh me'at*) before closing the patient's eyes out of concern that the patient has merely fainted and not actually died. R. Weisz understands Rambam as assuming some uncertainty as to the moment of death; as a result, since the patient may still be alive, any action that may potentially adversely affect or even possibly hasten his demise (such as closing his eyes) is prohibited. R. Weisz argues that Rambam derived this waiting period from the peculiar language of *Semahot*, forbidding touching the patient *"ad sha'ah she-yamut"* (until the hour/time of death) instead of the simpler *"ad she-yamut"* (until he dies).[12] The *"sha'ah she-yamut,"* argues R. Weisz, indicates a longer period than the actual moment of death, requiring the addition of a short waiting period to rule out the possibility of a reversible cause for the lack of respiration.

According to R. Weisz's understanding of Rambam's waiting period, the underlying assumption is that a patient who does not appear to be breathing cannot survive the waiting period without taking an additional breath. Once the requisite time had passed without a breath, the uncertainly is resolved – the patient has not merely fainted, but is considered certainly dead, and his eyes may be closed. This period can be termed the "time to apnea" (inability to breathe).

---

9 *Hilkhot Avel* 4:5.
10 Mishnah *Shabbat* 23:5.
11 *Masekhet Semahot* 1:4.
12 Interestingly, R. Shaul Yisraeli reaches the same conclusion based on the comments of Shemuel in Talmud *Shabbat* 151b, arguing that the time of *"im yetziat ha-nefesh"* (with the time of the departure of the soul) requires waiting a short period after death before initiating post-mortem practices. See "Regarding Permitting Heart Transplants Today" (Hebrew) in M. Halperin (ed.), *Kevi'at Rega ha-Mavet*, 2nd edition (Jerusalem: Schlesinger Institute, 2007), 305.

R. Weisz argues that this contradicts a different ruling of Rambam regarding a woman dying during childbirth. Citing Talmud *Erkhin* 7a, Rambam writes[13] that one should attempt to surgically remove the fetus from the mother's womb – even violating Shabbat prohibitions in the process if necessary (such as carrying through the public domain) – since saving the baby's life constitutes *pikuah nefesh*. This *halakhah*, its relevance to current practice, and the controversies that surround it have been discussed in chapter 5. The focal point of the present discussion is R. Weisz's claim that it appears to contradict Rambam's previously cited position.

If both of these rulings are taken at face value, we are left with a conundrum. If it is forbidden to even close the eyes of a dying patient out of fear of hastening his death, why do we allow surgically removing a fetus from its mother's womb at that same moment? Is it not obvious that the surgical procedure is potentially more dangerous to the dying woman than merely closing her eyes? If closing the eyes must wait until the waiting period has passed, certainly the surgery should wait as well! How could Rambam have recorded both positions?

R. Feinstein addresses this proposed contradiction by re-analyzing the necessity for the requisite waiting period and its ramifications for closing the eyes vs. surgically removing the fetus. R. Feinstein agrees with R. Weisz's assumption that the waiting period is intended to rule out the possibility that the patient will take a breath, but he notes that proving a negative – that breathing is not taking place – is challenging. When a person appears to have stopped breathing, it can be either because he has died (meaning that the last observed breath was, in fact, his absolute last) or because a serious illness has impaired his respiratory drive. In the latter case, the patient will certainly die without an additional breath, but until that additional breath becomes physiologically necessary – for the next several moments (seconds? minutes?) – the patient remains (tenuously) alive. Since we can never be absolutely certain which breath will be a patient's last, we can only declare death after this period has passed, not retroactively from the time that the last breath was observed.

---

13 *Hilkhot Shabbat* 2:15.

R. Feinstein explains that while it is true that death can be determined after the "time to apnea" has elapsed, we must be certain that the patient did not take an additional breath during that time. This, argues R. Feinstein, requires vigilant and unyielding observation during the entire period, since even subtle shallow breaths are indicative of continued life.

R. Feinstein argues that some level of uncertainty clearly extends even beyond the "time to apnea" delineated by Rambam. The Talmudic discussion in *Niddah* 69b, indicates that the uncertainty of fainting vs. death can sometimes linger for several days, with ramifications regarding ritual impurity. The reasoning for this extension, R. Feinstein contends, is out of concern that an observer did not enforce due diligence in verifying that the patient did not take an additional breath.

This longer "time to absolute certainty" is quite understandable in light of the grave ramifications. However, even this extended period must end at some point; once it has passed with normal, perhaps even casual (but not necessarily hyper-vigilant) observation, the concern for hastening death is obviated, as the patient is certainly dead by all accounts.[14]

---

[14] Current data shows that "neurologically intact" patients may spontaneously return to both circulatory and neurological functioning even 10 minutes after both have stopped and CPR was tried but failed, known as the "Lazarus Phenomenon." See W.H. Maleck, S.N. Piper, J. Triem, et al., "Unexpected return of spontaneous circulation after cessation of resuscitation (Lazarus phenomenon)," *Resuscitation* 39 (1998): 125-8; K. Hornby, L. Hornby, S.D. Shemie, "A systematic review of autoresuscitation after cardiac arrest," *Critical Care Medicine* 38 (2010): 1246-53. Some patients recover for only minutes, some for several hours and even days, and a small percentage recover completely. The second review cited calculates the time from the end of CPR efforts until autoresuscitation. However, the period that may be more halakhically relevant is the time between when the patient's heart stopped – when CPR was initiated – until autoresuscitation. The data shows that some patients may return to consciousness even 45 minutes after initial cardiac asystole and CPR is initiated. It would appear that such patients should be considered halakhically alive during this interim period.

These data are only marginally relevant to the issue of "brain death," as "brain dead" patients are certainly not neurologically intact, although their hearts and lungs may be working optimally. Given the criteria necessary for donating organs, many of the potential patients under discussion are young and previously healthy, having suffered some

Closing Eyes and Delivering Babies

In analyzing Rambam's rulings, R. Feinstein describes the "time to apnea" as one of uncertainty (*safek*). The prohibition of closing the eyes, contends R. Feinstein, is not exactly equated with murder, as would seem from the language of the *mishnah*. Rather, Halakhah is concerned that closing the patient's eyes **may** hasten death, even though this is far from certain.

R. Feinstein contrasts closing the dying patient's eyes with other activities, which certainly do hasten death and are therefore clearly forbidden. *Shulhan Arukh* categorizes various activities done to and around a *goses* as either permissible or prohibited.[15] *Shakh*,[16] attempting to identify a unifying theory behind these rulings, argues that certain fine movements (*ni'anu'a kal*) of the *goses*'s body are permitted, as these gentle motions will not generally hasten his demise. Thus, *Shakh* explains, *Shulhan Arukh* permits removing salt from the *goses*'s tongue but forbids removing a pillow from beneath his head; the former is classified as a fine, gentle movement, while the latter is more aggressive and may adversely affect the patient straddling the fence between life and death. R. Feinstein argues that closing a patient's eyes is most certainly a "fine motion" and is no worse than removing salt from the tongue; moreover, it also qualifies as one of the needs of the deceased (*tzorkhei ha-meit*). Indeed, if closing the patient's eyes certainly hastens the patient's death, it would obviously be prohibited, without needing the *mishnah* to spell it out. R. Feinstein argues that the *mishnah* mandates a cautionary rabbinic prohibition (*gezeirah*) intended to reduce even remotely possible harm caused by closing the patient's eyes – an act that would otherwise have been permitted.

By putting all these pieces together, R. Feinstein explains that closing the patient's eyes is permitted after the shorter time period ("time to apnea") has lapsed. Since the requirement for the "time to absolute certainty" (well after the "time to apnea") is only a stringency, coupled

---

acute neurological insult. Precise data for resuscitation success rates in "brain dead" patients are unavailable at this time.

15 *Shulhan Arukh*, YD 339:1.
16 *Nekudat ha-Kesef*, YD 339.

with the fact that closing the eyes is only prohibited by rabbinic decree because the likelihood of it causing harm is remote, the Rabbis limited the decree of not closing the eyes specifically only up until the "time to apnea." Thus, Rambam rules that one may close the patient's eyes after the short waiting period has elapsed.

R. Feinstein claims that Rambam similarly permits (and perforce requires) surgically removing the fetus from its mother's womb after the "time to apnea" has passed. As noted above, this allowance requires hyper-vigilant observation of the mother during this shorter period so as to ensure, beyond a shadow of a doubt, that she has indeed stopped breathing. This would be universally accepted as normative Halakhah were in not for the rabbinic concern for lack of sufficiently vigilant observation, the stringency that practically forbids most actions until after the "time to complete certainty" has passed. R. Feinstein argues that Rambam's position disregards, predates, or argues with the universal applicability of this rabbinic concern.

Almost all halakhic decisors, starting with the *Ge'onim*[17] and most notably represented by Rama,[18] maintain that current practice forbids (*ein nohagin*) surgically removing the fetus since "we are not experts at determining the [moment of] death of the mother accurately, such that the fetus will survive (*de-ein beki'in be-mitat ha-em be-kiruv kol kakh she-efshar la-velad lihyot*)." R. Feinstein explains that this uncertainty is similar to the general rabbinic concern for less than hyper-vigilant observation. He contends that Rama's ruling, representing normative Halakhah, views modern-day man as too inexperienced and too easily distracted for the requisite hyper-vigilant observation. Surgical removal of the fetus must therefore wait until the longer "time to absolute certainty" has passed – a time by which, Rama claims, the fetus is unfortunately no longer viable, and the practice has therefore been discontinued.

According to R. Feinstein, closing the eyes of a dying person and extracting a fetus from a dying woman are very different. Closing the eyes of a dying person, while forbidden, **will almost certainly not** hasten his death and is forbidden only by Rabbinic decree; since, in

---

17 *Teshuvot ha-Ge'onim*, no. 248 (see chapter 5, n.49).
18 Rama, *OH* 330:5.

addition, it qualifies as a "need of the deceased," it is permitted after the earlier "time to apnea." Surgically removing a fetus, in contrast, **will certainly** shorten the mother's life (if she is still alive). Modern man's ability to be faithfully hyper-vigilant in observing her during this time is rabbinically doubted, and extraction therefore may not begin until the "time to absolute certainty" has passed – which presents practical impediments.

Disagreement

Many have challenged these points, specifically R. Feinstein's understanding of the prohibition to close a dying person's eyes. R. Shaul Yisraeli notes that the prohibition seems absolute, not merely a precaution against something highly unlikely.[19] The language of the *mishnah*, "*harei zeh shofekh damim*" ("this person commits murder"), is quite explicit and does not resort to similes or other metaphorical devices. The concern is certainly real, R. Yisraeli argues, that any movement may cause harm to a seriously weakened patient. Closing the eyes must therefore wait until death can be absolutely ascertained.

According to R. Yisraeli, there is only one period of uncertainty – the "time to apnea" – and after this relatively short period has elapsed, the patient is certainly dead and his eyes may be closed. Indeed, Rambam rules that at that same point, a fetus may be extracted as well; there is no longer any concern of hastening the mother's death, as she is dead.

If death is certain after the "time to apnea" has passed, why do later authorities permit closing the eyes but forbid surgically extracting a fetus? Quoting a responsum of Rama,[20] R. Yisraeli suggest that the Talmudic sages, based on empirical evidence, determined that there is no chance for the fetus to survive even mere moments after the mother's death can be absolutely ascertained; the window during which the surgery is permissible and fetal survival is possible is exceedingly narrow. R. Yisraeli claims that in the past, people in fact tried to deliver fetuses under similar circumstances, but were always unsuccessful. Since they could not precisely

---

19 "Permitting Heart Transplants," 305.
20 Responsa of Rama, 40.

identify the moment of death and therefore could not accurately know the moment that the uncertainty had passed (since they did not precisely know from when to start measuring), they were unsuccessful in timing the procedure to the narrow window of potential success.

This, R. Yisraeli argues, is what Rama means in stating that we cannot accurately determine the moment of the mother's death with enough precision so that the baby will live. Although theoretically permissible to surgically remove the fetus after the "time to apnea" according to all opinions, it is practically impossible because of our inability to determine that time precisely.

Evaluating Reversibility

This long excursion may help alleviate Dr. Abraham's concern. As Dr. Abraham noted, the question of reversibility is axiomatic in determining death; for death to be absolute, it must also be final. In outlining his position regarding the "time to apnea" and "time of absolute certainty," R. Feinstein makes this very point. He maintains that proving a negative – the cessation of cardiac and respiratory function – always requires a heightened burden of proof. Since we can never be sure which breath will be the person's last, after each breath, uncertainty prevails until an additional breath is taken or the "time to apnea" (or in modern times, "time to absolute certainty") has passed; the same is true of the heartbeat. The notion of reversibility is necessary for this definition. Whenever reversibility – that is, potential resuscitation – is possible, by definition, the patient has not yet taken his last breath. This is true even when reversibility is only possible by external means (CPR, etc.).[21]

It seems that R. Feinstein entertains the notion of two possible tracks for determining death in Halakhah – cessation of cardiac/respiratory activity and decapitation – and applies the reversibility criterion unequally –

---

21 An interesting question relates to R. Feinstein's evaluation of the status of a patient who has the potential for resuscitation, but for whom it is not performed. When is he considered to have died – when his heart stopped initially or when the time for potential resuscitation has passed? While thought provoking, the question lies beyond the scope of the current endeavor; see chapter 4, n.56.

invoking it in the case of an asystolic, pulseless patient (at least) when resuscitation efforts are successful, yet setting it aside in the theoretical case of reversible decapitation. The difference is that decapitation is absolute; there is no uncertainty regarding the precise moment of death, and hence reversibility is not a mitigating factor. The cessation of cardiac/respiratory activity, however, is not absolute; uncertainty regarding the precise moment of death remains, and the test of reversibility resolves that uncertainty. The criterion of reversibility is in effect relevant only when death is uncertain — such as the few minutes after the heart stops beating — as it ascertains whether or not an additional breath will occur and thereby accurately identifies the patient's actual last breath.

This dichotomous definition for determining death fits well with the two major Talmudic discussions of this topic — decapitation derived from Mishnah *Ohalot* and cessation of cardiac and respiratory function from Talmud *Yoma*. It also neatly explains R. Feinstein's split in applying the reversibility standard.

Dr. Abraham takes issue with both sides of this analysis. In his view, for death to actually be absolute and final, it must by definition be irreversible. Irreversibility is not simply a tool to resolve uncertainty in particular situations, but part and parcel of the very definition of death. He is therefore unwilling to accept a dichotomous application of reversibility to decapitation vs. cessation of cardiac/respiratory function.

One might argue that the question of reversibility depends upon how one views decapitation. If one argues, as R. Feinstein appears to, that decapitation **defines** halakhic death, whatever may happen to the person post-decapitation is irrelevant, since it would be occurring in a dead body, and reversibility is therefore not called for. In contrast, if one were to maintain that decapitation is simply **indicative** of some other death-defining process, whether physiological (such as cessation of effective circulation) or spiritual (such as departure of the soul), one could argue that when these other processes are reversible, decapitation in and of itself does not automatically warrant a certain determination of death (although this is not practically possible even today).

Dr. Abraham rejects this distinction. He argues that whether one adopts a single halakhic determination of death (cessation of cardiac/respiratory function) with other indications (decapitation) or multiple options for halakhic determination of death (cessation of cardiac/respiratory function **and** decapitation), all must incorporate irreversibility for death to maintain the intended definition. Death by definition must be irreversible.

Further Discussion

R. Feinstein dedicates the rest of this responsum to addressing some of the additional issues raised by R. Weisz. He is chiefly concerned with whether or not one may (or is perhaps required to) give up his life or limb to save his fellow and whether one is obligated to attempt to save or rescue someone who has attempted to take his own life or taken some action to hasten his demise. As regards the local issue, R. Feinstein is quite clear that it is certainly forbidden to sacrifice one life to save another – halakhically validating the DDR.

As a whole, while validating cessation of both cardiac and respiratory function as criteria for death, it is hard to ascertain with confidence how to extrapolate his position to patients in whom these events occur at discrete moments. Furthermore, while this responsum clarifies R. Feinstein's view of the determination of death in various contexts, it does not appear to shed light on whether or not he maintains that there actually are multiple definitions or one uniform halakhic definition of death.

CHAPTER 11:

Rabbi Moshe Feinstein – Second Responsum:

Iggerot Mosheh, Yoreh De'ah 2:146

On 24 *Menahem Av*, 5730 (August 26, 1970), R. Feinstein penned a responsum directly dealing with the question of "brain death." Although written after the responsum discussed in the previous chapter, this responsum is printed earlier in the fifth volume of *Iggerot Mosheh*.

The Condition of the Patient in Question

This letter was written to R. Chaim Dov Ber Gulevsky in response to his questions about determining death by neurological criteria. Specifically, R. Feinstein notes that he will analyze the validity of "that which the doctors say that the signs of life and death depend upon the brain – that if, according to their assumptions, the brain is no longer functioning, the patient is considered dead even though he is still breathing (*hu kevar nehshav le-meit af she-adayyin hu noshem*)."

R. Feinstein does not provide further detail as to the medical status of this hypothetical patient, leaving many questions unanswered.

Specifically, what does R. Feinstein mean when he describes the patient as "still breathing" – does he mean spontaneously or ventilator dependent? The simple usage of the term *noshem* seemingly refers to spontaneous respiration, although the point is never fully clarified. This technicality is essential, as spontaneous respiration indicates a functioning brainstem – meaning that the patient under discussion here is not "brain dead." In that case, the subsequent analysis is somewhat irrelevant to the question of "brain death"/irreversible cessation of spontaneous respiration (ICSR).

R. Tendler, R. Feinstein's son-in-law, in fact argues that this responsum deals with a patient whose brainstem is fully intact and can therefore breathe spontaneously, but has suffered irreversible cerebral damage, causing a persistent vegetative state (PVS).[1] This, argues R. Tendler, is the only plausible definition for R. Feinstein's description of the patient as "*adayyin noshem.*" He therefore dismisses any ramifications derived from this responsum as irrelevant to "brain dead" patients, who have all irreversibly lost the ability for spontaneous respiration.

R. Tendler's contention is difficult on two fronts. First, a broader study of *Iggerot Mosheh* shows that R. Feinstein employs the verb *noshem* to refer to ventilator assisted breathing as well, going so far as to write that "with the machine [ventilator], it is possible [for a patient] to breathe, even though he is already dead."[2] R. Feinstein's choice of language, in this responsum as well as other technical contexts, is not meant to relay particular medical facts, but rather to depict the situation as he saw it; the patient appears to be breathing, even when he is mechanically ventilated. Therefore, despite the simple connotation of *noshem*, its technically precise meaning in this context remains elusive.

Importantly, this responsum was written in 1970, two short years after the publication of the guidelines of the Ad Hoc Committee of

---

1 M.D. Tendler, "Halakhic Death Means Brain Death," *Jewish Review* (January-February 1990), 20 and quoted by R. Yitchak Breitowitz, "The Brain Death Controversy in Jewish law," *Jewish Action* (Spring 1992), 65.
2 *Responsa Iggerot Mosheh, YD* 3:132.

Harvard University. The change in medical practice that ensued – recognition of someone as dead who two years before would have been deemed alive – appears to be the impetus for the question. Logically, R. Feinstein is responding to the issue of "brain death," and the patient described is not breathing spontaneously.

Additionally, later in this responsum, R. Feinstein **explicitly** describes a patient who can no longer breathe on his own as alive ("*ve-hu ha-hai mamash af* ***she-eino noshem***"), since his heart continues to beat. This significant statement not only clearly describes a non-breathing patient with a heartbeat as halakhically alive, it explicitly describes the patient in question as *"eino noshem."* Even if this statement describes a different patient than the one R. Gulevsky inquired about (R. Tendler's contention) and the original patient in question was not "brain dead," the point is moot. Whether or not the patient originally described as *noshem* was able to breathe on his own or only through mechanical means, with this forceful declaration, R. Feinstein is quite clear in describing a non-breathing patient as alive by virtue of his continued heartbeat. R. Feinstein is clearly willing to address more "global" issues than simply the matter at hand, with implications far beyond the limited confines of the original question. Thus, this is an important responsum regardless of the precise implication of *"noshem"* in the query.

The reverse question is also important – what does R. Feinstein mean in describing a patient as *"eino noshem"*? Is a patient who is ventilator dependent considered to be breathing? Elsewhere, R. Feinstein is quite clear that complete mechanical ventilation does not qualify as breathing.[3] In the present responsum, however, it does not appear to make much difference either way, as R. Feinstein does not address the point head on. For purposes of consistency, the following analysis will assume that when R. Feinstein writes *"eino noshem,"* he refers to a patient who is not able to breathe spontaneously, regardless of whether he is being mechanically ventilated.

---

[3] *Responsa Iggerot Mosheh, YD* 3:132. While written later, there is no substantive reason to assume that that responsum reflects a change in attitude or opinion.

The Role of the Brain in Determining Death

One of the prevailing themes in R. Feinstein's writings is that changes to or pathologies of the brain *per se* are of little concern with respect to determining death. He states clearly:

> The truth is, the fact that the brain has ceased functioning is irrelevant – so long that the patient is breathing, he is still considered to be alive... Neither the Talmud nor the halakhic decisors mention the brain or neurological function as signs of life... and it is clear that the brain functioned the same then as it does now.[4]

It is therefore permissible, and perhaps even proper, to pray for the recovery of a patient with a severe brain injury, just as one would for all other patients. While total brain dysfunction will ultimately lead to a person's death, R. Feinstein rules that it does not constitute death in and of itself. Accordingly, the patient in R. Gulevsky's question (regardless of his status) is still alive, despite the doctors' diagnosis that the brain is no longer functioning.

Clearly, for R. Feinstein, any argument for the halakhic recognition of "brain death" must rely upon elements other than total neurological impairment. In his view, total brain dysfunction is not an independent determinant of death.

What Qualifies as Proof?

Quoting from *Responsa Hatam Sofer*, YD 338, R. Feinstein explains that the Talmudic debate in *Yoma* 85a as to where on the body a person must check to determine death is really a question of **test** sensitivities; evaluation of respiration, the Talmud concludes, is the best indication of whether the person is still alive.

As we saw in chapter 9, *Hatam Sofer* cites *Masekhet Semahot*'s (8:1) story of the man who was buried and subsequently found to be alive and questions why we are generally not concerned with such phenomena.

---

4 *Responsa Iggerot Mosheh*, YD 2:146.

Why may we rely on any signs of death at all if even sometimes they are found to be non-reliable? He responds by explaining that the standard determination of death by respiratory exam is so highly sensitive that we need not concern ourselves with the very few and highly improbable (*mi'uta de-mi'uta*) cases in which it may not be sufficiently accurate. The story related in *Semahot* tells of one of these rare occurrences – its exceptional rarity being the impetus for recording the story in the first place.

According to *Hatam Sofer*, we normally rely completely on the respiratory test's exceptional sensitivity; Halakhah assumes that the likelihood of not breathing but still maintaining a functioning heartbeat is so rare that it is irrelevant. Lack of respiration normally determines death because we presume that no other signs of life exist. R. Feinstein notes, however, that when there is evidence that a certain case is an exception to the rule, we may no longer blindly follow the standard protocol. When proof of life exists – such as when there is evidence of a continued heartbeat – the presumption underlying the respiratory test is undermined. This patient has effectively identified himself as an exception to the standard "set," and he is most certainly considered to be alive, even though no longer breathing – "*ve-hu ha-hai mamash af she-**eino noshem**.*"

In his question, R. Gulevsky wonders whether EKG evidence of a continued heartbeat is sufficiently significant proof to constitute an exception to this rule. He notes that normally, Halakhah takes cognizance only of visually perceptible phenomena, routinely ignoring the subclinical world as irrelevant to the halakhic process. R. Gulevsky suggests that without additional physical evidence, a heartbeat detected by EKG alone – being imperceptible to the naked eye – should be regarded similarly. Since the electrical activity of the heart is not perceptible by natural, unaided human means, it should be of no halakhic consequence. R. Gulevsky concludes that an irreversibly non-spontaneously breathing patient should accordingly be considered dead if the only sign of continued life is EKG evidence of a heartbeat.[5]

---

5 From a medical perspective, a healthy heart rhythm as displayed on EKG should always be accompanied by a pulse, which should be considered halakhically significant by all accounts. This particular discussion is therefore theoretical, but the underlying principles may have more universal applicability.

R. Feinstein disagrees with R. Gulevsky's reasoning, arguing that when it comes to matters of life and death, we take cognizance even of subclinical phenomena that we normally disregard. If the EKG shows that a person's heart is still functioning, it is completely inappropriate to ignore it, since it reveals the assumption upon which determining death is predicated to be wrong. The presumption that irreversible inability to breathe assumes a concomitant cessation of cardiac activity cannot be taken normatively when objective evidence indicates otherwise. R. Feinstein thus argues that when an EKG rhythm strip shows a continuous heartbeat, the patient is most certainly alive even though he is no longer breathing ("*af she-**eino noshem***").[6]

Respiration as a Test for Life

According to R. Feinstein, when Talmud *Yoma* 85a requires removing the avalanche rubble until a rescuer reveals the victim's nose, it does not mean to ascribe any life or death determination to the nose *per se*; the nose is simply the landmark at which breathing can be most easily assessed. More dramatic signs of life – including those found in the heart, stomach/chest, and certainly brain activity – are often imperceptible. Halakhah concludes that a respiratory examination is the most sensitive test that these other indications are present.

While Halakhah normally ignores subclinical phenomena and often treats them as non-existent – even while cognizant that they actually

---

6 EKG is able to detect cardiac electrical activity whether or not it produces a pulse – meaning, whether or not the heart activity leads to effective circulation. Medically, the heart can experience "electro-mechanical dissociation," in which electrical activity continues, but it is insufficiently coordinated/powerful/directed to produce a pulse. While R. Feinstein does not specifically address the question of these patients, it appears likely that he is referring to **effective** cardiac activity, which produces a sufficient pulse to perfuse the other organs. R. Feinstein's reference to EKG data is his way of describing evidence of continued cardiac function, proof that the heart is still working despite the lack of visual or otherwise observable evidence. He does not appear to intend that EKG indication of ineffective cardiac activity should be taken into account. (Ventricular fibrillation and tachycardia, in which a pulse may be palpable [at least to experienced medical personnel] but not necessarily indicative of effective circulation, would seemingly be more appropriately labeled as *pirkus*, since it cannot provide effective circulation.)

exist – when making life and death determinations, any and all signs of life are halakhically relevant, regardless of the exquisite technological expertise necessary for their detection. R. Feinstein explains that the Talmud relies on a respiratory based determination of death because "we" (especially in Talmudic times) are not sufficiently versed in checking for other signs of life, such as the heart, the *tabbur*, and certainly not the brain. Not breathing is the ultimate determinant of death, argues R. Feinstein, because it is the ultimate and final **perceptible** indication of death.

As we saw in chapter 8, *Hakham Tzvi*, in arguing for the primacy of the heart in determining death, similarly explains Talmud *Yoma*'s reliance on respiration as a practical means of assessing the heartbeat. Since the heart is "hidden" beneath the flesh and may be beating weakly, a negative superficial chest examination may not indicate that the heart has stopped functioning. The Talmud therefore requires checking for respiration, which according to *Hakham Tzvi*'s physiological assumptions, is completely intertwined with and dependent upon continued cardiac activity.

R. Feinstein disagrees with *Hakham Tzvi*'s interpretation and argues for what he believes is a simpler solution. He claims that even when the heart stops beating **completely**, it still provides some minimal "life force" to the body (*"adayyin hu noten ko'ah hiyyut me'at le-ha-guf"*), and a person can continue to breathe. Breathing indicates that the heart is still "doing the work of providing life to the body" (*"avodato liten hiyyut le-ha-eivarim"*), even if it no longer beats. He argues that Talmud *Yoma* refers to a person who has no heartbeat at all – not just an imperceptible one, as per *Hakham Tzvi*. Nonetheless, since it is possible to continue breathing without a heartbeat, the nose must be checked as well.

Death, R. Feinstein argues, is dependent upon the complete cessation of **all** functions of the heart, both its pumping as well as its *"avodah."* When the heart no longer beats, continued respiration is the sole indicator of the heart's continuing *avodah*. Therefore, once breathing stops, there is no longer any proof for **any** of the heart's continuing functions, and only then can a person be declared dead. It is only because breathing indicates continued cardiac function that the (irreversible) cessation of respiration is determinant of death.[7]

From a scientific perspective, R. Feinstein's solution presents many difficulties. On the most basic level, a person cannot breathe without an effective heartbeat. But even granting that the heart may possess additional abilities that may sustain respiration, what is the precise physiological correlate of what R. Feinstein describes as the heart's *avodah*? Aside from pumping blood, the heart can sense changes in blood volume/pressure and secrete a hormone (atrial naturietic peptide) to help maintain volume balance, but it is highly unlikely that R. Feinstein is describing these functions as the heart's *avodah*. Atrial naturietic peptide was not even identified as a cardiac hormone until 1981, years after the writing of this responsum; regardless, it is not secreted unless the heart is pumping.

While speculative, perhaps one way of understanding R. Feinstein's position is by viewing this claim in its larger context. Previously, R. Feinstein references as support the many sources cited by *Hakham Tzvi* as indicative of the primacy of the heart in sustaining the body. Quoting from *Moreh Nevukhim*, *Sha'ar ha-Shamayim*, *Kuzari* and others, *Hakham Tzvi* passionately argues for the primacy of the heart as the ultimate determinant of life in that the life-force (*hiyyut*) of all other organs depends upon the heart's continued functioning. R. Feinstein appears to be distinguishing between the heart's role as the central circulatory pump and its role in sustaining the *hiyyut* of the body.

Even if that is possible, what complicates the matter further is that R. Feinstein does not discuss the matter scientifically or relate this claim to otherwise-known principles. Given his previous conclusion that EKG monitoring is reliable to determine heart function, the reader is left wondering whether R. Feinstein was aware of an EKG correlate to the heart's *avodah* when no longer beating. After all, EKG measures electrical currents generated by the heart while contracting

---

[7] R. Feinstein suggests that *Hakham Tzvi* did not offer this interpretation because he likely felt that so long as the heart continues its *avodah*, there must be some accompanying heartbeat, even if it is not externally perceptible; R. Feinstein however, thinks that this is simply not true.

and relaxing; in the absence of a heartbeat, an EKG should record only asystole (flat-line).[8]

Breath and Heartbeat

One point deserves further clarification here, as it relates to understanding this responsum in its entirety. As we noted in chapter 6, *Kesef Mishnah* apparently had a variant text of Talmud *Yoma* 85a, in which the *libbo* opinion is mentioned first and the *hotmo* opinion is mentioned as an alternate (*"yesh omerim"*). *Kesef Mishnah* explains that even though Rambam ordinarily would have ruled in accordance with the first opinion instead of the alternate, he ruled that one checks until *hotmo* as predicated upon the principle of *safek nefashot le-hakel* – choosing the more "lenient" position when faced with an uncertainty concerning matters of life and death.

In explaining this approach, R. Feinstein offers two alternatives, noting his preference for the second:

1. The Tanna who requires checking up until *hotmo* maintains that a cardiac exam is insufficiently specific to reliably detect the heart's activity. Even if there is no observable sign of cardiac function, it is still possible that the heart is beating and the victim is still alive. The rescuer must therefore continue to uncover the body – and in doing so, necessarily violate any Shabbat prohibitions – until he reaches the nose. The alternate opinion argues that a cardiac exam is sufficiently sensitive; once found without a heartbeat, the victim is presumed dead, therefore forbidding any continued rescue efforts. The principle of *safek nefashot le-hakel* indicates that we rule like the former opinion and violate Shabbat prohibitions in order to perform the more sensitive test.

---

8 R. Feinstein describes a patient without any heartbeat but breathing as living; when found beneath rubble in such a manner, he must be saved on Shabbat. It is clear that he is not describing a physiological state that is present for only a few moments – such as ventricular tachycardia, which would be detectable by EKG – but rather something more sustained.

2. Even the Tanna who requires checking the nose admits that a negative cardiac exam is of high specific value. However, because additional tests are readily available that, when combined, will lead to increased specificity (*birur*) – namely the nasal/respiratory exam – they must be investigated even at the expense of additional Shabbat violations. The other Tanna disagrees, arguing that given the exceptional specificity of a negative cardiac exam, further clarification – while encouraged on weekdays – is forbidden on Shabbat when necessitating Shabbat violations. The principle of *safek nefashot le-hakel* indicates that we rule like the former opinion and violate Shabbat prohibitions in order to achieve greater specificity.

The implication of the second interpretation of *Kesef Mishnah* is that all agree that a negative respiratory exam is so highly specific that a cardiac exam is unnecessary if the victim is discovered head first.

R. Shaul Yisraeli claims that by siding with the second approach, R. Feinstein is arguing that the nasal/respiratory exam is more highly specific than the cardiac exam and can therefore either serve to further clarify a negative cardiac exam or stand on its own.[9] If a victim is encountered head first and found not to be breathing, he is halakhically considered dead, according to R. Yisraeli, regardless of whether or not his heart continues beating; upon discovering that the victim is not breathing, the Talmud does not require any further exams. R. Yisraeli argues that nothing else is required because nothing else is relevant. He therefore concludes that R. Feinstein would agree that "brain dead" patients are considered halakhically dead because they cannot breathe independently regardless of a continued heartbeat.

Proving this questionable point from R. Feinstein's responsum is difficult as it leads to a number of difficulties that alternate explanations largely avoid. On the simplest level, R. Yisraeli's proposal directly contradicts what R. Feinstein writes earlier in this very responsum, where he

---

[9] "Regarding Permitting Heart Transplants Today" (Hebrew) in M. Halperin (ed.), *Kevi'at Rega ha-Mavet*, 2nd edition (Jerusalem: Schlesinger Institute, 2007), 303.

argues that a patient with a heartbeat, even when detectable only by EKG, is alive – even if completely incapable of breathing (*"af she-eino noshem"*).

To avoid this contradiction, R. Yisraeli proposes differentiating between two groups of patients – those for whom we cannot identify a reason for their respiratory arrest and those who suffer respiratory arrest resulting from traumatic brain(stem) injury. Since we do not know why a patient in the former group stopped breathing, when EKG evidence shows a continued heartbeat, it is possible that the patient stopped breathing simply because of an "external force" (*sibbah hitzonit*) that might be amenable to reversal. Because of the ambiguity in determining the etiology of the person's apnea, we cannot definitively determine that it is truly irreversible; as long as the person's heart continues to beat, the doubt remains unresolved. R. Yisraeli argues that R. Feinstein rules that such a patient considered alive, even though he cannot breathe.

The second type of patient, argues R. Yisraeli, is one who was "killed" (*neherag*; perhaps more precisely, mortally wounded); in this case, head trauma and brain(stem) injury are the cause for his inability to breathe. Given the context, such as the building collapse described in Talmud *Yoma*, R. Yisraeli argues that other causes for not breathing are remote at best; the brain(stem) injury is clearly the cause of his condition. In these situations, R. Yisraeli argues that R. Feinstein rules that the inability to breathe is clearly irreversible and should qualify as clear and convincing evidence that the victim has died, regardless of whether his heart continues to beat.

R. Yisraeli's resolution is difficult, however, because there is no textual evidence indicating that R. Feinstein differentiated between these or any causes of respiratory arrest. Furthermore, while the question of whether or not criteria of death must be defined contextually is possibly subject to debate (see chapter 9), R. Yisraeli himself later quotes *Hatam Sofer* as arguing that any determination of death must be universally applicable; the nasal/respiratory exam detailed in Talmud *Yoma* is not limited to avalanche victims. If respiratory arrest is the criterion for death, as R. Yisraeli argues, then it should qualify as death regardless of its cause and regardless of any continued EKG activity. Once R. Yisraeli endorses *Hatam Sofer*'s position of universal criteria for determining death, it is somewhat ironic to then offer a suggestion that limits it in just that way.

Finally, why assume that Talmud *Yoma* specifically describes a person who is not breathing because of irreversible brainstem dysfunction, a medical condition unknown in the time of the Talmud? There are many reasons that a building collapse victim may not be breathing, many of which are, in fact, reversible.[10] R. Yisraeli's assumptions therefore seem unnecessarily forced.

A seemingly more compelling reading of this responsum argues that finding an avalanche victim incapable of breathing is sufficiently specific to determine death because checking for a heartbeat will not practically add anything to the diagnosis. All R. Feinstein said was that according to the second approach of understanding *Kesef Mishnah*, a negative respiratory exam is so highly specific that a cardiac exam is unnecessary. R. Yisraeli understood "unnecessary" to mean that evidence of a heartbeat is irrelevant; even if the heart is still beating, death is determined solely by the capacity for respiration. A more attractive alternative understands R. Feinstein as simply describing reality. Given the medical facts of the time, whenever an avalanche victim was found to be unable to breathe for some time, the chances of finding a heartbeat – especially given the available primitive means of doing so – were practically nil (indeed, a likelihood that *Hatam Sofer* would have likely relegated to the realm of *ma'aseh nisim*; see chapter 9). Relying on a respiratory exam alone was therefore both an appropriate and practical means of determining the cessation of breathing and heartbeat.

This approach differs significantly with R. Yisraeli's when it comes to actual practice. According to R. Yisraeli, R. Feinstein rules that failure of a respiratory evaluation obviates any need for a cardiac test (at least in the case of traumatic brain injury). According to this explanation, however, the cardiac exam is "unnecessary" only because it almost certainly will not show evidence of a heartbeat given the negative respiratory exam. Given that R. Feinstein states quite clearly that continued cardiac function **is** indicative of life, even in a patient who is no longer breathing, when evidence of heart function is staring us in the face – in the form of

---

10 See D.Y. Sue, J.R.E. Vintch, "Respiratory failure" in F.S. Bongard (ed.), *Current Diagnosis & Treatment – Critical Care*, 3rd edition (New York: McGraw-Hill, 2008), ch. 12.

an EKG rhythm – we cannot simply ignore it. When it is clear that the patient's heart continues to beat (regardless of how this is ascertained), it cannot and must not be ignored, since it proves that the person is still alive. These situations exist today because of intensive medical interventions that maintain certain body functions even in extreme circumstances – techniques that were unknown and unavailable even 100 years ago – and the Talmud therefore does not consider them.

This approach may provide a more substantive and reasonable reading of this responsum and avoids the problems and difficulties raised regarding R. Yisraeli's approach.

Current Medical Realities

R. Feinstein concludes his discussion by reiterating the same notion with which he opened his previous responsum – performing a heart transplant constitutes a double murder. The donor is killed when his heart is removed prior to his death and the recipient is "killed" by having his life shortened by an (as of then) utterly futile and unsuccessful operation. In further emphasizing the danger to and prohibition upon the recipient, R. Feinstein describes a hypothetical case of an available heart recovered from a donor after certain death according to all accounts (*"she-neherag vaday u-meit kodem she-hotzi'u ha-lev mimenu"*). While avoiding the problem of murdering the donor (*"she-leika mishum retzihah al zeh she-lakehu mimenu ha-lev"*), R. Feinstein still prohibits the surgery because of the extreme risk to the recipient's life, a risk so high that R. Feinstein equates it with suicide. R. Feinstein's point is clear – while a "double murder" is certainly forbidden, a "single murder" is no less heinous.

R. Feinstein's conclusion in this closing paragraph is entirely consistent with his previous analysis. He repeatedly refers to an apneic (no longer breathing) patient with a continued heartbeat as alive and demands medical assistance to meet his needs. The point of this hypothetical case is to focus on the unacceptable risk to life of the recipient even were the heart to be obtained through "non-murderous" means. The point is didactic – to drive home the unacceptability of the risk – and is directly relevant to the medical realities of 1970.

The extended analysis of these few lines is important because of R. Yisraeli's seemingly overly creative interpretation, which leads to the exact opposite conclusion. He writes:

> There is no doubt that R. Feinstein was aware that potentially transplantable hearts must be still beating during their recovery, but he nonetheless refers to such a patient as certainly dead (*vaday meit*); therefore, one does not commit murder by removing this heart. This is certainly because such a patient suffers from ICSR and is therefore considered dead; a continued heartbeat is insignificant in such a clinical context.

This reading cannot be correct, however, as it contradicts the very point R. Feinstein was trying to make. The whole purpose of this concluding paragraph is to demonstrate that practically speaking, determining death is largely irrelevant for cardiac transplants, since even when it is not an issue – when the heart comes from a cadaver – the transplant is still forbidden. The goal was to create a hypothetical case in which R. Feinstein could focus on the acceptability of the transplant from the recipient's perspective alone.

Moreover, R. Yisraeli's interpretation contradicts two of R. Feinstein's other responsa in which he describes heart transplants as a "double murder."[11] One of the two murders certainly refers to the recipient because of the unacceptably high surgical and post-surgical risk, as is abundantly clear from R. Feinstein's closing remarks in this responsum. Who, then, is the second murder victim? According to R. Yisraeli, it cannot be the heart donor, since he interprets R. Feinstein as claiming that "brain dead" patients are halakhically dead. Since "brain dead" patients are the only potential cardiac donors, why would R. Feinstein describe removing this

---

11 *Responsa Iggerot Mosheh*, YD 2:174 (analyzed in the previous chapter) and *HM* 2:72. The present responsum (*YD* 2:146) was written chronologically between the other two, ruling out the possibility that R. Feinstein changed his mind in the interim – *YD* 2:174 was written on 19 *Tamuz*, 5728 (July 15, 1968), this responsum is dated 24 *Menahem Av*, 5730 (August 26, 1970), and *HM* 2:72 was written on 1 *Adar* II, 5738 (March 10, 1978).

patient's heart as murder? It is clear that R. Feinstein maintains that the "brain dead" donor is alive and ending his life by removing his heart constitutes murder.

Conclusion

This responsum, while often overlooked in the context of R. Feinstein's position on "brain death," contains a wealth of information and data, guiding the reader in understanding R. Feinstein's approach. Although R. Tendler argues that R. Feinstein's conclusions do not apply to "brain dead" patients, the status of the patient in the original question is actually largely irrelevant to the discussion. In analyzing and discussing the manifold related (and sometimes tangential) aspects of this inquiry, R. Feinstein makes it quite clear – at least twice – that a patient with a continuous heartbeat is alive, regardless of whether or not he continues to breathe.

However, in stating this position but not offering a detailed analysis, R. Feinstein leaves himself open to various interpretations. While clearly advocating the inclusion of cardiac criteria in determining death, some claim that he required this only in certain contexts. Thus, R. Yisraeli argues that cardiac criteria are necessary only when the patient's respiratory status is unknown; even though not breathing right now, the potential for reversibility may still exist. This is very reminiscent of R. Zalman Nehemiah Goldberg and R. Moshe Sternbuch's interpretation of *Hatam Sofer*'s concluding summary statement (discussed in chapter 9). This approach and its application to this responsum will be more fully analyzed in chapter 14.

CHAPTER 12:

Rabbi Moshe Feinstein – Third Responsum:

Iggerot Mosheh, Yoreh De'ah 3:132

This responsum, written to R. Moshe Tendler on 5 *Iyyar*, 5736 (May 5, 1976), has spurred animated and often heated controversy both regarding its conclusions as well as its potential implications. According to some interpretations, this is R. Feinstein's clearest discussion of the status of an organ donor and that which is unique about brainstem failure – continued heartbeat in a mechanically ventilated patient suffering from the irreversible cessation of spontaneous respiration (ICSR). Even then, there is no mention of organ donation whatsoever. Because of its importance in understanding R. Feinstein's position and the prominence this responsum has played in the "brain death" controversy, it will be translated and analyzed in detail.

The Non-Breathing Patient

R. Tendler, the recipient of this responsum, published an interpretive translation in the course of analyzing many of R. Feinstein's positions relating to end of life matters.[1] The translation below is adapted from R. Tendler's, noting his interpolated commentary (as *RMT*):

> Our knowledge of when a man is considered to be dead is recorded in Talmud *Yoma* 85a: "If a house collapses [and buries] a man [within], we are required to remove the debris in an attempt to find him, even on Shabbat. When he is found, he is examined *ad hotmo* [up to his nose]." This is the conclusion of both Rambam (*Shabbat* 2:19) and *Shulhan Arukh* (*OH* 329:4), declaring that if no [sign of] life is detected by the nasal/respiratory exam, [the victim] is deemed to be dead [solely on the basis of his inability to breathe – *RMT*]. Even if [the victim's] respiration is extremely shallow, he is still regarded as alive; this is determined by placing a feather or a thin piece of paper near his nostrils. If the feather or tissue paper does not move, the victim's death is halakhically established.

In this part of the responsum, R. Feinstein describes a patient without evidence of respiration (although the status of his heart function is unclear). Importantly, R. Tendler's addition that death is determined "solely on the basis on [the victim's]... inability to breathe" is an interpretation of R. Feinstein's position, not a translation of it. This is in line with R. Tendler's contention that R. Feinstein maintained that halakhic death is determined solely by ICSR. Given that this is the very question this responsum attempts to resolve, R. Tendler's commentary is simply noted at this time, with a more thorough analysis pending the possible conclusions of this responsum.

> However, it is necessary to examine [his breathing] several times, as I have already explained in *Iggerot Mosheh*, YD 2:174:2. There I explained Rambam's reasoning in *Hilkhot Avel* (4:5), where he rules that [death is determined on the basis of respiration – *RMT*], that one should wait a short while [before determining death], so

---

[1] M.D. Tendler, *Responsa of Rav Moshe Feinstein: Care of the Critically Ill* (Hoboken, NJ: Ktav Publishing House, 1985), 32-35.

as to [rule out other causes for a similar, but non-lethal patient presentation] such as fainting. [The required waiting] period is the length of time possible to live without breathing. This is true only when the patient was carefully observed during this whole period without even momentary interruption without observing any [signs of] respiration. Since it is very difficult to maintain a concentrated effort for any significant length of time without the eyes wavering, there is always a possibility that sporadic, shallow respiration still continues. Therefore, this examination must be repeated several times. If there is no evidence of independent respiration, this is an absolutely reliable sign of death.

I refer you also to the responsum of *Hatam Sofer* (*YD* 138) [where the principle that death is determined by the absence of spontaneous respiration is – *RMT*] explained in great detail.

Adding interpretation and clarification to his translation, R. Tendler repeats a similar sentiment as the one noted above, arguing that death should be determined solely by respiratory criteria. In making reference to *Hatam Sofer*'s famous responsum, however, R. Feinstein does not indicate what he believed to be its conclusions; as noted in chapter 9, *Hatam Sofer*'s actual conclusion is fiercely debated. Given R. Feinstein's current focus on the victim's respiratory status, R. Tendler reads R. Feinstein's reference as referring to *Hatam Sofer*'s discussion of respiration as determinant of death.

This reading, however, leads to two problems. In his conclusion, *Hatam Sofer* requires the cessation of heartbeat as well as respiration; ICSR is a necessary, but not sufficient, determinant of death. Perhaps R. Feinstein was referring to this conclusion in referring to *Hatam Sofer*'s presentation.

Furthermore, even if R. Feinstein adopted respiratory criteria for death, are they still sufficiently reliable when faced with objective evidence of continued cardiac function? As noted in the previous chapter, R. Feinstein previously ruled (*Iggerot Mosheh*, *YD* 2:146) that EKG evidence of persistent cardiac activity cannot be dismissed as irrelevant even when a patient cannot breathe ("*af she-**eino noshem**"*). This means that even when a patient is no longer breathing, if his heart continues to function – even if only detectable by technological means – it is certainly a sign of continued life. Precisely in that context, R. Feinstein quoted *Hatam Sofer*, whom he read as arguing that lack of observable respiration is sufficient to determine death because in the overwhelming majority of people it is indicative of death. The tiny minority (*mi'uta de-miu'ta*) who do in fact survive represent a very limited set of patients, and Halakhah requires us to follow the overwhelming majority, even when it comes to *pikuah nefesh*. However, where there is objective evidence that a given patient is in fact part of that limited set – and R. Feinstein states explicitly that EKG data of continued cardiac functioning qualifies as such evidence – we may certainly **not** determine death based on a lack of observable respirations alone.

We are thus left in somewhat of a quandary: What did R. Feinstein mean when he referenced *Hatam Sofer* in this responsum? Did he intend to argue, as R. Tendler suggests, that respiratory criteria alone are sufficient for determining death even in the face of a continued heartbeat? Or did R. Feinstein mean to refer to his previous explanation of *Hatam Sofer*, declaring that evidence of cardiac activity constitutes life even in the face of a lack of observable respirations? While both positions are plausible, neither is certain.

The Mechanically Ventilated Patient

The next passage is one of the most difficult to understand and interpret. Because his interpretation plays a central role in the debate regarding R. Feinstein's intent, we will first present R. Tendler's reading of this section:

The preceding discussion refers to a terminally ill patient who is not on a ventilator. Some people, however, do require the aid of a ventilator to support their breathing. [With such a device,] it is possible to continue breathing even though the patient is already dead. Breathing of this kind is not regarded as a sign of life. [The "breath of life" test requires that the patient breathe on his own. Breathing by means of a machine does not satisfy the halakhic definition of respiration, and therefore the patient is considered to be dead so long as the other criteria are met – *RMT*]. If the patient demonstrates no other signs of life (*le-lo simanei hiyyut*), [the patient] does not appear to feel anything, even a pinprick [completely unresponsive], such as [in a state] called a coma, it is forbidden to remove the ventilator for fear that he may be alive and [removing it] will kill him. However, when the oxygen tank is being replaced [if oxygen is being used rather than having oxygen piped in – *RMT*], [the ventilator] should not be restarted until [the patient] can be observed for approximately fifteen minutes [while the ventilator is off because the tank is being replaced – *RMT*]. If there is no evidence of respiratory activity during this period, it is certain that [the patient] is dead. If [the patient] shows any signs of respiration, the ventilator should be restarted[2] and the machine allowed to assist him. This procedure should be followed until the patient's status improves or he is completely apneic [with the ventilator off], at which point he is considered to be dead.

---

2   R. Tendler's translation reads, "If [the patient] shows any sign of respiration, he should be reintubated." Reintubation refers to placing a new endotracheal (ET) tube into the patient's throat. As noted in chapter 2, when the ventilator is shut off and disconnected from the patient during the apnea test, the ET tube is not removed from the patient's airway, since both placing (intubating) and removing (extubating) the tube are somewhat traumatic processes that are best avoided when not required. Instead, the tube is disconnected at a convenient location somewhere between the patient and the ventilator. Turning the ventilator back on does not require reintubation, but merely reconnection, which should not exacerbate the patient's condition. The original Hebrew text does not refer to the ET tube at all, but merely to the connection to the ventilator. The only room for slight concern in the process under discussion is that while remaining in place, the ET tube narrows the airway both by a factor proportional to the thickness of the tube itself as well as the diameter of the cuff necessary to hold the tube in place. As a result, slightly more inspiratory force is necessary to initiate a breath than would be necessary were the tube removed. Given R. Feinstein's concern that patients with even very shallow breathing and minimal independent effort must be continuously medically supported, leaving the ET tube in place in order to conduct an apnea test may pose a problem. While extubation and reintubation (if deemed necessary) is a possible solution, doing so may cause more stress – and hence greater impediment to independent respiration – to the patient than simply leaving the ET tube in place.

Glaringly absent from this discussion of a mechanically ventilated patient is any mention of the patient's heart function. R. Tendler observes that R. Feinstein must have been referring to a patient with a persistent heartbeat, since patients without heartbeats are not ventilated – they are dead. While a ventilator can provide oxygen, it cannot make the heart pump. If doctors determined that it was appropriate to support this patient's breathing when the patient otherwise could not, his heart clearly must have been beating.

The clinical scenario best fitting this patient description is a patient suffering from ICSR. In such a patient, it makes sense to ventilate, yet to be unclear whether or not the patient maintains any spontaneous respiratory effort. Continued ventilation could possibly mask a completely apneic patient (with no independent respiratory drive), with his condition only evident by looking for signs of breathing while the ventilator is shut off. R. Feinstein specifically excludes a similar patient who maintains weak respiratory effort, for whom the ventilator is only providing respiratory assistance but is not completely replacing the patient's own respiratory drive. The only type of patient who could continue to be ventilated in spite of ICSR is a patient with a heartbeat.

One of the main difficulties with this passage, already noted by Dr. Abraham S. Abraham, is R. Feinstein's description of such a patient as having "no other signs of life" (*lelo simanei hiyyut*) – a term that is difficult to reconcile if describing a patient with a beating heart.[3] Assuming that this responsum refers to an actual medical scenario means interpreting this phrase as referring to absence of other signs of life, such as the examples explicitly mentioned by R. Feinstein – complete unresponsiveness and a comatose state – despite a continued heartbeat. While an admittedly unorthodox usage of the term "*lelo simanei hiyyut*," Dr. Abraham notes that it is the only interpretation that makes any physiological sense.

Nonetheless, reading this into the text stretches the bounds of interpretive limits. Since R. Feinstein does not mention the patient's heartbeat at all, it is more straightforward to assume that he in fact lacks one

---

[3] "Determining the Moment of Death: On the Editor's Notes to the Decision of the Israeli Chief Rabbinate" (Hebrew) in M. Halperin (ed.), *Kevi'at Rega ha-Mavet*, 2nd edition (Jerusalem: Schlesinger Institute, 2007) (henceforth *KRhM*), 325.

(despite the lack of making physiological sense). The possibility of this interpretation will be explored below.

Some technical comments are also in order in analyzing this paragraph. As R. Tendler implies in his comments, today, unlike when R. Feinstein wrote this responsum, oxygen is usually supplied systematically to the entire hospital; all patient rooms have oxygen ports into which equipment can be connected. There is therefore no longer any need to replace oxygen tanks, and there is rarely any servicing that would entail shutting off the machine. While ventilators are now sophisticated enough to detect independent respiration efforts, their ability to do so is limited, forcing almost all "brain death" determination protocols to require an apnea test – deliberately turning off the ventilator for a period of approximately five minutes to allow for an accurate apnea determination (as detailed in chapter 2). Given his argument in this paragraph, whether or not R. Feinstein would allow such a procedure is debatable out of possible concern that shutting off the ventilator may remove necessary supportive care that such a patient, so tenuously hanging on to his last moments of life, desperately needs. In other words, even if ICSR indeed defines death, making that diagnosis requires turning off the ventilator, which is not necessarily permissible.

A seemingly technical, but actually quite far-reaching problem is the complete lack of any discussion of organ donation in this or any other paragraph within this responsum. R. Shelomoh Zalman Auerbach considered this point to be quite telling, a criticism taken up more fully in the next chapter.[4]

Evidence of Cardiac Function

A final substantive issue with this paragraph is how it relates to R. Feinstein's previously expressed opinions, specifically R. Feinstein's

---

[4] One practical point relevant to the current discussion is that were organ donation to proceed, the patient would need to be reconnected to the ventilator after determining that the patient cannot breathe spontaneously. As noted earlier, organs can only be effectively recovered when they are adequately perfused until moments before their removal; ventilation is a necessary prerequisite for this to take place.

ruling that EKG evidence of persistent cardiac activity cannot be dismissed even when a patient cannot breathe. According to R. Tendler's reading of this responsum, the patient in question's heart must necessarily be beating and circulating blood effectively for ventilation to be supportive. An EKG is not even necessary to confirm cardiac activity; in fact, even if an EKG were deemed halakhically immaterial, this patient's heart function would still be evident. How can we resolve R. Tendler's insistence that R. Feinstein argues here for determining death by ICSR alone – despite a continued heartbeat – with R. Feinstein's earlier claim that EKG evidence of cardiac function indicates life even when a patient can no longer breathe? While this question was raised by Dr. Abraham, it has not received sufficient attention or discussion. It may, in fact, be the key to deciphering R. Feinstein's position, as we will see below.

If we are to take R. Feinstein's position as advocated by R. Tendler at face value – that ICSR constitutes halakhic death – perhaps a creative explanation is possible. Maybe R. Feinstein insisted that EKG evidence of continued cardiac function should be considered indicative of continued life only based on principles of resolving uncertainty (*birur ha-safek*). Some small group of people who do not appear to be breathing may, in fact, still be alive; the chance is small, but it is a chance nonetheless. While we are not ordinarily concerned with such small likelihoods, even when it comes to *pikuaḥ nefesh*, when objective evidence indicates that a specific patient is indeed a member of this subset, we must take it seriously and declare such a patient to be alive.

According to this argument, in his earlier responsum, R. Feinstein did not mean to say that the continued cardiac function, as evidenced by EKG, **defines** the patient as alive, but rather **indicates** such. While all agree that complete irreversible cessation of cardiac activity certainly indicates death, its persistence is **necessary, but not sufficient** for sustaining life. Continued heartbeat is simply an indication that something "larger" is taking place in this patient that is availing him of continued life – described as persistence of the soul (*neshamah*), life-force, or otherwise.[5]

---

5 What this "something larger" is and how to define it are not explored, nor is the definition necessarily important.

According to this logic, negative evaluation of cardiac activity is an **indication** of death in the absence of clarity regarding the irreversible nature of respiratory failure. When a patient is found to have stopped breathing and had not previously suffered from brainstem failure, the prognosis of his continued respiratory status is, at first, almost always unknown. Will this patient ever be able to breathe again on his or her own? The answer depends on a whole host of factors – ranging from the patient's general health, co-morbid conditions, and, most importantly, the reason that he stopped breathing in the first place. There are many reasons that a person may stop breathing, certainly not all of them fatal, and a great majority amenable to medical reversal.[6]

Accordingly, R. Feinstein's point in *Iggerot Mosheh*, YD 2:174 was that while cessation of respiratory activity defines death, it only qualifies as such when it is completely irreversible. When it cannot be determined to be irreversible, then perhaps evidence of continued cardiac activity is indicative of continued life; it resolves our doubt and establishes that while the patient may be dying, he is not yet dead. Because of the presence of cardiac activity, we have not – or cannot – determine the patient to be suffering from ICSR.

However, this line of reasoning argues, when the condition of ICSR can be confirmed by hard facts, Halakhah defines the patient as dead. Persisting cardiac function is not indicative of life when there is objective – meaning halakhic – evidence to the contrary. Being necessary, but not sufficient, to maintain life, persistent cardiac activity in the face of objective/halakhic evidence of death is not meaningful.

Based upon the above argument, what would R. Feinstein rule if the patient described in *Iggerot Mosheh*, YD 2:174 suffered from both respiratory and cardiac arrest? It seems that his ruling would not change; determination of death would have to wait until proof of irreversibility is ascertained. Since cardiac activity is necessary (although not sufficient) to maintain life, the converse is also true – its absence is determinant of death. The condition of irreversibility is of prime importance here,

---

6 See D.Y. Sue, J.R.E. Vintch, "Respiratory failure," in F.S. Bongard (ed.), *Current Diagnosis & Treatment – Critical Care*, 3rd edition (New York: McGraw-Hill, 2008), ch. 12.

however; only irreversible cardiac arrest qualifies as death. In non-brainstem failure patients, at the moment of arrest, the prognosis of both respiratory and cardiac function are unknown; both may be amenable to reversibility. Therefore, at the time of the arrest the patient cannot be determined to be dead. Only when the patient's heartbeat is determined to be unable to return or his respiratory failure to be hopelessly irreversible is death established.[7]

If a heartbeat is indeed reestablished, it is likely that determining the patient's respiratory prognosis will be postponed until he is more stable and a more extensive and thorough exam is available. If cardiac activity is reestablished and the patient is ventilated and a later exam shows ICSR, the patient would then be considered halakhically dead.

This argument builds off of R. Yisraeli's suggestion discussed in the previous chapter. While possibly plausible in the context of understanding the present responsum, it is not necessarily true in either context. As noted in the last chapter, there is an alternative explanation that works rather well in understanding *Iggerot Mosheh*, YD 2:146, and it works in this responsum as well.

The question ultimately comes down to the relationship between respiration and cardiac failure and their status vis-à-vis **determining** or **indicating** death. The simpler and arguably more compelling reading of the sources suggests that R. Feinstein insisted on lack of respiration because it is **indicative** of a lack of a heartbeat – and in most "normal" cases of death, this is indeed an accurate indication. However, as a mere indication, when objective evidence points to the contrary – when there is a clearly evident heartbeat – the indication of lack of respiration is meaningless, and such a patient cannot be determined to be dead. Again, this reading suggests that R. Feinstein is discussing a ventilated patient without a heartbeat in this responsum (discussed more fully below).

---

[7] It is certainly interesting to explore the status of a patient while the resuscitative efforts are continuing, both if they are and if they are not successful. Is a final determination of death applied retroactively to the time of the original arrest? While both fascinating and provocative, this discussion will be saved for another time.

Another problem arises regarding R. Tendler's reading as well. Given the novelty and the significant ramifications of arguing for ICSR as death even in the context of a persistent heartbeat, it would have been both appropriate and prudent for R. Feinstein to have spelled this out clearly and unambiguously. Regardless of how one reads the sources, it is certainly not intuitive to identify a patient with a heartbeat as dead; that alone should have prompted clarification to the contrary. If R. Feinstein intended to determine death in such circumstances despite continuous heartbeat, he should have said so forthrightly. Instead, R. Feinstein does the complete opposite, not mentioning the heart at all throughout the entire responsum. This alone is cause for concern and should evoke serious hesitation in applying these assumptions in practice.

Regardless of whether respiratory failure is determinant or indicative of death, R. Feinstein reiterates that it must be absolutely irreversible in order to qualify:

> The above halakhic considerations apply to a patient who is deteriorating from a chronic debilitating disease. In [a trauma case, however, such as – *RMT*] an automobile accident or a fall from a window, [the victim] may not be breathing because of a [temporary – *RMT*] nerve shrinkage (*hitkavtzut*) near the lungs and respiratory organs. [It is possible that] with the passage of time and with the necessary [reliance on a] ventilator, the nerves will "open up" (*yitpashtu mekomot ha-nikvatzim*) and allow [the patient] to breathe on his own. [In the interim,] these patients, even though they cannot breathe on their own and other signs of life are absent, are possibly not [considered to be] dead.

R. Feinstein's clinical scenario of "nerve shrinkage" and "opening" is rather vague; to date, medicine has been unable to regenerate injured neurons. While the specifics of the neuronal injury described may remain a mystery, the intention is clearly to describe a reversible cause of respiratory arrest, whatever the physiological mechanism. In such a case, despite the patient's symptoms, we cannot declare him dead until respiration is proven to be irreversible.

The Connection Between the Brain and the Body

In the next paragraph, R. Feinstein introduces a new idea – the comparison to decapitation – which presents several interpretative challenges:

> Since you tell me that now it is possible to inject a substance intravenously [nuclide scan test] to determine that the connection between the brain and the body has been interrupted – if the [radioisotope] does not appear in the brain, it is clear that the brain no longer maintains any connection to the body and the brain has already completely rotted (*she-kevar nirkav ha-mo'ah le-gamrei*), and this is [comparable to] forceful/potential decapitation (*hutaz ha-rosh be-ko'ah*). In such patients – even those who cannot feel anything [completely unresponsive] and cannot breathe independently without ventilator assistance – we should be strict and not determine death until this test has been performed. If [the nuclide scan] shows a [continued] connection between the brain and the body – even if [the patient is] unable to breathe – the ventilator should be maintained even for an extended period. Only when the [nuclide scan] shows a lack of any connection between the brain and the body can they determine [this patient's] lack of respiration to be [irreversible and hence] dead.

R. Tendler argues that R. Feinstein is introducing an entirely new definition of death in this paragraph. The nuclide scan test, he argues, proves "that the brain no longer maintains any connection to the body" – essentially, "brain death" – and that a patient in this condition is considered death.

As straightforward as this sounds, however, the actual situation is far more ambiguous. Can the nuclide scan test described by R. Feinstein actually prove total brain dysfunction, "that the brain no longer maintains any connection to the body"?

A nuclide scan test is performed by injecting a small amount of radioactive dye into the patient's bloodstream; the dye is completely harmless and has no perceivable effect on the patient, and the test can be performed by the patient's bedside if necessary. After a certain period of time (which varies by protocol), the dye should have distributed equally throughout the patient's bloodstream and should therefore be "found" (by special equipment for detecting the specific radioisotope) in all organs being perfused. When the dye is not detected in the brain after the requisite time-period, this test provides evidence of lack of blood flow to the brain with exceedingly high clinical accuracy, reaching a sensitivity of about 98.5%.[8] The assumption behind this test is that the brain cannot continue to function without blood flow for more than a few short minutes; if there is no dye in the brain, the patient is therefore "brain dead."

As noted in chapter 1, "brain death" is essentially a clinical diagnosis; it is determined by examination and observation of visible indications of life that do not require technological equipment or techniques. The nuclide scan (and more modern adaptations) is performed, when requested, as a confirmatory test thereafter, presumably many hours after blood flow has actually ceased. Even as confirmation, neither this nor any other imaging study is necessary to pronounce a patient "brain dead" in the United States; "brain death" remains a purely clinical diagnosis.

As further noted in chapter 1, there is a growing body of evidence for continued brain activity in "brain dead" patients – even those confirmed by nuclide scan to have no detectable brain perfusion. The President's Council report from 2008 is quite clear that current diagnostics do not show the complete or total lack of function of the brain in "brain death;" indeed, such a situation rarely exists. According to the simple understanding of R. Feinstein's words – that the nuclide scan proves that "the connection between the brain and the body has been interrupted" – he assumed, based on medical information current at the time, that a negative nuclide scan indicates a complete break between the brain and the rest of the body, but this is now known to be inaccurate. Thus, the test noted by R. Feinstein does not confirm – and is not used to determine – either the complete lack of brain function or the physical destruction of brain cells.

---

8 W.M. Flowers, B.R. Patel, "Radionuclide angiography as a confirmatory test for brain death: A review of 229 studies in 219 patients," *Southern Medical Journal* 90 (1997):1091-6; S. Al-Shammri, M. Al-Feeli, "Confirmation of brain death using brain radionuclide perfusion imaging technique," *Medicine Principles and Practice* 13 (2004): 267-72.

Given the discussion of this diagnostic test immediately after the description of a patient who has questionable irreversible loss of spontaneous respiration, a different reading of this section is more plausible. The general sense of this section represents R. Feinstein's reliance on a diagnostic test to determine the reversibility status of the patient's respiratory failure. This section thus follows directly from the description of a patient with a potentially/questionably reversible respiratory failure. Since R. Feinstein ruled that respiratory arrest does not qualify as a determination of death until it is confirmed to be irreversible, it stands to reason that any test that can accurately and precisely determine such a status should carry significant weight.

Accordingly, the fact that the nuclide scan test does not and cannot indicate total brain dysfunction is irrelevant; R. Feinstein is not truly interested in the functioning of the brain. Assuming he defines death as ICSR, his interest relates only to the respiratory centers, not the brain in its entirety. Although he writes that the nuclide test indicates that "the connection between the brain and the body has been interrupted," for his purposes, it is sufficient to prove that the brainstem, which controls independent respiration, no longer functions. According to this argument, once the test has indicated that there is no "connection" between the body and the brainstem – that the brainstem is no longer perfused by blood flow and will therefore never recover – it is clear that the cessation of respiration is indeed irreversible. The viability or functioning of other areas of the brain is not important; since the apnea is proven to be irreversible due to brainstem failure, the patient should be considered dead.

According to this reading, the purpose of the nuclide test is not to establish that the brain is no longer functioning – something that the President's Council determined is not true in "brain dead" patients – but rather to confirm the irreversible nature of clinical diagnosis of respiratory failure, the actual determinant of death. R. Feinstein is not concerned with the presence or lack of neurological control of the body's functions, as R. Tendler argues, but rather with the lack of blood flow to the brainstem – without perfusion, the brainstem has hopelessly and irreversibly failed. There is no reason, according to R. Feinstein's logic in this or any other responsum, to assume that he viewed the brain as dissociated from the rest of the body in the case he describes. R. Feinstein maintains that cessation of respiration alone – when proven by nuclide scan to be irreversible as a result of brainstem failure – is determinant of death.

This perspective also raises problems, however. Recent evidence has shown that there is no "perfect" test of brainstem failure, as all have biases in terms of sensitivities to various areas of the brain;[9] some studies indicate that more advanced imaging systems are able to detect flow even when traditional devices cannot.[10] R. Hayyim David ha-Levi expressed this concern early on, when first presented with the idea of a nuclide scan. Even if the test shows no flow, "how do we know that tomorrow, a new test will not come out, more sensitive than the first, that might in fact show continued blood flow into the brain?"[11] Perhaps, then, even a nuclide scan would fail to conclusively prove that the brainstem is without flow and thus completely devoid of continued viability.

It is important to keep in mind that this entire approach hinges upon R. Tendler's assumption that this responsum describes an accurate medical reality of a ventilated patient with a continued heartbeat – an assumption that may not necessarily be true. If R. Feinstein is discussing the case of a ventilated patient without a heartbeat, our conclusions based on this responsum may be entirely different, as we will see below.

Comparison to Decapitation

The proposed comparison between "brain death" and decapitation requires additional clarification as well, as it has been the focus of repeated halakhic analyses. R. Feinstein writes that a negative nuclide scan indicates that "the brain has already **completely rotted**" (*she-kevar nirkav ha-mo'ah* **le-gamrei**) and is [comparable to] forceful/potential decapitation (*hutaz ha-rosh be-ko'ah*)." This rather complicated sentence must be parsed carefully to be completely understood.

---

9 L. Zuckier, J. Kolano, "Radionuclide studies in the determination of brain death: Criteria, concepts, and controversies," *Seminars in Nuclear Medicine* 38 (2008): 262-73.
10 E.F.M. Wijdicks, "The case against confirmatory tests for determining brain death in adults," *Neurology* 75 (2010): 75, 77-83.
11 *Responsa Aseh Lekha Rav* 8:64.

It is interesting to note R. Tendler's translation of these lines:

If it is determined that the blood circulation does not reach the base of the brain, it is obvious that the brain must have begun to show the physical signs of destruction referred to as lysis. When the brain shows extensive lysis, it is as if the head had been removed from the body or the person decapitated.

This information is culled from pathology research from the late 1970's describing a phenomenon known as "respirator brain." The term represents necrotic and lytic changes to the brain cells caused by the long-standing lack of brain perfusion. During that time-period, the scientific literature was replete with such accounts, including many pathology studies from "brain dead" patients – indeed indicating observably visible areas of necrosis and lysis.

However, without delving into the details of cell biology, current pathology data has shown that the notion of "total brain necrosis," or "respirator brain," is no longer found. Recent studies have demonstrated widespread **microscopic** ischemic injury to various areas of the brain, but have failed to show any diagnostic or characteristic changes consistent throughout the samples. While it is certainly true that in "brain death" many brain cells are no longer functioning, the number of such cells, their previous function, and the ability to visually observe such changes unassisted is quite variable. Just as *Hatam Sofer* had done before him, R. Feinstein relied on then current scientific knowledge in employing this description. Given the more recent studies, however, while we cannot be sure, it is likely that R. Feinstein would not have employed the description "the brain has completely rotted" (*nirkav ha-mo'ah le-gamrei*). But does this point make any difference halakhically?

R. Feinstein writes that the changes he describes are "[comparable to] forceful/potential decapitation" (*hutaz ha-rosh be-ko'ah*). According to R. Tendler, R. Feinstein is drawing a comparison between the situation described – complete lack of connection between the body and a "rotted" brain – and decapitation, described in Mishnah *Ohalot* as clearly indicative of death. Invoking the notion of decapitation indicates the complete and total death of the entire brain, parallel to actual decapitation, in which the brain is severed from the body. The "death" of the brain is intended to parallel its complete absence.[12] It seems, however, that R. Feinstein reached this conclusion based on the faulty scientific information he had available; if the brain, in fact, has not "completely rotted," it cannot be compared to decapitation.

R. Tendler's interpretive note potentially avoids this problem. He writes that "when the brain shows extensive lysis, it is as if the head had been removed from the body or the person decapitated." By inserting the description of "**extensive** lysis," he argues that complete and total death of the entire brain is not necessary. Although unbeknownst to him while writing these words, R. Tendler thus guarded himself from the arguments of the President's Council; by never requiring "complete lysis" of the entire brain, any new research suggesting still functional brain areas does not necessarily contradict his hypothesis. Nonetheless, current research indicates that even the term "extensive" is inappropriate to describe the inconsistent and microscopic cellular damage in "brain death."[13] Furthermore, is R. Feinstein's description of "the brain has completely rotted" indeed the same as "the brain shows extensive lysis"?

Complicating the matter further, R. Tendler first speaks of a negative scan being indicative that the brain has "**begun** to show the physical signs of destruction referred to as lysis," but then immediately equates a negative scan with "**extensive** lysis" in an attempt to equate the latter with Mishnah *Ohalot*'s description of decapitation. What does "extensive lysis" imply, and how does it differ from only "beginning to show physical signs of destruction"? How much of the brain must be non-functional to constitute virtual decapitation? Is this measured by looking at the "dead" areas as a proportion of the total brain, or should certain areas be more significant than others?

R. Tendler's interpretation further requires a non-literal reading of the phrase *"hutaz ha-rosh be-ko'ah."* According to the simplest reading, R. Feinstein is suggesting that once there is no connection between the

---

12 This point was later developed by R. Shelomoh Zalman Auerbach; see chapter 16.
13 E.F.M. Wijdicks, E.A. Pfeifer, "Neuropathology of brain death in the modern transplant era," *Neurology* 70 (2008): 1234-7.

body and the brain (or some part thereof), it is comparable to forceful decapitation – that is, complete separation of the brain from the body. Such separation, however, is not necessary according to R. Tendler's interpretation. He therefore explains that *hutaz ha-rosh be-ko'ah* refers to "theoretical" decapitation, translating *"be-ko'ah"* as "potentially," as opposed to "forcefully."

An Alternative Criterion?

Concluding his translation with an interpretive clarification, R. Tendler adds to R. Feinstein's original text:

> The requirements are evidence of brainstem death as evidenced by total cessation of respiration and a break in the connection of the brain to the rest of the body as evidenced by the total cessation of all independent respiratory activity.

Providing a clarification to what may have otherwise been understood differently, R. Tendler writes that "extensive brain lysis," however defined, is indicative of complete "physiological decapitation," and that in itself serves as a definition of death. These words and ideas do not appear in the original Hebrew text of R. Feinstein's responsum; they are part of R. Tendler's interpretive translation.

Before analyzing R. Tendler's position further, a more basic question must be asked: Why is this concluding discussion of the equivalence to decapitation necessary in the first place? R. Feinstein previously explained that death is halakhically defined as ICSR. Because the potential for reversibility is sometimes unclear at first, he suggested a test that would differentiate reversible from irreversible causes of respiratory failure. Why, then, introduce a second definition of death without even explicitly stating that he is doing so?

Indeed, this discussion is so completely unnecessary in this context that it cannot be given serious weight. Introducing such a novel concept as "physiological decapitation," as R. Tendler puts it, requires far more rigorous discussion than a comment made in passing, without even explicit reference to Mishnah *Ohalot* from which the phrase is meant to be borrowed. Even R. Feinstein, with his generally terse style, devotes at least some explanation to his completely novel rulings. It seems inappropriate for R. Feinstein to so succinctly redefine death in a way never discussed previously in the rabbinic literature without explanation or comment – a redefinition that would potentially permit organ donation, described elsewhere in *Iggerot Mosheh* as murder! Arguing that this line represents a separate "new" track for defining death is thus highly problematic.

Not only is such a new definition unnecessary, it does not even help in arguing this responsum's main point. According to what R. Feinstein just finished arguing, if the only section of the brain that was "completely rotted" (*nirkav le-gamrei*) was the respiratory center of the brainstem, that would be enough to diagnose ICSR – which he argues means death. The rest of the areas of the brain and their various functions are completely irrelevant to R. Feinstein's analysis and were therefore not mentioned at all previously, neither in this or any other of his responsa.

Indeed, in *Iggerot Mosheh*, YD 2:174, R. Feinstein stated explicitly that brain function is not relevant to determining death ("*lo zeh she-pasak ha-moah lif'ol hu mittah*"), as it lacks any reference in Talmudic or rabbinic literature. Clearly, however, he must accept Mishnah *Ohalot*'s description of decapitation as death. Were "physiological decapitation" to constitute a secondary independent definition of death, R. Feinstein would need to clearly differentiate between brain function and actual "decapitation" (that is, brain absence) – a notion that he never develops here or in any of his responsa.

Defending his interpretation, R. Tendler argues that the preceding analysis is fundamentally flawed. He claims that when R. Feinstein referred to the nuclide scan proving the dissociation between the brain and the body, it was precisely for that very reason – to show a break between the brain and the body. It is therefore logical, R. Tendler argues, to then reference, albeit obliquely, Mishnah *Ohalot*'s description of decapitation as death. R. Tendler's explanation requires reading this paragraph somewhat differently: When there are patients who are in respiratory failure but the potential for reversibility is yet unknown, a determination must be made, on the basis of the nuclide scan, whether or not this patient meets **alternative** criteria for death. Since declaring this patient dead based on respiratory criteria alone is not possible (since doctors cannot yet tell if it is irreversible), we must then ask whether or not this patient meets additional definitions of death, such as decapitation, or as R. Tendler puts it, "physiological decapitation."

There are several difficulties with this argument. First is the necessity for multiple definitions of death. Although not unheard of in rabbinic thought, especially in light of the differences between Talmud *Yoma* and Mishnah *Ohalot*, there is no indication that R. Feinstein agreed to such a dichotomous notion. Given his assertion at the start of this very responsum that death is halakhically defined as ICSR, it is far simpler to explain decapitation as an application of what he said previously, rather than a completely independent and unrelated definition. Accordingly, decapitation qualifies as death not by a unique, separate criterion, but rather as an example of ICSR.

Second is the problem mentioned previously – adding a second definition of death at this point in the responsum simply does not flow from the previous discussion. It is more likely that after describing a patient whose respiratory status is uncertain, R. Feinstein suggests a method of resolving that uncertainty. He understood, and therefore recommended, the nuclide scan as a means to determine whether a patient's cessation of spontaneous respiration was reversible or not. Why only introduce it here otherwise? According to R. Tendler's reading, this test does not aid in the previously uncertain diagnosis, but rather provides a completely new one – one that was unheard of until now.

There are also several linguistic and grammatical problems with R. Tendler's suggestion. R. Feinstein continuously refers to the connection (*kesher*) between the brain and the body, but only once describes it as decapitation. Moreover, it is somewhat difficult to read *"be-ko'ah"* as suggested by R. Tendler to mean "potential." If that is indeed what R. Feinstein meant, he would be positing a never-before heard of halakhic concept with no explanation before simply moving on. It is far simpler to understand *"be-ko'ah"* as "forceful" decapitation – indicating that the brain is completely absent.

Finally, R. Tendler's reading raises some more fundamental issues. First and foremost, we now know that the facts as presented are simply not true, as noted above. The brain is simply not "completely rotted," and R. Tendler's (foreshadowed) avoidance of this question raises even more problems, some of which were noted previously. "Extensive lysis" has no halakhic meaning; there is no source in Halakhah that differentiates between any of the brain's functions (other than possibly respiratory). Regardless of how R. Tendler describes "extensive brain lysis," anything less than complete necrosis/lysis of the entire brain is completely arbitrary. How can we determine which specific functions determine life and which are seemingly unnecessary in that determination? Who should make that decision in areas that have never been halakhically explored? There are indeed more and less important areas of the brain when it comes to preserving life – such as for example, areas that control finger movements as opposed to those that control liver function – effectively neutralizing measuring anything "extensive" by mere proportions. Lastly, other than the phrase *hutaz ha-rosh be-ko'ah*, there is absolutely no reference or indication of a notion of "physiological decapitation" anywhere, and the phrase itself is not entirely revealing.

An Alternate Reading

Given the context, the notion of "physiological decapitation" is so completely unnecessary, it almost cannot be taken seriously – and perhaps it was not meant to be. But if the above criticisms are valid, what did R. Feinstein actually mean? While speculative, a "cleaner" reading of this responsum would assume that R. Feinstein invoked the nuclide scan test only as a means to resolve the question of potential reversibility of a given patient's respiratory failure. According to R. Feinstein's articulated position mere lines before this one, there is no need to determine the status of any other brain function since it will not aid in diagnosing ICSR.

The translation "forceful decapitation," if taken literally, leaves many other questions unanswered, however. Why does R. Feinstein use such strong language to describe the cessation of blood flow to the brainstem? While not without drawbacks, the most likely explanation that preserves the flow, argument, and logic of this responsum interprets this phrase as a mere literary flourish (often described as *"lav davka"*). Given the complete lack of focus on what it would mean for the brain to be completely separated from the body and the halakhic ramifications of such a determination – coupled with no mention (other than possibly the word *"beko'ah"*) or discussion of the fact that in reality there is no actual separation (requiring R. Tendler to coin the phrase "physiological decapitation") – it is far more likely that R. Feinstein did not mean this phrase to be taken literally. It stretches the limits of the interpretive imagination to assume that R. Feinstein used this phrase as an oblique reference to "physiological decapitation" as an alternate definition of death. Referencing an idea makes sense when that idea is either well known or was previously discussed, not when it is something so completely novel and unheard of until now.

The greatest weakness of this argument is that it asks the reader to reinterpret what appears to be the simplest understanding of this difficult phrase – a task that most will undertake only with great hesitation. However, it is only through making such a "leap" that this responsum can be read with any consistency and clarity. While it can unfortunately no longer be validated after R. Feinstein's passing in 1986, since it provides what appears to be the most convincing reading of this responsum, it will be used from here on.

The logic of this reading is reinforced by R. Feinstein's concluding statement in this responsum, which reiterates a notion raised earlier – uncertainty as to the question of reversibility:

> You also noted that patients who have taken certain drugs, such as overdoses of sleeping pills, may not be able to breathe [on their own] and therefore should be ventilated for as long [as is necessary] for the drugs to be cleared, which can be determined by a blood test. Then the doctors could [assess his respiratory status] by not turning the ventilator back on [after replacing the oxygen tanks and] see if he shows no signs of respiration, in which case he is dead; if he can breathe [spontaneously] at all, even [only] with great difficulty, he is alive and the ventilator should be turned back on.

Reflecting his continuous insistence on requiring irreversibility in any determination of death, R. Feinstein rules, just as he did previously, that everything medically possible must be done for such patients until such time that they recover or an accurate determination of ICSR can be made.

Cardiac Criteria

Two basic alternatives have been presented for interpreting this responsum. While both approaches agree that in this responsum, R. Feinstein argued for ICSR as a certain determination of death, the notion of "brain death" or "physiological decapitation" as death is heavily debated.

Even assuming "physiological decapitation" to be a valid interpretation of R. Feinstein's position, its relationship to ICSR is still vague. Similarly, the notion of "physiological decapitation" as death in R. Feinstein's other responsa is also somewhat unclear. These and other more thematic issues will be analyzed in chapter 14, where we approach all of these responsa from a broader perspective.[14]

The entire previous discussion presupposes that R. Feinstein intended to describe the medical condition known as "brain death" – referring to a patient suffering from ICSR but maintaining a continuous heartbeat. As noted, however, R. Feinstein makes absolutely no mention of the patient's heartbeat at all, describing only a patient who must be ventilated as long as it is unknown whether or not he has irreversibly lost the ability to breathe spontaneously. Understanding R. Feinstein's intent and conclusion depends on interpreting this glaring omission. R. Tendler argues that R. Feinstein's depiction of such a patient was meant to be in accordance with the accurate medical reality – namely, that all ventilated patients have continuous heartbeats.[15] This in turn means that R.

---

14 See "Halachic Issues in the Determination of Death and Organ Transplantation, Including an Evaluation of the Neurological 'Brain Death' Standard *Sivan* 5770 – June 2010: A Study by the Vaad Halacha of the Rabbinical Council of American of the Halachic and Medical Issues Relating to Organ Transplantation from Both Live & Cadaver Donors, and the Determination of Death in Halacha" (2010), 49-54, for a similar, but somewhat nuanced analysis of this responsum.
15 Also see S.K. Rappaport, "An Explanation of R. Moshe Feinstein's Opinion Regarding Brain Death" (Hebrew) in *KRhM*, 226-7.

Feinstein determined such a patient to be dead based on the ICSR despite continued cardiac activity.

Given the glaring omission of one of the most integral factors of this case, however, another interpretation is also possible – that R. Feinstein describes a patient **without** a heartbeat. While R. Tendler is correct that no physician would ventilate such a person (and would instead describe him as a corpse), the issue R. Feinstein was dealing with was not an actual case, but rather the theoretical question of determining death in the abstract. According to this reading of the responsum, R. Feinstein identified ICSR with death only in the absence of "signs of life... in other areas," including a heartbeat. Since a heartbeat is perhaps the most intuitive sign of life, reading this phrase to specifically exclude the heartbeat is quite difficult. A patient with a heartbeat would certainly be considered alive even after ICSR; the status of the hypothetical patient in this responsum was in question because he lacked a heartbeat.

Although this suggestion appears strange at first, as it refers to a non-realistic situation – a ventilated patient without a heartbeat – it is actually consistent with R. Feinstein's comments and theory of cardiac physiology delineated earlier. In *Iggerot Mosheh*, YD 2:146, in the course of analyzing Rashi's comments to Talmud *Yoma* 85a that "sometimes life (*hiyyut*) is not perceptible in the heart, but is noticeable in *hotmo*," R. Feinstein suggests that the heartbeat is not perceptible because in fact it no longer exists. Nonetheless, argues R. Feinstein, the heart still retains some function (*avodah*) even when not beating, as is evidenced by the fact that the patient is still breathing (*"adayyin hu notten ko'ah hiyyut me'at le-ha-guf, de-lakhen hu noshem be-hotmo adayyin"*). Since this *avodah* is not clinically perceptible, the most accurate indication and therefore determinant of life under such circumstances is respiration. The lack of respiration proves both ultimate respiratory and cardiac failure, which is why it is determinant of death. Leaving the matter of interpreting Talmud *Yoma* aside for the moment, it is clear that R. Feinstein conceives of the possibility of continued breathing despite the lack of a heartbeat, which is why he suggests that the respiratory exam is necessary to determine death even after a negative cardiac exam.

Given the prospect of breathing despite lacking a heartbeat in R. Feinstein's theory of physiology, it is certainly possible that R. Feinstein describes a similar situation in the present responsum. Since, according to his reasoning, a person could breathe even without a heartbeat, it makes perfect sense to him that physicians would attempt augmenting and treating such a patient's respiration when it is weak and not quite up to par by placing him on a ventilator (perhaps even in the hopes of eventually recovering a heartbeat). In such a situation, the only indication and hence determinant of life is the patient's ability to breathe; absent that, given the lack of heartbeat, the patient would be deemed dead. ICSR determines death because it indicates that the heart has **completely** stopped functioning – both its beating as well as its *avodah* have stopped.

The patient described by R. Feinstein, according to this interpretation, is ventilated but without a heartbeat. It is only under these circumstances that R. Feinstein argues for determining death based solely on ICSR. While he makes no explicit comment with regard to determining death in a patient with a heartbeat, the implicit assumption is that death requires the cessation of **both** respiratory and cardiac activity – completely precluding a determination of death in patients medically diagnosed as "brain dead." Accordingly, any and all mention or discussion in this responsum of ICSR as a determinant or definition of death was only referring to the theoretical patient without a functional heartbeat or pulse – and thus completely irrelevant to the "real world," in which patients cannot breathe without functioning hearts. According to this approach, the nuclide scan test is indeed meant to assess the potential reversibility of the patient's respiratory failure (as argued above), but is only determinant of death in the patient we are describing – one who suffers from ICSR (as proven by this test) **and** lacks a heartbeat.

Understanding the responsum in this manner completely avoids the difficulties raised by R. Feinstein's earlier insistence that EKG evidence of a heartbeat constitutes a certain sign of life even in the absence of respiration (*Iggerot Mosheh*, YD 2:146). EKG evidence is indicative of life because a heartbeat is indicative of life; accordingly, death as ICSR cannot be determined in the face of a continuous heartbeat.

Which approach is correct in understanding this responsum will never be known with certainty, given R. Feinstein's passing. Recognition of the doubt, however, may have serious ramifications for future discussions, and most certainly for practical application. How these issues relate to each other in light of all of R. Feinstein's relevant responsa will be analyzed in chapter 14.

R. Dovid Feinstein's Clarification

After R. Feinstein's passing, some apparently took issue with the authenticity of this third responsum (published in R. Feinstein's lifetime), prompting his son, R. Dovid Feinstein, to publish a letter vouching for the responsum's authenticity.[16] Dated 1 *Kislev*, 5753 (November 26, 1992), R. Dovid Feinstein, frustrated with responding to repeated questions as to its validity and strongly requesting an end to the debate, reports that it is most certainly authentic and that he even heard parts of it from his father himself. After signing the letter, R. Dovid Feinstein adds in a comment, "for additional clarification" (*le-birur ha-devarim*), that if a patient "lies like a corpse and exhibits no motion, even though his heart continues to beat (*af she-ha-lev po'em*) – because he is not breathing, he is considered to be absolutely dead (*me-ahar she-eino noshem – hu ke-meit gamur*)." In this context, R. Dovid Feinstein does not mention whether this represents what his father wrote in *Iggerot Mosheh*, YD 3:132 or if this is his interpretation and extension of his father's opinion. However, in a letter to R. Tendler from January 3, 1990, R. Dovid Feinstein states quite clearly that "I never spoke to my father about his halakhic ruling on 'brain death'"[17] – meaning that this "additional clarification" represents his own reflections on the topic (which are nonetheless significant in and of themselves) and not those of his father.[18]

Assuming that "not breathing" refers to lack of spontaneous respiration (as opposed to completely ventilator mediated breathing [as explicit in *Iggerot Mosheh*, YD 3:132]), the plainest meaning of R. Dovid Feinstein's letter is that ICSR defines death. A "brain dead" patient, who by definition suffers from ICSR, would thus be considered dead. Yet, in a published interview, R. Dovid Feinstein repeatedly states simply

---

16 "Determining Death with a Beating Heart" (Hebrew), in *KRhM*, 232.
17 M.D. Tendler, "Brain Death: Torah, Medicine, and Intellectual Integrity," *Jewish Review* 3 (April-May 1990): 8.
18 See also A.S. Abraham, *Nishmat Avraham*, 1ˢᵗ ed., vol. 4, 133-4.

that "my father said breathing," unwilling to extend the notion to "brain death" or organ donation. Given the logical conclusion from this letter, R. Dovid Feinstein's hesitance during the interview likely related to other matters, although he effectively admitted (in the previously cited letter to R. Tendler) that these reflect his and not his father's opinions.

R. Dovid Feinstein does not explain how or even if his conclusion fits in with his father's other responsa, which seem to argue for the opposite conclusion. While his opinion can stand on its own, it creates serious difficulties for explaining the simple meaning of *Iggerot Mosheh*, YD 2:146 and 2:184, published earlier, as well as *HM* 2:82, published some years after *YD* 3:132.

CHAPTER 13:

Rabbi Moshe Feinstein – Fourth Responsum:

Iggerot Mosheh, Hoshen Mishpat 2:72 and Beyond

R. Feinstein wrote his last responsum on the issue of cardiac transplants on 1 *Adar* II, 5738 (March 10, 1978), two years after penning the previous one. It is the shortest of the group and largely reiterates his earlier points.

Written to R. Kalman Kahana (rabbi of Kibbutz Chafetz Chaim in Israel), R. Feinstein repeats his description of cardiac transplantation as a "double murder" (*retzihah be-yadayyim li-shenei nefashot*). He references his previous responsum in *Iggerot Mosheh*, YD 2:184 (written in 5728 [1968]), noting that his opinion has not changed. (Interestingly, he makes no mention of his more recent responsum, YD 3:132, an omission of unclear significance.)

Focusing on the transplant recipient, R. Feinstein reports that his son-in-law, R. Moshe Tendler researched the medical literature and found that transplant survival rates were still grim, with few if any cardiac transplant recipients surviving for more than a few months. Even those who did manage to survive for this short time suffered greatly and were continuously tethered to hospital machinery.

R. Feinstein directs his outrage at "one state" (California) that continued to permit a "single physician" (who R. Tendler identifies as Dr. Norman Shumway of Stanford University[1]) to perform transplants despite the professional moratorium. He argues that given the current survival rates, it can only be surgeons' reckless disregard for the sanctity of life that "allows" them to consciously continue with these procedures.

In his defense, Dr. Shumway was one of the first to discover the beneficial uses of cyclosporine A, one of the first immunosuppressive drugs that helped limit and almost eliminate the recipient's rejection of the donated organ. These discoveries were just coming into the fore in 1978, and R. Feinstein was likely unaware of their benefits.[2]

Although written in 5738 (1978), this responsum was only published in 5745 (1985) in the seventh volume of *Iggerot Mosheh*. In the introduction to that volume, which R. Feinstein signed on 15 *Shevat* of that year, he thanks all those who assisted in publishing this work. As is widely known, R. Feinstein was elderly and unable to deal with many of the finer details of publication, even dictating many responsa for others to write.

The issue is relevant because of the time lapse of almost seven years between the original writing and eventual publication of this responsum. This is especially important in light of the advances in transplant medicine during those years. For example, while in 1980, the one, two, and three-year survival rates for cardiac transplants at Stanford University (where Dr. Shumway practiced) were 63%, 56%, and 52%, five years later in 1985, with the widespread usage of immunosuppressive therapy, the survival rates increased significantly to 83%, 75%, and 70% respectively.[3] For comparison purposes, today survival rates are no longer even measured in one, two, and three-year intervals, but rather at one, three,

---

[1] M.D. Tendler, *Responsa of Rav Moshe Feinstein: Care of the Critically Ill* (Hoboken, NJ: Ktav Publishing House, 1985), 38. That text refers to a Dr. Shulman, but this appears to be a typographical error.

[2] Without legal backing, the moratorium did not stop others from performing transplants during this time either, although Dr. Shumway was one of the most famous of the group.

[3] D.J. DiBardino, "The history and development of cardiac transplantation," *Texas Heart Institute Journal* 26 (1999): 198-205.

and five-years. According to the US Department of Health and Human Services, as of July 2011, the Kaplan-Meier Patient Survival prediction rates were 88%, 79%, and 73% respectively for males and 86%, 77%, and 69% respectively for females.[4] It is unclear if R. Feinstein was aware of the more recent data prior to printing this responsum in 1985.

Who is the Donor?

This responsum is primarily a vocal condemnation of physicians who insist on continuing to perform surgeries in the face of miserable outcomes. R. Feinstein does not discuss the donor much at all, other than noting that the procedure involves a "double murder" – of both donor and recipient. While in his third responsum (*YD* 3:132), R. Feinstein describes the physiological state of a ventilated patient in some detail – albeit not without ambiguity – this responsum is silent on the matter. Since R. Feinstein describes the donor as alive, the critical question is what the medical condition of this patient was, or more accurately, what R. Feinstein knew about his status.

The simplest reading is that since the question was about cardiac transplants, the donor is question was "brain dead." These patients can no longer breathe on their own, having failed an apnea test as part of the standard "brain death" protocol, and are suffering from the irreversible cessation of spontaneous respiration (ICSR). Supported by mechanical ventilation, these patients continue to maintain a sustained heartbeat. While R. Feinstein's conclusion in his third responsum (*YD* 3:132) may be somewhat unclear, leaving room for speculation, this responsum – written and published later – leaves little room for ambiguity, specifically describing a "brain dead" patient as alive and describing the removal of his heart as murder.

However, as was R. Feinstein's practice, he refrains from using specific medical terminology and does not describe the actual medical condition of the potential donor, condemning the practice only in general terms. In doing so, R. Feinstein leaves himself open to widely varying interpretations.

---

4 http://optn.transplant.hrsa.gov/latestData/rptStrat.asp, accessed 9 July 2011.

R. Tendler, in an introductory note to his translation of this responsum, claims that "the question concerns a patient referred to in Israel as a *tzemach*, i.e., a person in a persistent vegetative state" – specifically not a "brain dead" patient.[5] Patients in persistent vegetative states (PVS), while deeply unconscious, are capable of spontaneous respiration – not meeting the "Harvard Criteria" – and considered alive by all legal standards.

In making this argument, R. Tendler effectively removes this responsum from the entire discussion of "brain death" in Halakhah. He maintains that R. Feinstein accepts "brain death" as halakhically meaningful and yet describes the removal of organs from the particular donor in question in this responsum as murder. Were the donor to actually be "brain dead," argues R. Tendler, R. Feinstein would have even encouraged removing his organs to save a potentially salvageable recipient. Interestingly, R. Feinstein never published a responsum to this effect.

While technically possible and with no explicit contradictory indications, interpreting this responsum as R. Tendler suggests raises several difficulties.

First, R. Feinstein compares the patient in the question to those operated on by Dr. Shumway. All of Dr. Shumway's donors were determined to be "brain dead" prior to donation, having met the "Harvard Criteria," including a negative apnea test.[6] R. Tendler appears to be claiming that (at least in some circles), organs were procured from patients who were not legally dead according to any definition, legal or otherwise. Even if this were true, in referring to Dr. Shumway's patients in particular as alive (as per R. Tendler's identification of the "single physician"), R. Feinstein is clearly referring to "brain dead" patients, and yet he describes harvesting their organs as murder.

Furthermore, accepting R. Tendler's reading effectively claims that R. Feinstein had two motivations in writing this responsum. The first was to describe PVS patients as alive and the removal of their hearts as

---

5 *Responsa of Rav Moshe Feinstein*, 37.
6 A.K. Rider, J.G. Copeland, N.E. Shumway, "The status of cardiac transplantation, 1975," *Circulation* 52 (1975): 531-9; S.W. Jamieson, E.B. Stinson, N.E. Shumway, "Cardiac transplantation in 150 patients at Stanford University," *British Medical Journal* 1 (1979): 93-95.

murder. The second goal was to prohibit the procedure on the grounds of inappropriately high risk to the recipient, using Dr. Shumway's experience simply as an example of procedures that are performed despite unacceptably high levels of risk to the recipient. "Coincidentally," R. Feinstein chose to illustrate unacceptable risk by discussing "brain dead" mediated organ donation from patients whom R. Tendler claims that R. Feinstein thought were dead. According to R. Tendler, R. Feinstein's charge of "double murder" is only relevant to part of this very short responsum. It relates specifically to some abstract PVS patients – who are deemed alive by all accounts – and not to Dr. Shumway's patients, whom R. Feinstein actually mentions. This reading indeed seems forced.

If any of these suggestions were true, it would have behooved R. Feinstein to explicitly list these distinctions, rather than leaving this important point open to the very opposite interpretation. Additionally, in the course of his short discussion, R. Feinstein references his previous responsum (*YD* 2:174), in which he writes explicitly that a patient is considered alive with a heartbeat alone despite no longer breathing ("*hu ha-hai mamash af she-**eino noshem***") – deeming "brain dead" patients alive.

Because of the imprecision in describing the donor's medical state, R. Feinstein's conclusion itself is therefore open to interpretation. While the simple reading certainly indicates that he is referring to a "brain dead" donor and that he views removal of any organs from such a donor as murder, R. Tendler strenuously objects. The former reading insists that R. Feinstein clearly denies the halakhic validity of "brain death," while R. Tendler's argues that this responsum has nothing to do with "brain death" at all – and, in fact, that R. Feinstein embraced such criteria. The actual conclusion of this responsum therefore remains clouded.

A Posthumously Published Letter

Further complicating the matter is a letter published only after R. Feinstein's death. The letter from R. Moshe Feinstein to Dr. Elliot Bondi is dated 1 *Kislev*, 5745 (November 25, 1984); it was eventually printed in a posthumously published volume of *Iggerot Mosheh* (1996) as number 54 in the *Yoreh De'ah* section. A note appended to the published letter appearing in *Sefer Assia* 7 reports that Dr. Bondi showed this letter to the Tendler family (in 1992), who were up until then completely unaware of it. The note continues that the letter was dictated by R. Feinstein in Yiddish and was typed and translated by his student, a son-in-law of R. Mordechai Savitsky. The note concludes by noting that R. Feinstein reviewed the letter in its entirety prior to affixing his signature.[7]

This letter is quite explicit in its acceptance of "brain death" as halakhically meaningful, describing the "Harvard Criteria" as halakhically appropriate (*"gam mutzdak le-dina"*). The letter continues that even though a "brain dead" patient maintains a continuous heartbeat (*"af she-ha-lev adayyin yakhol lidhof kamah yamim"*), he is considered dead because of his (irreversible) lack of spontaneous respiration (*"kol zeman she-ein le-ha-holeh ko'ah neshimah atzma'it nehshav ke-meit"*), making reference to one of his previous responsa (*YD* 3:132).

While defending the "Harvard Criteria" as consistent with the halakhic determination of death as ICSR, a couple of paragraphs later, the letter offers a second, additional explanation, describing a patient meeting the "Harvard Criteria" as decapitated (*"she-nehshav mamash ke-mehtakh* [sic] *rosho"*), since "the brain is already actually rotting" (lit., being digested) (*"she-ha-mo'ah kevar ... mamash mit'akel"*). Concerned about further liberalization of standards for determining death, the letter goes on to argue that were state law to declare as dead a person who is still halakhically considered alive, Jewish physicians would be obligated to continue caring for him just as they did previously, even at great personal expense.

Leaving the last sentiment aside, on the face of it, the letter appears to support R. Tendler's position; it indeed sounds like a resounding support of "brain death." There are, however, many difficulties with this particular responsum – difficulties so significant that some dismiss it entirely when attempting to determine R. Feinstein's opinion.

Published posthumously and completely unknown prior to 1992, some have questioned the authorship of this letter. This hesitation is strengthened by R. Tendler's own admission that "for the last 15 years of his [R. Feinstein's] life, I photocopied and dispatched every sig-

---

[7] *Sefer Assia* 7 (Jerusalem: Schlesinger Institute, 1993), 148-148a.

nificant responsum he composed,"[8] and yet was completely unaware of this responsum's existence until it was shown to him six years after R. Feinstein's passing. Others, acknowledging the letter to have been reviewed by R. Feinstein, note that it was written during the last years of his life, when he was frail and less than active, leading some to question whether it accurately represents R. Feinstein's full cognitive faculties.

There is, however, a much more significant difficulty – that of chronology. As noted above, the introduction to the seventh volume of *Iggerot Mosheh* is dated 15 *Shevat*, 5745 (February 6, 1985); this letter, dated 1 *Kislev*, 5745 (November 25, 1984), was written a few short months prior. In and of itself, the fact that R. Feinstein chose to leave this letter out of that volume is not highly significant, as he may not have felt it fit to publish for one reason or another or perhaps hoped to publish it at a later time. The problem is that the seventh volume **does** include the fourth responsum (*HM* 2:72), discussed above, which arguably makes the opposite point. Although that responsum was written seven years earlier (1 *Adar* II, 5738 [1978]), in his introduction to the volume, R. Feinstein explicitly takes complete responsibility for its entire contents, having reviewed all of the galleys prior to publication.

Thus, in 1985, R. Feinstein clearly stood by his 1978 responsum, effectively repeating his prohibition on organ transplantation as a "double murder" of both donor and recipient. While R. Tendler argues to the contrary, the simplest reading of that text is that a "brain dead" patient is alive and that removing his heart therefore constitutes murder. Why would R. Feinstein have decided to publish this particular responsum (*HM* 2:72) – forbidding organ donation and describing "brain dead" patients as alive – if several months prior, he wrote a letter to the opposite effect? If he indeed supported "brain death" as halakhically meaningful on 1 *Kislev*, why on 15 *Shevat* of that same year did R. Feinstein openly declare his continuing support for a position to the contrary? This question is not easily or comfortably resolved.

---

8 M.D. Tendler, "Brain Death: Torah, Medicine, and Intellectual Integrity," *Jewish Review* 3 (April-May 1990): 8.

It is theoretically possible that R. Feinstein simply changed his mind in his later years. However, R. Tendler notes that R. Feinstein told him mere weeks before his death that he was "proud, even boastful" that he never had to retract or withdraw any of his written responsa.[9] Changing his mind would necessitate retracting his earlier argument (*YD* 2:146) against the brain having any role in determining death. R. Dovid Feinstein similarly notes that he is unaware of any evidence that his father ever reversed any of his positions on determining death.[10]

R. Auerbach's Reading – Withdrawing Support vs. Organ Donation

Addressing the issue of content more than chronology, R. Shelomoh Zalman Auerbach notes the lack of any mention of organ donation in the newly discovered letter.[11] While it discusses criteria for death and what actions physicians should undertake should they change, it does not mention organ donation even once. R. Auerbach argues that since in *Kislev* of 1984, the "whole Torah world" was discussing organ donation, if R. Feinstein really felt that "brain dead" patients are halakhically dead, he certainly would have explicitly permitted and even encouraged organ donation as a form of *pikuah nefesh*. R. Auerbach further notes that even in his third responsum (*YD* 3:132), R. Feinstein never makes any mention of organ donation, limiting his discussion to determining the moment of death and removing/withdrawing therapy. He finds this consistent omission quite telling.

R. Auerbach was unwilling to believe that R. Feinstein would have considered "brain death" as halakhically meaningful and yet completely neglect any mention of organ donation. He therefore suggests that R. Feinstein was uncomfortable relying on scientific studies to prove death when not otherwise clinically apparent, and was therefore hesitant to apply the notion of "brain death" to practical matters.

---

9 M.D. Tendler, "Halakhic Death Means Brain Death," *Jewish Review* 3 (January-February 1990): 20.

10 Cited by D. Schorr, "The Opinion of R. Moshe Feinstein *zt"l* Regarding Determining Death and Cardiac Transplants," *Ha-Pardes* 62:1 (5748): 14; A.S. Abraham, *Nishmat Avraham*, 1ˢᵗ ed., vol. 4, 134.

11 A.S. Abraham, *Nishmat Avraham*, 2ⁿᵈ ed., *YD*, (henceforth, *NA*), 477-8.

R. Auerbach suggests that in this letter, R. Feinstein merely allows cessation or withdrawal of treatment/therapy from patients diagnosed as "brain dead," but never permits organ donation. In the former case, the death of the patient results from the passive action of the physician (not continuing care), while in the latter case, the death of the patient is at the direct hands of the surgeon removing his heart.[12]

Responding to R. Auerbach's interpretation, R. Shabtai Rappaport (R. Tendler's son-in-law) argues that R. Auerbach's contention is at odds with R. Feinstein's broader positions regarding end-of-life care.[13] R. Rappaport claims that R. Auerbach reached his conclusion because he permitted disconnecting a respirator from a *goses* patient. Following the ruling of Rama that one may remove an impediment to death from such a patient,[14] R. Auerbach did not consider removal of the ventilator to be prohibited euthanasia. R. Feinstein, R. Rappaport argues, felt otherwise, viewing disconnecting a ventilator as euthanasia – actively removing necessary vital support – and certainly forbidden. While R. Feinstein permits withholding medications that merely prolong the *gesisah* process without providing any hope for recovery, he nonetheless insists on providing continued nutrition and ventilation, regardless of the circumstances:

> It is clear that one must feed [such a patient] foods that cause no harm, since they certainly strengthen the body a little, even if the patient himself or those around him cannot appreciate [this strengthening]... And the reason is simple; since eating is a natural [activity], we must eat to maintain life (*she-mukhrahin le-ekhol le-hahazik ha-hiyyut*).[15]

---

12 *Ru'ah Ya'akov*, sec. 60, makes a similar claim, arguing for differentiating between stopping/withdrawing therapy and organ donation, echoing R. Auerbach's interpretation of this last letter and finding further support for such a distinction.

13 "Explanation of R. Moshe Feinstein's Opinion Regarding Brain Death" (Hebrew) in M. Halperin (ed.), *Kevi'at Rega ha-Mavet*, 2nd edition (Jerusalem: Schlesinger Institute, 2007), 235-8.

14 Rama, *Shulhan Arukh*, YD 339:1.

15 *Responsa Iggerot Mosheh*, HM 2.74. R. Feinstein interprets Rama's permission to "remove an impediment to death" as limited to cases of great suffering; only under such circumstances does Halakhah allow a person to stop seeking medical care. However,

Earlier in the same paragraph, R. Feinstein discusses the imperative to continue artificial ventilation, leading R. Rappaport to argue that the same reasoning underlies both applications – both disconnecting a ventilator and withdrawing nutrition are tantamount to active euthanasia.

Accordingly, R. Rappaport argues, even if all that R. Feinstein permits for a "brain dead" patient is removal of ventilation, it must be because the patient is dead; otherwise, such removal constitutes murder. While he cannot comment as to why R. Feinstein neglected to make any mention of organ donation in this letter, R. Rappaport argues that R. Feinstein viewed "brain dead" patients as halakhically dead and would certainly have permitted transplanting organs from them to potentially salvageable patients.

Seemingly compelling, there are a number of difficulties with R. Rappaport's analysis. First, while not related directly to this issue, is his assumption regarding R. Auerbach's opinion. R. Auerbach, in fact, never allowed disconnecting a ventilator from any patient, except in the rare circumstance in which the patient was almost certainly – but not yet conclusively proven to be – dead (see chapter 16 for a more in depth analysis). More substantively challenging, however, is R. Rappaport's presentation of R. Feinstein's position.

In *Iggerot Mosheh*, *HM* 2:73:1, R. Feinstein explains that all patients must be ventilated, since he believes that providing oxygen lessens the patient's suffering.[16] Building upon this idea, in the next responsum (*HM* 2:74:3), R. Feinstein describes all forms of nutrition as natural needs (even when artificially administered) and life-sustaining; whether visibly apparent or not, they certainly strengthen the patient. R. Rappaport **assumes**

R. Feinstein argues, we have a tradition that the state of *gesisah* itself entails tremendous (psychic, spiritual, or otherwise non-physical) suffering as the soul departs from the body. Therefore, Rama applied this permissive ruling broadly to all *gosesim*.

16 This is true even for a *goses*, from whom one is generally permitted to withhold therapies that merely extend the *gesisah* without providing an actual cure. Since the entire permission to withhold therapy from a *goses* is predicated upon reducing his suffering, anything that increases suffering is certainly forbidden. While certain medications may be withheld (possibly even withdrawn), R. Feinstein argues that ventilation (ignoring its status as a medical therapy) must be continued out of fear of violating that which the permissive ruling was meant to prevent.

that a similar logic applies to ventilation, but R. Feinstein himself – even when comparing ventilation and nutrition – never makes this suggestion. R. Feinstein provides a different rationale for insisting on continuing ventilation and nutrition respectively, predicating the former on alleviating misery and the latter on increasing the patient's strength. He specifically explains each differently even in the same paragraph.[17] Thus, while R. Rappaport's suggestion is most certainly cogent in the abstract, it does not appear to fit within the plain meaning of R. Feinstein's words.

In R. Feinstein's presentation, supplying oxygen alleviates suffering, a concept possibly derived from a medical theory popular in the 1970's that stopping ventilation actively causes additional suffering, known as "physiological trauma." Regardless of the possible medical basis, his ruling is inherently dependent upon mitigating suffering, in whatever way it is accomplished. Today, alleviating dyspnea (the agonizing feeling of difficulty breathing) may sometimes be more appropriately and effectively addressed with carefully dosed morphine, not necessarily increased oxygen. This may lead to the possibility that according to his own logic, R. Feinstein would not require ventilating such a patient. Furthermore, even while certain amounts/levels of oxygen may indeed eliminate suffering, this may be sufficiently accomplished with an oxygen facemask, and may not necessitate intubation and mechanical ventilation. Accordingly, if prevention of suffering can be accomplished in a manner other than through using a ventilator, withdrawal of ventilation would **not** constitute euthanasia in R. Feinstein's view.

It is thus possible to read this letter in line with R. Auerbach's comment, limiting R. Feinstein's halakhic recognition of "brain death" to withdrawing/withholding therapy when doing so would not increase the patient's suffering. According to this reading, the most important "novelty" of the letter is identifying a "brain dead" patient as one for whom discontinuing ventilation would not cause suffering. While R. Rappaport's position is certainly possible, it is not necessarily compelling.

However, even taking the letter at face value – as deeming "brain dead" patients dead and allowing withdrawal/withholding of ventilation – presents

---

17 A possibly differentiating case might be when providing continued nutrition in and of itself induces great pain. R. Feinstein does not address this question.

several difficulties, mostly resulting from the dual reasoning given for possibly halakhically recognizing "brain death." Why, in fact, did R. Feinstein offer two reasons – both ICSR and a parallel to decapitation? Is it because either is sufficient, but both not necessary, to determine death? Or is only the combination of the two rationales sufficiently compelling to acknowledge "brain death" as halakhically meaningful? Requiring both criteria may possibly stem from some inherent doubt in relying on either alone – arguing that in tandem, reliability is more assured, either because of medical/scientific issues or for halakhic reasons. Determining this question is of paramount importance in the modern era, since we now know that even in "brain death," the brain retains some function and in many cases maintains blood flow. The brain can therefore not be described as "completely rotted," which R. Feinstein requires as part of the determination.

Oral Record

There is a rich oral record of numerous conversations and pronouncements by R. Feinstein regarding "brain death" – spanning views from total acceptance to complete rejection, with some even describing some befuddlement as to the precise medical facts. For each person claiming to have heard one opinion, another offers a contrary testimony. While certainly fascinating and perhaps revealing in resolving many of the doubtful and difficult issues within these responsa, all oral records are fraught with questions of accuracy and precision. If the oral record were uniformly accepted as authentic and reliable, perhaps it might help resolve some of these questionable matters, but given the extent of disagreement and almost vitriolic tone that these discussions often engender, it is not likely that this can or will happen.

This is especially true in this case, given the historical context of changing medical realities and increasing scientific complexities emerging with every technological advancement. While perhaps a scholarly desideratum, undertaking an analysis of the oral record would need to take the form of investigative journalism, with its own standards and methods, rather than halakhic analysis. As discussed in the introduction, in this book's focus on **understanding** the halakhic attitudes and approaches to "brain death," it adds little and will not be discussed further.

CHAPTER 14:

Rabbi Moshe Feinstein – Putting it All Together

The last four chapters have presented R. Feinstein's legacy on determining death in Halakhah. As one of the preeminent halakhists of modern times, R. Feinstein's opinion was eagerly sought on all matters, including medical issues. Living during the early days of organ transplantation, R. Feinstein formed negative biases towards the procedure in particular and to the medical establishment in general. Disenchanted with recurring unfulfilled promises about the potential success of cardiac transplants, as well as the repeated mantra that practice would eventually breed success, R. Feinstein strenuously objected to all transplants as a matter of principle. The risk to life was simply too high, with all recipients dying mere days after surgery. He simply could not fathom sacrificing recipients' lives – patients who by all estimates still had at least several months to live – for the sake of developing and perfecting a procedure that was so unsuccessful. In fact, because of such poor outcomes in the 1960's and 1970's, many professional medical societies declared a moratorium on cardiac transplants in the United States, lasting until the discovery and development of effective immunosuppression. R. Feinstein therefore dedicated a portion of each responsum to state in no uncertain terms that irrespective of how one determines the death of the donor, transplant surgeries are absolutely forbidden because of the unacceptably high risk to the **recipient**'s life.

With his objections predicated upon statistical facts, R. Feinstein would certainly have viewed the matter differently today, with one-year survival rates from cardiac transplant surgery reaching 86-88%.[1] With improvements in medical practice, the risk to the recipient is vastly different and certainly mitigated today. The real issue thus comes down to accurately identifying the status of the donor – that is, determining the moment of death in the context of "brain death" more precisely. It is in this regard that R. Feinstein's opinion is largely debated.

While frequently quoted by advocates for recognizing "brain death" as halakhically significant, the written record presents a clouded picture. The first two of R. Feinstein's responsa on the topic (*YD* 2:174 and 2:146) are quite firm in describing any patient with a continued heartbeat as alive, irrespective of respiratory status (R. Yisraeli's comments notwithstanding). The third responsum (*YD* 3:132) may be the most flexible in terms of allowing for varying interpretations, while the fourth (*HM* 2:72) is largely a statement of complete dissatisfaction with the medical establishment.

Irreversible Cessation of Spontaneous Respiration (ICSR)

The key issue in understanding R. Feinstein's position regarding "brain death" is deciphering what he recognized as the halakhic criteria for death. R. Feinstein is quite clear (*YD* 2:146) that the brain *per se* plays no role in defining or determining death, lacking absolutely any Talmudic or later halakhic source. Accordingly, if "brain death" is significant, it is not because of brain injury or dysfunction, but only because "brain dead" patients suffer from ICSR.

Acceptance of ICSR as the halakhic criterion for death requires reading Talmud *Yoma* 85a as debating the **criteria** for death and concluding that respiratory failure alone is definitive – largely sidelining Rashi's comments, which appear to indicate otherwise. Furthermore, to maintain this position, R. Feinstein would need to focus on the earlier sections of

---

[1] http://optn.transplant.hrsa.gov/latestData/rptStrat.asp, accessed July 14, 2011.

Hatam Sofer's famous responsum. He would have to read the concluding statement with some caution and precision, being unable or unwilling to take it as face value for its inclusion of cardiac asystole in determining death.

R. Feinstein does not address each of these sources systematically, but rather only touches upon some of them. For example, he quotes from *Hakham Tzvi*, who, building off Rashi's comments, argues that the lack of breathing *per se* does not define death at all, but is rather the most sensitive indication of a continued heartbeat (at least in Talmudic times). R. Feinstein does not, however, explain how he understood this ruling and what role it should play in the debate.

Those arguing for ICSR as death cannot accept *Hakham Tzvi's* interpretation of the Talmudic passage; they must claim that respiration is significant in its own right. Dr. Steinberg, who argues that R. Feinstein supported determining death solely by ICSR, claims that since *Hakham Tzvi's* ruling relied on scientific assumptions that are now known to be incorrect, his position vis-à-vis the importance of the heart in determining life and death should be summarily ignored;[2] *Ru'ah Ya'akov* offers a similar argument.[3] R. Feinstein however, took *Hakham Tzvi's* position seriously enough to analyze and argue with parts of it – indicating that it is, in fact, currently relevant and cannot be summarily dismissed.

Recognizing ICSR as halakhically significant, regardless of the reasoning, must assume that a patient who is completely reliant on mechanical ventilation is not considered breathing in the traditional sense. On this point at least, R. Feinstein is rather clear – the determination is properly focused on the ability for **spontaneous** respiration, a status that is often unknown with certitude in a ventilated patient.[4]

---

2 "Determining the Moment of Death and Cardiac Transplants" (Hebrew), in M. Halperin (ed.), *Kevi'at Rega ha-Mavet*, 2nd edition (Jerusalem: Schlesinger Institute, 2007) (henceforth, *KRhM*), 50.
3 *Ru'ah Ya'akov*, sec. 75. Alternate approaches to *Hakham Tzvi's* responsum in light of current science were discussed in chapter 8.
4 *YD* 3:132. One last point of universal agreement is R. Feinstein's belief (*YD* 2:184) that death must, by definition, be irreversible. Whether we determine death by cardiac or respiratory criteria, these functions must have **irreversibly** ceased in order to qualify as death (regarding all determinations of death except for decapitation – see chapter

Practical Challenges

In addition to halakhic challenges, positing ICSR as an exhaustive criterion for death creates a serious conceptual difficulty. This approach identifies death with the irreversible inability of a person to engage in the **work** of breathing – meaning the physical movement of air into and out of the lungs. The criterion is predicated upon a specific physiological **function**; the only relevant determination is whether or not a patient is able to or will ever be able to breathe on his own. As a functional definition, the specific etiology causing the lack of function is irrelevant. Otherwise, it would be the specific cause or reason that is the true criterion for death; the inability to breathe would not be a criterion in and of itself, but merely an indication that some other criteria (that specific cause) has been met.

As noted above, R. Feinstein clearly does not consider the status of the brain as a determining factor of death; if he considers "brain death" significant at all, it is only because of ICSR. The logical conclusion is that any patient suffering from ICSR is dead, even without any concomitant brain injury. However, there are patients who suffer from ICSR from causes other than brainstem failure. These are patients who, by all accounts, should most certainly qualify as living, not least of all because they can effectively state so on their own. If one accepts ICSR as death, then any patient who has irreversibly lost the ability to breathe on his own should be considered dead, since the definition is functional and independent of any particular pathophysiology. The difficulty lies in the fact that these patients otherwise appear quite alive –

---

10 for a fuller discussion). This raises a more general philosophical issue of the precise chronology of making this determination. Cf. J. Lynn, R. Cranford, "The persisting perplexities in the determination of death," in S.J. Yougner, R.M. Arnold, R. Schapiro (eds.), *The Definition of Death: Contemporary Controversies* (Baltimore: The Johns Hopkins University Press, 1999), ch. 6. Often, the moment that a given physiological function is known or proven to have irreversibly ceased occurs much later in time than when the function has actually irreversibly ceased. What is the status of a patient during the interim? Should his status be reevaluated retroactively once the latter time point has passed? The question of irreversibility was touched upon in chapter 4.

with not only beating hearts, but retaining the ability to communicate as well.

A more detailed discussion of these types of patients and the particular physiology leading to this situation is presented in chapter 18. Only the relevance to R. Feinstein's responsa will be mentioned here.

One possibility for solving this problem is to argue that ICSR is not really an exhaustive criterion for death at all, but rather simply the absence of "an indicator of the living state." As a coauthor of a 1977 paper, R. Tendler argues that ultimately, spontaneous respiration

> [c]annot be considered... [death's] definition, since a respirator patient whose sole defect is paralysis of the motor neurons to the muscles of respiration due to neurologic disease is surely fully alive despite his inability to breathe spontaneously. Therefore, to define death in biblical terms, loss of respiration must be combined with... complete and irreversible destruction of the brain."[5]

Accordingly, the Biblical and Talmudic reliance on ICSR as death (per this approach) was meant solely as "a crucial criterion for determining whether complete destruction of the brain has occurred," not because the lack of respiration is in and of itself meaningful. While intriguing, R. Feinstein's 1973 responsum (*YD* 2:146) explicitly rejects this notion, noting that "in the times of the Sages, the brain functioned just as it does today... and yet a person was not considered dead when his brain stopped functioning, and it is clear that the same is true today." While R. Tendler's approach can certainly stand independently, it appears to conflict somewhat with his father-in-law's opinion.

Another approach employs part of the above suggestion, but does not take it quite as far – agreeing that ICSR does not actually define death (or more accurately, is not the sole criterion for death), but rather only indicates that some other death-defining moment or process has occurred. Whereas R. Tendler identified that "something else" as the destruction of the brain, this alternative offers the more vaguely described "departure

---

5 F.J. Veith, J.M. Fein, M.D. Tendler, "Brain death I: A status report of medical and ethical considerations," *Journal of the American Medical Association* 238 (1977): 1651-5.

of the soul." As a metaphysical notion, a precise time cannot necessarily be determined for this event; it is ascertainable only when it has not yet taken place or when it has long passed. Accordingly, Dr. Steinberg argues that when there is "objective" evidence that a person's soul persists within him, he cannot be declared dead even when suffering from ICSR.[6]

Broadly speaking, this idea boils down to arguing that ICSR is equivalent to death only in the context of dying – namely, the soul's departure. Regardless of how one describes "brain dead" patients, even if they are not dead right now, they soon will be. When a patient is dying, argues Dr. Steinberg, the criterion of ICSR is determinant and therefore appropriate for "brain dead" patients.

This approach not only lacks solid halakhic support, it suffers from a more fundamental problem as well. Shifting ICSR from a **definition** or **criterion** for death to merely an **indication** of some other death-defining event is tantamount to conceding that ICSR is not equivalent with death. In other words, relying on ICSR is a good "rule of thumb" that is rooted in tradition and is rigorously defensible in **most** cases. Everyone, regardless of how they understand "brain death," agrees to this point. After all, without medical intervention, respiration, cardiac function, and almost all other vital functions stop within moments of each other in a dying patient. The question is how to determine the cases when medical technology has managed to tease apart these various vital functions, supporting some but not all at the end of life. These types of patients highlight these distinctions in an intriguing and relevant way.

Physiological Decapitation

In interpreting *Iggerot Mosheh*, YD 3:132, R. Tendler introduces the notion of "physiological decapitation" in an attempt to compare "brain death" with decapitation as death, as described in Mishnah *Ohalot*.[7] This argument is largely based on R. Feinstein's description of a negative

---

6 A. Steinberg, "Determining the Moment of Death and Cardiac Transplants, A Response to Critiques" (Hebrew), *Or ha-Mizrah* 36 (5748): 283.

7 M.D. Tendler, *Responsa of Rav Moshe Feinstein: Care of the Critically Ill* (Hoboken, NJ: Ktav Publishing House, 1996), 72.

nuclide scan test as parallel to "forceful decapitation." The merits and difficulties of this argument in the context of this particular responsum were discussed in chapter 12. Even granting "physiological decapitation" as a possible interpretation of that responsum, however, the very notion raises many concerns. The first is whether "physiological decapitation" stands alone as a definition of death or if it must be part and parcel of ICSR to qualify. This question was raised earlier (chapter 13) specifically with regard to the posthumously published letter to Dr. Bondi. Requiring both factors avoids the difficulties raised by conscious but non-breathing patients, but one must begin to wonder why these dual criteria are necessary and how they should be practically applied to other cases.

The question of general applicability is significant in light of the President's Council's report explaining that in "brain dead" patients, the "whole brain" cannot be described as completely "dead."[8] Since decapitation describes the separation of the head from the body, "physiological decapitation" should parallel this notion. Focusing more specifically on the brain, "physiological decapitation" should refer to a situation in which the brain can be considered completely absent, such as when the entirety of the brain can be considered "dead." This scenario may exist in the hypothetical case in which each and every cell of the brain is dead (a position more carefully articulated by R. Shelomoh Zalman Auerbach and described in more detail in chapter 16), but not in the "standard" medical diagnosis of "brain death," as noted by the President's Council.

It is particularly difficult to read both criteria (physiological decapitation and ICSR) as absolutely necessary in R. Feinstein's first two responsa, which do not appear to mention the notion of "physiological decapitation" at all.

This tension as to whether both criteria are necessary or if either is sufficient was recently discussed in the pages of *Tradition* (a publication of the Rabbinical Council of America). The journal hosted a pair of articles questioning whether the status of "brain death" in Halakhah should be

---

8 D.A. Shewmon, "The brain and somatic integration: Insights into the standard biological rationale for equating "brain death" with death," *Journal of Medicine and Philosophy* 26 (2001): 457-78, cited by President's Council of Bioethics, *Controversies in the Determination of Death: A White Paper by the President's Council on Bioethics* (2008), 56.

readdressed in light of advances in scientific research. Dr. Joshua Kunin, adopting R. Tendler's notion of "physiological decapitation," seriously calls previous determinations into question, citing recent evidence for the viability of the hypothalamus in "brain dead" patients.[9] R. Dr. Edward Reichman (while not taking a position on the matter himself) responds by arguing that R. Feinstein predicated death upon ICSR alone, with "brain death" serving only as confirmatory evidence for the irreversibility of the condition.[10] In essence, Dr. Kunin and R. Dr. Reichman debate this very point – are both criteria necessary or is either sufficient on its own? If both "physiological decapitation" and ICSR are necessary, recent research should have serious practical ramifications on the determination of "brain death" as halakhic death. If only ICSR is necessary, the fact that parts of the brain may continue to function after "brain death" is irrelevant.

This question is even more relevant for R. Tendler's position described above, as he argues that ultimately, the singular definition of death is "brain death." In his view, cessation of respiration and cardiac function only serve as surrogates or indicators of "brain death."[11] If the "brain death" that R. Tendler posits as the ultimate definition for death is meant to parallel decapitation as per Mishnah *Ohalot*, then it should refer to a state where the brain can be considered completely absent – parallel to the death of the entire brain and cessation of all brain function. This medical reality does not exist according to recent research – strongly calling R. Tendler's premises into question.

Some have tried to resolve this difficulty by narrowly focusing on the hypothalamus, one area of the brain still functioning in many "brain dead" patients. While other "nests of cells" may still be functional throughout the brain, the hypothalamus is likely the most significant, as it often continues to function in a physiologically important manner by maintaining thermoregulation and blood pressure regulation, among other functions. R. David Ben Zazon suggests that the parallel between "brain death" and decapitation need not refer to the brain's complete absence,

---

9 "Brain Death: Revisiting the Rabbinic Opinions in Light of Current Medical Knowledge," *Tradition* 38:4 (2004): 48-62.
10 "Don't Pull the Plug on Brain Death Just Yet," ibid., 63-69.
11 "A Status Report," 1653-4.

but rather to the "death," destruction, or irreversible dysfunction of only particular parts of the brain.[12] Since many of the hypothalamus's endocrine functions can be artificially maintained (by providing the appropriate hormones intravenously), its destruction or death may be considered unnecessary for defining the entire brain as completely absent. While R. Ben Zazon offers this as a possible explication of R. Auerbach's understanding of Mishnah *Ohalot*, it applies equally to R. Tendler's description of "physiological decapitation."

R. Ben Zazon himself, however, notes both fundamental and practical difficulties in accepting this proposal. Just because a physiological function can be artificially replaced does not render that function, when present, as not necessarily indicative of continued life. Indeed, if that were the case, the same argument could be made for the brainstem, which controls respiration, since respiratory function can be replaced by a ventilator, leading to the conclusion that a patient may be considered "brain dead" even if his brainstem is functioning. This is not a viable argument, R. Ben Zazon claims, and it is therefore questionable whether it can be considered valid with regard to the hypothalamus.

Dr. Steinberg, responding to a request from R. Shelomoh Amar, the Sephardic Chief Rabbi of Israel, also focuses on the endocrine functions of the hypothalamus, suggesting that the parallel between "physiological" and absolute decapitation need only be true of the brain's neurological functions.[13] Dysfunction of the hypothalamus is largely dealt with by endocrinologists, not neurologists, argues Dr. Steinberg, concluding that the criteria for "whole brain death" are met even in the presence of a functional hypothalamus.

This distinction suffers at two major points. The first (already addressed by R. Ben Zazon) is that the hypothalamus is not limited to endocrine function, but includes neurological functions as well, including thermoregulation. Leaving technical issues aside, this argument also raises a more fundamental issue in suggesting a distinction based on histological or cellular functioning in the brain, whereas Halakhah does not

---

12 D. Ben Zazon, "Brain Death According to R. Shelomoh Zalman Auerbach *zt"l*" (Hebrew) in *KRbM*, 242-5.
13 Unpublished responsum of R. Amar, originally dated 10 *Av*, 5763, p. 29.

(and frankly may not even have the tools to) derive conclusions based on non-visual differences in the inner workings of cells. Even granting an expansive definition of decapitation – encompassing the "death," destruction, or irreversible dysfunction of the entire brain as halakhically appropriate definitions of death (and not because decapitation fits some other death-defining criteria) – Dr. Steinberg's anatomical distinction between brain functions does not appear to be halakhically relevant.[14]

R. Tendler offers a different distinction, arguing that "Rambam in his commentary to Mishnah *Ohalot* 1:7 [1:6 in different editions] defines the 'halachic brain' as the control center for bodily movements."[15] Accordingly, R. Tendler argues that when the cortical (controlling voluntary movements) and brainstem (controlling breathing) areas of the brain are no longer functional, a person is dead. Whether or not other areas of the brain remain viable and functional is irrelevant according to his approach. He can therefore discount the viability of the hypothalamus and other vegetative function-controlling areas of the brain as unimportant to this determination.

---

14 Others attempt to negate the notion of "physiological decapitation" as death by noting that "brain dead" patients are capable of digesting nutrients, fighting infections, and gestating a baby. R. Leizerson (*Mishnat Hayyei Sha'ah*, 68) claims that had this information been available to R. Auerbach, he would certainly not have defined death as the death of each and every cell of the brain. These and other physiological functions, argues R. Leizerson, are indicative of continued life – and, if present in a "brain dead" patient, effectively preclude defining such a patient as dead. The same argument is leveled against those who understand R. Feinstein as endorsing a definition of death predicated upon "physiological decapitation."

This position effectively boils down to refusing to recognize as dead someone who cannot be described as a corpse because he can still perform important physiological functions. While largely intuitive, this line of reasoning is valid with regard to **indications**, but not **definitions**, of death. If a given set of conditions indicates death even in the vast majority of cases, it may not be true in the context of continued biological activity. However, if "physiological decapitation" or the death of each and every cell of the brain defines death and are not merely indicative of death, continuing biological activity may, in fact, be irrelevant. Regardless, there is little support for the argument that many of these physiological functions are halakhically meaningful, particularly those that have no macroscopic, observable effect.

15 M.D. Tendler, *Responsa of Rav Moshe Feinstein: Care of the Critically Ill* (Hoboken, NJ: Ktav Publishing House, 1985), 97.

This is a difficult reading of Rambam, however. In the context of the comment cited, Rambam appears to be merely differentiating between controlled, integrated movements and spasmodic, jerk-like twitches (*pirkus*), the latter of which, he writes, do not stem from a "singular source." This does not seem to be an attempt to define the "halakhic brain," but rather an explanation of why *pirkus* occurs even when the brain is absent. While the brain certainly controls organized motion, there is no compelling reason to assume that this is the only brain function recognized by Halakhah.

Further probing this approach, Drs. Steinberg and Halperin question whether the parallel to decapitation necessitates the "death" of every single brain cell or perhaps is encompassed more appropriately by "total brain dysfunction," akin to the medically familiar description of "whole brain death" referring to "complete" dysfunction.[16] They compare "brain death" to death determined by cardiac criteria. In the latter, the heart must irreversibly stop beating; there is no requirement that each and every cardiac cell die. In fact, many cells may still be metabolically "alive" for some time after the heart has terminally stopped beating. Drs. Steinberg and Halperin argue that it is the **function** of the brain that is critical, not whether each individual cell can still metabolize nutrients. While not explicit, this argument interprets Mishnah *Ohalot* as describing decapitation as death because the brain no longer functions to control the body.

The difficulty is that Mishnah *Ohalot* does not provide a reason for why decapitation should qualify as death, only stating that it does – leaving Drs. Steinberg and Halperin's suggestion in need of support. What the *mishnah* does say is that severing the head constitutes death, which Rabbis Feinstein and Auerbach interpret as the absence of the brain in particular, not necessarily the other parts of the face. For the brain to be absent, however, it must be completely gone – either through the death and liquefaction of each and every cell or by being physically separated from the rest of the body. Especially in light of recent research, suggesting that the definition of "brain death" be functional and not anatomical begs the question of which functions are important and which are not.

---

16 Unpublished responsum of R. Amar, originally dated 10 *Av*, 5763, pp. 30-31.

This argument is true both for R. Auerbach's description of the death of each and every cell of the brain (described in chapter 16) as well for R. Tendler's interpretation of R. Feinstein's position as supporting a notion of "physiological decapitation."

Conclusion

Perhaps the most contentious aspect of the "brain death" debate is determining R. Moshe Feinstein's position. Writing four responsa during the tumultuous era of organ donation's infancy, R. Feinstein's writings reflect the uncertainty, ambiguity, and hesitancy that pervaded the moral and ethical foundations of the medical world. Adding to the written record are R. Feinstein's reported conversations and pronouncements, spanning the entire spectrum of options – from wholehearted acceptance of "brain death" to vigorous opposition. Where all can agree is that R. Feinstein strongly influenced both the religious as well as the bioethical community in insisting that death represents a value judgment that is to be decided by value-driven societies, be they legal, moral, or religious – but certainly not medical.

What R. Feinstein's actual position on "brain death" was and what his legacy has become may, in fact, be quite divergent. Advocates for three different approaches have emerged: those arguing that R. Feinstein firmly accepted "brain death," those arguing that he adamantly rejected it, and those hesitant to make any final determination due to the preponderance of conflicting evidence. These four responsa often reflect differing sentiments, some more elaborate and intricate than others, leaving the reader wondering how much weight to assign to each in appropriately distilling R. Feinstein's actual opinion. At best, it appears that the most accurate description is one of doubt (*safek*) – while some evidence points in one direction, alternate proofs and approaches exist for the other. In addition, R. Feinstein's conflicting personal statements not only create confusion, but often lead to setting his opinion aside as too ambiguous to decipher.

The practical question since R. Feinstein's passing really boils down to one of Halakhah – if and how to incorporate a difficult-to-ascertain but normally highly influential opinion when deciding a practical matter.

Because this is not just any opinion, but rather that of one of the greatest halakhic decisors of modern times, the question takes on additional significance. These last five chapters are intended only as a guide to help understand and analyze R. Feinstein's position on determining death, not to arrive at any conclusions. As in the rest of this book, these chapters do not propose or attempt to define, arbitrate, or determine halakhic practice. As a matter of Halakhah, deciphering R. Feinstein's position vis-à-vis the role it should play in adjudicating practical Halakhah is left to the traditional halakhic decisors.

CHAPTER 15:

The Israeli Chief Rabbinate

In 1971, the Chief Rabbis of Israel, R. Yitzhak Nissim and R. Isser Yehudah Unterman, made their opinion quite clear in rejecting any neurological based determination of death, and even doubted whether any rabbi would dare take such a stance.[1] Three years later, the subsequent Ashkenazi Chief Rabbi, R. Shelomoh Goren, published an essay in which he entertained the possibility that the absence of brain function may deem other continuing physiological functions irrelevant.[2] Even so, R. Goren merely speculates as to potential ramifications for "brain death" based organ donations, limiting any conclusions or applications only to withdrawal of care. All these however, were individual opinions of the various rabbis and did not necessarily reflect a policy statement of the Chief Rabbinate (*Rabbanut ha-Rashit*).

In 1986, in the course of establishing public policy in Israel, the Israeli Ministry of Health consulted with the Chief Rabbinate of Israel, then under the auspices of R. Avraham Kahana Shapira and R. Mordechai Eliyahu, for a halakhic opinion on the permissibility of cardiac transplants. In response, the *Rabbanut* issued their decision on 1 *Marheshvan*, 5747 (November 3, 1986). The social and political climate in Israel during

---

[1] "The Chief Rabbinate: Cessation of Brain Activity is Not a Sign of Death" (Hebrew), *She'arim* (19 *Shevat*, 5731/ February 14, 1971), 1.
[2] "The Definition of Death in Halakhah," *Shanah be-Shanah* (5734): 125-30.

this time greatly influenced and strongly affected this entire discourse. Dr. Naftali Moses, in his *Really Dead? The Israeli Brain-Death Controversy 1967-1986*,³ thoroughly details, surveys, and analyzes all of these aspects from a variety of perspectives, and will not be discussed here.

Because of its complexity and pivotal historical role, the decision and follow-up letter are presented here in their entirety:⁴

> Today, the first day of *Marheshvan* 5747 (November 3, 1986), the Chief Rabbinate Council has unanimously decided to endorse the recommendations of the Transplant Committee as follows:
>
> 1. The Ministry of Health asked the Chief Rabbinate to advise them regarding the position of Jewish Law regarding heart transplants in Israel. For this purpose, the Chief Rabbinate appointed a committee of rabbis and physicians to study the halakhic and medical aspects of the question. The committee consulted leading physicians specializing in this field at Hadassah and Shaare Zedek Medical Centers in Jerusalem.
>
> 2. Seventeen years ago, when the first heart transplants were performed abroad, both R. Moshe Feinstein and Chief Rabbi Isser Yehudah Unterman concluded that the procedure constituted a double murder, of both donor and recipient. The last ten years [however,] have seen fundamental factual and medical changes affecting heart transplants as follows:
>
>   a. Approximately 80% of cardiac transplant recipients live to reach *hayyei sha'ah* (surviving at least one year post-transplant) and approximately 70% survive for at least five years.

---

3 N. Moses, *Really Dead? The Israeli Brain-Death Controversy 1967-1986* (np: np, 2011).
4 The translation of the letter from the original Hebrew is adapted from *Assia – Jewish Medical Ethics* 1:2 (1989): 2-10. (The footnotes included in *Assia* are not part of the original document and are not included here.)

    b. There is now an accurate and reliable method to establish that respiration has completely and irreversibly ceased.
    c. We have received evidence that even R. Moshe Feinstein recently permitted a heart transplant in the United States. We also know of other leading rabbis who advise cardiac patients to undergo a transplant.

3. Since heart transplants are matters of life and death, we feel obligated to decide the question of their permissibility in a clear and definitive manner (*bi-behinat yikov ha-din et ha-har*).

4. Relying on principles in the Talmud (*Yoma* 85) and the decision of *Hatam Sofer, Yoreh De'ah*, no. 338, death is halakhically determined by respiratory arrest/failure (*hafsakat ha-neshimah*) (see *Iggerot Mosheh*, YD 3:132). Therefore, [one] must verify that respiration has permanently ceased in an irreversible manner.

    This can be determined by proving the destruction of the entire brain, including the brainstem (*heres ha-mo'ah kulo kolel geza' ha-mo'ah*), which controls (*maf'il*) spontaneous respiration.

5. The medical establishment accepts five conditions for arriving at such a determination (as per paragraph 4):

    a. Clear knowledge of the cause of the [cerebral] injury.
    b. Absolute cessation of natural breathing (*neshimah ha-tiv'it*).
    c. Detailed clinical proof for a destroyed brainstem.
    d. Objective proof for the destruction of the brainstem from scientific testing, such as BAER.
    e. Proof that the absolute cessation of respiration and inactivity of the brainstem is maintained for at least 12 hours, despite complete customary intensive care.

6. After examining the "Recommendation for Establishing Death" as proposed by the physicians of Hadassah Hospital in

Jerusalem on 8 *Tamuz*, 5745 [June 27, 1985] and submitted to the Chief Rabbinate on 5 *Tishrei*, 5747 [October 8, 1986], we find that [the "Recommendation"] could be halakhically acceptable if it will additionally include an objective, scientific examination (BAER) of the brainstem.

7. In light of the above, the Chief Rabbinate of Israel is prepared to permit heart transplants (from accident victims)[5] at Hadassah Medical Center in Jerusalem, under the following conditions:

   a. Fulfillment of all the conditions for determining the death of the donor, as outlined above.
   b. The participation of a representative of the Chief Rabbinate as a full member of the committee that determines the death of the organ donor.
   c. Written consent for donation from the donor or his family.
   d. The establishment of a Review Committee by the Ministry of Health with the participation of the Chief Rabbinate to examine all cases of heart transplants in Israel.
   e. The Ministry of Health will issue regulations in accord with all of the above conditions.

8. Heart transplants are prohibited in Israel until the conditions in paragraph 7 are met.

9. If permission will be granted as per the conditions outlined in paragraph 7, the Chief Rabbinate will [itself] establish a [separate] Review Committee to verify full compliance with these conditions.

Dr. Steinberg records the participants in this committee as the two current Chief Rabbis at the time, R. Avraham Kahana Shapira and R. Mordechai

---

[5] This parenthetical comment appears in the original document.

Eliyahu, as well as R. Shaul Yisraeli, R. Yisrael Meir Lau, R. She'ar Yashuv Cohen, R. David Hayyim Sheloush, and R. Zalman Nehemiah Goldberg; he and Dr. Mordechai Halperin served as medical consultants.[6] As a position statement, it does not include much in the way of halakhic justification other than mentioning Talmud *Yoma* 85a and the famous responsum of *Hatam Sofer* (*YD* 338), as well as advising the reader to see the third of R. Feinstein's responsa regarding determining the moment of death (*Iggerot Mosheh*, *YD* 3:132) without any elaboration or analysis.

To better explain their position, on 23 *Tamuz*, 5747, the "secretariat" of the Chief Rabbinate (*Mazkirut ha-Rabbanut ha-Rashit*) issued the following letter, addressed to "the honorable rabbis in each and every place" (*likhvod ha-rabbanim shlit"a di be-khol atar va-atar*):

> Since there is some confusion regarding the issue of cardiac transplants, which some are unfamiliar with, we are providing an outline, concisely explaining the halakhic sides of the debate, as well as the decision of the Chief Rabbinate, and a medical appendix.
>
> From this, each [person] should understand that there is a singular halakhic problem: [We are discussing] a person whose spontaneous respiration has completely ceased and there is absolutely no chance of [it] returning. The function of the organs, as well as the natural function of the heart, cease within several minutes. The continued heartbeat results only and completely from the ventilator, with no spark of/connection to life (*zik hayyim*)[7] or possibility for [the return of] any spark of/connection to life. The question therefore is whether mechanical ventilation creates (*yotzeret*) [*sic*] life or whether [such a patient] is dead and the machines are merely activating (*maf'ilot*) his muscles alone. All who [previ-

---

6 "The Decision of the Chief Rabbinate of Israel Regarding Cardiac Transplants" (Hebrew) in M. Halperin (ed.), *Kevi'at Rega ha-Mavet*, 2nd edition (Jerusalem: Schlesinger Institute, 2007) (henceforth, *KRhM*), 338-45.

7 The precise meaning of the phrase "*zik hayyim*" is unclear; while "*zikah*" is a "connection," "*zikim*" are sparks. The distinction between the alternative translations does not appear to be significant, however.

ously] discussed this issue did not address this point, but rather wrote simply that the heart still functions and [therefore] is a sign of life. However, as we said above, [under such circumstances,] there is no life nor any sign of life, and everything that they wrote does not address the focal question.

The decision of the Chief Rabbinate is only regarding cardiac transplants and not liver transplants.

This opening letter is quite striking in its presentation of a "singular halakhic problem." The (unnamed) letter writer assumes that since, under natural circumstances, the heart will stop beating a few moments after complete respiratory arrest, any continued heartbeat thereafter – stimulated, induced, or produced by any means – is no longer considered to be part of the heart's "natural function" and therefore halakhically meaningless. The writer is quite dismissive of those who seriously consider the continued heartbeat in their discussions, writing that they fail to understand this basic premise. The real question, argues the writer, is whether mechanical ventilation "creates" (*yotzeret*) life or merely activates/sets into motion the patient's muscles. Overly vague in its terminology, the question is posed is very stark terms. The writer most certainly never entertained the possibility that mechanical ventilation can "create" life – meaning that after a patient becomes apneic, doctors can resurrect the patient by providing oxygen. While possibly metaphorical and most certainly imprecise, this choice of language radicalizes the opposing view almost to the point of ridicule – painting the halakhic landscape with logic and common sense clearly supportive of the writer's position.

The writer also remains somewhat vague as to what he believes to be the role of the ventilator – "activating the muscles," presumably referring to the respiratory muscles. In reality, the ventilator merely provides oxygen at a given pressure or volume, enabling the native pulmonary system to engage in gas exchange; the ventilator neither contacts nor engages the muscles of respiration in any way. The letter writer seems to be trying to distinguish between ventilating a corpse, which does not promote "continued life," and ventilating a "brain dead" patient, where vital functions appear to continue; he suggests that the difference lies in the ventilator's ability to "activate" the muscles of the latter but not of the former. In truth, however, the difference lies in the corpse's inability to participate in gas exchange because of the concomitant lack of circulation. Ironically, it is the continued heartbeat – which the letter writer wishes to dismiss as completely meaningless – that allows the ventilator to have any effect at all in the "brain dead" patient but not in the corpse.

Leaving the actual function of the heart aside – as the letter writer describes its continued role as completely artificial and thus halakhically meaningless – the "real question" he claims, is whether or not the functions of the "other organs" are similarly considered to be artificial, and thus also halakhically meaningless, when supported by mechanical ventilation. While the letter writer does not indicate which "other organs" are under discussion, he presumably is not referring to the lungs, as respiration is one bodily function that all agree is completely artificial and non-intrinsic in a ventilated "brain dead" patient. Having excluded the heart and lungs, the letter writer never indicates which other organ functions are being artificially supported such that the question is even applicable. He is possibly describing the kidneys, liver, or even the pancreas, but there are no halakhic sources predicating continued life or attributions of death to their continued functioning.

Alongside this vague and rather unclear introductory letter, the rest of the document attempts to clarify and provide more detail as to the various "halakhic aspects relevant to the matter of transplants." The following is an adaptation of this appended document:

A.

1. A number of months ago, the Ministry of Health and Hadassah Hospital asked the Chief Rabbinate for a halakhic opinion on organ transplants. The Chief Rabbinate therefore appointed a committee of rabbis and experts to fundamentally deal with this matter, offer their opinions, and make a recommendation on how to proceed. On this committee were rabbis from all denominations who agreed to participate. The Chief Rabbis also asked several older, esteemed rabbis

of Jerusalem to investigate the matter and the experts on the committee visited with them as well…⁸

2. A position that is accepted by all is that death is only determined upon the cessation of spontaneous respiration, as explained in *Yoma* 85a that [when searching for] a person upon whom an avalanche fell, one checks until the *hotem*, [and if] no breath is found, then the victim is certainly dead. As determined by *Hatam Sofer*, this is considered a *halakhah le-Mosheh mi-Sinai* that is rooted in Scripture, [based on the verse] "*nishmat ru'ah hayyim be-appav*." However, while mechanically ventilated, we cannot determine whether continued respiration is [considered to be] artificial and not spontaneous/independent as granted by the Creator and therefore similar to ventilating a corpse or whether there is also some spontaneous/independent respiration and therefore [still some] spark of/connection to life, meaning that the patient is still alive.

Hadassah Hospital provided the Chief Rabbinate with documents detailing the examination of a patient who is a potential organ donor, [including] a requirement to stop mechanical ventilation for five minutes so as to determine during that time whether the patient is capable of spontaneous respiration or not, in which case he is considered to be dead. This is how it was always determined, although in our times, with the option for artificial respiration through mechanical ventilation, there is room to wonder that perhaps the ventilation will help the patient regain spontaneous respiration. However, if this examination is performed twice with at least a 12 hour interval between exams, this is proof that the brainstem is destroyed and the brain can no longer activate (*le-haf'il*) the spontaneous/independent respiration of

---

8 The document goes on to describe how the invitations were sent, the history of who was asked to participate, and other details of historical record – not overly relevant for our purposes.

the heart [*sic*] (*ha-neshimah ha-atzmit shel ha-lev*). Any ability to continue to breathe after this point is completely ventilator dependent and not considered respiration [granted] by the power of the Creator. Such a person does not have, nor will he ever have, the ability for spontaneous respiration. It is therefore clear that the lack of respiration during those five minutes was complete and the patient no longer has any spark of/connection to life as granted to him by his Creator.

In addition to the accepted examinations done at Hadassah Hospital, we also required performing a new test called BEAR [*sic*], which can verify the death of the "brainstem." We heard testimony from God-fearing physicians who stated that the test is new and can be completely relied upon if adhering to the other conditions set forth by Hadassah Hospital.

Since the exam is only performed in such patients, [meaning] accident victims who are potential cardiac donors, regarding all other ventilated patients where there is some doubt as to whether or not they still maintain spontaneous/independent respiration, this test is not performed. Therefore, these [latter] patients are considered alive for all matters and their physicians should be confident in treating them as such.

This is not true regarding a patient upon whom such an exam was performed and it was proven that there is no chance for spontaneous respiration and therefore is considered dead according to Halakhah. Death is determined by the cessation of respiration and not the destruction of the brain, [although] the destruction of the brain proves that the patient can no longer breathe spontaneously. Of course, stopping the ventilator must be done in a halakhically acceptable manner.

Anyone who has not seen nor analyzed the documents provided by Hadassah Hospital as well as the additional document written by an important physiologist regarding the BEAR exam cannot accurately arrive at proper conclusions on this matter. Such a person may even come to think that the issue is dependent on the disagreement between Rambam and Aristotle regarding the brain and the heart or to confuse this with regular clinical death (*mavet kelini stam*) and not understand that such a patient is halakhically proven to be dead.

Iggerot Mosheh, YD 3:132 deals with determining the moment of death. After explaining that death should be determined by a negative respiratory exam and that this is an accurate and reliable indicator of death, he writes, "Since you tell me that now it is possible to inject a substance intravenously [nuclide scan test] to determine that the connection between the brain and the body has been interrupted – if the [radioisotope] does not appear in the brain it is clear that the brain no longer maintains any connection to the body and the brain has already completely rotted (*she-kevar nirkav ha-mo'ah le-gamrei*) and is [comparable to] forceful decapitation."

We are dealing with a case of the destruction of the brainstem, which is comparable to decapitation and the absolute cessation of spontaneous/independent respiration. The exam was performed twice with an intervening 12 hour period prior to the transplant, in a person who, even if alive, would have been halakhically considered to be a *tereifah*. Therefore, there is no doubt that such a person is considered to be dead and his continued existence (*kiyumo*) is entirely artificial and is not considered to be a living person, since once a person has lost the *nishmat ru'ah hayyim* granted to him by the Creator, it cannot be returned to him by human means.

With regard to the transplant recipient, today we know that more than 80% survive for at least one year and approximately 70% survive five years or more, all of whom, had they not received the transplant, would have died within a few months. Previous decisors have ruled that it is appropriate to undergo surgery even when there is some concern that it may not be successful and that it may possibly be life-ending, as per *Ahi'ezer* 2:16.

Some have argued that through the transplant, the recipient is rendered a *tereifah* since a vital organ was removed. However, since an organ was replaced that fulfills the same function, the recipient is not considered to be a *tereifah*.

We also have the testimony of R. Moshe Feinstein's grandchildren and son-in-law that with the continued advances in preventing organ rejection and discovery of the destruction of the brainstem, R. Feinstein advised questioners to proceed with cardiac transplant procedures.

Here in Israel as well, *tzedakah* collections have been held with the approbation of important rabbis, including those from circles that forbid organ donation, to assist potential recipients to travel outside of Israel so as to find suitable organ donors. If this is considered to be a double murder, how can there be a mitzvah to travel abroad in order to be killed? We have also not heard that there is a mitzvah to raise money for the murder of the donor.

Most of the potential donors are accident victims and are considered to be *tereifot* before they die. However, since the matter is one of life and death, we cannot permit going ahead with a transplant without the approval of a representative of the Chief Rabbinate who knows Halakhah as a participant in the medical committee responsible for overseeing such surgeries. Without the participation of such a representative, the Chief Rabbinate cannot approve permitting such surgeries.

B.

The decision of the Chief Rabbinate relied upon documents provided by Hadassah Hospital regarding their proposed protocols for heart transplants and various medical tests, as well as an additional document by a famous, God-fearing physiologist. Whoever did not read or analyze them cannot issue a proper decision that appropriately relates to reality and may come to think that what is being discussed is "standard" clinical death or perhaps the situation of a *goses*, whereas we are discussing someone considered halakhically dead.

There are several medical principles necessary to determine the Halakhah and they were explained to us by expert physicians who are also Torah scholars and include the following:

1. The destruction of the brainstem causes the cessation of spontaneous/independent respiration.
2. Cessation of spontaneous/independent respiration causes, within a few minutes, the cessation of life functions in the heart (*pe'ilut hayyim ba-lev*) and all other organs, and such a person is considered dead.
3. As long as the brainstem is intact, it is possible that ventilation will help bring about a [respiratory] recovery and the return of spontaneous/independent respiration.
4. In a patient in whom it has been determined that his brainstem is destroyed, it is not possible for mechanical ventilation to ever bring about recovery or the return of spontaneous/independent respiration, and there are no known cases of this happening in the medical world. As a rule, with the cessation of mechanical ventilation, the patient remains dead.
5. Once spontaneous/independent respiration granted by the Creator has ceased, artificial respiration through machines cannot transform a dead man into a live one, and everything [that takes place in his body] is simply the [result of the] actions of the machine.

This determination was also approved in a committee of more than 30 senior staff members of Hadassah Hospital in Jerusalem, and we were not presented with the names of any reputable physician who disagrees. Therefore, if the examination was performed under the guidance of a rabbi or physician who is a Torah scholar and is worthy of rendering a halakhic opinion and after 12 hours the test was repeated, [proving] that the patient's spontaneous/independent respiration has ceased already for some while – as a result, the patient's independent life (*hayyim atzmiyyim*) has also ceased. If there remain any bodily movements at all, they are entirely those of the machines and not of a living person.

All of this is in accordance with that which R. Moshe Feinstein *zt"l* ruled on similar matters, that the destruction of the brainstem is comparable to decapitation. Therefore, since the aforementioned tests prove that the patient's respiration has ceased, they are practical proof for that which Halakhah describes as indications of death.

Summary of conclusions:

1. During the course of the test, the ventilator is stopped/removed for at least five minutes, so as to ascertain that the patient can no longer breathe on his own, which is the main indication of human life (*ikkar siman ha-hayyim shel ha-adam*).
2. Destruction of the brainstem will be determined by special clinical and physiological tests and will therefore also determine that the first proven cessation of spontaneous/independent respiration was absolute and is not subject to recovery, as explained in *Yoma* and *Hatam Sofer*.
3. As mentioned in *Iggerot Mosheh* 3, a destroyed brainstem is comparable to decapitation.
4. The entire protocol of examinations will be performed twice over the span of 12 hours, only after which will a transplant be permitted.
5. After these 12 hours, it is clear that this patient no longer has any independent life granted by the Creator but everything is instead the actions of the machines; these machines cannot grant life to a person from whom the Creator has already taken it. From a medical perspective, [to maintain the patient as a potential organ donor] it is sufficient that the heart not begin to rot and the "machine-dependent heartbeat" is enough to prevent this. However, from a halakhic perspective, what is important is whether such a person has independent life and respiration or whether his life has already ended.
6. A potential cardiac donor is considered to be a *tereifah*, even before his death.
7. With regard to the recipient, since we now know that the chance of surviving for at least a year is about 80%, from a

halakhic perspective, we are required to enable him to have this surgery, since without it, it is clear that he will die within a few months – meaning only if he stands no chance now of surviving a year or more, as per *Ahi'ezer* 2.

As is evident from all of the aforementioned information, it is clear that there is no complicated halakhic question that requires rigorous analysis of the Talmud and its commentaries, but rather the matter is in fact quite simple.

Whether the fundamental indication of death is cessation of respiration [and] the other two indications mentioned by *Hatam Sofer* – namely, bodily movements and heartbeat – are not absolutely necessary, or even if all three indications are necessary for such a determination, it is clear that they are all interdependent. Cessation of respiration causes the heartbeat to stop in a matter of moments, and thus the termination of bodily movements as well. Maybe this is the reason that *Yoma* relies on cessation of respiration in determining the death of an avalanche victim, or perhaps for other reasons. Regardless, once respiration has ceased, everything else will stop in a matter of moments.

Accordingly, from the times of *Hazal* until recently, before mechanical ventilators were introduced, once breathing stopped, even if only temporarily, without the assistance of mechanical ventilation, even if some spark of/connection to life remained (*adayyin hayah zik hayyim ba-adam*), it would certainly disappear rather quickly. The advent of mechanical respiration when applied to a patient whose loss of respiration was only temporary and still retained a spark of/connection to life allowed for the return of spontaneous respiration and the concomitant awakening of that very spark of/connection to life.

However, when the brainstem is found to be destroyed through an examination for 12 hours and stopping the ventilator for 15 [*sic*] minutes and there is therefore no hope for the return of spontaneous respiration – since, without a [functioning] brainstem, respirations will stop within a couple of minutes, and without mechanical ventilation, the other signs of life will also shortly cease as well, what appears to be a continued heartbeat is only a result of the machine blowing air into the patient. Since there is no hope for the return of spontaneous respiration, it is clear that there is no longer any possibility for retaining any spark of/ connection to life, which is completely dependent upon natural respiration as granted by God and not the product of machines. Therefore, we do not see any natural sign of any of the three indications enumerated by *Hatam Sofer*, and the patient is considered dead, since the machines are activating his lungs without any chance that spontaneous respiration, and therefore life, will return.

Regarding the other issue that the recipient is rendered a *tereifah* when his natural heart is removed and this should be forbidden – since we see that the transplanted heart assumes the role of the natural heart, thus "healing" the recipient, there is no prohibition at all. Rather, through the transplant, the patient become healthier and certainly not a *tereifah*.

Analysis

The polemical tone of this document and its downplaying of the most controversial elements of the decision are quite troubling. It attempts to preempt any criticism by noting that "it is clear that there is no complicated halakhic question that requires rigorous analysis of the Talmud and its commentaries, but rather the matter is in fact quite simple." As should be obvious from our discussion until this point (and evident from the fact that this letter was necessary in the first place), the issue is a far cry from "quite simple." Indeed, what led to this conclusion was likely the strong, rather one-sided approach and argument offered.

The main difference between the letter writer's approach and that of almost every other authority is what they view the actual problem to be. All others (spanning the entire spectrum of opinions) understand the question to be one of a patient with a continued heartbeat in the face of irreversible cessation of spontaneous respiration (ICSR). While mechanical ventilation provides for continued tissue oxygenation, including that of the cardiac muscle, it is not the mechanical respiration *per se* that "activates" the heart, but rather the inherent ability of the heart to continue to function without any neurological input. The letter writer paints the landscape much differently. He is only interested in "whether mechanical ventilation creates (*yotzeret*) life or whether [such a patient] is dead and the machines are merely activating (*maf'ilot*) his muscles alone" – having already dismissed any and all other indications of continued life as halakhically meaningless. He assumes that the real focus of the discussion is how one should halakhically view breathing while on a ventilator.

Admitting that others have focused and analyzed very different aspects of this question, the writer claims that "[a]nyone who has not seen nor analyzed the documents provided by Hadassah Hospital… cannot accurately arrive at proper conclusions on this matter. Such a person may even come to think that the issue is dependent on the disagreement between Rambam and Aristotle regarding the brain and the heart." In other words, other authorities erred in assuming that the real problem is one of continued heartbeat in the face of ICSR; in reality, the "singular halakhic question" is whether or not mechanical ventilation halakhically constitutes breathing.

This question itself is rather difficult to understand, and defending this position is far more challenging than the letter writer lets on. The letter writer takes for granted that all agree that death should be determined solely by ICSR even in the face of continued cardiac function. Merely referencing the discussion in Talmud *Yoma* 85a, the letter writer interprets that discussion as dealing exclusively with **criteria** for death, arguing that the Talmud concludes firmly in favor of respiratory criteria alone and citing *Hatam Sofer*'s responsum in defense of this thesis. Only later in the letter does the writer address *Hatam Sofer*'s inclusion of unresponsiveness and lack of heartbeat, ultimately dismissing these concerns as irrelevant to the current medical reality. The writer's only interest is therefore whether or not mechanical ventilation halakhically qualifies as breathing, as this is the only way he conceives to describe the patient as alive. He takes great pains to establish that in the context of ICSR, mechanical ventilation is not considered halakhically meaningful breathing, as opposed to other situations in which it is implemented to help a patient make it through some period until such time that he can recover respiratory function.

The letter writer accurately notes that after ICSR and **without** medical intervention, the heart can only continue to beat for a very short while. Powered by the remaining oxygen previously inhaled and without a new oxygen source, the heart muscle stops pumping once this supply is depleted; the letter writer describes the heartbeat during these moments as "natural." Once these moments have passed, the letter writer considers the patient dead, as he deems any subsequent motion, movement, or function as "artificially induced" and of no halakhic import. This is true, he claims, not only of continued "breathing" – which is completely mechanically (ventilator) dependent – but also of the continued heartbeat, since it is no longer "activated" by spontaneous respiration, but rather by mechanical ventilation. The letter writer argues that **even if** an absent heartbeat is necessary for determining death, this only refers to a "natural" heartbeat; once the few moments after ICSR have passed, any continued heartbeat is meaningless, as it is "unnatural." Despite what by all accounts appears to be a normal beating heart, the letter writer asserts that such a patient is considered dead also by virtue of the cessation of his "natural" cardiac activity. Nevertheless, while most authorities indeed agree in discounting mechanical ventilation as meaningful respiration, they nonetheless argue with the letter writer's conclusions.

In repeatedly insisting on ascertaining that the inability to breathe spontaneously is in fact irreversible, the letter writer never addresses the same question vis-à-vis the heart. He views the claim that the continuing heartbeat should be considered "natural" as tantamount to saying the same thing about continued respiration through mechanical ventilation, an argument that he strongly rejects. Most authorities, however, note an important physiological difference between respiration and heartbeat

– respiration requires neurological input for its continued activity, while the heartbeat does not. It is for this reason that brainstem dysfunction or "death" causes respiratory failure; without a neurological impulse (originating in the brainstem) to stimulate the respiratory muscles to contract, respiration is not possible. Mechanical ventilation can substitute for respiration by providing oxygenated air at a given pressure or volume and delivering it to the lungs' alveoli. Ventilation works because, unlike a corpse, "brain dead" patients still participate in gas exchange, extracting oxygen from the air into the blood stream and excreting carbon dioxide as waste. This gas exchange continues because the heart continues beating, enabling the circulation necessary for gas exchange to occur. Thus, in a ventilated patient, the heart continues to beat the same way after spontaneous respiration has irreversibly ceased as it did prior to that moment.

The letter writer, however, introduces an entirely new concept of a "naturally activated heartbeat" – one that functions solely as a result of spontaneous respiration – even at one point referring to "the spontaneous respirations of the heart." He argues that a heartbeat is only halakhically recognizable as an indication of life when it is powered by oxygen derived from spontaneous respiration. Practically, however, the source of oxygen used to "power" the heart is irrelevant for its continuing function as the circulatory center of the body; whether respiration is spontaneous or mechanical makes no difference with regard to the heartbeat. In fact, the letter writer does not explain or elaborate why the source of the oxygen should determine the status of the heartbeat. He does repeatedly note that the ventilator "activates" (*maf'il*) the lungs; although the concept does not appear to have a physiological correlate, he may have extended this same notion to the heartbeat as well. Almost all other halakhic decisors, even if not addressing the point directly, implicitly reject the letter writer's basic premise – accepting the continued function of the heart as meaningful, even if debating its halakhic significance.

There are several other difficulties in understanding this letter.[9] In describing the protocol for determining "brain death," the letter writer

---

9 There are several typographical errors in the original document that might mistakenly be read as having far-reaching implications, but are almost certainly unintentional. The letter writer likely meant to describe an apnea test performed for five minutes, as

details an apnea test, an examination intended to diagnose the existence of spontaneous respiration or lack thereof. He repeatedly asserts that the reason for the inability to breathe spontaneously is the destruction (*heres*) of the brainstem, which normally controls (involuntary) breathing. This is somewhat inaccurate, however; the apnea test only proves **dysfunction** of the brainstem, not necessarily **destruction**, the critical difference being that the former is possibly amenable to reversibility while the latter is not. The letter writer seems to accept that proof of brainstem dysfunction is sufficient while the Chief Rabbinate itself, in accepting this position in its original statement, required performing an additional study to "prove" the **destruction** of the brainstem, referring explicitly to the BAER exam[10] and later, when revisiting the issue in 2009, expanding this to include four additional tests.[11] The Chief Rabbinate is uncomfortable relying exclusively on two randomly timed apnea tests as sufficient evidence for the destruction of the brainstem, and thus effective permission for organ procurement.

The letter deviates from the Chief Rabbinate's position on other matters as well. The original proclamation of the Chief Rabbinate refers to the destruction of the **entire** brain as indicative of death. The letter writer omits this; in fact, this turns out to have been appropriate, since it is now known to be inaccurate.

---

in the original document, and not fifteen minutes. Similarly, the language of "spontaneous respirations of the heart" likely refers to cardiac muscular contractions and not to some unknown physiological function. Lastly, the letter refers to the BEAR exam (using Latin characters), which is more commonly referred to as BAER, but certainly refers to the same exam.

10 The BAER exam (brainstem auditory evoked responses) aims at detecting brainstem function via sound waves, examining the neurological response of the brainstem to a stimulus, with a negative test indicative of a neurologically dysfunctional brainstem. Just as the brain can no longer neurologically respond to auditory stimuli, it almost certainly can no longer control respiration. While the classic EEG can only register electrical activity in the most superficial areas of the cerebral cortex, the BAER exam (and sensory evoked potentials exam) can more accurately assess the functioning of deeper structures.

11 "The Decision of the Israeli Chief Rabbinate from *Tishrei* 5770" (Hebrew), *Assia* 87-88 (2010): 96-99.

Searching for support from other rabbinic figures, the letter writer refers to R. Feinstein's third responsum on the topic (*Iggerot Mosheh*, YD 3:132), which was translated, analyzed, and discussed in detail in chapter 12. As is evident from our discussion there, drawing a direct parallel between that responsum and the topic of this letter is not quite as simple as the letter writer implies.

In broadening his search, the letter writer notes that unnamed "important rabbis, including those from circles that forbid organ donation," helped arrange collections to assist patients in affording transplant procedures outside of Israel. The letter writer asserts this as incontrovertible evidence that even these rabbis, in their heart of hearts, really believe "brain death" to be halakhically meaningful. The Chief Rabbinate's original letter also makes mention of R. Feinstein permitting receiving a heart transplant, which is taken as evidence that R. Feinstein ultimately recognized "brain death" as the death of the individual.

This point, however, is far from certain and ventures into realms that are not the focus of this book; it is more a question of public policy and understanding the role of different voices within the halakhic world than understanding the halakhic approach to death. Even one who opposes viewing "brain death" as halakhically meaningful may recognize another person's right to do just that, especially if that other person is not bound by the strictures of Halakhah. This issue has far reaching public policy, ethical, moral, and political factors and implications, and as such will not be dealt with in this context. However, clear proof for the letter writer's position it is certainly not.

Some other technical difficulties are also apparent in this letter. The letter ends by limiting the Chief Rabbinate's permissive ruling to cardiac and not liver transplants, but does not provide any basis or explanation for this distinction. From a medical perspective, both organs are recovered from patients diagnosed as "brain dead," the diagnosis of which should not change depending on the organ to be explanted. Dr. Mordechai Halperin suggests that the limitation was implemented so as to prevent things from "getting out of hand," requiring re-consulting the Chief Rabbinate for any proposed expansion of current protocol.[12]

---

12 M. Halperin, A. Bush, "Responsa on the Matter of the Decision of the Chief Rabbinate Regarding Cardiac Transplants from 1 *Marheshvan*, 5747" (Hebrew), *Assia*

An additional point of difficulty is the letter writer's insistence that "stopping the ventilator must be done in a halakhically acceptable manner," without elaborating what qualifies as such. Given the vast rabbinic literature on disconnecting and stopping ventilators, this requirement without any explanation is neither instructive nor helpful. Moreover, the entire apnea exam itself is potentially problematic since it is not done for the benefit of the patient, but rather for the potential recipient.[13]

87-88 (2010): 83. This exchange is in response to a question posed to former Sephardic Chief Rabbi Mordechai Eliyahu, who asked Dr. Halperin to respond on his behalf.

13 Some safeguards are included in the exam in requiring 5-15 minutes of pre-oxygenation so as to limit hypoxia (deprivation of oxygen) during the five minutes in which the ventilator is disconnected, limiting potential harm to the patient. From a medical perspective, when appropriately pre-oxygenated prior to the exam, the apnea test has few complications. In a review of 212 clinically "brain dead" patients (E.F.M. Wijdicks, A.A. Rabinstein, E.M. Manno, et al., "Pronouncing brain death: Contemporary practice and safety of the apnea test," *Neurology* 71 (2008): 1240-4), the test was aborted in only 3% of patients, who when disconnected from the ventilator suffered from progressive hypotension (low blood pressure) or hypoxemia (low blood oxygenation); even in these patients, the complications occurred very shortly after disconnecting the ventilator and completely resolved with its reconnection. 7% of patients were deemed inappropriate candidates for an apnea test, mostly due to unstable blood pressure. Importantly, cardiac arrest or pneumothorax (air entering the chest cavity) was not observed in any of the patients in this series. Thus, when screened appropriately and when proper safety measures are employed, including pre-oxygenation and continuous blood pressure and pulse oximetry monitoring during the test, the apnea test carries little risk to the patient.

As noted previously, when disconnecting the ventilator, the endotracheal tube is not removed from the patient's throat; to further protect the patient, even when disconnected, oxygen continues to flow past the open end of the tube, so that should the patient initiate a breath, it will be more oxygen rich. Nevertheless, there are some potential problems. Since the endotracheal tube remains in place, the effective diameter of the trachea is diminished, and should the patient indeed initiate a breath, he would be required to generate a larger pressure gradient between his lungs and the atmosphere than were the tube removed completely. The tube cannot be removed, however, since the ventilator will ultimately be reconnected – even if negative, the results of the apnea test will not be known for several minutes, and in that period, the patient remains ventilated pending a possible positive test – and extubation and ultimate re-intubation would cause seemingly unnecessary trauma.

Additionally, as noted in the protocols provided by Hadassah Medical Center, the patient is monitored for breathing by direct observation as well as by measuring the partial pressure of carbon dioxide in the blood, searching for an uncompensated elevation.

The claim that the exam benefits the potential donor in that it can prove that he is still alive and therefore requires continuing medical care is not compelling; whatever medical care is available can be given even without the test. Were it not for the potential recipient awaiting the organ, it is highly unlikely that an apnea test would ever be performed.

The Chief Rabbinate's position statement makes clear, and the letter is quick to mention, that the donor pool is limited to "accident victims" alone. While only appearing in a parenthetical comment, the official position statement allows donation **only** from such patients; the letter writer writes, somewhat differently, only that "**most** of the potential donors are accident victims" [emphasis added] and that such a victim is considered a *tereifah*. Neither document elaborates as to the need for this limitation, but it appears to be an attempt to appeal to a wider base for leniency. While normative halakhic authorities throughout the generations have rejected this notion, a minority opinion exists that may allow sacrificing the life of a *tereifah* to save a potentially salvageable person (see chapter 1). This limitation should thus be viewed as a "back-up" plan; according to this minority opinion, even if the conclusion about "brain death" is incorrect, donating organs from a *tereifah* (thereby killing him) may be permissible even if he is alive.

Dr. Mordechai Halperin indeed suggests that while fully confident of the veracity of their approach, the Chief Rabbinate required this additional factor in order to garner support from even those opposed to their broader perspective.[14] As the ruling stood, however, only "brain dead" *tereifot* were deemed eligible organ donors, without caveat or stipulation. Neither Dr. Halperin nor other commentators address the discrepancy

---

Obtaining accurate blood-gas measurements requires collecting arterial blood. Many ICU patients have arterial lines in place already, intended to more accurately report blood pressure fluctuations, which may also be used to collect arterial blood; today, almost all "brain dead" patients fall into this category. Without an arterial line, however, collecting arterial blood requires an arterial puncture, usually at the wrist; this procedure is excruciatingly painful and should be forbidden when not done, in full faith, for the benefit of the patient himself. The letter writer makes no comment about this aspect of the test, assuming it to be always permissible.

14 "The Legal Ramifications of the Chief Rabbinate's Decision" (Hebrew) in *KRhM*, 328-31.

between the Chief Rabbinate's original position statement and the fact that now, with the passage of the Israeli "Brain and Respiratory Death Law – 2008," the requirement that potential donors specifically be accident victims has been dropped.

The Chief Rabbis

R. Avraham Kahana Shapira, the Ashkenazi Chief Rabbi, and R. Mordechai Eliyahu, the *Rishon le-Tziyon* and Sephardic Chief Rabbi, each separately penned their own defenses of the position published on their behalf. In a short reaction to the entire debate, R. Shapira reiterates the approach of the aforementioned letter writer in adopting the notion of the "natural function of the heart" (*yekholet ha-pe'ulah ha-tiv'it shel ha-lev*) as that whose energy source derives from oxygen inhaled only through spontaneous respiration.[15] R. Eliyahu largely agrees with this approach, although he presents it as one of several possible ways to understand the issue and does not provide proof or evidence for choosing this over any other understanding.[16]

R. Shapira responds to several other points, including the safety and permissibility of the apnea test and his interpretation of Talmud *Erkhin* 7a, discussed in chapter 5. R. Eliyahu relates to the issue of "brain death" as part of a larger essay about many "end of life" matters in Halakhah, culling and detailing the many different approaches on each of these issues. In this context, he analyzes Talmud *Yoma* 85a, offering two approaches to understanding respiratory cessation in the face of a continued heartbeat – whether it should qualify as an indication of continued life or not – without concluding either way.

The subsequent Ashkenazi Chief Rabbi, R. Yisrael Meir Lau, an original member of the committee appointed by the Chief Rabbinate, also published his views on the matter (discussed shortly), while R. Bakshi Doron, the *Rishon le-Tziyon* after R. Mordechai Eliyahu, has not made any public remarks on the matter.

---

15 "Determining Death According to Halakhah" (Hebrew) in *KRhM*, 247-9.
16 "Organ Transplantation According to Halakhah" (Hebrew), *Barkai* 4 (5747): 18-31.

R. Shelomoh Moshe Amar, the next *Rishon le-Tziyon*, changed course somewhat in attempting to incorporate the Chief Rabbinate's original position as part of the actual law of the land. For a variety of technical, political, and other reasons, although originally published in 1987, the Chief Rabbinate's position and recommendations were not incorporated into Israeli law until the passage of the "Brain and Respiratory Death Law – 2008."[17] Taking effect on June 1, 2009, the Chief Rabbinate endorsed the law several months later (4 *Tishrei*, 5770), with R. Amar requesting that their endorsement not reflect any stance on organ donation, but only on time of death.[18] Given the time gap and concurrent scientific advances since the publication of the Chief Rabbinate's original position, when it finally became law in 2009, it included additional imaging modalities, in addition to BAER, to further ascertain the destruction of the brainstem, keeping in step with the medical world. In publically supporting the bill that ultimately became law, R. Amar issued a proclamation on behalf of himself and his mentor, R. Ovadiah Yosef, that "brain death" is considered halakhic death due to ICSR and destruction of the entire brain,[19] a position that R. Yosef would later clarify and amend.[20]

In a lengthy responsum to R. Hershel Schachter (to be published in his upcoming *Responsa Shema Shelomoh* 7), R. Amar surveys the relevant halakhic literature and disagrees with R. Schachter's analysis (described in chapter 19). The latter half of this responsum articulates his own approach to understanding "brain death," supporting a comparison between "brain death" and decapitation. In explaining his stance more clearly during a lecture at Yeshivat Hazon Ovadiah, R. Amar explained that the complete destruction of the entire brain is parallel to decapitation, as described in Mishnah *Ohalot*, largely echoing the position of R. Shelomoh Zalman

---

17 For further discussion, see *Really Dead?*, 287-93.
18 "The Decision of the Israeli Chief Rabbinate from *Tishrei*, 5770," 98.
19 Printed in *Assia* 87-88 (2010): 78.
20 See A. Steinberg, "Brain and Respiratory Death Law – The Opinion of R. Ovadiah Yosef" (Hebrew), *Assia* 87-88 (2010): 77, for an excerpt from a discussion with R. Yosef on the matter. According to R. Yosef's grandson, R. Yaakov Sasson, with whom R. Yosef has held extensive discussions on the topic, both the particular language and the overall context of Dr. Steinberg's article are rather confusing and do not provide a coherent understanding of R. Yosef's approach.

Auerbach (discussed in chapter 16). While advocating relying upon respiratory criteria alone, he notes that a beating heart would appear to preclude a determination of death. Countering Rabbis Shapira and Eliyahu's dismissal of a continuously beating heart in a patient irreversibly incapable of spontaneous respiration, R. Amar argues that the heart's inherent ability to continue to function regardless of the respiratory status of the patient certainly indicates continued life; the source of the oxygen from which energy is ultimately derived to maintain the active pumping – whether from spontaneous or mechanical ventilation – is not a factor. R. Amar contends, however, that the entire question is largely irrelevant, since, in his opinion, even with a beating heart, a decapitated person – and in parallel fashion, one suffering from "brain death" – is considered dead by definition, regardless of anything else happening in his body.

During the course of his lecture, R. Amar frequently repeats the assertion that clinically diagnosed "brain death" is comparable to "total brain liquefaction," meaning the complete destruction of each and every brain cell. Himself not a physician, he attests that this was the information that he and R. Yosef were provided with. As mentioned previously, this does not reflect the accurate medical reality. Despite his and R. Yosef's early endorsement of the new law aimed at incorporating the updated guidelines from the Chief Rabbinate, R. Amar clarified that neither he nor R. Yosef ever intended to discuss organ donation; the only implication that they intended was that once a patient reaches such a state, it is permissible to withdraw any and all treatment if the patient's family so chooses.[21]

---

21 One difference between the two procedures is that withdrawing therapy can, and according to many must, be done through passive means alone; even when the patient dies as a result, the action cannot be directly attributed to the one who passively discontinued or did not renew whatever medical intervention was keeping the patient alive. Organ procurement, however, entails actively ending the life of the donor. While not providing an explanation for his hesitancy in allowing organ donation, since originally endorsing the new law, he learned that even when diagnosed as "brain dead," the patient's entire brain is most certainly not completely destroyed or liquefied. See also chapter 1, n.14.

Neither allows or instructs questioners to permit or facilitate organ donation as already noted in chapter 1.[22]

R. Shaul Yisraeli, an original member of the committee appointed by the Chief Rabbinate to analyze the issue, also published a defense of the Chief Rabbinate's position, providing what he calls "The Principles Underlying the Chief Rabbinate's Decision."[23] He analyzes R. Moshe Feinstein's various responsa, arguing that R. Feinstein ultimately accepted "brain death" as halakhically meaningful based on respiratory criteria alone. R. Yisraeli's various interpretations of R. Feinstein's positions were discussed earlier (chapters 10 and 11).[24] Further supporting his position, R. Yisraeli opts for interpreting Talmud *Yoma* 85a as specifically debating the **criteria** for death, with the Talmud clearly advocating for determining death based on respiratory criteria alone, regardless of any other continued bodily functions. As noted, this view represents one of several possibilities in interpreting the Talmud, as discussed in chapter 5. Additionally, in relying solely on a respiratory determination, the problem of conscious non-breathing patients (noted in chapter 14 and discussed extensively in chapter 18) looms large, without any indication of how R. Yisraeli would view such a case.

In analyzing *Hatam Sofer*'s opinion, R. Yisraeli focuses on *Hatam Sofer*'s insistence on relying on respiration alone and even reads *Hatam Sofer*'s concluding summary statement, in which *Hatam Sofer* includes cardiac criteria, as supportive of the overall position. As discussed earlier (chapter 9), R. Yisraeli reads *Hatam Sofer*'s claim that "any person who lies [still] like a stone (*munah ke-even domem*) and has no heartbeat (*defikah*)

---

22 This was attested to numerous times by R. Yosef's grandson, R. Yaakov Sasson (in several private communications), who has made it quite clear that R. Yosef absolutely forbids organ transplants and has instructed families to not allow organ harvesting from their relatives.

23 *KRhM*, 299-309

24 From a historical perspective, it is interesting to note the influence of R. Feinstein's responsa on future discussions of "brain death" in Halakhah. For further reading, see "Responsa on the Matter of the Decision of the Chief Rabbinate," 84, for the understanding of Dr. Halperin (a member of the original Chief Rabbinate's committee) of the relationship of R. Feinstein's opinion to the Chief Rabbinate's decision. See also *Really Dead?*, 236-41.

[possibly pulse], and then ceases to breathe" as chronologically specific. He explains *Hatam Sofer* to mean that if a person is lying still and has no heartbeat, he is still considered alive, since the true (i.e., respiratory) criteria for death have not (necessarily) been met; only when the patient is found to be irreversibly apneic is he halakhically determined to be dead. This is a highly questionable proposition, since breathing is not possible without a heartbeat. It is not likely that *Hatam Sofer* parsed his words so precisely so as to preclude something that is physiologically impossible.

R. Yisrael Meir Lau, upon assuming the mantle of Ashkenazi Chief Rabbi after R. Shapira, penned his own defense on the matter.[25] In surveying the vast literature on the topic, including Talmudic and recent discussions, R. Lau gives much weight to *Gra*'s commentary to Mishnah *Ohalot* 1:6. In the course of distinguishing between two types of moribund people (a *meguyyad* and a *goses*), R. Lau argues that *Gra* offers two indications of life – the potential to continue living and cognitive lucidity/consciousness (*da'ato tzelulah*) – and the existence of even one of the pair is sufficient for defining life. A patient lacking both qualities – who can certainly not live any longer (*eino yakhol od lihyot*) and who is no longer lucid – is dead. What R. Lau seems to be suggesting is that even before meeting the traditional definition of death, Halakhah considers an unconscious person who is imminently dying to be already dead. R. Lau argues that this is what the Mishnah intended when describing decapitation and is in fact consistent with the modern medical diagnosis of "brain death."

Noting that many disagree with this approach,[26] R. Lau is somewhat hesitant in applying this novel understanding to actual practice. In addition, his approach fails to address a key concern regarding the status of a "brain dead" patient. Before determining that a given patient is imminently dying, one must propose a definition, or at least criteria, for that upcoming death, which R. Lau does not. Thus, while he can read *Gra*'s description of "a person who can certainly not live any longer" as referring to an imminently dying person, this does little in elucidating the point

---

25 *Responsa Yahel Yisrael* 2:85-86; originally published as "Determining the Moment of Death" (Hebrew), *Assia* 53-54 (1994): 32-47.
26 See *Sidrei Taharot*, *Ohalot* 16a.

in time at which this becomes relevant. If life is identified by continued cardiac function, then there is no room for the blanket statement that "brain dead" patients are all imminently dying without adopting a more expansive definition of "imminence;" "brain dead" patients can continue living for days or even months. Additionally, R. Lau's approach is not the only possible interpretation of *Gra*'s comments (as discussed in chapter 17). It is difficult to rely solely on a contested interpretation of an admittedly difficult comment on a life and death issue.

The Rabbinate and the Law

While adopting a position advocating the halakhic acceptance and recognition of "brain death," the additional BAER exam required by the Chief Rabbinate was not incorporated into Israeli law until 2008. The "Brain and Respiratory Death Law – 2008," adopted by the Israeli Knesset on 17 *Adar II*, 5768 (March 24, 2008),[27] conditions the acceptance of "brain death" as death in accordance with the protocols set forth by the general director of the Health Ministry and upon the fulfillment of the following requirements:

1. There is a clear and known medical explanation for the cessation of cerebral activity.
2. There is clinical proof for the absolute cessation of spontaneous respiration.
3. There is clinical proof for the complete and irreversible cessation of brain function (*hafsakah melei'ah u-bilti hafikhah shel tifkud ha-mo'ah*), including brainstem function.
4. There is medical instrument-based evidence (*bedikah makhshiranit*) for the complete and irreversible cessation of brain function, including brainstem function.
5. All possible medical conditions that may interfere with the above requirements have been ruled out.

---

27 *Sefer ha-Hukkim* 2144, 24 *Adar II*, 5768 (March 31, 2008).

The Law defines "medical instrument-based evidence" (*bedikah makhshiranit*) as an objective test, independent of any clinical exam, that assesses the lack of blood flow to the brain or the lack of electrophysiological functioning of the brain. The first appendix to the Law defines "a medical instrument" as one of the following tests: BAER,[28] transcranial doppler (TCD),[29] sensory evoked potentials (SEP),[30] computerized tomography with angiography (CT-A),[31] or magnetic resonance imaging with angiography (MRA).[32] The inclusion of this section requiring more objective than clinical evidence of the lack of brain perfusion (blood flow) or function was added at the behest of the Chief Rabbinate. Although initially only recommending BAER in 1987, the Chief Rabbinate expanded the options for proving the lack of brain perfusion in accord with the many advances in medicine and medical technology in the 21 intervening years.

The protocols established by the health ministry detail the technical procedures necessary to fulfill the criteria set out by the Law.[33] Recognizing the debate and discussion of accepting "brain death," especially in the Jewish world, the protocol includes a notable addition to the Law:

> If a determination of brain-respiratory death is contrary to the religion or worldview (*hashkafat olam*) of a patient as reported by his family, the patient will not be disconnected from a mechanical ventilator, and therapy supporting his continued breathing will not be stopped until his heart has stopped beating. The location of this continued therapy will be determined by professional opinion.[34]

---

28 See n.9 above.
29 TCD is a test of the velocity of blood through blood vessels in the brain.
30 SEP is an electric potential recorded from the central nervous system in response to stimulating one of the senses.
31 CT-A is a CT exam with the ability to visualize arteries and veins.
32 MRA is an MRI technique used to image blood vessels.
33 "Guidelines for Implementing the Brain and Respiratory Death Law – 2008" (Hebrew), *Hozer ha-Minhal ha-Kelali*, no. 27/09.
34 Ibid., sec. 1.10.

This caveat effectively allows people to opt-out of having their death determined by "brain death" in favor of the traditional cardio-respiratory definition. The Law is somewhat unclear, however, as to the continued treatment of such patients, legally requiring only the continuation of supportive ventilation and leaving all else seemingly open to interpretation. For those who view such patients as alive, ventilation alone is often insufficient to even maintain the *status quo* without other treatments, such as nutrition, diuretics, and antibiotics should they become necessary. Of only recent applicability, it remains to be seen how this will ultimately play out in the Israeli medical and legal establishments.

After being in effect for less than a year, the Israeli daily newspaper *Haaretz* reported many difficulties and inefficiencies in applying this new law.[35] Spokespersons from the Israeli Ministry of Health claimed that out of 46 patients clinically diagnosed as "brain dead" from January-March, 2010, only 25 patients whose families agreed to organ donation were deemed to be eligible donors (54%) based on the Law's protocols. Before the law took effect and these additional tests became necessary, **all** of these patients would have qualified as potential donors. Why was there such a sudden drastic drop? Do these newly demanded tests determine that many of the patients who would previously have been considered dead are actually alive?

Lacking substantive scientific research on the matter, the Ministry of Health attributed the radical decline in number of potential donors to lack of accessibility to the specific mandated tests, a lack of technical personnel to perform them, and a number of patients in whom some of these tests were actually performed who were shown to have continuous cerebral blood flow. In addressing this problem, the Ministry of Health is lobbying to include additional testing modalities and training additional technical staff to address this shortage. Regarding the last group of patients, however – those deemed to be alive by these additional tests – the Israeli National Transplant Center has been rather coy in discussing actual num-

---

35 "Health Ministry to Reexamine Problematic Brain-Death Law" (Hebrew), April 26, 2010.

bers and has repeatedly refused any elaboration.[36] It is certainly in the public's interest to know how many of these 21 patients were ineligible to donate their organs because they were still alive, especially since what would have been considered legal donation under the old system is now considered murder. This is precisely the group of people for whom the Chief Rabbinate required further testing – those for whom no objective evidence of irreversible brainstem destruction exists. These patients, as per the Chief Rabbinate's own rules, are alive and must be fully medically supported. Refusing to identify what percentage of clinically diagnosed "brain dead" patients fit into this final category certainly does not build the public's trust and confidence in the transplant enterprise.

Furthermore, the Israeli National Transplant Center's "surprise" at these outcomes is itself surprising, as well as quite troublesome. Several recent studies from 2007-2009, cited by the recent review of "brain death" determination guidelines by the American Academy of Neurology (AAN), show evidence of cranial blood flow in many patients clinically diagnosed as "brain dead."[37] In a study of patients meeting clinical criteria for "brain death," 11% of clinically "brain dead" patients showed

---

36 Personal email correspondence with Ms. Yael Bistritz of the National Transplant Center in Israel and Ms. Tamar Ashkenazi, manager of the Center (May 2, 4, 5, 10, 13, 2010) and phone conversation (May 9, 2010).

37 E.F. M. Wijdicks, P.N. Varelas, G.S. Gronseth, et al., "Evidence based guideline update: Determining brain death in adults – Report of the Quality Standards Subcommittee of the American Academy of Neurology," *Neurology* 74 (2010): 1911-8. The American Academy of Neurology has in fact argued against performing any of these tests, with Dr. Wijdicks, the lead author of the AAN update, arguing that these tests are "not accurate, not conclusive, not pertinent, and not warranted" ("The case against confirmatory tests for determining brain death in adults," *Neurology* 75 (2010): 77-83) and that the technical problems that they pose because of their inaccuracies should give serious pause to requiring them for determining death. Dr. Wijdicks opposes these tests because according to the UDDA, once a patient meets the clinical criteria for death (unresponsiveness, lack of brainstem reflexes, and apnea), he is dead, with no need for – and even in spite of – any ancillary testing. He feels that these tests merely serve to confuse people, making them think that blood flow or brain necrosis (death of cells) are important or necessary for the diagnosis, which, according to American law, they are not. Cf. R.D. Truog, F.G. Miller, "Brain perfusion scans to diagnose death: More than meets the eye," *Pediatric Critical Care Medicine* 11 (2010): 527-8.

evidence of cerebral perfusion on CTA,[38] while a separate study found evidence for cerebral blood flow in an astounding 56% of patients clinically diagnosed as "brain dead."[39]

There is a more fundamental problem with the Chief Rabbinate's demand for these extra tests as well. The purpose of these additional tests is to confirm that the criterion for death (ICSR) is indeed irreversibly met. The fact that the brainstem is not functioning properly in a "brain dead" patient is already established through a negative apnea test, but by definition, this is an assessment of a specific point in time; a negative apnea test demonstrates that right now, the patient is incapable of breathing on his own. In and of itself, it does not necessarily indicate that the patient's apnea is irreversible and irrecoverable. Indeed, there are many possible causes of reversible apnea, in all of which the patient presents with a negative apnea test.[40] Thus, the fact that the patient is presently apneic does not demonstrate whether the patient's ability for spontaneous respiration will ever recover. It is true that from a statistical perspective, a negative apnea test in the context of "brain death" (complete unresponsiveness and negative brainstem reflexes) is almost universally viewed as irreversible; a study of 1,229 adult patients declared "brain dead" showed none to have recovered any brainstem function (reflexes or spontaneous respiration) upon repeat examination.[41] If the focus was simply on the chances of recovering spontaneous respiration however, then from a statistical perspective, a clinical diagnosis of apnea is sufficient, since when

---

38 D. Escudero, J. Otero, L. Marques, et al., "Diagnosing brain death by CT perfusion and multislice CT angiography," *Neurocritical Care* 11 (2009): 261-71.

39 E. Frampas, M. Videcoq, E. de Kerviler, et al., "CT angiography for brain death diagnosis," *American Journal of Neuroradiology* 30 (2009): 1566-70.

40 See D.Y. Sue, J.R.E. Vintch, "Respiratory failure" in F.S. Bongard (ed.), *Current Diagnosis & Treatment – Critical Care*, 3rd edition (New York: McGraw-Hill, 2008), ch. 12.

41 D. Lustbader, D. O'Hara, E.F.M. Wijdicks, et al., "Second brain death examination may negatively affect organ donation," *Neurology*, published online before print December 15, 2010. The one recently reported case of return of spontaneous respiration in a patient previously diagnosed as "brain dead" per AAN protocol (discussed in chapter 2) so far stands as an outlier. While it cannot be cavalierly dismissed, what effect this one case has on the larger statistical models remains to be seen. Cf. A.C. Webb, O.B. Samuels, "Reversible brain death after cardiopulmonary arrest and induced hypothermia," *Critical Care Medicine* 39 (2011): 1538-42.

it "finds evidence of brain death… no recovery of function has ever been documented."[42] Without addressing the reliability of statistical certainty in Halakhah, however, the Chief Rabbinate requires some additional confirmation for the irreversibility of apnea.

The acceptable tests detailed in the law (aside from BAER and SEP) show the absence of blood perfusion to various areas of the brain. These tests also only demonstrate the lack of cerebral perfusion at a particular moment in time, but they are nonetheless considered more predictive than the functional apnea test because without the oxygen supplied by continued cerebral perfusion, brain cells cannot survive. Dead brain cells do not recover, and dead cells therefore prove that the function previously controlled by those cells is irreversibly lost.

While the Chief Rabbinate's criteria of ICSR is **functional** – measuring the ability for breathing – the proof provided by these additional tests is **structural** or anatomic. Even though the absence of blood flow also indicates a functional problem – that the brainstem cells right now are not functioning properly – this was already proven by the negative apnea test. The assumption upon which these further tests are premised is that the lack of blood flow proves that the cells are dead (in the areas measured by that particular test), and when the cells of the brainstem are dead, they cannot recover and spontaneous respiration is irreversibly lost.

However, this underlying assumption – that a negative perfusion scan serves as a surrogate marker for brain cell death – is seriously flawed. A recent study of 41 patients diagnosed as "brain dead" shows that only about two-thirds showed evidence of moderate-to-severe neuronal ischemia (death from lack of blood perfusion) in the cortex (outermost segment of the brain), and less than half showed this finding in the midbrain and brainstem.[43] This study did not report whether or not these patient had absent cerebral perfusion, leading Dr. Truog to suggest one of two logical possibilities.

---

42 "The case against," 81.
43 E.F.M. Wijdicks, E.A. Pfeifer, "Neuropathology of brain death in the modern transplant era," *Neurology* 70 (2008): 1234-7.

1. If brain perfusion scanning can reliably diagnose the absence of cerebral blood flow, then more than half of patients currently diagnosed as "brain dead" would show the presence of perfusion if scanned. Therefore, this testing would show that most patients currently diagnosed as "brain dead" are actually still alive.

2. Conversely, if most of the patients in this study would, in fact, show an absence of flow on brain perfusion scanning, then this scanning is not sensitive enough to detect small amounts of flow sufficient to prevent neuronal necrosis and loss of function.[44]

Either option is problematic for the Chief Rabbinate, who added these **tests** to prove a **criterion** meant to be reflective of a **definition** of death – meaning that a negative scan proves that the brainstem is irreversibly destroyed. According to this study, about a third of the patients meeting the Chief Rabbinate's technical **test** for diagnosing "brain death" (lack of brain perfusion) do not fulfill the Rabbinate's **criteria** for death! Nonetheless, the Chief Rabbinate, both in 1987 and again in 2009, still requires an objective determination of brainstem destruction, thought to be adequately assessed by a negative perfusion scan. This recent research should evoke at least a moment of pause prior to proceeding with these tests, wondering whether or not they accomplish what the Chief Rabbinate intended.

Moreover, the tests designated by the Israeli law, even if sensitive in detecting cerebral blood flow, present several methodological difficulties in not accurately reflecting what the Chief Rabbinate set out to accomplish. Without delving into overly technical detail, several of these suggested exams do not accurately assess the irreversible destruction of the brainstem specifically. In fact, they are more appropriately categorized as proof for the lack of blood perfusion of the brain's cerebrum and internal capsule structures, not necessarily indicative of brainstem perfusion or function. According to the Health Ministry's "Guidelines," the sensory evoked potential exam should be performed on the median nerve of the forearm; even if negative, it is not necessarily indicative of complete

---

44 "Brain perfusion scans," 527.

brainstem destruction. The same is largely true of the BAER exam, which assesses the functional ability, and not the structural destruction, of the brainstem. The intravenous contrast-based tests, while indicative of blood flow, are often contraindicated in patients with renal problems or those in whom renal preservation is important (for example, for transplant), limiting the applicability of angiography based studies. Additionally, in post-brain surgery patients or head trauma victims, blood flow studies can often be misleading, requiring relying upon other methods. The transcranial doppler study appears to most directly assess brainstem perfusion, but as per the Israeli Transplant Network coordinator's report, is not widely available as yet.

Even more disturbingly, recent studies have shown significant discrepancies between the various tests, such as preserved flow on transcranial doppler (TCD) despite a negative CTA exam,[45] with another study showing CTA evidence of blood flow in 30% of patients with absent flow by traditional angiography.[46] The "Brain and Respiratory Death Law – 2008," however, allows performing any one of the five listed exams to accomplish the purpose of establishing death, placing them all on equal footing. Differences and discrepancies abound among these tests, leading to diagnosing death differently depending on which equipment is available – seriously questioning implementing these guidelines as sound public policy.

Even if professional consensus will select one specific test as the most highly sensitive, current experience shows that in the not too distant future, a more sensitive test will undermine that which was previously deemed the "gold standard" (as traditional angiography was). R. Hayyim David Ha-Levi raised this very concern early on in criticizing the use of the nuclide scan proposed by Prof. Hayyim Somer out of fear that a newer, more sensitive or accurate test will show that what we once thought to

---

45 D.M. Greer, D. Strozyk, L.H. Schwamm, "False positive CT angiography in brain death," *Neurocritical Care* 11 (2009): 272-5.
46 J.C. Combes, A. Chomel, F. Ricolfi, et al., "Reliability of computed tomography angiography in the diagnosis of brain death," *Transplantation Proceedings* 39 (2007): 16-20.

be death really was not.[47] This broaches the larger issue of how and when Halakhah may rely on current science, given the nature of the scientific enterprise's ability to continuously critique and refashion itself with each advance and breakthrough, which lies somewhat beyond the scope of the current endeavor.

Conclusion

With the eventual passage of the "Brain and Respiratory Death Law – 2008," the State of Israel formally incorporated the Chief Rabbinate's recommendations in updated form, expanding the requirement for BAER testing specifically so as to conform to advances in medical technology. Unanimous in their agreement that "brain death" should be halakhically recognized as death, the members of the Chief Rabbinate's committee adopted a novel approach to understanding and interpreting the traditional sources, making a bold statement in their support of organ donation. Predicated upon defining death as ICSR and less interested in brain function *per se*, the Chief Rabbinate, already in 1987, endorsed organ donation from "brain dead" patients as long as it is conclusively proven that lack of respiration is indeed irreversible.

While not necessarily accepted by the medical establishment as necessary for a diagnosis of "brain death," the Chief Rabbinate required additional objective proof for the irreversibility of the respiratory cessation, as evidenced by the dysfunction or destruction of the brainstem, initially requiring only the BAER test. The Law, as adopted in 2008, includes other testing modalities as well, all aimed at assessing blood flow to the brain or the electrophysiological functioning of the brain.

However, the outcomes of the other exams, as defined in the Health Ministry's "Guidelines," are more appropriately categorized as proof for the lack of blood perfusion of the brain's cerebrum and internal capsule structures, not necessarily indicative of brainstem perfusion or function. In the medical world, such proof is more than enough to establish a diagnosis of "brain death," since the focus is on "the whole brain" or whatever part thereof it has been interpreted to represent, and not necessarily on

---

47 *Responsa Aseh Lekha Rav* 8:64.

the brainstem or on respiration. In contrast, the Chief Rabbinate's insistence on an objective assessment of the brainstem has little to do with overall brain function, but rather only with the brainstem's function in controlling spontaneous respiration. As long as the patient is irreversibly unconscious, the existence of "nests" of still functioning cells throughout the brain is completely meaningless, as per the Chief Rabbinate's proposal, in the context of proven ICSR.

Even if these tests accurately examine the criteria set out by the Chief Rabbinate (although recent evidence suggests otherwise), current research would suggest that the Israeli transplant establishment should expect a drop of 11-56% of organ donors. The ramifications of this projected shortage on Israeli patients, physicians, and the medical system as a whole remains to be seen.

CHAPTER 16:

Rabbi Shelomoh Zalman Auerbach

R. Shelomoh Zalman Auerbach (1910-1995), one of the leading halakhic decisors in Israel in the late 20th century, was deeply involved in the application of Halakhah to modern medical realities. His influence on issues of medical Halakhah is still keenly felt to this day, 16 years after his passing. Although never completely addressing all of the issues relating to "brain death" in a single discussion, R. Auerbach's many letters, proclamations, and dictated position statements during the early 1990's paint a vivid description of the breadth and depth of his views. The current discussion will proceed chronologically, presenting his position as he developed it, in an attempt to decipher it correctly and alleviate what in the past may have led to confusion.

First Reports

Responding to recent discussion in the United States regarding the halakhic status of "brain death," Rabbis Feivel Cohen and Shmuel Kamenetsky visited R. Shelomoh Zalman Auerbach and R. Yosef Shalom Elyashiv to determine their position on the matter. Dr. Steinberg reports[1] that this visit prompted the Israeli decisors to

---

1 A. Steinberg, "Determining the Moment of Death – A Survey of Opinions" (Hebrew), in M. Halperin, *Kevi'at Rega ha-Mavet*, 2nd edition (Jerusalem: Schlesinger Institute, 2007) (henceforth, *KRhM*), 199.

issue the following proclamation, dated 18 *Menahem Av*, 5751 (July 29, 1991):

> We have been asked to give our opinion, *da'at Torah*, regarding a cardiac transplant for a very sick patient (*holeh mesukkan*) as well as transplanting other organs to sick patients (*holim she-yesh ba-hem sakkanah*). It appears that as long as the donor's heart is beating, even when the whole brain including the brainstem is no longer functioning, termed "brain death," it is our opinion that it is completely forbidden (*ein shum heter*) to remove even one of his organs and that [doing so] constitutes murder (*yesh ba-zeh mishum shefikhut damim*).

This proclamation was printed in the Orthodox newspaper *Yated Ne'eman* on 12 *Tishrei*, 5752 (September 20, 1991). In response, R. Moshe Tendler engaged R. Auerbach and R. Elyashiv in discussion, enquiring further into their position. This correspondence prompted the following response, aimed at eliminating any possible confusion or misinterpretation of their opinion. Dated during the *Aseret Yemei Teshuvah* of 5752, Rabbis Auerbach and Elyashiv wrote:

> We received his [R. Tendler's] letter from 23 *Elul*, 5751 (September 2, 1991), and after analyzing his position, we did not find any reason to change our opinion. It is completely forbidden (*ein shum heter*) to remove organs while the donor's heart is beating and [doing so] constitutes murder (*yesh ba-zeh shefikhut damim*).[2]

At this point in time (1991), Rabbis Auerbach and Elyashiv did not (at least publicly) offer arguments for their position.[3] From the little information that is available, and based on future discussions, it appears

---

2 *Nishmat Avraham*, YD, 2nd ed. (henceforth, *NA*), 459.
3 While cosigning the proclamation and forbidding cardiac transplants, R. Elyashiv would later include additional arguments against recognizing "brain death" as halakhically meaningful that were not originally voiced by R. Auerbach. R. Elyashiv's position will be analyzed separately in chapter 19.

that R. Auerbach did not accept irreversible cessation of spontaneous respiration (ICSR) as the halakhic determinant of death, maintaining that as long as the heart continues to beat, the patient is considered alive. Removing organs from such a patient therefore constitutes murder.

The Order of Death

R. Auerbach held many discussions with Dr. Avraham Steinberg, a pediatric neurologist by training, a noted Torah scholar, and an expert on medical ethics, about the many detailed scientific, medical, and halakhic aspects of "brain death." Learning of "brain dead" pregnant women being able to deliver healthy (if not somewhat premature) babies, R. Auerbach suggested (and then later retracted) a Talmudic proof against halakhically recognizing "brain death" – leading to one of the greatest medical-halakhic experiments of modern times.

Talmud *Erkhin* 7a relates that when a pregnant woman dies, her fetus dies first, since its grasp on life is more ephemeral (*zutar hiyyuteih*) than hers. The Talmud contrasts this to a traumatic death, in which the baby can outlive its mother. The assumption is that natural death is a process, with a gradual decline and eventual shutting down of organ systems. The fetus, being effectively "part" of its mother's body, without independent viability (loosely fitting the Talmudic description of *zutar hiyyuteih*), dies during that process, prior to its mother's ultimate demise. However, this logic is true only in the case of natural death; in a traumatic or sudden death, the mother dies (or at least can die) prior to the fetus.

R. Auerbach explained that this last statement only refers to the few moments after the mother was suddenly killed; while the fetus can certainly outlive the mother in the case of sudden death, it is only possible for mere moments. Shortly after the mother's traumatic death and without any support for its continued gestation, the fetus would surely die.[4]

In a letter to Dr. Abraham, R. Auerbach argued that according to this logic, if a "brain dead" woman can deliver a living child, it proves that she is still alive.[5] Unwilling to entertain the possibility that a corpse

---

4 *NA*, 459.
5 *NA*, 461.

could gestate a baby, he argued that the capacity for gestation is certainly indicative of life.

R. Auerbach wondered whether current intensive medical care could counter the Talmud's assumption regarding the ability of a fetus to outlive its mother, in which case his Talmudic proof against "brain death" would be invalid. Can modern medicine keep a pregnant woman who is dead by halakhic standards functioning long enough to enable the healthy delivery of her fetus?

While normally defining death as the irreversible cessation of both respiration and cardiac function, cognizant of Mishnah *Ohalot* (1:6), R. Auerbach also entertained a second track for defining death, that of decapitation. R. Auerbach therefore proposed an experiment in which a pregnant sheep would be surgically decapitated – qualifying as halakhically dead – and a delivery would be attempted. This experiment would test the Talmud's assumption that a fetus cannot outlive its mother for any significant period of time and help prove whether or not gestation is a certain indication of continued life. Even then, however, R. Auerbach hesitated taking this to its logical extreme, arguing that even if such an experiment proved that a dead body could function "merely" as a gestational incubator, the results would not necessarily have immediate relevance for humans.

The Sheep Experiment

As a result of the profound respect for R. Auerbach among physicians and scientists alike, the experiment he suggested was indeed arranged. This tremendous undertaking is certainly a profound testament to the pious, truth-seeking, and God-fearing doctors and other medical professionals who, eager to better understand and implement Halakhah, researched, arranged, and organized a most fascinating project. On 4 *Shevat*, 5752 (January 1, 1992), a special medical-surgical-veterinary team met with Dr. Steinberg, R. Yigal Shafran, Dr. Moshe Hirsch, Dr. Abraham S. Abraham, and Dr. Mordechai Halperin to conduct the test. The following description is adapted from Dr. Steinberg's account.[6]

---

6 "Determining the Moment of Death," 200-1.

A pregnant sheep at 19 (out of 21) weeks gestation was generally anesthetized and her neck was surgically opened, completely occluding her bilateral carotid arteries and jugular veins. Fetal monitoring was continuous throughout the procedure. The mother sheep's skull was opened and the whole brain was completely evacuated. The medical team stabilized the mother sheep in this condition – without a brain – for three hours, with normal cardiac function of both mother and baby. Attempting to go even further, a complete decapitation was then attempted; a tracheotomy was performed (inserting the breathing tube through the neck) and the vertebral column was dissected between cervical vertebrae one and two. Despite these aggressive measures, normal cardiac functioning of both mother and baby continued for an additional 20 minutes. The fetus's heart rate then suddenly dropped and an emergency Caesarian section was performed, ultimately delivering a stillborn; resuscitation efforts were ineffective. Despite the unfortunate outcome, it was clear that the fetus (and its mother) maintained a normal heartbeat for more than three hours after the mother had been deemed halakhically dead.

Armed with this data, Dr. Abraham, Dr. Steinberg, and R. Shafran met with R. Auerbach. After a long debate, an important methodological concern was raised. Although the fetal heart rate was monitored continuously until its ultimate demise long after its mother was already declared halakhically dead, some were concerned that relying on the fetal heart rate alone could not adequately prove that the fetus survived the mother's death. After all, if the mother's continued heartbeat was of no halakhic consequence, perhaps the same should be true of the fetus's. If the mother sheep was deemed dead even while maintaining a pulse, how can we rely on that very same indicator to establish that the fetus was still alive?

Dr. Steinberg argued that while a continued heartbeat is not the sole criterion for life (as evidenced by this very experiment), it should be assumed to be an indication of life absent any proof to the contrary. This is demonstrably true, as the great majority of people (and animals) with continued heartbeats are most certainly alive. As a statistical model, this explanation accepts and validates the possibility of exceptions. The mother sheep fit into this latter category; having been decapitated, her continued heartbeat was not indicative of life. There was no evidence for the death of the fetus, however, and we must therefore consider it alive until there is evidence pointing to the contrary.

Because of disagreement on this point, a second experiment was conducted under similar conditions, performed by the same surgical team and with the same witnesses and supervisors, on 25 *Shevat*, 5752 (January 22, 1992).

During this second attempt, the mother sheep was completely decapitated early on. Both mother and fetus maintained normal cardiac function for 25 minutes post-decapitation. At that point, rhythmic muscular contractions were noted throughout the mother's body, consistent with uterine contractions. A healthy calf was then delivered via Caesarian section, which continued living for years thereafter.

R. Auerbach was left with somewhat of a dilemma. How are we to understand Talmud *Erkhin*'s postulate regarding the order of death in light of current scientific realities? The experiment clearly indicated that an animal fetus (at the very least) can, in fact, survive its mother. In that case, the fact that a "brain dead" woman can gestate a healthy fetus does not conclusively prove that she is still alive.

Reacting to this data, R. Auerbach retracted his argument from Talmud *Erkhin* against halakhically recognizing "brain death." Writing to R. Feivel Cohen of Brooklyn, he explains that the Talmud's statement was limited to the then-current medical realities. In earlier times, without the benefit of intensive medical interventions, the fetus certainly died prior to its mother, and when the mother died suddenly or traumatically, the fetus died within moments thereafter. However, with the advent of mechanical ventilation, this premise is no longer necessarily true; with its mother attached to a ventilator, a fetus can certainly outlive her for some time.[7] Accordingly, the fact that a "brain dead" woman can gestate a baby is not proof that she is alive.

In re-analyzing Talmud *Erkhin*, R. Auerbach takes certain assumptions for granted:

1. The mother sheep was considered halakhically dead once decapitated (or when the brain was suctioned out in the first experiment).

---

7 *NA*, 463-4.

2. The experiment faithfully tested and challenged Talmud *Erkhin*'s premise that the fetus dies prior to its mother or immediately after death (in cases of traumatic death).
3. The ramifications from the decapitated sheep experiment have relevance to the question of "brain death."

The first assumption, taken for granted by R. Auerbach, is subject to challenge. Generally, R. Auerbach allowed for multiple definitions of death, including the traditional cardiopulmonary standard as well as decapitation. In "normal" situations, R. Auerbach defined death as the irreversible cessation of both cardiac and respiratory function – a classification that is inapplicable to "brain dead" patients who maintain a continuous heartbeat. Declaring such a patient dead must rely on a second set of death-defining criteria, distinct from the traditional signs and indications. According to R. Auerbach's reading of Mishnah *Ohalot* 1:6, decapitation is the other possible **definition** of death, and it defines death in all circumstances. Elsewhere, he argues that it is specifically the absence of the brain, and not the other organs of the head and neck, that determine death.[8] Accordingly, the mother sheep was dead, and yet her fetus outlived her; by extension, the fact that a "brain dead" mother's fetus survived does not prove that she is alive.

As discussed in chapter 6, some have taken issue with R. Auerbach's two-track approach, arguing for a single, unified definition of death, with decapitation merely an example of that broader principle. According to this view, decapitation is not automatically equivalent to death; since the sheep maintained respiratory (although mechanically produced) and cardiac function, she might, in fact, have been alive, in which case the experiment proves nothing.

The second assumption is also subject to dispute. Did this experiment indeed faithfully test and challenge Talmud *Erkhin*'s premise that the fetus dies prior to its mother? Dr. Abraham argues that the parallel

---

8 *Mishnat Hayyei Sha'ah*, 49. This was the reason that the brain was suctioned out of the skull during the first attempt prior to a complete decapitation. During the second attempt, R. Auerbach's equation of decapitation as absence of the brain was obviated in that a complete decapitation was performed initially.

between a diagnosis of "brain death" and that of decapitation was ultimately not met under the conditions of the experiment.[9] The sheep selected for this experiment was very close to the end of her pregnancy and once determined to be dead by decapitation – a sufficient criterion of death according to R. Auerbach – she only survived three hours in the first experiment and 25 minutes in the second. Despite efforts to keep the first sheep's fetus alive, its heart rate dropped after a short time and it ultimately died. This is quite different from "brain dead" pregnant women, who, with the assistance of intensive medical therapy, are sometimes able to carry babies to term. In the reported literature regarding successful pregnancies, women were determined to be "brain dead" anywhere from 15 to 27 weeks of gestation, far earlier in pregnancy that the decapitated sheep. Moreover, these women managed to continue carrying their babies for a much more extended period, from 24 to 107 days.[10] The scenarios are therefore decidedly not parallel; what is true of the decapitated sheep may very well not be true of a "brain dead" woman.

In fact, Talmud *Erkhin* differentiates between women during the middle of their pregnancies and those who are in labor. When a woman dies in the middle of her pregnancy, the Talmud assumes that the fetus will always predecease her; when she dies in childbirth however, the baby may indeed outlive her.[11] Accordingly, the Talmud itself recognizes the possibility that a fetus will outlive its decapitated mother at the end of

---

9 NA, 466.
10 D.J. Powner, I.M. Bernstein, "Extended somatic support for pregnant women after brain death," *Critical Care Medicine* 31 (2003): 1241-9. It is important to note that these numbers are almost certainly an underestimate, as "brain death" is frequently a "self-fulfilling prophecy;" these patients are usually not medically supported for extended periods, either because of withdrawal of ventilation or organ donation. If more pregnant "brain dead" woman were medically supported, there would most likely be an even greater number of successful gestations. While some advocate that it is appropriate to continue to support pregnant "brain dead" women for longer periods, as this may represent the best interests of the fetus (A.I. Applbaum, J.C. Tilburt, M.T. Collins, et al., "A family's request for complementary medicine after patient brain death," *Journal of the American Medical Association* 299 (2008): 2188-93), it is unclear whether and how often this theory is actually put into practice.
11 Cf. Responsa of Rashba 1:87 and Responsa of Rama, 40.

pregnancy. The experiment therefore proves nothing about what would happen in the middle of pregnancy under the same circumstances.

Furthermore, the experiment only calls into question R. Auerbach's original novel interpretation of Talmud *Erkhin* 7a, according to which it is possible for a fetus to outlive its mother when she dies suddenly/traumatically, but only for a few moments. However, many challenge R. Auerbach's interpretation of this Talmudic passage. Accordingly, the experiment merely proved the second half of the Talmudic dictum – that when a pregnant mother is traumatically killed, her fetus can still survive. According to this view, R. Auerbach's initial Talmudic "disproof" of the halakhic recognition of "brain death" still stands; when the mother dies naturally, her fetus cannot survive, and the fact that the "brain dead" woman's fetus can live indicates that she is quite alive.

The last assumption presumes some parallel between "brain death" and decapitation. As noted previously (chapter 6), R. Auerbach compares the death (meaning complete liquefaction or decomposition) of each and every cell of the brain to decapitation. Only under these circumstances can the brain be considered absent, just as it is in decapitation. R. Auerbach explains that according to the medical report he received, a contrast based radiographical scan showing the complete absence of perfusion in both the carotid and vertebral arteries is indicative of the complete "death" of all brain cells; since direct observation of brain cell viability is (as of yet) impossible, radiographical perfusion studies act as surrogate markers.[12] As already noted, however, modern medicine no longer accepts this premise. Even patients with negative perfusion scans have areas of their brains that are still functional – indicating that either the perfusion studies are not sufficiently specific or that the assumption that lack of perfusion equals the complete absence of function is incorrect.

This research however, calls the **test** for "brain death" into question, not R. Auerbach's **criteria** for death. His argument that the "death" of every single brain cell is equivalent to physical decapitation is unchanged by the emerging evidence. Practically, however, modern science has shown that the **tests** once thought capable of diagnosing these **criteria** are unreliable. Thus, R. Auerbach's theory – that death of every cell of the

---

12 *NA*, 461.

brain is equivalent to decapitation and therefore death – still stands, but its practical implementation awaits future developments.

Some have challenged R. Auerbach's comparison between decapitation and the death of each and every cell of the brain from the other direction, arguing that it is far too strict. Even according to R. Auerbach, the "standard" definition of death depends upon the heart ceasing to beat – focusing on its function, not the death of each and every cardiac cell. Even after the heart has irreversibly stopped beating, many of its cells still retain the capacity for metabolism and cellular functions. Why require a more stringent definition for the brain?

R. Shelomoh Amar responds to this claim by noting the scientific lack of a complete and comprehensive understanding of brain function, arguing that as long as some brain cells retain viability, the possibility for recovery has not been completely ruled out.[13] While perhaps true, however, this does not address a more fundamental issue. While determinations of death according to cardiac criteria consistently refer to the **lack of function** of the heart, the *mishnah* specifically focuses on the **absence** of the head/brain. It is only when the head/brain is completely missing – detached from the body – that the *mishnah* describes the person as dead. The *mishnah* makes no mention of function, only structure. Interpreting this *mishnah* as describing death as decapitation because of the loss of cerebral function instead of its absence raises significant challenges. How should one halakhically determine brain function? Are all functions important to this determination or only some? How should newly discovered functions or newly discovered sources for known functions be understood? No halakhic source addresses any of these questions – likely because they are not halakhically relevant.

The inability to provide consistent and coherent responses to these difficulties seriously raises the specter of undermining the validity of the entire approach. Halakhah does not provide answers to these questions because it seemingly does not recognize the very premise upon which they are predicated. From the halakhic perspective, it is the actual absence of the brain that determines death, not the lack of any of its particular functions.

---

13 Unpublished responsum, dated 10 *Av*, 5763, p. 31.

How to Practically Proceed?

Recognizing that a "brain dead" patient is not necessarily comparable to a healthy living person, but hesitant to equate such a patient with a corpse, R. Auerbach ruled that any such patient be treated as a *safek goses* (possibly moribund and possibly dead). He therefore permitted removing/disconnecting/shutting off such a patient's ventilator (whichever method would prevent moving the patient in any way). Even then, the heart may continue to beat for some time until all the oxygenated blood in circulation is used up; how long this takes is not easily predictable and depends on many variables. R. Auerbach therefore writes that after observed apnea, eventual complete asystole (flat-line on EKG), and then – and only then – after waiting the "accepted period of time" (*shi'ur ha-zeman ha-mekubal*), the patient can be declared dead.[14]

Since death is by definition irreversible, once determined, R. Auerbach permitted restarting the ventilator and reanimating the heart, if medically possible, for the purpose of eventual organ recovery. Without restarting circulation, the organs would likely be unrecoverable, being starved of oxygen for too long. Aware of current medical limitations to recovering hearts only from patients in whom they remain beating until stopped intraoperatively, R. Auerbach allowed doctors – after waiting the as of yet undetermined but "accepted" waiting period – to attempt to reanimate the heart, in the hopes of enabling the effective recovery and transplant of that heart into a potential donor.[15]

In requiring waiting "the accepted waiting time" after asystole, R. Auerbach was clearly not referring to the customary waiting period of 20-30 minutes after determining death prior to initiating preparations for burial. Instead, he turned to several physicians to assist in determining what was medically "accepted" as appropriate. On 24 *Adar II*,

---

14 NA, 466. In R. Auerbach's initial response to Dr. Abraham (NA, 461), he mentions only apnea, leaving open the important question of continued heartbeat. However, in his response to a letter from Drs. Schulman, Fleishman, and Schechter (NA, 467), he takes it as a given that declaring death is only possible after the heart has stopped beating. This is in accordance with his previous positions on the issue and represents an application of his generally held thesis; it is not a novel determination of death.
15 Ibid., 468.

5752 (March 29, 1992), Drs. Robert Schulman, Yaakov Fleishman, and Yaakov Schechter gave their collective professional opinion that based on currently available information, if a patient is declared "brain dead" by both clinical and radiographic criteria, once his heart stops beating after disconnection from the ventilator, they would be willing to sign a death certificate after 15-20 seconds of asystole.[16] This was based on their best assessment at the time, with little available research as to the time after which autoresuscitation (spontaneous return of heartbeat) is no longer possible. Even today, while autoresuscitation has been documented for up to seven minutes after (proven) asystole and subsequent CPR, there is no data available for "brain dead" patients or for others in whom CPR is not initiated.[17]

Responding the next day (25 *Adar II*, 5752), R. Auerbach reconfirmed his opinion that until such time passes, the patient qualifies as a *safek goses* and nothing may be done that may even possibly hasten his death. Accordingly, in R. Auerbach's opinion, the only way to permit organ donation requires disconnecting the ventilator, waiting until the heart completely stops and the person appears absolutely motionless for 30 [*sic*] seconds, and only then initiating the process of organ recovery.[18]

For someone who normally equates death with the cessation of the heartbeat, as R. Auerbach does, this position seems quite perplexing, as he is willing to declare the patient dead despite the potential for the

---

16 Ibid., 461-2.

17 Cf. K. Hornby, L. Hornby, D. Shemie, "A systematic review of autoresuscitation after cardiac arrest," *Critical Care Medicine* 38 (2010): 1246-53.

18 For some reason, in his response, R. Auerbach increases the waiting time to 30 seconds while the physicians themselves only stated 15-20 seconds. R. Auerbach does not give any reason or explanation for this change and it remains of unclear significance. It is important to note that many such patients' hearts might, in fact, be amenable to reanimation (depending on the clinical situation, of course). Many potential organ donors – and they are the patients that are of primary interest for this discussion – particularly those who suffered traumatic brain injury, often have otherwise healthy organs; this is why it makes sense to transplant them into someone else. A relatively healthy heart stands a decent chance of reanimation after only 30 seconds of complete asystole. In fact, this notion frames a similar debate regarding donation after cardiac death (DCD) as to how much time must pass between the onset of asystole and beginning the organ recovery effort.

reversibility of his heartbeat. In determining death in non-"brain dead" and non-ventilated patients – that is, most people – R. Auerbach indeed required that their hearts **irreversibly** stop beating. Patients suffering from heart attacks and with flat-line readings on an EKG are not automatically assumed to be dead, and all resuscitative measures must therefore be undertaken (even on Shabbat) in an effort to save them.[19] If these interventions are successful and the heartbeat returns, the patient is considered resuscitated – never having died – not resurrected. Why should the "brain dead" patient be treated differently? In fact, even the language used to illustrate this scenario seems rather forced, describing the heart as being "reanimated," as opposed to "revived" or "resuscitated," so as to avoid the connotation that the patient – now with a beating heart – is actually alive.

While R. Auerbach did not directly address this issue, for R. Auerbach, aside from the traditional cardiopulmonary determination, decapitation represents an independent and *sui generis* additional criteria for death, not necessarily corresponding to parameters and limitations of the traditional cardiopulmonary approach. Because decapitation fulfills the alternate criteria for death according to R. Auerbach, any post-decapitation functions or movements are meaningless insofar as indicating continued life. These are what Mishnah *Ohalot* describes as *pirkus*, movements devoid of significance and consequence, since they occur after death is unequivocally determined.

Thus, once the sheep's brain was removed (which R. Auerbach equated with decapitation), she was dead by Scriptural fiat, irrespective of her continued heartbeat. This does not mean, however, that the heartbeat is always irrelevant in determining death – quite the contrary. Rather, the sheep was dead because decapitation meets a secondary, completely independent set of criteria for death.

But once comparing a "brain dead" patient to the decapitated sheep, why consider the "brain dead" patient alive so long as his heart continues beating (prohibiting organ recovery until 30 seconds after asystole) but characterize the sheep as dead in spite of her continued heartbeat?

From a methodological perspective, there are a number of problems in directly comparing the decapitated sheep with a "brain dead" patient.

---

19 *NA*, 456.

Even while equating decapitation with the death of each and every brain cell, R. Auerbach was hesitant in making the parallel complete. The first sheep "lived" for three hours and the second for 25 minutes, whereas "brain dead" patients can survive for much longer – making it quite difficult to describe such a patient's heartbeat as mere *pirkus*. Coupled with this incomplete parallel, R. Auerbach was similarly hesitant to halakhically rely solely on a scientific test to determine death, when not otherwise determined visually or perceptibly.[20]

In conjunction with these methodological reservations, R. Auerbach also had doubts regarding the absolute accuracy and precision of the medical diagnosis. In his letter to R. Feivel Cohen, R. Auerbach writes that even without radiographic evidence, it is far more likely than not ("*karov le-vaday*") that a patient exhibiting the clinical signs of "brain death" is indeed dead.[21] However, even after hearing back from the aforementioned doctors, who effectively confirmed the validity of the diagnosis of "brain death" as death, R. Auerbach was still hesitant – continually concerned that as long as the patient's heart continues to beat, there may be some area of the brain that retains function. He was worried that even when tests detect no brain perfusion at all, there may be some areas of the brain that are still "living" and functioning. If so, the **tests** do not accurately gauge the **criteria** for which R. Auerbach intended them – diagnosing the death of each and every brain cell – and he was therefore reluctant to apply the category of decapitation to "brain dead" patients. (While R. Auerbach's concerns were ultimately proven correct, this information was unknown at the time.)

This concern lingers so long as the heart continues beating; once it stops and blood ceases circulating, R. Auerbach felt confident in describing the brain as having completely died. When there is no bodily circulation at all, he was sufficiently satisfied that even those brain cells that he thought might continue living or functioning even in "brain death" could do so no longer. He was so satisfied, in fact, that after 30 seconds passed, he was willing to describe the patient as effectively decapitated, so that even if his heartbeat returned thereafter, it would be of no

---

20 *NA*, 461.
21 Ibid., 463-4.

consequence (as per the *sui generis* definition of decapitation). The waiting period was meant to ensure that the brain cells had all died beyond any reversible potential. R. Auerbach could then be confident that the patient met the criteria of Mishnah *Ohalot* and that this status would not change, as there are currently no therapies available to "revive" dead brain cells.[22]

Reaffirming Principles

While news of the "sheep experiment" was making rounds in the Torah world, R. Auerbach's response and reaction to it were not as well publicized. Rumor and speculation filled the air, with some suggesting that R. Auerbach completely reversed his opinion on "brain death," permitting organ recovery and transplants. Regardless of the precise impetus, Rabbis Auerbach and Elyashiv issued a second proclamation on the matter, signed on 4 *Iyyar*, 5752 (May 7, 1992) (published in *Yated Ne'eman*, 8 *Menahem Av*, 5752 [August 7, 1992]):

> We have been asked to give our opinion, *da'at Torah*, regarding a cardiac transplant for a very sick patient (*holeh mesukkan*) as well as transplanting other organs to sick patients (*holim she-yesh ba-hem sakkanah*). It appears that as long as the donor is being ventilated and his heart is beating, even when the whole brain including the brainstem are no longer functioning, termed "brain death," it is our opinion that it is completely forbidden (*ein shum heter*) to remove even one of his organs and there is a concern for [the prohibition of] murder (*yesh ba-zeh hashash shefikhut damim*).

---

22 This was, in fact, the rationale for the physician's assessment as well. Although not appearing in the text of their letter, Dr. Robert Schulman explained (personal communication, November 23, 2009) that their goal was to try to figure out how long after a complete lack of perfusion they could be certain that all remaining brain tissue had "died." He explained that at the time, there was no available evidence proving their assertion; it was based on their best analysis and estimate of the then-current medical knowledge. Even today, such studies are somewhat lacking and it is a rather difficult assessment to undertake.

While almost entirely identical to their proclamation from 18 *Menahem Av*, 5751 (July 29, 1991), there is a small difference between the two. In referring to the prohibition, the final phrase of the first proclamation states, *"yesh ba-zeh mishum shefikhut damim"* – "[doing so] constitutes murder" – while the later proclamation states, *"yesh ba-zeh* **hashash** *shefikhut damim"* – "there is a **concern** for [the prohibition of] murder," or alternatively, "it is an act of questionable murder." It is unknown whether in formulating this second proclamation, Rabbis Auerbach and Elyashiv had the text of their previous proclamation available to them for comparison purposes or whether or not this change was intentional – and if so, what it should mean.

Dr. Mordechai Halperin finds great significance in this linguistic shift, noting that since it was written specifically after the famous "sheep experiment," it represents a modification in R. Auerbach's understanding of "brain death."[23] In essence, he echoes the conclusion that what was previously discussed – the experiment helped solidify the notion that a patient can continue to exhibit signs of bodily function despite being dead as defined by decapitation. Previously, R. Auerbach was completely opposed to the notion of halakhically recognizing "brain death" in any way, describing a "brain dead" patient as alive and recovering organs from him as full-fledged murder. After the experiment, however, he referred to a "brain dead" patient as a *safek goses safek meit* (possibly a *goses* and possibly dead). Harvesting organs from such a patient only constitutes murder on the assumption that the patient is in fact a *goses*; removing organs from a corpse, however, is certainly not murderous. Since R. Auerbach considered the patient's status to be uncertain, he then wrote that organ harvesting is only "questionable" murder.

Dr. Halperin's chronological assessment of the evolution of R. Auerbach's thought flows quite well from the previous analysis. The fact that Dr. Halperin was one of the key players in the debate, as well as his close relationship with R. Auerbach, strongly supports this approach as accurate.

---

23 M. Halperin, "The Torah's Opinion Regarding 'Brain Death:' Two Opinions of R. Shelomoh Zalman Auerbach and R. Yosef Shalom Elyashiv, Before the 'Sheep Experiment' and Afterwards" (Hebrew), in *KRhM*, 265-73.

New Discoveries

In the early 1990's, great strides were made in better understanding and characterizing severe brain injuries. One area of serious exploration was what exactly happens to a "brain dead" patient's brain. With more sensitive diagnostic tests available and with increasing public support for the notion of equating "brain death" with death, more tests and autopsies were performed on these patients, furthering basic principles and understandings of the inner workings of the brain and its functions.

Scientists began to learn that even in "brain death," parts of the brain continue to "live" and even support whole-body oriented functions. More than just random nests of cells, important brain structures were also found to be spared, especially within the inner portions of the brain, most notably portions of the hypothalamus. Responding to these discoveries, R. Auerbach wrote to Dr. Abraham on 1 *Menahem Av*, 5753 (July 19, 1993):

> After some time, I learned that in a patient such as one we discussed [a "brain dead" patient whose ventilator was disconnected], even when 30 seconds have passed after his heart has stopped, it is **possible** [emphasis added] that part of the brain known as the "hypothalamus," which controls all [*sic*] of a person's organs, is still viable. If [physicians] will reconnect the ventilator and restart the patient's heart and breathing, it [the hypothalamus] could continue to function (*yukhal od le-hamshikh u-le-tafked*) for many days. Therefore, I am unsure (*mesupkani*). It is possible that it is insufficient to wait only 30 seconds [after asystole before organ retrieval], but rather [one must wait for] a [longer] time, so that this section of the brain will also have "died" – since [otherwise] it is possible that a significant part of the brain (*helek hashuv ha-mo'ah*) can still survive and function. Therefore, even if it is proper to sign a death certificate after waiting [only] 30 seconds, it is [an insufficiently short time] to remove organs. Therefore, I am writing explicitly to you that I retract what I wrote [previously] and it is if I said nothing at all.[24]

---

24 *NA*, 468.

This appears to be simply an application of R. Auerbach's previously established principles, now faced with new scientific evidence. Since, as was argued, R. Auerbach equated Mishnah *Ohalot*'s decapitation with the complete destruction of the entire brain, it must be just that – the complete destruction of the **entire** brain. The **criteria** remain unchanged even in light of this research; it is only the **tests** to determine whether these criteria have been satisfied that the research calls into question. The new research did not alter R. Auerbach's thinking about the fundamental issue, but merely changed the medical facts that he needed to take into consideration. Since the hypothalamus may "possibly" be alive, he was unwilling to characterize a brain as entirely irreversibly "dead" until he could be certain that even the hypothalamus was no longer functional and had no chance of ever becoming functional again; he therefore retracted his ruling that it was necessary to wait only 30 seconds before harvesting organs.

While not entirely free of ambiguity, it appears that R. Auerbach did not make any other changes to the protocol he initially proposed. Even with the possibility of the viability of the hypothalamus despite the apparent destruction of much of the rest of the brain, R. Auerbach allowed physicians to disconnect such a patient's ventilator; he only changed the requisite waiting time required after asystole prior to organ retrieval.

According to Dr. Halperin's model of R. Auerbach's evolving position on "brain death," in his final position, R. Auerbach equated Mishnah *Ohalot*'s description of decapitation with the death of each and every cell of the brain. Therefore, R. Auerbach described a patient in whom it is uncertain whether or not every brain cell has died as *safek goses safek meit* and not as certainly *meit*. The discovery of the possible viability of the hypothalamus bolstered R. Auerbach's initial hesitation to completely rely on a diagnostic test to identify the death of each and every brain cell. The possibility of a functioning hypothalamus negates the comparison of "brain death" to decapitation, and the independent track of determining death by decapitation is therefore no longer applicable. Once the parallel no longer exists, determining death must rely on the traditional cardiopulmonary standard. Accordingly, death can only be determined when the heart irreversibly stops beating, requiring an extended waiting period.

Indeed, if the heart is reanimated in another person's body, this raises serious questions as to the irreversibility of its functioning.

Since even when after stopping, a heartbeat is still potentially reversible for some time, R. Auerbach required the organ recovery team to hold off until death was determined by the alternate criteria. Once sufficient time has passed so that the hypothalamus has also "died," however, the patient now meets Mishnah *Ohalot*'s description of decapitation as death, regardless of whether or not his heart could possibly restart.

This increased waiting period is predicated upon a **doubt** as to whether this patient's hypothalamus remains viable; if it is indeed viable, death is not determined until it is no longer viable. Given all of his reservations, both methodological and technical, R. Auerbach required certainty that each and every cell of the brain had died, including the hypothalamus – something that an increased waiting time would assure. If, however, a diagnostic test were to accurately diagnose a completely destroyed hypothalamus, R. Auerbach would seemingly revert to his previously stated opinion; if the entire brain is proven to be "dead," one need only wait for 30 seconds of asystole before declaring death.

What would R. Auerbach say if the hypothalamus or other parts of the brain were shown to **certainly** be viable? What if most "brain dead" patients' brains could not be described as having each and every cell dead? Diagnosing a viable hypothalamus is actually not particularly clinically challenging. The hypothalamus controls temperature homeostasis, the ability to keep the body's core temperature hovering around a set point despite outside influence or environmental factors.[25] This is easily assessed by taking the patient's temperature; a consistent body temperature in a "brain dead" patient is a strong indication of a functioning hypothalamus. Other simple tests are available, such as the direct measure of serum ADH levels or its effects by serial measurements of sodium and water balance in blood and urine. Normal or even stable levels appear to indicate not only continued ADH secretion by the posterior pituitary

---

25 Frequently, "brain dead" patients' body temperatures are less than the "normal" 37C (98.6F). Regardless of the reason, these patients manage to maintain this lower temperature, called thermoregulation. Effectively, this is a reset of the set point, not a malfunction of the thermoregulatory homeostatic mechanism.

gland, but also continued regulation of total body water balance, including sensing the body's current status and reacting appropriately to changing conditions.

Certainly, clinical conditions may make these tests unavailable or possibly even alter their results, while a decision may need to be made on the spot by the patient's medical team. But even when these indicators are not found, pathology research has shown that up to a third of patients diagnosed as "brain dead" do not show any signs of moderate to severe signs of cell death (neuronal ischemia) in their cerebral cortices.[26] Only 40% of these patients had moderate to severe ischemic damage to neurons of the deeper brain structures, such as the medulla (which contains the respiratory center). This means that a full 60% of clinically diagnosed "brain dead" patients' brainstems appear normal to only mildly ischemic, and even then, not in each and every cell of each and every brain. These data preclude recognizing the clinical diagnosis of "brain death" as the "death of each and every cell of the brain."

In the case of a "brain dead" patient whose hypothalamus is clearly functional (that is, most cases of "brain death"), R. Auerbach would certainly require the increased waiting period after complete asystole prior to engaging in organ recovery as a matter of principle, not out of doubt. But would he even allow the patient to get that far? In other words, would he permit disconnecting a ventilator from a patient with a proven functional hypothalamus?

Initially, R. Auerbach permitted disconnecting a ventilator from a patient diagnosed as "brain dead" when it is "absolutely certain" (*she-yod'im be-vada'ut muhletet*) that the brain is no longer perfused and is "completely rotted" (*nirkav betokh ha-gulgolet*),[27] the assumption being that the brain cells cannot survive without blood flow. The discovery of a functioning hypothalamus does not change the patient's grim prognosis, but does beg the question as to whether he qualifies as "brain dead" under these conditions. Regardless of what perfusion studies show, a viable hypothalamus prevents describing a patient's brain as "completely rotted" – failing R. Auerbach's limiting criteria.

---

26 E.F.M. Wijdicks, E.A. Pfeifer, "Neuropathology of brain death in the modern transplant era," *Neurology* 70 (2008): 1234-7.
27 *NA*, 461.

Generally, R. Auerbach opposed discontinuing therapy for "standard" (i.e., not "brain dead") terminal patients. He interpreted Rama's permission to remove impediments to the departure of a *goses*'s soul[28] as limited to out of the ordinary, non-routine (*shigrati*) medical procedures that do not provide for the patient's basic needs. Intravenous fluids, antibiotics, and in some cases even hemodialysis are all considered to be routine interventions and may not be withheld or withdrawn,[29] whereas resuscitation attempts (CPR) and limb amputating surgeries are not considered routine and may be avoided if the patient (or his proxy) desires.[30] For R. Auerbach, stopping replacement insulin injections and mechanical ventilation are completely forbidden; these therapies replace natural body processes and are certainly not within the gamut of Rama's intention. Withdrawing respiratory life-support from a "brain dead" patient was a clear exception. His permissive stance in this case is specifically limited to patients for whom there is absolutely no hope of any recovery and the likelihood is that their entire brains are "almost certainly" (*karov le-vaday*) destroyed.[31] Thus, according to his own standards, R. Auerbach should prohibit disconnecting a ventilator from a patient who shows evidence of continued hypothalamic function.

Although R. Auerbach permits disconnecting a ventilator from a "brain dead" patient, he explicitly refers to a patient with only **questionable** hypothalamic viability. Removing therapy, according to R. Auerbach, is "permissible only on condition that one knows with **absolute certainty** that the brain is not receiving any blood supply whatsoever and is decayed within the skull" (emphasis added).[32] If it is known with certainty that any part of the brain is still "alive" or that the brain is not completely decayed (which is almost always the case nowadays), the patient is certainly alive according to R. Auerbach and his conclusion would be radically different – prohibiting the withdrawal of life-support.

---

28 Rama, *YD* 339:1.
29 See D. Shabtai, "End of Life Therapies," *Journal of Halacha and Contemporary Society* 56 (2008): 42-43.
30 *NA*, 487.
31 Ibid., 464.
32 Ibid.

With the "certainty" of the brain's destruction severely clouded by increasing evidence for the continued functioning of the hypothalamus, R. Auerbach's criteria for withdrawing life-support are simply not met.[33] For R. Auerbach, disconnecting the ventilator and waiting for the heart to stop beating is a prerequisite for any organ retrieval; forbidding this step derails the entire process. In practice, Dr. Abraham S. Abraham has asserted (in multiple personal correspondences) that R. Auerbach categorically forbade removing life-support from "brain dead" patients after learning of the evidence that many areas of the brain were still functioning in these patients.

Death of the Entire Brain

Before analyzing how this position fits in chronologically, it is important to analyze some other features of R. Auerbach's letter. The first is a matter of slight medical inaccuracy. R. Auerbach states that the "hypothalamus… controls all of a patient's organs." While physiologically imprecise, however, this point is not relevant to his conclusion. The hypothalamus does indeed regulate and control many, but certainly not all, bodily functions, and by all standards, it constitutes "a significant part of the brain" (*helek hashuv ba-mo'ah*).

Some, in an attempt to read R. Auerbach as not demanding complete brain destruction, have focused on this latter phrase, wondering which areas of the brain qualify as sufficiently "significant" (*hashuv*) so as to prevent an equation with decapitation.[34] According to R. Auerbach, however, it is the fact that **any** part of the brain is still viable that precludes the parallel to decapitation, not the possible function of a particular brain segment. While it is true that in today's medical environ-

---

33 See A. Tatz, *Dangerous Disease and Dangerous Therapy in Jewish Medical Ethics: Principles and Practice* (Southfield, MI: Targum Press, 2010), 128, 136, who differs regarding this conclusion, although without any elaboration or discussion. One could question his understanding based on the above analysis. Cf. M. Halperin, A. Bush, "Responsa on the Matter of the Decision of the Chief Rabbinate Regarding Cardiac Transplants from 1 Marheshvan, 5747" (Hebrew), *Assia* 87-88 (2010): 84.
34 D. Ben Zazon, "Brain Death According to R. Shelomoh Zalman Auerbach" (Hebrew) in *KRhM*, 242-5.

ment, brain viability is often assessed by function, for R. Auerbach, the question is one of structure. Whether or not the patient can be considered halakhically decapitated, he argues, depends on the complete destruction of each and every brain cell, regardless of its function. R. Auerbach argues that just as the complete brain is absent in actual decapitation, each and every cell of the brain must be destroyed in a parallel case; function is tangential at best, and more likely simply irrelevant. His word choice of *"helek hashuv"* (significant part) most likely represents his understanding of hypothalamic function, not a limitation of his general principles.

Dealing with a Goses

There is another tangential, but practically relevant aspect of R. Auerbach's position. In discussing the contrast-based radiographical imaging used to diagnose the presence of brain perfusion, R. Auerbach argues quite emphatically that the testing itself is prohibited because it constitutes a medical intervention that does not benefit the patient; it is therefore not halakhically justifiable.[35] The only "benefit" would be to "prove" that the patient is still alive and support the continuation of all medical measures. But the same "benefit" can and should be accomplished by treating the patient as if he were still alive anyway. The test is performed not to help the patient himself, but rather prove his death – certainly not serving his own needs.

R. Auerbach is concerned with a more serious halakhic infraction as well. The *mishnah* prohibits closing the eyes of a *goses* (moribund person), for fear that even such an action, as gentle as it might be, may inadvertently harm a patient who is so tenuously hanging on to life and may possibly even hasten his death.[36] R. Auerbach understands this as a blanket prohibition, encompassing even routine measures that do not directly promote the patient's comfort or health (such as routine blood work).[37] While medically

---

35 *NA*, 461.
36 *Shabbat* 23:5. See chapter 10 for further discussion of this *mishnah*.
37 *NA*, 481. R. Auerbach understood this prohibition to be so universally applicable that he felt obligated to defend a permissive ruling for an emergency room physician to

presenting no appreciable risk to most patients, R. Auerbach views injecting intravenous dye as "moving" the patient internally, even when using an already existing intravenous line (requiring no additional needle sticks), and he therefore summarily forbids the practice. In fact, R. Auerbach understands the intentional injection of a dye dispersed throughout the body to be even worse than merely moving a limb ("*hu harbeh yotter hamur mi-lehaziz ketzat et ha-guf... de-vaday asur*"), possibly because of the systemic effect that an injection has, more so than simply moving a *goses*'s arm or leg.[38]

Practically, while giving specific halakhic weight to the determination of "brain death" as he understands it – the complete death of each and every brain cell – since he views a "brain dead" patient as a *safek goses*, R. Auerbach completely forbids the radiological imaging necessary to make such a diagnosis. Even in accepting the notion of "brain death," he is not comfortable with taking it to the next level. In addition, he raises technical, although more philosophical, opposition, questioning whether relying on "scientific studies," as opposed to clinically observable phenomena, is appropriate for determining death.

In contrast, it appears that R. Feinstein is supportive of such testing. In his responsum on the issue (*Iggerot Mosheh*, YD 3:132), R. Feinstein

---

gently move a *goses*'s stretcher to allow another patient to get to the operating room for emergency surgery. Unlike the *goses*, he argued, the second patient's life is potentially salvageable. His assumption was that moving a *goses* is tantamount to murder, and one may not murder one patient – even a *goses* – to save another. However, even R. Auerbach was unwilling to take this argument to its logical extreme – forbidding moving the *goses* in this circumstance – seemingly appreciating that the *mishnah*'s concern is not always completely applicable. He permitted moving the *goses* gently in an effort to save another patient's life, apparently arguing that the likelihood of hastening the *goses*'s life in such a manner is rather remote.

It appears, however, that other than for immediate reasons of *pikuah nefesh* (in this case, to save the life of another patient), R. Auerbach completely forbade moving a *goses*. Nonetheless, he seemed willing to accept the position of *Shevut Ya'akov* (no. 13) allowing actions necessary to prolong life or alleviating suffering. He did not view saving the life of a potential organ recipient – while certainly noble – as sufficient cause to permit touching or otherwise handling a *goses*. The potential recipient's medical needs are not considered to be sufficiently immediate to warrant possibly hastening the death of the *goses*.

38 Ibid., 461.

discusses performing the radiological exam on a *goses* to assess for the possibility of reversal in apparent brainstem failure.[39] While he does not directly address the potential problems of injecting the contrast, but rather assumes its permissibility, R. Feinstein likely maintains a more limited or practical view of the prohibition of moving a *goses* – either injecting contrast into an existing intravenous line does not constitute forbidden movement, or since the contrast presents no significant medical danger, it is not included in the prohibition.

Even in prohibiting the necessary testing, however, R. Auerbach is aware that his rulings are not universally accepted by medical practitioners. Given that these exams are performed – in his opinion, in opposition to normative Halakhah – R. Auerbach is prepared to accept the findings of these imaging studies as fact, clearly stating that he was told that a negative test indicates that each and every cell of the brain no longer functions and can be described as dead – a claim that is now known to be inaccurate.[40]

"Principles and Conclusions"

In response to the widespread confusion regarding R. Auerbach's final opinion, Dr. Avraham Steinberg attempted to set the record straight by drafting a set of principles and conclusions, written in collaboration with R. Auerbach, to clarify and provide accurate guidance to those who sought R. Auerbach's perspective. After some back and forth, R. Auerbach returned the draft to Dr. Steinberg with his final revisions on 29 *Menahem Av*, 5753 (August 16, 1993). These "Principles and Conclusions" first appeared in *Assia* in 1994[41] and were subsequently republished in Hebrew several times. Dr. Steinberg added footnotes to the various sections, providing background information so that the piece could stand completely on its own. The following translation will attempt to be as accurate to the text as possible (emphases not in original).

---

39 Interestingly, the countervailing force permitting this testing in R. Feinstein's analysis is not saving another patient's life, but rather expediting burial. Nowhere in that entire responsum does R. Feinstein even mention organ donation.
40 *NA*, 463.
41 Vol. 53-54, pp. 5-16.

Principles

1. Since the dawn of time, Halakhah determined a person to be dead when he was completely unresponsive (lit., still as a stone) and with the complete cessation of his respiration and heartbeat. This determination was made after all resuscitative attempts had failed and after a waiting period of 20-30 minutes.

2. In principle, a person whose entire brain has completely "died," including each and every brain cell, is possibly (*yitakhen*) dead even if his heart continues to beat [through the help of] mechanical ventilation. [This is true] even for a pregnant woman whose fetus is still alive, since in such a circumstance, her body is functioning merely as an incubator.

3. A person whose brain has "died" can only be considered dead when it is absolutely clear, with no possibility for doubt (*be-ofen muhlat u-lelo kol safek*), that his **entire** brain has "died." The "death" of the brainstem is necessary, but not sufficient; inasmuch as it is part of the brain, it too must be "dead" so that the person can be considered so, but proving the "death" of the brainstem alone cannot determine death. It is specifically the death of the **entire** brain [that is necessary].

4. When a person has been clinically diagnosed as "brain dead" but his heart continues to beat, it is very likely (*karov le-vaday*) that the heartbeat is solely a function of the machines (i.e., the ventilator), although it is possible that this is proof that the entire brain has not [yet] "died."

5. Therefore, a person who has been clinically diagnosed as "brain dead" by all modern criteria, but is receiving mechanical ventilation and whose heart continues to beat, has the halakhic status of *safek meit safek goses* (possibly dead and possibly a *goses*).

6. Even though today we do not know how to define *Hazal*'s notion of a *goses*, a person clinically diagnosed as "brain dead" is like a *safek goses*, with all the *halakhot* regarding a *goses* being applicable. Therefore, it is forbidden to move the patient when it is not for his own benefit, but rather for the benefit of someone else. As such, all of the tests necessary to diagnose "brain death" that require moving the patient are forbidden (*harei hen be-geder ha-issur*). [Even] tests that do not cause any actual movement, but require injecting any substance into his body, are similarly forbidden.

7. It is forbidden to hasten the death of any person, even one considered to be a *safek goses*, even if the purpose is to save the life (*hatzalat hayyim vada'it*) of another "known" patient (*holeh lefaneinu*).

8. In such a *goses*, if the physicians violated section 6 above and proved through testing that the patient's brain had "died" – it is permissible to rely on their determination to permit disconnecting the ventilator (i.e., withdrawing life support), following the notion of removing an obstacle [to the soul's departure]. However, the final determination of death can only be made after the patient's heart has completely stopped and he lies completely still as a stone and he is no longer breathing at all, and only after waiting a half-minute (30 seconds). After this point, even if doctors will successfully reanimate the heart, the determination of the patient's death is unchanged.

These "Principles" flow quite well from a thorough analysis of R. Auerbach's positions as described above.

From a chronological perspective, R. Auerbach gave his final "go-ahead" to this piece approximately a month after writing to Dr. Abraham about the halakhic ramifications of the discovery of the continued viability of the hypothalamus. While not mentioned in the text, Dr. Steinberg raises this issue in a footnote to principle 3, recording that R. Auerbach had written to him (seemingly after having submitted his revisions in a separate document) that with the discovery of the possible continued viability of the hypothalamus, he was uncertain whether or not one is halakhically required to wait additional time for that brain tissue to "die" as well. This is completely consistent with R. Auerbach's letter to Dr. Abraham. When there is the possibility for the continued viability of brain tissue, the equation between decapitation and total brain destruction is tenuous – prompting R. Auerbach's hesitation. In a footnote to principle 8, Dr. Steinberg takes R. Auerbach's position to its logical conclusion, stating that a longer waiting period than 30 seconds may be appropriate if there is some doubt as to possible continued hypothalamic activity.

The text of the "Principles" and its technical requirements clearly reflect R. Auerbach's position prior to learning about the potential for continued hypothalamic viability. Importantly, Dr. Steinberg's footnotes reflect the change in mindset after this new information was provided to him, describing a patient with **possible** continued hypothalamic activity. In such a patient, R. Auerbach permits disconnecting the patient's ventilator, but questions whether a lengthened waiting period is required prior to initiating organ recovery. Neither the text nor the footnotes discuss what is now the more common situation – when continued hypothalamic function is **known** with a significant degree of certainty (as argued by the President's Council to be prevalent in most cases). In these circumstances, the technical specifications of his conclusions are not relevant; what are applicable are the principles as just described. When continued brain function is known with certainty, R. Auerbach would not only certainly forbid organ retrieval, but even disconnecting a ventilator (never even getting to a point where organ removal even becomes a question); such a patient/potential donor, in his view, is still alive.

The second half of the document lists the practical ramifications of these principles:

Conclusions

1. "Brain death," as it is currently diagnosed, is insufficient to determine a patient's death; such a patient has the halakhic status of *safek meit safek goses*. It is therefore forbidden to hasten such a patient's death in any way, and it is forbidden to remove

any organs from such a patient while his heart continues to beat out of concern that it would hasten his death. Removing organs [from such a patient] is forbidden even for the purpose of saving the life of another "known" patient (*holeh lefaneinu*) who will certainly die [without the transplant].

Therefore, in Israel, where the physicians do not adhere to all of these limitations and it is known that they must act in accordance with Halakhah (*ve-harei yod'im she-hayyavim le-hitnaheg al pi ha-halakhah*) – one is forbidden from being an organ recipient.

2. In certain circumstances, it is sometimes permitted to recover organs, and in others to receive organs, from a patient diagnosed as "brain dead." They include:

   a. Outside of Israel, where the majority of physicians and patients are non-Jewish and act in accordance with medical opinion and local laws, a Jew is permitted to receive a life-saving organ, even if he knows that the donor is Jewish as well.

   b. When a donor's head has been completely decapitated or his brain has completely liquefied (*ke-she-kol ha-mo'ah nishpakh ha-hutzah*), even though his heart is still beating.

   c. When clinically diagnosed as "brain dead" using all the currently accepted medical criteria and testing, when it is permissible to disconnect the ventilator – and subsequently the patient lies still as a stone and cannot breathe, and waiting 30 seconds after the heart has completely stopped – if afterwards physicians are successful in reanimating the heart, they may recover organs for transplant.

   d. If, in the future, there will exist such a test that will accurately and reliably (*be-vada'ut gemurah u-be-meheimanut melei'ah le-lo kol safek*) determine that each and every brain cell has "died," and after stopping the ventilator they will see that the patient is not breathing at all for 30 seconds – on condition that the test will not violate the *halakhot* of a *goses*, meaning that it will not require moving the patient in any way or injecting anything into his body – there will be room to deliberate (*yehei makom li-shkol*) whether this state is parallel to decapitation and thereby permit organ recovery from such a patient, even though his heart is still beating.

In a testament to R. Auerbach's tremendous humility, as a footnote to the last conclusion, Dr. Steinberg notes that R. Auerbach requested that he indicate that these "Principles and Conclusions" are merely his personal opinion and should not be acted upon unless other great Torah scholars agree with them.

The other footnotes deal with more substantive issues. In a footnote to conclusion 2a, Dr. Steinberg discusses the complex issues of person and place – meaning, to whom these conclusions were addressed and where they were expected to be followed. He quotes R. Auerbach's rationale in distinguishing between Israel and abroad, explaining that it is predicated upon several variables. Since outside of Israel the vast majority of physicians and patients (i.e., potential donors) are not Jewish, they do not abide by the *halakhot* relating to a *goses*, as evidenced by their willingness to perform the various examinations necessary to determine "brain death." The non-Jewish medical establishment, as well as the donors (as expressed by their proxies), accept a diagnosis of "brain death" as determinant of death. This diagnosis is made while the patient is still mechanically ventilated and his heart is still beating – which, for R. Auerbach, present insurmountable obstacles to organ recovery. Nevertheless, since the organs will be recovered from this patient in any event, the recipient is not the proximate cause of the effort. Thus, while R. Auerbach normally describes organ recovery in such a patient as possible murder, the recipient does not violate the prohibition of facilitating or being an accessory to any violation (*lifnei iver*), neither in declaring himself a transplant candidate, nor in actually receiving a transplanted organ recovered in such a manner. In contrast, R. Auerbach contends that in Israel, no recovery efforts would be made if all Jews would refuse to receive transplanted organs. Therefore, in Israel, a recipient's willingness to accept a transplanted organ qualifies as *lifnei iver*.

Debating this issue and responding to the many questions that it raises, or even attempting to do so, requires a separate discussion and analysis and is beyond the scope of this current work (*ve-od hazon la-mo'ed*).

Challenges

The only truly challenging element of the "Principles and Conclusions" is the question of determining the death of the entire brain, as previously described. As noted above, this entire discussion is relevant only when there is only the **potential** or chance for continued brain viability, not when it is **known** for certain. When there is **proof** for continued "life" or function of any area of the brain, principle 2 should be strictly adhered to – waiting for the "death of the entire brain, including each and every cell" prior to engaging in any of these efforts.

However, recent pathology research (discussed earlier) calls even this into question. For R. Auerbach, a negative brain perfusion study is useful and necessary as diagnostic of the death of each and every cell of the brain, because without oxygen (carried by the blood), brain cells cannot survive for more than mere minutes. It is important not to invest too heavily in the **tests** themselves, however, because it is rather what they show, what they represent, and the **criteria** they fulfill that is R. Auerbach's true focus. If pathology studies show that up to 60% of "brain dead" patients have normal to only mildly ischemic neurons in their brainstems, one has to question what this means for R. Auerbach's position. If any, or even some, would show a lack of perfusion, would R. Auerbach have changed his position? After all, this would indicate that lack of perfusion, as demonstrated by the **tests** he mentions, does not automatically represent death of brain cells. At some point, at some percentage, R. Auerbach would need to reassess whether or not these **tests** accurately represent the **criteria** he assumed that they address.

Clarity or Confusion?

The preceding analysis of specific technical issues notwithstanding, these "Principles and Conclusions" appear quite straightforward. R. Auerbach was willing to accept the notion of "brain death" as halakhically significant only in extremely limited circumstances – with evidence for the destruction of each and every brain cell. This is not and never has been the medically or legally accepted definition of death in any jurisdiction; practically, organs are routinely recovered from patients in whom these criteria have not been met.

However, a well-popularized misunderstanding of these "Principles and Conclusions" arrived at the entirely opposite conclusion. R. Auerbach responded to it himself in the strongest terms, arguing for the conclusions as described above. This discussion is important to analyze because it had far-reaching ramifications and caused much confusion, in particular in the American Jewish community.[42]

In the spring of 1994, Rabbi Tendler and Dr. Fred Rosner wrote a letter to the editor of *Tradition*, arguing for a "growing consensus for the halakhic validity of brain stem death."[43] As examples of this widening consensus, they cite the opinions of R. Auerbach and R. Eliezer Yehudah Waldenberg. Supporting this contention, they carefully and selectively quote from the "Principles and Conclusions," giving an impression opposite of that which R. Auerbach actually maintained.

The publication of this letter caused widespread confusion in the American Orthodox community, especially among those more familiar with R. Auerbach's opinions. Dr. Robert Schulman attempted to clarify the matter. On 10 *Kislev*, 5755 (November 13, 1994), R. Auerbach responded:

> I have received your letter and I am informing you that I have not changed my mind from that which I previously wrote to you (the

---

42 It was during this time that the Rabbinical Council of America endorsed organ donation from "brain dead" donors (see M. Angel, "The RCA Health Care Proxy: Providing Responsible Halakhic Leadership to our Community," *Jewish Action* [Spring 1992]: 60-62), with R. Tendler serving as the chairman of the Biomedical Ethics Committee that prepared the document. What role, if any, this interpretation of R. Auerbach's position had in formulating this ruling is unclear.
43 *Tradition* 28:3, 94-96.

"Principles and Conclusions" piece, published in *Assia* 1994). I still think that a person diagnosed as "brain dead" has the halakhic status of *safek goses*; one who moves a *goses* is considered as if he murdered him. All the more so that it is forbidden to remove any organs [from such a patient], as I have already written to Dr. Abraham.

A similar letter, revealing his shock that someone would arrive at such a conclusion, was quickly forthcoming from R. Waldenberg as well (discussed in chapter 19). In the Winter 1995 issue,[44] *Tradition* published a letter to the editor by Dr. Schulman citing this correspondence. With R. Auerbach's own final assertion in clarifying his position, any uncertainty should be put to rest.

Dr. Halperin notes in several instances that R. Auerbach urged him (in his capacity as the editor of *Assia*) to publish the "Principles and Conclusions" promptly, as it faithfully represented his views on the matter. This confirmation was echoed in R. Auerbach's letter to Dr. Schulman responding to R. Tendler's and Dr. Rosner's misunderstanding.

Final Thoughts

As one of the greatest halakhic decisors of his day, R. Auerbach's opinion was highly influential in understanding "brain death" in Halakhah. With his extensive relationships with physicians and scientists, R. Auerbach tried to obtain the fullest picture and the widest perspective possible on the complex issues of determining death from clinical, physiological, and pathological perspectives.

Dr. Halperin presents several defined stages in the progression of R. Auerbach's thought, interestingly demonstrating that in the end, R. Auerbach came full circle – realizing the truth of his first impressions. He suggests the following chronological model: Initially, while opposed to any type of organ recovery, R. Auerbach accepted a broadened definition of Mishnah *Ohalot*'s definition of decapitation as death to encompass the complete destruction of the entire brain. Later, however, in what

---

44 *Tradition* 29:2, 102-3.

Dr. Halperin describes as R. Auerbach's "first retraction," R. Auerbach countered his initial assumption, arguing that Halakhah would not recognize this expanded form of decapitation. In learning of the several instances of live births from "brain dead" mothers, R. Auerbach suggested that Talmud *Erkhin* 7a is sufficient proof against halakhically recognizing "brain death." These thoughts prompted the famous "sheep experiment," which ultimately led to what Dr. Halperin describes as R. Auerbach's "second retraction." Armed with scientific evidence that a dead body could function merely as a gestational incubator, R. Auerbach's proof from Talmud *Erkhin* had been neutralized. He then reverted back to his initial assumption, allowing, in theory, for an expanded understanding of the Mishnaic decapitation as parallel to the complete destruction of the entire brain.

It is appropriate to add a "final clarification" to Dr. Halperin's model, specifically regarding the issue of the hypothalamus. In the end, this is simply a restatement of R. Auerbach's initial principles, permitting withdrawing life support and organ removal only from patients whose brains are completely destroyed – meaning each and every cell. In reaffirming this stance, R. Auerbach similarly made clear that it is absolutely forbidden, according to his opinion, to withdraw life support or remove organs from a patient with evidence of continued brain function – any function – since it indicates that the entire brain has not been destroyed and is therefore not parallel to the *mishnah*'s description of decapitation as death. Practically, this "final clarification" is of utmost importance, since many patients clinically diagnosed as "brain dead" today maintain at least some hypothalamic function, and up to 60% may not experience complete cellular death of their brainstems.

There are two other points that deserve comment regarding R. Auerbach's general approach. The first is his insistence on continuing life-supporting treatment for a patient clinically diagnosed as "brain dead" but evidencing continued brain function (e.g., of the hypothalamus). R. Auerbach joins the company of almost all halakhic decisors in prohibiting withdrawing life-supporting ventilation from a terminal, moribund, living patient. With each authority providing his own reasoning, the majority consensus is that removing life-support is tantamount to murder and should not qualify as merely removing an obstacle preventing the soul's departure (as per Rama, *YD* 339:1). There have been, however, prominent opponents of this idea – such as R. Hayyim David ha-Levi[45] and R. Zalman Nehemiah Goldberg[46] – who argue that in very limited circumstances, withdrawing life-support is permitted, and sometimes even appropriate. This discussion is beyond the scope of the current study; suffice it to say that the general modern consensus is with the majority opinion.[47]

Another, far more fundamental critique analyzes R. Auerbach's definition of death more precisely. In attempting to accurately parallel the *mishnah*'s determination of decapitation as death, R. Auerbach understood that whatever the clinical scenario, it must be analogous to the absence of the entire head. His first novel interpretation was to argue that the *mishnah*'s decapitation is particularly aimed at the brain; it is the absence of the brain, and not necessarily the other organs of the face and head, that constitute death according to the *mishnah*.[48] His second step was to effectively accept R. Tendler's description of "physiological decapitation." Putting these elements together, R. Auerbach defined it as the death or destruction of every single cell of the brain. While eminently plausible, R. Auerbach's theory raises a great many practical difficulties that may in effect undermine his fundamental assertion.

How are we to determine that a brain cell has died, let alone every single brain cell? Is cell "death" determined functionally – when a cell is no longer able to use energy? Or is it defined structurally – when it is completely burst open (lysed) or when none of its sub-segments (organelles) or contents move about in any meaningful way? Perhaps it requires the more familiar halakhic standard of tissue that crumbles to the touch (*basar she-nifrakh be-tzipporen*) or tissue that a physician scrapes away (*basar she-ha-rofe gorero*), meaning gangrenous tissue? Halakhah does not appear to have a clear position on the issue, yet the precise defini-

---

45 *Responsa Aseh Lekha Rav* 5:30.
46 "On Saving Life and Choosing One Life Over Another" (Hebrew), *Moriah* 4-5:88-89 (Elul, 5738) 48-56
47 Cf. Shabtai, "End of Life Therapies," 22-48.
48 *Mishnat Hayyei Sha'ah*, 49.

tion of cellular death has important implications for the method of its diagnosis.

Whatever the answer to this question, a second is not far behind. Given criteria for determining the death of a single cell, how are we to determine that **every** single cell of the brain has met those criteria? Radiographically? For R. Auerbach, this poses serious concerns, as accuracy in radiographical imaging is often achieved by using intravenous contrast – forbidden by R. Auerbach in a *goses*. Indirect means of reaching such a diagnosis have historically not borne fruit, with the discovery of continued hypothalamic viability in spite of negative blood flow scans.

Finally, how does Halakhah define the "entire brain"? Already different than "standard" decapitation, R. Auerbach's approach allows for the continued viability of parts of the head and face. But what precisely defines the brain? Do the cranial nerves that exit the brain count (all other nerves emerge from the spinal cord)? The optic nerve in particular embeds itself in the retina – does Halakhah require making a histological diagnosis, separating nervous tissue from ophthalmologic tissue in determining which needs to be "dead"?

As a halakhic determination, the answers to these questions must find answers within the halakhic system. However, the tools for addressing these notions do not appear in the Talmud or halakhic literature. While Halakhah can and does define the parameters for the physical absence of the brain in decapitation, the extension of this notion to the death of each and every brain cell, while intellectually intriguing, practically appears to be more in the world of philosophy than Halakhah. While we may speculate as to the precise parameters that govern a parallel to physical decapitation, admitting that it effectively is an extra-halakhic notion limits its practical applicability.

While questions abound, R. Auerbach's greatness was clearly evident on many fronts – personal, halakhic, and innovative – not least of which was his willingness to engage modern science and medicine head on. This allowed him to offer a fresh perspective on this complex matter, developing and sharpening his approach throughout.

CHAPTER 17:

Cardiac Function and Vital Motion

In the course of the last few chapters, we analyzed the positions of R. Moshe Feinstein, the Chief Rabbinate of Israel, and R. Shelomoh Zalman Auerbach regarding the halakhic validity of defining "brain death" as death. While R. Feinstein's position is open to interpretation, the Chief Rabbinate and R. Auerbach assume that some form of "brain death" is acceptable, although their definitions do not correspond to the current medical diagnosis. Supporters of accepting "brain death" as a halakhic definition of death either consider the irreversible cessation of spontaneous respiration to be the sole halakhic criterion of death (as proven by a "dead" brainstem) or equate "brain death" with the inherently death-defining decapitation.

However, a substantial number – and possibly even a majority – of modern halakhic decisors reject the notion of "brain death" as the death of an individual. They form a large, although not necessarily cohesive voice in arguing for determining death only upon the irreversible cessation of all natural motion. These opinions are united in their disagreement with defining death by respiratory standards alone and their unwillingness to accept R. Auerbach's comparison between decapitation and "brain death" (for either halakhic or scientific reasons, or both). In essence, proponents of this approach insist that a person defined as dead must look and "feel" like a corpse, nothing less. Any bodily movement – most notably a heartbeat – contradicts this status and is considered a continued sign of life – perhaps ephemeral life, but life nonetheless.

Among the principle proponents of this group are R. J. David Bleich, R. Yosef Shalom Elyashiv, R. Hershel Schachter, R. Moshe Sternbuch, R. Eliezer Yehudah Waldenberg, and R. Yitzhak Yaakov Weisz. While each takes a subtly distinctive approach, their positions will first be discussed as one unit so as to analyze and understand the approach more generally; later, we will explore the individual opinions.

From a historical perspective, accepting "brain death" as halakhically relevant is certainly a novelty, not in the least because the condition simply did not exist in the past. Many of these halakhic decisors take a conservative approach, not necessarily defining or describing a comprehensive halakhic determination of death, but rather reacting to, arguing with, and dismissing proofs and arguments offered for changing the *status quo*. Others cite specific proofs and evidence to the contrary and adopt a more aggressive approach, rallying support against accepting "brain death" as halakhically meaningful. The last group, most vocally represented by R. J. David Bleich, posits a unified halakhic definition of death dependent on cardiac failure, but not necessarily limited to it, reviewing the halakhic literature to develop a definition applicable in all situations and reflective of all sources. The main spotlight is on the specific interpretation of the various sources, focusing particularly on the cardiac-centered elements. R. Bleich has developed one of the more extensive discussions, engaging in debate with "brain death" proponents and responding to critiques, thereby forming a comprehensive and organized framework to discuss these issues. The subsequent analysis will therefore largely follow R. Bleich's outline while incorporating the wide spectrum of opinions where appropriate.

The original sources and various analyses were presented in earlier chapters. The following discussion will highlight the salient points relevant to the current approach and expand on them where appropriate.

Talmud Yoma 85a

Proponents of "brain death" interpret the discussion in Talmud *Yoma* 85a as relating to possible criteria for death, ultimately concluding that

ICSR is the sole determining factor. Opponents, in contrast, focus on Rashi's interpretation of this passage, according to which the Talmud concludes that a negative respiratory exam is a sufficient test to determine death because "sometimes life (*hiyyut*) is imperceptible in the heart but is perceptible by the nose." Accordingly, all agree that appropriate **criteria** for death must include cessation of heartbeat; the opinions in the Talmud disagree only as to which **test** most accurately ascertains cardiac status.[1] Supporting this approach, R. Bleich quotes *Hatam Sofer*'s conclusion (*Responsa Hatam Sofer* 338), in which he defines death only when a person lies completely motionless and is unresponsive – suffering from **both** irreversible respiratory and cardiac failure.

Relating to the focus on respiration more generally, many in this camp adopt the position of R. Shalom Mordechai Schwadron,[2] who argues that Talmud *Yoma* never intended to establish the irreversible cessation of spontaneous respiration (ICSR) as a **definition** or even necessary **criteria** for death, but rather only as an **indication** of death. As a general rule, a person suffering from ICSR is in fact dead – not because of his inability to breathe *per se*, but rather because ICSR coincides with some other death-determining criteria.

R. Schwadron was specifically asked about a person whom the *hevra kadisha* was preparing for burial when a certain sound or grunting was heard from the "body." The *hevra kadisha* was perturbed by the possibility that he was not quite yet dead and immediately called for a doctor. The doctor said that in all likelihood the noise came from the emptying or mixing of gastric juices and was certainly not indicative of life. Since it was Friday afternoon, the *hevra kadisha* quickly prepared the body for burial before Shabbat. Later in the week, some of the *hevra kadisha* members had second thoughts as to whether or not they acted appropriately and turned to R. Schwadron to ask if repentance was warranted. It is in this context that R. Schwadron explained that even though death can normally be determined when signs of respiration are no longer perceived, when there is objective evidence to the contrary – such as when the not-yet-dead person emits a groan or sigh – declaring death is certainly inappropriate.

---

1 *Bi-Netivot ha-Halakhah* 3 (henceforth, *BNhH*), 119-22.
2 *Responsa Maharsham, YD* 6:124.

Similarly, although we normally rely upon the perceived lack of respiration to determine death, when there is evidence to the contrary – such as when the heart continues to beat – we must question whether the respiratory test accurately represents the determinant criteria for death.

Understanding Talmud *Yoma* in this light greatly limits the impact of the role of respiration in determining death; ICSR only determines death in the absence of any other signs of life. According to R. Bleich's interpretation of Rashi's comments,[3] the Talmudic discussion is a purely practical matter, completely limited to the appropriateness of the **test** used to assess whether the **criteria** for death have been fulfilled. It is specifically not a discussion of the **criteria** of death, which, according to Rashi, must include a cardiac component. Checking the *hotem* is acceptable and appropriate because it is (or more correctly, was) the most sensitive diagnostic **test** for cardiac function, not for any essential or intrinsic reason.

This presents somewhat of a methodological difficulty, however, as it seems strange for the Talmud to cite Biblical proof for a purely practical matter. In presenting the parallel disagreement regarding the origins of fetal development, the Talmud comments that the dispute is limited to the question of embryological origins, specifically noting that in the context of matters of *pikuah nefesh*, all agree that "the essence of one's life-force is found in the nose/face" (*ikar hiyyuta be-appeih*) and citing the verse, "All in whose nostrils was the breath of the spirit of life" (*kol asher nishmat ruah hayyim be-appav*)."[4] If, from a practical perspective, respiration is the best or most sensitive determinant of cardiac function – which according to this view is a certain indication of life – then logic dictates and Halakhah requires that respiration be assessed prior to diagnosing death. Why require a proof-text at all? Rashi must interpret this discussion as proof for the circumstantial reality. The Talmud records Biblical proof for specifically relying on the test in question; in the context of *pikuah nefesh*, a rescuer may/must rely on respiration as the indication of life. The verse teaches us that despite its lack of any inherent indication

---

3 *BNhH*, 97, 107-8, 131.
4 *Bereishit* 7:22.

of life, checking respiration is not only appropriate, but also may (and perhaps must) be relied upon to make life and death determinations.[5]

Relying on Rashi

Those who read Talmud *Yoma* 85a as advocating ICSR as the sole criterion of death note that in codifying the rulings of the passage, neither Rambam (*Hilkhot Shabbat* 2:18-19) nor *Shulhan Arukh* (OH 329:4) mention Rashi's comment[6] – indicating that they implicitly reject his reading. This conclusion is not necessarily true, however, and this point touches upon the broader issue of the status of Rashi's positions.

In authoring one of the first great works of Talmudic commentary, Rashi's style and format were precisely that – commentary. This allowed him to explore and interpret the text, encountering multiple and often opposite approaches within a halakhic debate, as well as explaining similar material contextually in different circumstances. This is important, as his preferred style has led many to wonder whether Rashi intended for his comments and interpretations to be taken as halakhic positions.

Authors of the classic works of Halakhah often do incorporate Rashi's positions, but this question is of even greater relevance and concern when they do **not** do so. Is the omission intentional – arguing against Rashi's position even though not necessarily providing an alternative? Or was Rashi's interpretation assumed to be so elementary that it was deemed unnecessary to reference it altogether? It is certainly possible that Rambam and *Shulhan Arukh* assumed that Rashi's comment reflects a halakhic position and accordingly took it for granted.

---

5 Rashi must also interpret the phrase *"ikkar hiyyuta be-appeih"* as referring to the crucial location for practically determining or ascertaining life as being in the nostrils/face. While perhaps not the simplest reading of this discussion, the Talmud often cites Biblical proof-texts as supportive of practical, realistic questions, such as searching for Biblical proof that blood is red (*Shabbat* 108a). In interpreting the passage in this way, Rashi relies on his knowledge that the heart is the ultimate indicator of life and any mention or reference to respiratory function is merely intended as a practical assessment of cardiac function. He takes this as a given without elaboration or discussion.
6 For a fuller analysis of their presentation of this ruling, see chapter 5.

Textual Variants

As discussed in chapter 5, two different textual variants were available to the medieval commentators. Rashi's text presents the Talmudic debate regarding the proper extent of excavation efforts permitted on Shabbat before declaring an avalanche victim dead as *hotmo* (nose/face) vs. *libbo* (heart). Almost all others, including Rabbeinu Hananel, Rif, Ran, and Rosh, refer to the text as debating *hotmo* vs. *tabburo* (navel), making no mention of Rashi's text at all, and Yerushalmi *Yoma* (8:5) similarly presents the debate as *hotmo* vs. *tabburo*. The classic Vilna Shas, however, follows Rashi's text.

Proponents of ICSR as the criterion of halakhic death attribute great importance to these variants, asserting that according to the more prevalent version, all opinions agree that assessment of cardiac activity is entirely irrelevant. Accordingly, *tabburo*, like *hotmo*, must indicate some sort of respiratory examination.

R. Bleich argues, in contrast, that there is in essence no difference between the two texts, explaining that checking the navel refers to palpating the abdominal aortic pulse.[7] The goal is the same – attempting to diagnose continued cardiac activity as expressed through a palpable pulse – with each text merely suggesting a different anatomical location for examination. However, while an abdominal pulse can be felt by pressing deeply, it is often difficult to find, frequently to the point of being impossible. The navel certainly seems a strange choice of location for determining cardiac activity, particularly in the Talmud's context, in which further search efforts would be forbidden once the abdomen is uncovered. Given that abdominal pulse is a profoundly insensitive indicator for cardiac function, it seems highly unlikely that an opinion in the Talmud would allow depending on it for life and death decisions.[8]

---

7 *BNhH*, 133.
8 Physical diagnosis guidelines often recommend assessing the abdominal aorta through palpation, examining for abnormal pulsations indicative of abdominal aortic aneurysms (AAA). Due to the lack of sensitivity of such an exam, current United States Preventive Services Task Force guidelines recommend routine ultrasound exams for individuals at increased risk for developing AAA's, such as male smokers older than 65 (http://www.ahrq.gov/clinic/uspstf05/aaascr/aaars.pdf, accessed July 22, 2010).

Having said that, the navel or abdomen is an equally strange choice for examining respiration, especially in light of the obvious alternative of examining the nose or mouth. Indeed, although most medieval commentators cited this alternate text and apparently decided practical matters accordingly, all major halakhic codifications rely upon Rashi's text, framing the debate as *hotmo* vs. *libbo* and uniformly siding with *hotmo*.

The Physical Orientation of the Discovered Avalanche Victim

The Talmud concludes with R. Pappa's claim that the original Talmudic debate is only relevant when the victim is discovered feet-first. When rescuers first uncover the victim's head, everyone agrees that the rescue effort must end with a negative respiratory exam of the nose. Rambam and *Shulhan Arukh* rule in accordance with this conclusion. Interpreting R. Pappa's conclusion, however, depends upon the different methodological approaches regarding whether the entire discussion debates the **criteria** for death or the merits of various **tests** assessing whether or not those criteria have been met.

R. Bleich argues that upon closer analysis, the Talmud cannot possibly be debating the criteria for death.[9] According to R. Pappa, the disputed case is one in which rescuers uncover the chest before the face and find no heartbeat. The *libbo* approach argues that without a heartbeat, the person is dead, and further rescue efforts are therefore prohibited. But what does the *hotmo* approach assume? If they are debating criteria, the *hotmo* opinion must maintain that even without a heartbeat, rescuers must assume that the person is still alive until they determine whether or not he is breathing, as this is the real determining factor. This cannot be true, since it is impossible to breathe without a heartbeat. This is likely what prompted Rashi to explain (as per R. Bleich's understanding) that the Talmudic argument is only about the sensitivity of the different **tests** – all geared toward determining whether or not the heart is beating. The *hotmo* approach argues that direct cardiac exam is insufficiently sensitive to reliably and accurately detect a heartbeat; he therefore always requires a respiratory exam, even when the victim is discovered feet-first. The *libbo* approach claims that a direct cardiac exam is sufficiently sensitive to

---

9 *BNbH*, 120, 130-1.

detect a heartbeat, but agrees that a respiratory exam is at least equally as sensitive, and therefore agrees that examination of *hotmo* is sufficient when the victim is discovered head first. According to the *libbo* approach, when either **test** is negative (no detected heartbeat or no detected breathing), the person is dead, and no further rescue attempts can be made on Shabbat. Rambam and *Shulhan Arukh*, in ruling in accordance with the *hotmo* opinion in all cases, attest that a respiratory exam is always necessary, as this is the best evaluation of cardiac activity.

R. Bleich understands the Talmud as consistently assuming cardiac criteria for death to the point that it was never even subject to debate (as per Rashi); the Talmud's discussion of examining *hotmo* is merely a **test**, not a **criterion** for death.

Concluding similarly, R. Eliezer Yehuda Waldenberg offers a somewhat different analysis.[10] R. Waldenberg consistently argues that the Talmud requires both the cessation of respiration and cardiac function to determine death. He explains that the Talmud assumes that under normal conditions, continued respiration is a sure sign of continued heartbeat, and the absence of respiration indicates irreversible cardiac failure (per Rashi). The victim is therefore determined to be dead upon negative results of a *hotmo* test, but only as long as there is no other proof or evidence for continued life. As R. Schwadron argues, when there **is** evidence to the contrary – meaning that death is not an absolutely forgone conclusion – rescuing must continue. In such a case, apparent lack of respiration cannot be relied upon to declare the victim dead.

R. Waldenberg explains that the Talmud assumes that a lack of respiration indicates a lack of cardiac function under most circumstances, and the Talmud therefore relied on a respiratory test to determine both respiratory and cardiac failure. If, however, there is any evidence for a continued heartbeat – even via an EKG recording – this certainly precludes a diagnosis of death.

R. Waldenberg limits the application of this discussion, however, suggesting that R. Pappa's rule applies only on Shabbat and only when there are absolutely no indications of continued life. Only then, argues R. Waldenburg, does the Talmud permit relying on a respiratory test to determine death without examining the rest of the body. Since the

---

10 *Responsa Tzitz Eliezer* 17:66.

possibility for continued life under such circumstances is so miniscule (*mi'uta de-mi'uta*), searching for it does not warrant desecrating Shabbat law. R. Shemuel Wosner rules similarly, arguing that a check for respiration is only reliable and permitted in the case of a building collapse on Shabbat.[11] On any other day of the week, R. Waldenberg and R. Wosner agree that all efforts must be made to discover any possible signs of life and continue to support those signs of continued life – especially cardiac function – regardless of whether or not the patient is able to breathe on his own.

Hakham Tzvi: The Relationship Between Respiration and Heartbeat

As discussed in chapter 8, *Hakham Tzvi* explains Rashi's comments based on then-current physiological basis, concluding that life can only be

---

11 *Responsa Shevet ha-Levi* 7:235, 8:86. While the Talmudic discussion specifically deals with rescue efforts on Shabbat, this contention is rather novel, as it suggests different thresholds for allowing potentially life-saving efforts depending on which *halakhah* is at stake. While parallels to such a notion exist, particularly when it comes to Shabbat (allowing violating only Rabbinic prohibitions for lesser concerns and limiting violations of Torah law only to persons and cases that are potentially life threatening), when it comes to saving lives, there are usually no distinctions made among different prohibitions save the three cardinal sins – and removing rubble on Shabbat is certainly not among them. Distinctions do exist between permissible, but not required, weekday activities that by dint of their lack of incumbent obligation are forbidden on Shabbat. While potentially conceivable, models for requiring certain actions on weekdays for life-saving purposes but prohibiting them on Shabbat appear to be lacking.

One possible answer would be to argue that when a person is found to be completely apneic, the likelihood of still finding a heartbeat is so low that if falls beneath the halakhic radar screen and is effectively ignored. However, when despite the small chances of being true, it is easy to ascertain the matter with greater precision, one should certainly do so. When not possible, either because of physical or halakhic impediment, the Halakhah defaults back to assuming that since the possibility of such an occurrence is so small, it has no halakhic relevance. Therefore, during the week, one should attempt to continue a rescue effort, searching for a heartbeat even though the chances of finding one are so small that they are in all other respects halakhically irrelevant. However, when ascertaining a more precise or accurate determination of an otherwise halakhically ignored likelihood entails violating halakhic precepts (such as Shabbat restrictions), it is summarily forbidden. Neither R. Waldenberg nor R. Wosner offers this solution explicitly, but this may be along the lines of what they intended.

determined by cardiac activity. Many question the relevance of *Hakham Tzvi*'s position in light of its faulty assumptions.

However, many halakhists who reject "brain death" as death largely incorporate and accept at least part of *Hakham Tzvi*'s conclusions, although their approach is not uniform in doing so. R. Shemuel Wosner, for example, wholeheartedly accepts *Hakham Tzvi*'s conclusions regarding the centrality of cardiac function, arguing that it is not in the realm of science to distinguish life from death. The halakhic position – whatever one argues it should be – is not based on physiology, but rather on tradition. R. Wosner argues that *Hakham Tzvi*'s sources (including the *Zohar* and R. Sa'adyah Gaon) are not debatable, being accurate on both actual (seemingly scientific/medical) and halakhic grounds. R. Wosner therefore concludes that *Hakham Tzvi*'s assertion that life can only be determined by cardiac activity is halakhically binding, and perhaps even the impetus for *Hatam Sofer*'s (otherwise un-sourced) mention of the cessation of heartbeat in his concluding summary statement (see chapter 9).[12]

While not analyzing *Hakham Tzvi*'s sources directly, R. Wosner does not mention that almost all of them (including R. Sa'adyah Gaon, R. Gershon b. Shelomoh [author of *Sefer Sha'ar ha-Shamayyim*], R. Meir Aldebi [author of *Shevilei Emunah*], and R. Yehudah ha-Levi), other than the *Zohar*, offer physiological explanations for their positions. Aware of the changed scientific realities, R. Wosner nonetheless accepts these opinions as binding, seemingly arguing that physiology only served a supporting role for an otherwise independent conclusion. Accordingly, he argues that decisions on these matters cannot be affected by changes in medical knowledge; these are matters of Halakhah, not science.[13]

---

12 *Responsa Shevet ha-Levi* 7:235:1.
13 R. Wosner distinguishes these questions from those entirely reliant on ascertaining facts, such as anatomical positioning. For example, *Hatam Sofer* (*YD* 167) argues for accepting the current scientific view of reproductive anatomy regarding matters of *niddah*. Based on then-current (but now known to be inaccurate) science, *Hatam Sofer* endorses the description of female anatomy found in Rambam (*Hilkhot Isurei Bi'ah* 5:2-5), as opposed to that of Rashi (*Niddah* 17b, s.v. *heder*), *Tosafot* (*Niddah* 42b, s.v. *shehotzi*), and *Maharam Lublin* (Responsa, no. 110). This is a question of reality, describing the correct and accurate diagram of female anatomy, and is certainly subject to validation by medical science. Upon learning that the *Hatam Sofer*'s analysis is not based on

R. Waldenberg takes a different approach, arguing that the merits of *Hakham Tzvi*'s scientific arguments are not the proper focal point. Even if we reject the science of *Hakham Tzvi*, argues R. Waldenberg, the more important question is what the Talmud meant when it discussed respiration. If, as *Hakham Tzvi* argues, respiration was then understood to be part and parcel of cardiac function, Rashi's comment is far more understandable and quite compelling. Breathing, as a means of providing the heart with its necessary "ventilation system," was understandably viewed as a surrogate marker for continued cardiac function. Therefore, when the Talmud discusses breathing, it really means cardiac function, using respiration as a more accessible and simpler means of assessing the heartbeat. The Talmud relies on checking respiration precisely because it indicates cardiac function – meaning that cessation of heartbeat is the ultimate determinant of death.[14]

According to R. Waldenberg, how the Talmud came to rely on a respiratory test is not relevant, and the fact that its reasoning (and that of *Hakham Tzvi*) is inaccurate is immaterial. The "science" only explains why the Talmud insisted on checking for respiration, as opposed to any other sign; what was really at stake was the heartbeat. The fact that the science is now known to be incorrect does not affect the Talmud's presupposition that death requires the irreversible cessation of both respiration and cardiac function. The proper focus should not be on the technical **test** advanced by the Talmud for determining death – meaning checking for respiration – but rather on the **criteria** of death presupposed by the entire discussion – the irreversible cessation of both respiratory and cardiac function. Ancient science is only responsible for the (faulty) assumption that respiration is indicative of cardiac function.[15]

---

fact, we are not bound by it. In contrast, questions of values and judgments, such as those of determining the moment of life and of death, are not determined by the conclusions of medical science.

14 *Responsa Tzitz Eliezer* 9:46.

15 This raises an important methodological question related to the relevance of an author's historical intent. The Talmud is quite clear in focusing solely on respiration, while Rashi elucidates and *Hakham Tzvi* elaborates that respiration was understood as a means to allow for continued effective cardiac function. R. Waldenberg argues that the intent of the Talmud was to diagnose continued cardiac function and through that means to

Mishnah Ohalot 1:6

As discussed in chapter 6, Mishnah *Ohalot* 1:6 describes a decapitated person as dead, leading to the conceptual question of how this definition relates to the more "standard" or mundane definition of death by respiratory and/or cardiac criteria. Regardless of one's position on the inclusion of cardiac criteria in this determination, it is important to note that a decapitated person's heart will most likely continue to beat for at least some time after the head is completely severed. Nonetheless, the *mishnah* describes such a person as dead immediately upon decapitation, despite the continued (but certainly soon to be extinguished) heartbeat. The *mishnah* continues to describe any further movements exhibited by such a person as *pirkus* – uncontrolled, unorganized, and not-precisely-definable motions.

For those who rely on cardiac criteria alone to determine death, this certainly presents a paradox. Indeed, proponents of ICSR as the sole criterion of death use this *mishnah* to show that heartbeat is completely irrelevant to the determination; supporters of "brain death" extend it to refer to "physiological decapitation" and/or interpret it as a distinct definition of death.

R. Bleich relates to this question on two levels. First and foremost, he rejects any comparison between a "brain dead" patient and a decapitation victim.[16] For decapitation to qualify as death, the brain must be physically separated from the rest of the body or otherwise be physically absent

---

determine death; the method the Talmud suggests at arriving at that conclusion is not of concern, and hence irrelevant, as it is now known to be predicated on incorrect physiological assumptions. Others would argue, however, that the Talmud focuses solely on respiration and brings a Biblical proof text as support, effectively mitigating any argument that the Talmudic discussion is dependent on then-current scientific theories. The Bible is assumed to be ubiquitously and timelessly true; its precepts therefore cannot be dependent on any amount of science, neither ancient nor modern. It is perhaps for this reason that the then-current scientific assumptions are purposely left out of the Talmudic discussion, leaving such gaps to be filled by Rashi and the later commentators.

16 J.D. Bleich, "Of Cerebral, Respiratory, and Cardiac death," *Contemporary Halakhic Problems*, vol. IV (Hoboken, NJ: Ktav Publishing House, 1995): 318-23

(such as if liquefied or otherwise excised). As discussed in chapter 2, the clinical realities of "brain dead" patients do not meet these criteria.

While R. Bleich believes that this first contention stands independently in rejecting "brain death" as parallel to decapitation, he capitalizes upon the general difficulty as a springboard for a more general approach to the halakhic definition of death, as discussed extensively in chapter 6.[17] R. Bleich explains that no one ever intended to focus on the heart as the **exclusive** determinant of death, but rather simply to exclude any patient with continued cardiac function as dead. It is not the heart *per se* that is the focus, but rather what a continued heartbeat represents – what R. Bleich terms "vital motion." The continued pumping of the heart identifies a patient as alive only as an example of "vital motion." Conversely, it is not the stoppage of the heart *per se* that constitutes death. Rather, death is defined by the irreversible cessation of "vital motion," with the heartbeat being just one of many examples. The heart is most often the focus simply because in many circumstances, it is the last sign of "vital motion" to remain, so that upon its irreversible cessation, no further "vital motion" exists at all – defining a state of death.

Accordingly, decapitation is not a separate definition of death, but rather only an application of this broader principle. R. Bleich explains that normally, the heart exhibits "vital motion" – repeated and continuous muscular contractions (pumping) that result in **effective circulation** – which in and of itself contributes to continued life. A heartbeat that does not succeed in effectively pumping blood throughout the body does not qualify as "vital motion." Upon the decapitation-induced severing of the head, all organized motion throughout the body ceases, with subsequent muscular contractions completely involuntary, sporadic, and convulsive at best – certainly not "vital" – constituting what the *mishnah* refers to as *pirkus*. This is also true, argues R. Bleich, of the post-decapitation short-lived continued heartbeat. With a gaping wound just inches above the heart, the circulatory system collapses, unable to maintain functional blood flow, rendering the heartbeat ineffective and therefore irrelevant. It is not the simple contraction of cardiac muscle that defines life, but

---

17 *BNhH*, 109, 199-22.

rather the heartbeat viewed in the context of its appropriate intended consequence – supporting a functional circulatory system.

Applying this conceptual model more broadly, R. Bleich interprets Talmud *Yoma* 85a in a similar light.[18] While the Talmud mentions respiration and Rashi explains that it is used merely as an easily assessable surrogate for heartbeat, R. Bleich argues that it is neither of these physiological functions themselves that are determinant of death. The focus is instead on what they represent – the last vestiges of "vital motion" present in an avalanche victim. When they irreversibly cease, the victim is dead because he no longer exhibits "vital motion." This is why Rashi prefaced his comments regarding cardiac activity with the additional condition that the victim must be "lying still as a stone," completely unresponsive (*mutal ke-even*); any coordinated (non-*pirkus*) movement would indicate that the victim is still alive.[19]

Limitations of This Approach

R. Bleich's suggested interpretation is not without difficulties. According to R. Bleich, breathing, heartbeat, and muscular movement all constitute "vital motion," but only when they are natural or spontaneous. No one would consider lifting the hands of a corpse and bringing them together repeatedly as proof that the corpse is clapping; similarly, any organ whose motion is maintained completely artificially cannot be described as exhibiting "vital motion." What, then, would be the status of an artificial heart?

---

18 *BNhH*, 106, 119-21.
19 In a similar vein, R. Bleich analyzes the status of a patient who has received a heart transplant (*BNhH*, 111-25). This patient's own heart can certainly no longer be described as providing any "vital motion" upon its removal; according to a strict application of R. Bleich's criteria, the patient should therefore be described as dead. However, once the anesthesia wears off and the patient is successfully weaned from the ventilator, any and all volitional motion is certainly considered "vital" and certainly life confirming. Therefore, even during the surgery and the subsequent moments when no "vital motion" is perceived, the patient is still considered alive. It is not the patient's actual heart or continued heartbeat that constitutes life, but rather the potential for continued "vital motion," which the successful recovery from surgery proves never irreversibly stopped.

Put more broadly, modern medicine provides "replacement therapy" for many organs that no longer function adequately, such as ventilators for respiratory failure, hemodialysis for renal failure, and ventricular assist devices and even (still experimental) artificial hearts for heart failure. Many of these therapies are instituted prior to the complete collapse and failure of the organ they intend to replace, leading to an important question as to when these natural organs are considered to be contributing to "vital motion" and when their functions are deemed completely artificial. The question becomes more complex since a given organ may be functioning at only 5% or 10% of what is necessary to maintain life, with the other 95% or 90% maintained artificially. While the artificial intervention is entirely necessary to maintain life, the native organ still functions minimally. Should that be termed "vital motion"?

Other questions that push the "vital motion" envelope even further abound, specifically as regards what is considered "vital." With continued advances in "organ replacement therapies," one must wonder at what point, if any, enough organ systems have been artificially replaced so that the patient can no longer be described as having any independent "vital motion." Put differently, what bodily functions constitute "vital motion" so that replacing enough of these functions transforms the person into a "cyborg," whose movements are most certainly not indicative of "vital motion"? It is just as important to identify which, if any, organs or functions do not qualify as "vital motion," so as to negate the notion that their continued functions signify life.

Even assuming that the function or organ involved is deemed "vital," one must also ponder the limits and extents of what constitutes "motion." Normally, Halakhah takes cognizance only of clinically perceptible phenomenon, disregarding microscopic or molecular interactions as insignificant. Indeed, it is possible to conceive of a case in which a patient exhibits no clinically visible "vital motion" at all, yet we would intuitively consider him alive.

Imagine a patient who received an artificial heart transplant for some congenital anomaly 15 years ago and has been free from any cardiovascular disease ever since. He now experiences a serious medical insult and suffers from localized lesions in the brainstem, therefore finding himself unable to breathe without the aid of mechanical ventilation. In his "locked in" state, the patient is aware and awake, maintaining full conscious and cognitive abilities, but he is completely unable to move. In such a condition, while almost all voluntary muscles are incapacitated, the muscles of the eyes and eyelids are often spared, prompting some ambitious patients to develop blinking-based communication systems.[20] Were a patient with an artificial heart and suffering from "Locked In Syndrome" to lose even this ability, he would, according to R. Bleich's strict definition, no longer exhibit any clinically perceptible "vital motion" – despite the fact that he maintains his mental faculties. The patient's brain operates to the same degree before and after he loses eyelid movement; the only difference is that there was previously perceptible clinical evidence to that effect. Once no longer able to blink, would R. Bleich describe such a patient as dead, even though just a moment before he was most certainly alive? Due to completely external reasons and although desperate for and even retaining the mental capacity for communication, this patient cannot physically make his communicative desires known to others. Can such a patient be defined as dead due to lack of "vital motion"?

This situation may seem so unlikely as to be irrelevant, but a precise definition of what constitutes "vital motion" is certainly important in clearly and accurately defining what death means and when it occurs. This question has recently even taken on increased relevance.[21] In patients suffering from persistent vegetative (PVS) and minimally conscious (MCS) states (not "brain dead"), doctors have been able to detect meaningful thought patterns evident through functional MRI (fMRI) technology. Because different parts of the brain process different types of thinking, when healthy ("normal") people are asked to perform motor imagery or spatial imagery tasks, they use different particular patterned areas of the brain, characterized by increased blood flow to those areas and visualized

---

20 Jean-Dominique Bauby, an editor-in-chief of *Elle* magazine, suffered a stroke in 1995, leaving him in a locked-in state. He developed a monocular based Morse Code (one eye was sewn shut due to irrigation problems) and described and detailed his feelings and emotions during that time in a best-selling book, *The Diving Bell and the Butterfly* (New York: Vintage, 1998).
21 M.M. Monti, A. Vanhaudenhuyse, M.R. Coleman, et al. "Willful modulation of brain activity in disorders of consciousness." *New England Journal of Medicine* 362:7 (2010): 579-89.

by fMRI technology. All of the patients in the study, who were unconscious and otherwise thought to be unable to communicate, exhibited the "appropriate" fMRI pattern when asked to visualize the different imagery tasks.

Taking this one step further, the clinicians instructed one such patient to picture himself performing a motor imagery task as an affirmative answer to a question, or "yes," and to picture himself performing a spatial imagery task as a negative answer, or "no." Using this method, the patient, who had not communicated with anyone for more than five years, accurately answered a series of yes/no questions.

While all PVS and MCS patients are considered to be alive by all standards, the possibility of "communication" in unconscious patients raises important questions regarding what constitutes "vital motion." Does the ability to "communicate" through modern technological (and rather creative) means constitute "vital motion," or must proof for life be perceptible to a technologically-unaided observer? The future potential of these technologies is yet unknown, but may lead to more elaborate communicative abilities beyond affirming and denying statements. If possible, would a patient similar to the one described above – with an artificial heart implanted years earlier for unrelated reasons and now suffering a spinal cord injury severing the phrenic nerve and preventing spontaneous respiration – be considered dead, even while "communicating" that he wishes to continue living?[22]

---

[22] Along the same lines, how would one describe a clinically imperceptible phenomenon that was able to create/effect/induce some clinically perceptible effect external to itself? New emerging technology attempts to harness brain waves to control electronics – in more simple systems, adjusting the power of a fan by concentrating more or less intently, thereby affecting EEG wave frequencies, or even by controlling certain aspects of video games in conjunction with the more standard hand-held controllers. Researchers are working on adapting these techniques to communication, and the day it is not far off when a person will be able to communicate by means of brain waves alone – with absolutely no "vital motion" whatsoever.

Would R. Bleich consider a person who can utilize only such methods of communication to be dead? It would be quite strange to do so, especially since the person can hear the pronouncement of his death and "respond" to it with his futuristic "brain wave into language" machine, protesting that he prefers not yet to be buried just yet.

All of these cases are (still) within the world of science fiction, unlikely to be relevant in the near future, and they have not yet been analyzed or discussed by contemporary halakhic decisors. Even while not realistic at this point, however, the questions that these hypothetical cases raise and difficulties that they evoke are important in that they require sharpening current definitions.

Even while these questions may not be answerable as yet in terms of defining "vital motion," and particularly as they regard "brain death," the application to current situations, R. Bleich argues, is most certainly clear. Current realities are far simpler – a "brain dead" patient's continuing functional, spontaneous, and natural heartbeat most certainly qualifies as "vital motion," rendering such a person as living and completely forbidding the life-ending removal of any organs.

Importantly, R. Ahron Soloveichik regarded continued brain activity as a certain sign of continued life.[23] Determining death, in his opinion, requires the irreversible cessation of three basic functions – cardiac, respiratory, and neurological. While not elaborating on his understanding of the source material, R. Soloveichik cites Mishnah *Ohalot* as also requiring the cessation of brain activity for determining death. He does not explain how the various sources relate to each other, but clearly assumes that each adds an indispensible element to the final determination.

Assuming these criteria to be correct – as R. Soloveichik does not offer rigorous analysis – he does not relate to the issue of subclinical phenomena directly. Nonetheless, he argues that they should be accorded halakhic import. Most halakhists who identify continued cardiac activity

---

In a different context, R. Auerbach argues (*Responsa Minhat Shelomoh* 2:100:7) that microscopic cellular components should be considered "visible," and thus halakhically meaningful, since "people deal with these particles (*anashim metaplim be-helkikim ha-eleh*) and transfer them from one species to another." Expanding this approach to encompass all subclinical phenomena that have macroscopic effects would mean that even R. Bleich would regard these EEG readings as signs of "vital motion," since their effect, even if not their source, is certainly of halakhic import.

23 A. Soloveichik, "Death According to the Halacha," *Journal of Halacha and Contemporary Society* 17 (1989): 41-48. This article was written as an answer to several short questions and is not a thorough analysis of all the issues. As a position statement, R. Soloveichik is abundantly clear in rejecting "brain death" as death. Because of the absence of rigorous analysis, R. Soloveichik main thesis is presented here only briefly.

as a sign of continued life recognize EKG evidence as sufficient proof of function, even when a pulse or heartbeat is not palpable. So too, argues R. Soloveichik, EEG evidence of continued brainwave activity should serve as sufficient proof of continued brain function. This, he argues, should be true even in the absence of any macroscopic signs for brain activity or even visible effects of the continued function.

Hatam Sofer: Interpretation and Role in Crafting the Halakhah

While one of the most often quoted sources in the halakhic literature discussing "brain death," *Hatam Sofer*'s famous responsum is rarely analyzed in its entirety. While ICSR and "brain death" proponents focus on the discussion in the main part of this responsum, those arguing for including cardiac criteria in determining death quote almost exclusively from *Hatam Sofer*'s concluding summary statement:

> [A]ny person who lies [still] like a stone (*munah ke-even domem*) and has no heartbeat (*defikah*) [possibly pulse], and then ceases to breathe – we must rely on the determination of our Holy Torah that he is dead – his burial should not be delayed and *kohanim* who come into contact with him violate a prohibition...

R. Bleich stresses the literal understanding of this concluding sentiment. *Hatam Sofer* describes three criteria that must all be met to properly pronounce a person as halakhically dead: 1) completely unresponsive; 2) no heartbeat; 3) not breathing. Ostensibly, lacking any one of the three should preclude such a pronouncement.

While seemingly relevant to the discussion, *Hatam Sofer* makes no mention of *Hakham Tzvi*'s published responsa (74, 76-78) on the primacy of the heart and circulatory system in determining death. Nonetheless, R. Wosner argues that it was precisely *Hakham Tzvi*'s forceful stance that convinced *Hatam Sofer* to determine death only upon the (irreversible) cessation of cardiac function.[24]

---

24 *Responsa Shevet ha-Levi* 7:235:1. See the concluding section of chapter 9 for a fuller discussion of this relationship.

Coming from a different perspective, R. Bleich argues that *Hatam Sofer* specifically included these three elements because he was attempting to identify a state of the complete absence of "vital motion." Any motion not qualifying as *pirkus* – be it voluntary movement, respiration, or even simply an effective heartbeat – qualifies as "vital motion;" all three must be irreversibly absent to accurately determine death. It was simply inconceivable for *Hatam Sofer* to even begin to imagine declaring dead someone who by simple observation appears to be not so. Even in attempting to shorten the time between death and burial, it was beyond what *Hatam Sofer* deemed possible to consider burying someone who exhibits continued signs of life – including a heartbeat.[25]

Rama, Orah Hayyim 330:1 - Inability to Precisely Define the Moment of Death

Describing the tragic case of a woman dying in childbirth, Rama (*OH* 330:1) rules that despite the noble intention of saving lives, our inability to precisely define the moment of death prevents an observer from attempting to surgically remove the fetus emergently (and certainly not to violate Shabbat prohibitions in doing so). The mother may still be alive, albeit dying, and the radical surgical procedure may unintentionally hasten her death.[26]

Traditionally, in fact, in most "standard" or "normal" cases, the recently deceased is not moved for a period of 20-30 minutes, reflecting, among other notions, a hesitant approach to precisely defining the moment of death.[27] This presents a difficulty for any determination of death; regardless of how one identifies it, it should be able to be practically actionable. This is true not only of cardiac, but also respiratory-based determinations. Even though a patient's last breath can only be identified retroactively, after some time, it should be clear that the patient is indeed irreversibly no longer breathing – permitting emergent surgery that stands the chance of saving the life of a fetus.

---

25 Cf. *Responsa Aseh Lekha Rav* 8:64.
26 Rama's opinion and its basis in Halakhah were discussed in chapter 5.
27 See, for example, Y.M. Tukachinsky, *Gesher ha-Hayyim* 1, 48.

R. Waldenberg argues that it is incorrect to interpret Rama's comment as reluctance to determine death based on the absence of respiration (which, according to R. Waldenberg, means no perceivable heartbeat as well). Rather, Rama is clear that his concern regards a lack of expertise in making this determination – *"ein anu beki'in"* – for fear that death be confused with fainting or syncope. As *Hatam Sofer* records, distinguishing between these states, especially during a person's final hours, requires significant expertise and experience, normally relegated to members of the *hevra kadisha*. Complicating the matter is the presumed "fact" that the fetus can only survive for a few moments after its mother's death, necessitating an immediate decision and highlighting Rama's reluctance to rely on our meager ability to make speedy and accurate determinations.[28]

Understood more generally, Rama is not making a halakhic determination that we are in principle incapable of accurately determining the moment of death. Rather, he is stating that practically, most people are not sufficiently versed or experienced to make an "on the spot" decision when the potential for murder hangs in the balance. R. Waldenberg therefore concludes that Rama's comments are not relevant to the discussion at hand. While it is necessary to proceed cautiously, appropriate, accurate, and practically actionable criteria for death are to be found within Halakhah.

---

28 *Responsa Tzitz Eliezer* 10:25:4. R. Waldenberg mentions the opposite suggestion as well. Assuming that fetal survival is only possible for several moments after its mother's death, given our practical inability to accurately diagnose death, perhaps once we finally make that ultimate determination, we should be concerned that the mother died only moments prior. If so, we should certainly try to remove and rescue the fetus, since it may have a substantial chance of survival. R. Waldenberg responds that by the time that Halakhah is comfortable confirming the mother's death, she most certainly must have died a long while before the determination. It is only our hesitation to even possibly speed up this process that is cause for such a long delay, after which the fetus can no longer survive.

CHAPTER 18:

Challenging ICSR as Determinant of Death

Since, according to many opinions, recognizing "brain death" requires accepting purely respiratory criteria for death, resulting in a radical change from the *status quo*, many opponents have dedicated significant efforts to analyzing, dissecting, and ultimately rejecting possible proofs for this notion. Additionally, many advocates for cardiac-oriented criteria find difficulties with the solely respiratory-based approach, including conceptual problems, practical challenges, and specific textual proofs.

Conceptual Difficulties

First and foremost, R. Bleich rejects ICSR as the sole determinant of death as not representative of the irreversible cessation of "vital motion."[1] As long as "vital motion" continues – and all "brain dead" patients' hearts continue to beat unabated – life continues. R. Bleich continues to argue that even if ICSR is, in fact, the sole criteria of death, ventilated patients need not necessarily meet criteria of being irreversibly incapable of breathing. The physiological inability to breathe spontaneously,

---

1 *Bi-Netivot ha-Halakhah* 3 (henceforth, *BNhH*), 120-1.

R. Bleich argues, is not necessarily equivalent to "halakhic ICSR," when the patient is being mechanically ventilated.

R. Bleich explains that when the Talmud discusses breathing, it refers to more than just the muscular work of inhalation and exhalation, but rather the human body's ability to interact with, incorporate, and extract oxygen from the environment.[2] It is the purpose, ultimate goal, and outcome of respiration – meaning gas exchange (or ventilation) – that is considered "vital," not the physical work of forcing air into the lungs' alveolar spaces.

In brainstem failure, the problem is that the patient cannot move air in and out of his lungs; once that hurdle is overcome with the assistance of a mechanical ventilator, the body accomplishes the rest of the breathing process on its own. When air reaches the lungs, oxygen is absorbed across the lung alveoli into the blood and carbon dioxide carried by the blood is unloaded into the lungs to be exhaled. Gas exchange in a "brain dead" patient is unaffected by the neurological injury.

A ventilator provides air to the lungs of a patient who is unable to obtain it on his own in much the same way that "Meals on Wheels" provides food for the homebound, who are otherwise unable to obtain it on their own. Neither has a problem appropriately using that which they could not have otherwise obtained – the elderly person can certainly eat the food and the patient with brainstem failure can certainly participate in gas exchange – but each has a physical impediment preventing them from accessing that which their body naturally needs. No one would consider the homebound person to be dead and only kept alive by the kind couriers of "Meals on Wheels." The same is true, R. Bleich argues, of "brain dead" patients. Breathing in Halakhah means naturally actualizing the person's interaction with the gases in the atmosphere. A patient suffering from brainstem failure should therefore be considered alive even according to those who determine death based on the irreversible inability to breathe alone.

R. Bleich contends that it is therefore inappropriate to describe mechanical ventilation as artificially supporting a dead patient's continued

---

2 Ibid., 108.

vegetative functions. R. Yitzhak Zylberstein reports that R. Elyashiv argues similarly.³

Practical Challenges: Superman and Other Men of Steel

From a practical perspective, when pushed to the limit, death based solely on the inability to breathe leads to conclusions that are difficult to accept as true. As mentioned in chapter 14, there are certain situations in which a patient can suffer from ICSR, but otherwise seem very much alive.

In 1995, Christopher Reeve, the actor who played Superman, suffered a spinal cord injury after falling from a horse, severing his spinal cord between vertebrae C3 and C4. The injury paralyzed him from the neck down, deeming all nerves stemming from the spinal cord at and below this level – including the phrenic nerve – non-functional. The phrenic nerve consists of fibers from spinal cord levels C3, C4, and C5 and stimulates the diaphragm to contract and physically initiate inspiration; Mr. Reeve was therefore incapable of breathing on his own. Eventually, he was fitted with an external "phrenic nerve stimulator" (diaphragmatic pacer), which stimulated his respiratory muscles to contract and allow breathing without any mechanical ventilator support.⁴

While rigorously researched, current medical practice can offer no cure for severed nerves, relegating Mr. Reeve's inability to breathe as

---

3 Y. Zylberstein, "Transplanting Hearts and Livers – Determining the Moment of Death" (Hebrew), *Ha-Hug li-Refu'ah ve-Halakhah* (5768): 1-6.

4 In actuality, the work of breathing depends upon additional accessory muscles of respiration as well, including the intercostals and certain neck muscles. These are innervated by different nerves, of which Mr. Reeve likely retained functionality. While insufficient to solely support respiration for any significant period of time, these accessory respiratory muscles probably played some role in Mr. Reeve's incredible recovery. From a technical and engineering perspective, however, the "phrenic nerve stimulator" should prove therapeutic even in a patient who has lost control of both his central (diaphragmatic) as well as accessory respiratory muscles. As a thought experiment, we will assume that Mr. Reeve fits into this latter category – lacking any ability for spontaneous respiration whatsoever – even though this is not completely synchronous with the historical record.

irreversible. The reason that Mr. Reeve made any "recovery" at all was because his brain was unaffected by the riding accident.

If one accepts ICSR as death, Mr. Reeve – having irreversibly lost the ability to breathe on his own – should be considered dead. Since the definition is functional and independent of brain pathophysiology, Mr. Reeve met the criteria for ICSR quite nicely. The problem is that Mr. Reeve "survived" for nine years – he retained full mental capacity, was able to communicate with others, and even starred in documentaries. Could someone possibly declare Mr. Reeve dead even while he himself vocally protested to the contrary? The question is vital, since if the criterion fails in certain circumstances, it raises major concerns as to its applicability more generally – especially when other, more encompassing criteria can withstand similar scrutiny.

The same problem arose years ago in polio victims, when the polio virus eventually affected the nerves that normally stimulate the respiratory muscles, rendering these patients irreversibly incapable of breathing on their own. While maintaining full mental faculties, these patients were connected to "iron lungs," primitive equivalents of modern ventilators. Patients suffering from ALS (amyotrophic lateral sclerosis, also known as Lou Gehrig's disease) similarly lose neuromuscular function starting peripherally and slowly moving more centrally, eventually affecting their respiratory muscles. Retaining consciousness as well as the unique ability for eye movements, these patients ultimately also require mechanical ventilation when they can no longer breathe on their own. All present a serious challenge to accepting a purely respiratory criterion for death.

If ICSR merely **indicates** that death has occurred, then it makes sense to say that this is true only under certain circumstances. When it is plainly obvious that a person has not in fact died – which, in Mr. Reeve's case, was evidenced by him actually stating so – then the indication is not accurate. While this **criterion** may be true and accurate in almost all circumstances, when common sense proves otherwise, it is inapplicable. But defending "brain death" as halakhically meaningful, argues R. Bleich, demands that ICSR **define** death, giving it universal applicability. For a definition to be rigorous, it must account for all situations. Even if ICSR only indicates that it is likely that death has occurred, who is to say what qualifies as an exception, and on what basis are these "rare" occurrences classified and identified? The appeal to common sense – "no one would declare him dead under such conditions!" – is irrelevant in a rigorous attempt to precisely identify what determines halakhic death. A definition that applies only when "common sense" dictates but fails under strict scrutiny cannot form the basis for Halakhah.

Indeed, while common sense dictates that Christopher Reeve was most certainly alive, this "feeling" cannot have any halakhic import unless rooted in Halakhah itself. R. Bleich argues that both premises cannot stand – either Mr. Reeve was dead or the criteria of death by ICSR fails scrutiny and ultimately falls. This does not necessitate a clash between Halakhah and common sense, but rather a re-evaluation of what Halakhah in fact says. For R. Bleich, the solution is quite simple – relying on his approach to determine death only upon the irreversible cessation of "vital motion." Since Christopher Reeve maintained "vital motion" even after his accident – evidenced by his ability to communicate and continued heartbeat – he cannot, should not, and was not considered dead. For R. Bleich, there is no clash because the halakhic underpinnings are squarely in accordance with common sense thinking.

R. Tendler and Dr. Steinberg offer a possibility for resolving this problem by claiming that ICSR is not really an exhaustive criterion for death at all, but rather just the absence of "an indicator of the living state." These positions were more fully developed an analyzed in chapter 14 in the context of R. Feinstein's responsa.

Conscious Communication as Life

There are two options in responding to the paradox presented by Mr. Reeve while maintaining ICSR as the definition or exhaustive criterion for death: arguing that communication is unique in indicating continuation of life, despite ostensibly meeting criteria for death, or arguing that any sign of significant movement is indicative of life, except for a beating heart.

The first approach claims that Christopher Reeve differed from a classic "brain dead" patient in that he retained the capacity for conscious communication. Dr. Steinberg argues that ICSR is essentially a "rule of thumb," the criterion which, in the context of dying, is almost always determinant of death. Consciousness, however, precludes relying on the "rule of thumb" in declaring death because it most certainly is a sign of continued life. While other vegetative functions are ignored in the context of ICSR, Dr. Steinberg suggests, the ability for communication stands out as manifestly proving that the person is still alive.[5]

In defending the uniqueness of communication, Dr. Steinberg cites the comments of R. Eliyahu of Vilna (*Gra*) to Mishnah *Ohalot*. In describing the ritual defilement of a corpse, the *mishnah* notes that as long as a person is still alive, he does not engender any impurity; this is true even while dying (but not yet dead) and even if considered a *goses* or a *meguyyad*. In interpreting the latter term, *Gra* describes a person "who can no longer live (*she-eino yakhol od lihyot*) [but] does not engender impurity since he is of sound mind (*da'ato tzelulah*); and even a *goses* who is not of sound mind (*she-ein da'ato tzelulah*) does not engender impurity, since he can still live" for another short while. Dr. Steinberg focuses on the fact that one who is *meguyyad* and "can no longer live" should be described as dead, were it not for the prototypical contraindication to declaring death – being of sound mind. Dr. Steinberg argues that even if a person meets the strict criteria for death, objective evidence of continued life in the form of intelligent consciousness precludes this determination.

Others, however, understand *Gra's* comments very differently. R. Hershel Schachter contends that *Gra* merely meant to explain the difference between the two categories of dying patients – a *goses* does not engender impurity because he can still live, but a *meguyyad* is even better off and certainly does not engender impurity, since he is still of sound mind.[6] This explanation interprets the *mishnah* and *Gra's* commentary in the familiar Mishnaic format of listing the more novel position second, following the more obvious position (*lo zu af zu*). However, this does not appear to be entirely true, as *Gra* explicitly describes a *meguyyad* as one who "can no longer live," and in that regard, he is certainly worse off than his *goses* counterpart, who can – leading one to question whether the literary structure suggested by R. Schachter is applicable.

---

5   Ibid.
6   *Be-Ikvei ha-Tzon*, no. 36.

From a more fundamental perspective, R. Bleich argues that in terms of Halakhah, there are no sources indicating that life should be determined or measured solely by mental capacity or ability.[7] The *mishnah* makes clear that a *meguyyad* is certainly alive, prompting *Gra* to comment that his death is nevertheless imminent. Reading *Gra*'s comments as suggested by Dr. Steinberg requires not only literary creativity, argues R. Bleich, but also making many seemingly unfounded assumptions about a *meguyyad*. Furthermore, in drawing an arbitrary line between communication and all other functions, especially when largely based on logical and not halakhic sources, one must wonder whether the line should be more appropriately drawn elsewhere. Why is communication special? Are these unique characteristics evident in other physiological functions as well? What about a futuristic unconscious patient who is completely unresponsive but can communicate via a "brain scanner" that can interpret the electrical activity in his brain as coherent thoughts? Is he alive because of his "ability" to "communicate"?[8] Most importantly, and deserving of reiteration, is that a distinction between communication and other functions is not based on halakhic principles and therefore cannot form the basis for a halakhic determination of death.

Discounting the Heartbeat: Decapitation and "Brain Death"

A second approach to resolving the "Christopher Reeve problem" focuses less on what qualifies as a sign of life and more on what does not. According to this position, some continuing physiological functions qualify as signs of life even in the face of ICSR and some do not. This approach argues that a line must be drawn somewhere along that spectrum between these various functions – the precise location of that line is irrelevant so long as cardiac activity stands firmly on the side that no longer qualifies as life.

R. Avraham Shapira and R. Mordechai Eliyahu, former Chief Rabbis of Israel (1983-1993), proposed the notion that only a "natural" heartbeat

---

7 *BNhH*, 143-4.
8 See the discussion of PVS and MCS patients' ability for potential communication in the previous chapter.

qualifies as a true sign of life.[9] They define a "natural" heartbeat as one that is powered by energy derived solely from spontaneous respiration. This would include the heartbeat of a spontaneously breathing patient, and possibly that of a patient during the few moments after respiration has ceased, when the heart continues beating until in runs out of energy. Even though the heart of a ventilated patient suffering from ICSR continues to function autonomously, Rabbis Shapira and Eliyahu argue that mechanical ventilation is considered an artificial impetus for cardiac function; such a heartbeat is not "natural" and therefore not indicative of life. They describe the heartbeat of a patient suffering from ICSR more appropriately as *pirkus* (defined in chapter 6).

This position is quite difficult on several levels and is analyzed more fully in chapter 15. Briefly, it assumes that the halakhic significance of a heartbeat depends upon the source of the oxygen from which energy is derived to promote cardiac muscular contraction – a distinction with logical, but not necessarily Talmudic or halakhic basis. Additionally, it seems difficult to describe the rhythmic, continuous, and effective heartbeat as *pirkus*, as per *Hakham Tzvi* (discussed more fully in chapter 8).

Dr. Steinberg notes that Rashi, commenting on the discussion in Talmud *Yoma*, states that determining death is only appropriate when the avalanche victim is "lying still as a stone" (*mutal ke-even*). One does not even begin to search for signs of respiration or even cardiac activity when it is clear that a person is still moving, since that is sufficient proof of life.[10] Dr. Steinberg must argue that a person with the ability/capacity to communicate cannot be described as one who is *"mutal ke-even domem,"* and applying ICSR as death is therefore inappropriate under the circumstances. The same is true of a person capable of voluntary movements, who, regardless of his ability to breathe, cannot be considered dead as long as he displays characteristics of the living.

---

9 A.K. Shapira, "Determining Death According to Halakhah" (Hebrew) in M. Halperin (ed.), *Kevi'at Rega ha-Mavet*, 2nd edition (Jerusalem: Schlesinger Institute, 2007), 247-9; M. Eliyahu, "Organ Transplantation According to Halakhah" (Hebrew), *Barkai* 4 (5747): 18-31.
10 A. Steinberg, "Determining the Moment of Death – Responses to Critiques" (Hebrew), *Or ha-Mizrah* 36 (5748): 283.

R. Bleich flips this notion, arguing that Rashi's requirement of "lying still as a stone" specifically refers to the complete absence of "vital motion."[11] When an avalanche victim is found to motionless and unresponsive, it is then appropriate to search for more subtle signs of "vital motion," including respiration and heartbeat. R. Bleich believes that by adding this caveat, Rashi intentionally alluded to Mishnah *Ohalot*, defining death specifically by the irreversible cessation of "vital motion."

Indeed, Dr. Steinberg's argument is difficult when taken to its logical conclusion. If, as Dr. Steinberg assumes, a moving victim does not qualify as *mutal ke-even domem*, and is therefore considered alive regardless of his ability to breathe, Dr. Steinberg must also make the assumption that a person with a beating heart **is** described as *mutal ke-even domem*. If communication is meaningful and voluntary motion is meaningful, why is the heartbeat different? If a person maintains a functional cardiac rhythm, is that a sufficient characteristic of life to claim that death by respiratory criteria not apply in such circumstances? In essence, this really comes down to the question of whether a persistent heartbeat is a sufficient indicator of continued life, as discussed previously in chapter 4, with R. Bleich and all others in this camp strongly arguing in the affirmative.[12]

---

11 *BNbH*, 119-22, 139-41.

12 Conceptually, Dr. Steinberg argues that it is perfectly plausible for a definition to be applicable only in certain circumstances, with R. Bleich, as noted previously, strongly standing in opposition. Granting Dr. Steinberg's conceptual point, however, he must claim that ICSR qualifies as death only when the determination of death is not contraindicated by additional evidence of continued life, such as the ability for communication. What Dr. Steinberg appears to be stating is that a person meeting the purely respiratory criteria is dead, except for when he is not dead. A patient irreversibly incapable of ever breathing on his own is defined as dead, except when the definition fails – meaning that the definition is circular. Dr. Steinberg is left with **criteria** for death that are not dependent upon a **definition** of death – since no meaningful definition can account for all of these caveats – but rather with criteria for death that seem to stand on their own. Adding more and more caveats – claiming that ICSR qualifies as death only in the absence of the ability to communicate and exhibiting no voluntary muscular motion – simply begs the question of what these criteria actually represent. When a person meets these criteria, he is dead, and when failing to do so, he is alive, even though it is hard to define or give meaning to the fundamental difference between the two.

In and of itself, this is not conceptually problematic. Dr. Steinberg is proposing a "rule of thumb" that applies to the vast majority of all cases, regarding which everyone

Ru'ah Ya'akov suggests an additional reason for discounting a continuing heartbeat as a sign of life in the context of ICSR based on R. Auerbach's "sheep experiment" (discussed in detail in chapter 16).[13] Having been decapitated, *Ru'ah Ya'akov* argues that the sheep was dead, and no matter how it may have appeared, any and all continued biological functioning – including her heartbeat – must have been the result of medical interventions and not indicative of continued life. He argues that the same phenomenon is true in "brain dead" patients. Since the vast majority of all people who cannot spontaneously breathe are dead, a "brain dead" patient is dead as well; his persistent heartbeat is simply an artifact of medical intervention and therefore considered *pirkus*. Mr. Reeve, in contrast, was not decapitated, and his heartbeat therefore does not constitute *pirkus*.

While intellectually intriguing, this argument suffers from a number of drawbacks. As noted in our discussion of this experiment, a "brain dead" patient is not necessarily comparable to the decapitated sheep. From a purely medical perspective, the sheep's continued biological functions lasted for only a short while and likely could not be sustained for very much longer. Dr. Abraham points out that regardless of how one views these remaining, short-lived biological functions, they are fundamentally distinct from the organized, coordinated, and – most importantly – **sustained** biological functions of a "brain dead" patient.[14] The experiment was repeated twice, with the first sheep surviving for three-and-a-half

---

agrees to rely on ICSR as sufficient criteria for death, as it coincides with irreversible cardiac arrest. However, this approach connotes a lack of a meaningful **definition** of death; although not fundamentally problematic, this does not seem very compelling.

Based on these criteria, Dr. Steinberg takes the general "rule of thumb" and applies it to extreme cases, differentiating between "brain dead" patients and Christopher Reeve – the former meeting criteria for death while the latter does not. The difficulty lies in the absence of such a distinction in the Mishnah, Talmud, *Hatam Sofer*, *Hakham Tzvi*, or any other sources discussing the moment of death. Dr. Steinberg must therefore introduce a novel proposition – that a continuous heartbeat is not necessarily an indication of life – basing this distinction on logical, not Talmudic principles. Having admitted that, it is upon him to prove this assertion convincingly, since the question at hand is one of murder if he is incorrect – leaving ample room for disagreement.

13   *Ru'ah Ya'akov*, sec. 66.
14   *Nishmat Avraham, YD*, 2nd ed., 466.

hours and the second for a half hour; "brain dead" patients can survive for months and (rarely) even years.

"Brain dead" patients differ from the decapitated sheep conceptually as well. *Ru'ah Ya'akov* assumes, as did R. Auerbach, that the decapitated sheep was dead, as per Mishnah *Ohalot* 1:6. This premise is necessary for describing any continuing biological functions as *pirkus*. However, determining the status of the sheep depends upon the reason why decapitation as death fits in with the general definition of death in Halakhah. Indeed, *Ru'ah Ya'akov*'s comparison between a "brain dead" patient and the decapitated sheep fails according to all views.

According to the position that ICSR is the exclusive halakhically sanctioned criterion for death, decapitation defines death not in and of itself, but because it renders the victim irreversibly incapable of spontaneous respiration. Just as a continuing heartbeat (or any other biological function, for that matter) post-decapitation is not indicative of life but is rather considered *pirkus*, the same is true of any continued functioning after "brain death" induced ICSR.

Acknowledging the "Christopher Reeve problem," however, this approach understands ICSR to be only an **indication** of death, one that is indeed accurate in the vast majority, but not necessarily all cases. Applying this understanding to the decapitated sheep appears quite straightforward; severing the head caused the irreversible failure of her respiratory system. It is the next premise that is open to challenge – assuming that all continuing biological functions after ICSR in "brain dead" patients are similarly considered *pirkus*. This presumption is certainly not true by definition, since the determination of death by ICSR was only made by an **indication** – meaning that it is highly likely, but certainly not necessary, that death has occurred.

Moreover, the biological functions that continued in the decapitated sheep do not necessarily fall within the rubric of *pirkus*. Rambam defines *pirkus* as disorganized, uncoordinated, and un-sustained movements, the random, spasmodic, and involuntary twitches and jerk-like motions sometimes exhibited immediately after death.[15] The coordinated, integrated, and sustained function of the cardiac muscles within the context of an

---

15 *Commentary to the Mishnah, Ohalot* 1:6.

intact circulatory system does not appear to fit this description. The assumption, therefore, that since indications of death are present, anything occurring thereafter is considered *pirkus* and not indicative of life is simply not true. When an indication for death is present (ICSR), one must then begin to analyze whether any continuing functions qualify as *pirkus* or signs of continued life despite indications (but not absolute proof) to the contrary.

Even after ICSR ensues, it is still possible to maintain coordinated, integrated, and sustained physiological activity – seemingly not considered *pirkus* – as was exhibited by the decapitated sheep. When a biological function is not *pirkus*, it is in fact an indication of continued life and, more importantly, proof that this patient is one of those few for whom ICSR does not necessarily indicate death. Comparing a "brain dead" patient to the decapitated sheep, one should arrive at the exact opposite conclusion of *Ru'ah Ya'akov* – while both the sheep and the "brain dead" patient seemingly fulfill criteria for an indication of death (ICSR), the continued organized, integrated, and sustained biological functioning of their hearts is evidence for continued life, contradicting and precluding any determination to the contrary.

In addition, the very presumption of *Ru'ah Ya'akov* in his argument is somewhat inaccurate. *Ru'ah Ya'akov* argues that since the overwhelming majority of all people who cannot spontaneously breathe are dead, it is far more likely that a "brain dead" patient with ICSR is also dead, and his continued heartbeat should thus be considered artificially maintained (and therefore halakhically irrelevant). It is certainly true that most people with ICSR are indeed dead, regardless of how one defines death, since they exhibit no signs of life whatsoever (including no heartbeat). The vast majority of people with ICSR are completely unresponsive and utterly lifeless. When these patient exhibit a questionable sign of life, it is far more likely to be externally induced than an actual indication of continued life that was previously misdiagnosed as death.

A "brain dead" patient, however, is not included in this set. He is different because he is connected to a mechanical ventilator that allows him to maintain sustained biological functioning. When a "brain dead" patient exhibits signs of life, we cannot assume that they are externally induced because we know that the only externally induced functions are inhalation and exhalation. Thus, while the original presumption of *Ru'ah Ya'akov*'s argument is true in most "standard" dying patients, it is not true for a ventilated patient, whose many biological functions continue throughout this entire process.

Furthermore, according to the view that decapitation is not in and of itself a death-defining state, a heartbeat that persists thereafter is significant. According to R. Bleich, for example, it is not decapitation *per se* that qualifies as death, but the fact that any continued cardiac function is effectively worthless – not "vital" – as it no longer serves as the body's central circulatory pump. A decapitated person is dead despite his continued heartbeat because his head was severed from its body, causing massive hemorrhage and relegating any remaining circulation and cardiac function ineffective. According to R. Bleich's approach, effective circulation is an indication of life in the "brain dead" patient.

Coming from a different perspective, R. Hershel Schachter concurs with this approach (as discussed in the next chapter). Discounting the automatic presumption of death upon decapitation has also recently garnered support in the bioethical literature.[16]

Ru'ah Ya'akov's conclusions based on the sheep experiment are difficult even according to R. Auerbach, who maintained that there are two independent definitions of death – one based on cardiac and respiratory function and one defined by decapitation. In this view, the latter is not necessarily limited by the former's criteria, nor by any other halakhic parameters, but is rather *sui generis*. A two-track approach to defining death posits decapitation as a type of Scriptural decree (*gezeirat ha-kattuv*), not necessarily corresponding to parameters known from elsewhere. It is likely that for this reason, many halakhists, R. Auerbach among them, describe the decapitated sheep as dead even though normally describing a heartbeat as a sign of continued life. Understood in this way, any post-decapitation movements or biological functions cannot indicate life, since by definition, the decapitated sheep is identified as dead by Scriptural fiat.

---

[16] F.G. Miller, R.D. Truog, "Decapitation and the definition of death," *Journal of Medical Ethics* 36 (2010): 632-4.

Ru'ah Ya'akov effectively argues that since these functions can exist in a decapitated (and therefore dead) sheep, they qualify as *pirkus*. Therefore, even when found in an anatomically intact person, they do not necessarily indicate continued life. The comparison, however, is faulty. Aside from the difficulty of describing a regular, sustained heartbeat as *pirkus*, labeling it in this way in a decapitated sheep says nothing about its status in a "brain dead" patient, whose head is still attached. The heartbeat's "irrelevance" in decapitation stems from the *sui generis* nature of decapitation qualifying as death according to R. Auerbach; decapitation means that the sheep is dead regardless of what functions may be continuing in her body. This is not because these functions are always irrelevant, but rather because death is determined here by a *gezeirat ha-kattuv*, a secondary, completely independent set of criteria. Because of the unique status of decapitation in determining death, any lessons learned from the sheep experiment are limited to cases where the head or brain is actually absent.

Unless one equates "brain death" with actual decapitation and the absence of the entire brain, this experiment says nothing about the status of a "brain dead" patient's heartbeat. A heartbeat always qualifies as evidence of life, except in the context of actual decapitation; **only** then, is it described as *pirkus*.

Thus, *Ru'ah Ya'akov*'s comparison of a "brain dead" patient to the decapitated sheep, leading to negating the significance of a continued heartbeat, is seriously questionable.

Textual Proofs

There are some Talmudic discussions, admittedly difficult to understand, that seem to call into question determinations of death reliant entirely upon respiratory-oriented standards. Talmud *Gittin* 70b describes a person who was ritually slaughtered (*shehitah*) as still alive inasmuch as he can gesture to a bystander to issue a *get* (divorce writ) to his wife on his behalf. The Talmud concludes that while the victim's death is certainly imminent, he is considered alive for at least a short period after the attack. The difficulty is that *shehitah* requires the transection of both the trachea and esophagus (or at least a majority of their diameter), which would seem to inevitably lead to inability to breathe. While in this case, the brain can still send "messages" to initiate a breath and the respiratory muscles can indeed contract, the trauma makes this effort completely futile, given the gaping hole in the victim's neck. According to the respiratory-based approach, this victim should be considered dead, but the Talmud explicitly describes such a person as alive and recognizes a *get* he instructs to send as halakhically meaningful.

While seemingly proof against those advocating ICSR as death, this Talmudic discussion is fraught with difficulty. While perhaps difficult to imagine, it is at least conceivable that a person injured in such a manner still retains the ability to offer some gesture in the few seconds thereafter that would indicate his desire to divorce his wife. However, this case is merely the beginning of a more complex discussion, with the Talmud continuing to discuss a case in which *shehitah* is performed on a person who then subsequently runs away/disappears (*barah*), questioning whether witnesses to the event can testify that the victim is in fact dead so as to allow his widow to remarry. The Talmud concludes that while the witnesses cannot testify that they saw that the man was dead, they can testify that he suffered such a serious injury that he would most certainly die fairly soon, "freeing" the widow from a potential levirate marriage.

While also seemingly evidence against determining death solely by respiratory standards, the story itself is rather difficult to imagine. It is hard to understand how a person no longer capable of spontaneous respiration could possibly escape and flee so far that he could no longer be found. Running or any other vigorous exercise requires oxygen, and the fact that the Talmud questions how to proceed in the victim's absence indicates that the victim had indeed escaped. It seems that the first unstated assumption – that *shehitah* is necessarily equivalent with irreversibly inhibiting the ability for spontaneous respiration – is not true, at least in this Talmudic context, as this assumption makes the facts of the case incomprehensible. Importantly, accepting this interpretation makes the case irrelevant to the discussion of determining the moment of death in the context of "brain death."

CHAPTER 19:

Opposing Brain Death

As noted in the previous two chapters, many modern halakhic decisors have objected, some vehemently, to acceptance of "brain death" as a halakhic determination of death, interpreting the sources differently than their opponents and suggesting evidence that their arguments are faulty. In this chapter, we will analyze the positions of several halakhists separately, as they often differ in approach. They are presented in alphabetical order.

Rabbi Yosef Shalom Elyashiv

Considered to be one of the most influential halakhic decisors today, R. Elyashiv has not penned a written exposition on his position regarding "brain death," other than publishing very succinct opinion statements. Often quoted by Drs. Abraham and Steinberg as staunchly rejecting "brain death" as halakhically meaningful, he has not offered much explanation for his stance.

Nevertheless, he and R. Auerbach publicized concise position statements expressing their complete disapproval for determining a patient's death in the face of a persistent heartbeat (cited in chapter 16). Since R. Auerbach's passing, R. Elyashiv published an additional position statement on 5 *Adar I*, 5758 (March 3, 1998), referencing the previous statement and declaring in no uncertain terms that his position has not changed. More recently, his son-in-law, R. Yitzhak Zylberstein, himself a noted expert in areas of medical Halakhah, responded to a request from R. Moshe Elyakim Brooks of Ma'ayanei HaYeshua hospital in Bnei Brak to put into writing what he understands to be his esteemed father-in-law's thinking and rationale.[1] R. Zylberstein presents R. Elyashiv's reasoning as rather consistent with R. Bleich's analysis, specifically focusing on ICSR as an **indication** of death and inapplicable to a patient whose heart continues to beat.

According to R. Zylberstein's report, R. Elyashiv adds an additional element as well, countering the approach of R. Auerbach. As discussed in chapter 16, R. Auerbach endorsed the idea that the death of each and every cell of the brain, were it to become medical reality, is comparable to decapitation, and therefore death. R. Elyashiv argues against this position based on a ruling of *Shulhan Arukh*, who declares as kosher an animal whose brain "decomposed somewhat (*nirkav me'at*) or was smashed (*nitma'ekh*), but the outer membrane remains intact... [However,] if [the brain] spills [entirely] like water or wax, [the animal is rendered] a *tereifah*."[2] Accordingly, R. Elyashiv argues that even if every brain cell were to decompose and completely liquefy, the animal would still be considered alive – the *Shulhan Arukh* specifically rendering such an animal a *tereifah* and not a *neveilah*. While such extensive tissue destruction does not, in fact, occur in clinical "brain death," R. Elyashiv argues that the point is still instructive. Since the brain tissue in clinical "brain death" does not spill "like water or wax," it certainly cannot qualify as a determinant of death.

While R. Auerbach never addressed this specific concern (at least in print), a possible response is certainly forthcoming. In analyzing this point, *Ru'ah Ya'akov* explains[3] that the animal discussed by *Shulhan Arukh*, whose brain was discovered to be "liquefied," has just undergone *shehitah* – meaning that just moments earlier the animal was most certainly alive, for otherwise *shehitah* would be meaningless. Presumably, the animal was breathing and had a heartbeat, and we can safely assume

---

1 Y. Zylberstein, "Transplanting Hearts and Livers – Determining the Moment of Death" (Hebrew), *Ha-Hug li-Refu'ah ve-Halakhah* (5768): 1-6.
2 *Shulhan Arukh, YD* 31:2.
3 *Ru'ah Ya'akov*, sec. 70.

that the animal's brain did not spontaneously completely lyse at the very moment of *shehitah*. It is impossible, however, for a farm animal to act completely normally while its brain completely "spills like water or wax." Rather, in the *Shulhan Arukh*'s case, there must be some extant brain tissue organizing and coordinating these functions; he cannot mean that the entire brain, including the brainstem, "spills like water or wax." The animal described in *Shulhan Arukh* never reached the threshold for what R. Auerbach considered determinant of death, namely the death of **each and every cell** of the brain – mitigating its challenge to R. Auerbach's position. While R. Auerbach allows for defining death by decapitation or the equivalent death of each and every cell of the brain even in the face of continued physiological functions, these scenarios only exist in intensive care units, where monitoring and advanced life-supporting therapies are available.[4]

Rabbi Hershel Schachter

Agreeing generally with requiring cardiac criteria in determining death and rejecting a sole respiratory standard, R. Hershel Schachter adopts a unique approach.[5] R. Schachter identifies life with circulation, citing the many Biblical and Talmudic references to "blood" and its ability to flow as indicative of and defining life. For R. Schachter, just as blood flow constitutes the definition of continued life, the cessation of flow is determinant of death.

R. Schachter argues that Halakhah also recognizes the death of individual organs, citing a responsum of R. Moshe Feinstein as proof.[6] R. Feinstein differentiates between a gangrenous arm and the arm of a stroke victim; the former is considered halakhically "dead," as no blood reaches it, while the latter is "alive." R. Feinstein therefore exempts plac-

---

[4] Seen in this light, this question does not really pose a difficulty even for those who argue for a purely respiratory based criteria for death (regardless of the state of the brain tissue), since the animal in question must have been breathing prior to *shehitah*; otherwise, it would have been considered dead long ago.

[5] *Be-Ikvei ha-Tzon*, no. 36.

[6] *Responsa Iggerot Mosheh*, *OH* 1:8.

ing *tefillin* on the gangrenous arm (and likely requires placement upon the other, healthy arm), but requires it on the paralyzed arm (noting that his father, after suffering a stroke, in fact continue to place his *tefillin* upon his affected left arm). Mishnah *Bekhorot* 37a, as elaborated upon in Talmud *Hullin* 46b, similarly identifies "dried out" organs as completely lacking circulation, which R. Feinstein describes as dead.

R. Schachter further notes that in a number of different contexts, the Talmud identifies certain organs/body parts as vital (lit., "those upon which the soul depends," *eivarim she-ha-neshamah teluyah bahem*) and as limited in number – differentiating them from the less vital organs/body parts, such as arms and legs.[7] In identifying these organs, Rambam lists the head/brain, heart, and liver.[8] R. Schachter wonders how to properly understand that there are three organs upon which life depends. Does Halakhah require that all three function properly for a person to qualify as alive, or are two or even one sufficient? He suggests that this question forms the subtext for the discussion of whether an animal without a heart (whether missing or removed) is rendered a *tereifah* or a *neveilah*.[9] Those who deem such an animal a *tereifah* necessarily believe that even without a heart, the animal is still halakhically considered alive. They would argue that all three organs are not necessary to halakhically qualify as living, so that in the absence of even one of them (the heart in this case), the animal is still considered alive. In contrast, those who describe such an animal as a *neveilah* argue that the halakhic status of continued life depends on all three organs and that missing even one of them defines halakhic death.

Putting the two discussions together, R. Schachter employs R. Feinstein's definition of "organ death" in a rather novel manner. R. Schachter argues that an organ should be defined as "dead" when it is no longer perfused, leading him to wonder whether the complete absence

---

7 See *Nazir* 21b; *Temurah* 10b, 20a.
8 *Commentary to the Mishnah*, *Erkhin* 5:3, *Hilkhot Ma'aseh ha-Korbanot* 15:2. While the heart is never listed in any of the Talmudic texts in their current printings, R. Schachter argues that it is likely that Rambam had a variant text of at least one of these sources, in which the heart was mentioned.
9 See chapter 8.

of cerebral circulation – thereby causing the "death" of one of the three vital organs – establishes the death of the individual. In other words, is the "death" of the head alone sufficient to determine the death of the individual, or must circulation cease in the heart and liver as well to accurately make such a diagnosis?

R. Schachter argues that accepting "brain death" as halakhically meaningful requires accepting both R. Feinstein's premise that lack of perfusion defines "organ death," as well as the position claiming that the "death" of even one of the "three vital organs" defines the death of the individual. These are both matters that R. Schachter believes to be subject to serious halakhic controversy. He therefore concludes that while this conclusion is possible, there is no practical way to take a definitive position on this debate, leading to a state of objective doubt (*safek*). As such, R. Schachter forbids declaring death under such circumstances and equates organ procurement from "brain dead" patients with possible murder (*safek retzihah*).

However, it is important to note that R. Schachter's doubt is only relevant where the brain can be described as completely dead – parallel to a gangrenous arm. Only then is R. Schachter's analysis of how many vital organs need to function to qualify as life even relevant. The actual medical reality however, as noted numerous times previously, does not support this pathological description. The brains of "brain dead" patients are decidedly not completely "dead" and most certainly cannot be compared to gangrenous tissue. As a matter of practical application therefore, R. Schachter would describe actual "brain dead" patients as certainly living – with all three of their vital organs still "alive" – and harvesting organs from them as absolute murder.

Dr. Daniel Malakh takes issue with several of R. Schachter's assumptions.[10] He notes that the Talmudic notion of "vital" organs is always discussed in the context of assessing the "value" (*erekh*) of a person or organ. These organs, because of their importance, can represent the person as a whole, so that if a person pledges to donate "the value of his head, heart, or liver," he effectively obligates himself in the total "value" of himself (however that is to be determined). There is no mention of life-saving

---

10 *Assia* 65-66 (1999): 112-20.

or death-defining matters in the Talmudic context of this discussion, precluding introducing them into criteria for death. R. Shelomoh Amar argues similarly, in his (as of yet) unpublished responsum to R. Schachter on this very issue.[11]

While not addressing this concern directly, R. Schachter reads this Talmudic notion simply – as describing organs that are necessary for life. By definition, were they to be missing, in part or in whole, life could not continue. Although admittedly not noted in any life-saving context, the very definition of cessation of cardiac activity or the reliance on cessation of respiration as indicative of cessation of cardiac activity are predicated upon these very ideas. Far from irrelevant, R. Schachter would argue, these are the very premises underlying all other discussions, Talmudic and beyond.

Dr. Malakh is also critical of R. Schachter's insistence on blood flow as the ultimate indication of life. While aware of debate on the matter and realizing that most interpretations are mutually exclusive, R. Schachter adopts R. Moshe Feinstein's approach, which he feels to be the most compelling. Dr. Malakh's point raises the broader issue of adjudicating matter of practical Halakhah in the context of a multitude of opinions. As halakhic decisors, these are issues that Rabbis Schachter and Feinstein deal with on a constant basis – each with their unique approach – and this is certainly not an aspect particular to this issue.

By defining life by the continued flow of blood, R. Schachter comes very close to R. Bleich's definition of "vital motion," since physiologically, spontaneous motion is not possible without blood flow. While particular differences may exist, in today's medical context, they are few and far between.

R. Moshe Sternbuch

As one of the earliest halakhists to deal with organ donation,[12] R. Sternbuch revisited this discussion in his later publications. While in an early responsum, R. Sternbuch appears to argue for a solely respiratory-oriented determination of death,[13] he later clarifies his opposition to "brain

---

11 Unpublished responsum of R. Amar, originally dated 10 *Av*, 5763, p. 5-9.
12 *Be'ayot ha-Zeman be-Hashkafat ha-Torah*, 10, published in 5729 (1969).
13 *Teshuvot ve-Hanhagot* 3:351, published in 5757 (1996-1997).

death" dependent organ donation.[14] Offering a somewhat historical perspective, he notes that whereas Talmud *Yoma*, *Hatam Sofer*, and years of tradition all indeed support determining death by respiration alone, *Hakham Tzvi* disagreed and has firmly swayed the modern rabbinic consensus to avoid determining death in a patient with a heartbeat.[15] Even though quite sympathetic to relying solely on respiratory standards, R. Sternbuch is unwilling to argue with the rabbinic consensus (*da'at gedolei hora'ah*).

It is of further historical interest to note that much of this later responsum is predicated on R. Sternbuch's assumption that a "brain dead" patient's heart, and in fact his "entire life force" (*kol hiyyuto*), are "entirely artificial" (*melakhuti bilvad*). He wonders how to halakhically classify an artificially induced heartbeat, since while it does effectively circulate blood throughout the body, it cannot necessarily be ascribed to the patient himself. A similar difficulty is presented by artificial ventilation; while a mechanical ventilator oxygenates blood quite adequately, the work of breathing can certainly not be ascribed to the ventilated patient. While irrelevant if death is solely determined by cardiac standards, R. Sterbuch is quite unnerved by the revelation that, in reality, a "brain dead" patient's heartbeat is not artificially induced, but rather beats autonomously, without any connection to the ventilator whatsoever. He leaves the matter unsettled, to be determined by rabbinic consensus.[16]

Rabbi Eliezer Yehudah Waldenberg

R. Waldenberg is quite clear in completely rejecting any suggestion that the Talmud's reliance on checking *hotmo* means determining death by ICSR.[17] Clarifying his position even more explicitly, R. Waldenberg

---

14 Ibid. 4:268.

15 While *Hakham Tzvi* lived earlier than *Hatam Sofer*, R. Sternbuch is referring to the impact of the various position on "the rabbinic consensus," not the chronological sequence of these positions' original formulations.

16 See, however, A. Steinberg, "The Brain and Respiratory Death Law – Opinion of R. Moshe Sternbuch (1)" (Hebrew), *Assia* 87-88 (2010): 79 and M. Peleg, "The Brain and Respiratory Death Law – Opinion of R. Moshe Sternbuch (2)" (Hebrew), ibid: 80, which describe more recent, but contradictory claims as to R. Sternbuch's position.

17 *Responsa Tzitz Eliezer* 10:25:4.

explains that the Talmud requires checking for respiration as the most sensitive means available for assessing cardiac function. What really matters is whether the heart continues to beat; however, since this is sometimes difficult to assess, the Talmud allows (and perhaps even requires) checking for continued respiration as a surrogate marker for cardiac activity.[18] He specifically means to preclude an argument made by some physicians (the responsum was written in 1967) arguing that since the ability for spontaneous respiration resides in the brain, determining life and death should in fact depend on continued brain function.[19]

R. Waldenberg responds to this assertion on two fronts. He begins by noting that since the heart can continue to beat long after the brain has been declared "dead," using brain-oriented criteria for death would deem patients with active heartbeats as dead – all of whom, R. Waldenberg argues, are most certainly still alive. He then goes on to quote extensively from *Hakham Tzvi*, proving that in Talmudic parlance, respiration is simply an easily assessed marker or **test** for cardiac function. As discussed in chapter 17, R. Waldenberg maintains that the fact that the medical premise of the Talmud/*Hakham Tzvi* is inaccurate is irrelevant; while their choice of **test** may not properly reflect their criteria, those criteria remain unchanged.

R. Waldenberg is quite fierce in his complete and total opposition to any form of organ donation.[20] In his view, it is not only a direct violation of Torah law, but also reveals utter disrespect for God, His world, and His creations:

> We must be shocked and shudder at the deterioration of [our society]… for in front of us, there is the murder of two people, something that should terrify each and every person. And one should not think that he is unaffected by this, but rather stand up and oppose this with all our strength and raise a tremendous unending ruckus (*le-har'ish olamot al kakh hashkem ve-ha'arev*), and not allow these murderers and those who support them to rest.

---

18   Ibid. 17:66.
19   Ibid. 10:25:4.
20   Ibid. 6:66:2:7.

It is the ancient evil inclination of "Let us make a name for ourselves" that resides within that pushes these evil-doers to travel down such dangerous paths and prevents them from seeing the truth. These transplants are the ways of death and open a door for the general disregard for human life to a degree which we have never seen before – may God have mercy!... O, that the eyes of the blind who traverse perilous paths were opened so that they could see and understand what they are really doing, and then the righteous will watch and rejoice.

R. Waldenberg's tone and rhetoric are severe and seemingly meant to shock. In fact, in each of his many responsa on the topic, he makes sure to include an ethical treatise on the horrors of organ donation and why he believes that it degrades human dignity. He also frequently appends a fervent prayer that the proponents of such transplants "see the light" and that they cease entirely, certainly in the Land of Israel.

It is against this backdrop of passionate diatribe against organ donation that R. Moshe Tendler and Dr. Fred Rosner claim that toward the end of his life, R. Waldenburg changed his mind – finally agreeing to accept "brain death" as halakhically meaningful.[21] (As noted in chapter 16, they make a similar [erroneous] claim regarding R. Auerbach's position.) Citing one of R. Waldenberg's later responsa, they infer this fundamental policy change from his position concerning a separate, but related matter.

In this responsum,[22] R. Waldenberg responds to a request from Dr. Eli Schussheim regarding the case of a "brain dead" woman in her seventh month of pregnancy. Her physician wished to emergently deliver her fetus because of the mother's rapidly deteriorating condition. The father opposed the early delivery, arguing that the physicians could offer no guarantee that the child would be healthy and develop normally after the mother suffered the "brain death" causing injury during pregnancy. He therefore wished to remain passive and allow nature to take its course. The matter came before an Israeli judge, who sided with the husband as

---

21 "Letter to the Editor," *Tradition* 28:3 (1994): 94-6.
22 *Responsa Tzitz Eliezer* 18:31.

proxy for his wife's wishes; the mother's heart stopped two days later, and both she and her baby died. R. Waldenberg was asked for his halakhic insight into the matter, and he concludes that as a matter of Halakhah, the possibility for physical disability or developmental impairment should not matter at all when it comes to saving lives. R. Waldenberg argues that even if it were certain that this child would suffer from such difficulties, Halakhah still mandates that every effort be expended to save his life.

R. Tendler and Dr. Rosner note that all recorded cases of children born to "brain dead" mothers required Caesarian sectioning, since the mothers could not actively participate in a natural birth.[23] In a rapidly deteriorating "brain dead" patient such as the woman described in the question, the surgical procedure would almost certainly cause the mother's death. R. Tender and Dr. Rosner conclude that since Halakhah forbids choosing one life over another, and yet R. Waldenberg clearly advocates for trying to save the fetus at the expense of the certain death of its mother, it is "clear" that he felt that the "brain dead" mother was no longer alive. Whether or not the procedure would cause her heart to stop was completely irrelevant since, according to this logic, she was already dead.

R. Tendler and Dr. Rosner's argument is not only cogent, but rather convincing. How indeed could R. Waldenberg have suggested the procedure if he considers a "brain dead" woman to be alive? Yet, in a letter to Dr. Robert Schulman, R. Waldenberg vigorously and explicitly denies R. Tendler's and Dr. Rosner's claim, stating as clearly as ever that he has most certainly not reversed his opinion.[24] So as to leave no possibility for misinterpretation, he emphatically repeats that harvesting organs from "brain dead" patients constitutes murder.[25] How can both of R. Waldenberg's positions stand? Are they not contradictory?

A point that is important to note – and which R. Tendler and Dr. Rosner do not mention – is that nowhere in this responsum does

---

23 See, for example, D.J. Powner, I.M. Bernstein, "Extended somatic support for pregnant women after brain death," *Critical Care Medicine* 31 (2003): 1246.
24 Originally written on 25 *Marheshvan*, 5755 (October 30, 1994), R. Waldenberg's unequivocal rejection of R. Tendler and Dr. Rosner's position was published in *Tradition* 28:2 (Winter 1995): 102-3.
25 *Responsa Tzitz Eliezer* 21:28.

R. Waldenberg explicitly address "brain death." Moreover, R. Tendler and Dr. Rosner specifically focus on that which was specifically **not** mentioned in Dr. Schussheim's question. Nowhere is the question broached of possible harms to the mother resulting from this early-induced delivery. In fact, the method of delivery itself is not mentioned anywhere, simply referring to the outcome of removing the fetus from its mother's womb. Neither Dr. Schussheim nor R. Waldenberg makes any mention of possible risks to the mother, and it is highly likely that R. Waldenberg was completely unaware that the delivery of the fetus would cause the mother's heart to stop beating. His focus is entirely on whether or not it is prudent to expend efforts to save a child who might suffer from medical and mental disabilities.

Indeed, one could only imagine that one of the most vociferous opponents of accepting "brain death" would preface his supposed "reversal" with some sort of explanation for this radical shift – or at the very least note that he has indeed changed his opinion and reversed his earlier ruling. Instead of presuming that R. Waldenberg completely reversed his staunch opposition to "brain death" without as much as even a word, it is far more likely that he did not relate to the issue at all because he did not know that the mother would die (her heart would stop) as a result of the procedure under discussion. His analysis presumes that while the mother was certainly dying even while being ventilated, the delivery would have no effect on this outcome.

In fact, in a later responsum,[26] R. Waldenberg writes specifically that no efforts may be taken to save a fetus when they may pose a serious risk to the mother's life; when it comes to a choice as to whom to save, Halakhah demands that we save the mother. R. Waldenberg appends two caveats to this position. The first is that the risk to the mother by saving the child must be considerable, or at least serious – applying almost exclusively to cases of the severely ill. Second, he notes that if the woman is expected to die along with her child, then efforts must certainly be directed to saving the fetus – referencing the aforementioned responsum. Clearly, according to his understanding of the case presented by Dr. Schussheim, the mother was alive and efforts to excise her fetus would not have killed her. With

---

26 Ibid. 22:60.

this understanding in mind, it is clear that R. Waldenberg's position to save the fetus does not contradict his staunchly held opinion that "brain death" is halakhically meaningless.[27]

Rabbi Yitzchak Yaakov Weisz

Writing around 1968, R. Yitzhak Ya'akov Weisz was one of the first to deal with the issue of organ transplantation.[28] Many of the details of this responsum specifically relate to more fully understanding R. Feinstein's positions and were presented earlier (chapter 10). Of current relevance is his discussion – or actually, the lack thereof – of determining the moment of death.

R. Weisz, citing the (unnamed) questioner's analysis, claims that ascertaining the precise moment of death is of prime importance for a detailed halakhic discussion. He notes, however, that

> practically, it is impossible to "coincide" the moment of the donor's death with the moment that the recipient is ready to receive the organ (*i efshar le-tzamtzem et ha-rega shel mittat ha-nodev im ha-rega she-bo mukhan ha-mekabbel li-shetilat ha-ever*). Instead, they keep the donor alive... through artificial means [without which he would have naturally died], and in the meantime prepare the recipient... Only when the recipient is ready do they stop the resuscitative efforts of the donor and take out his organs immediately.

The focus of the rest of this responsum analyzes whether or not one may sacrifice the life of a dying patient to save a patient with a greater chance of survival. R. Weisz thus skirts the entire issue of determining the moment of death, avoiding the complex questions of "brain death"

---

27 Written on 9 *Adar II*, 5757 (March 18, 1997), this later, clarifying responsum (22:60) was unavailable to R. Tendler and Dr. Rosner when penning their letter in *Tradition*.

28 *Responsa Minhat Yitzhak* 5:7. While his responsa are not dated, R. Moshe Feinstein (*Responsa Iggerot Mosheh*, YD 2:174) specifically addresses the points raised by R. Weisz in a letter to him, and his responsum is dated 19 *Tamuz*, 5728 (July 15, 1968).

and whether cardiac or respiratory arrest is necessary or sufficient to halakhically determine death.

Interestingly, R. Weisz assumes that all agree that while the "resuscitative efforts" continue, the donor is considered alive. Only after they have ceased – coinciding with the heart stopping to beat – is the patient dead. What R. Weisz describes appears to be more akin to "donation after cardiac death"[29] (DCD) than to donation after "brain death." He therefore delves into whether or not it is appropriate for physicians to maintain the life of a person who naturally would have died without these interventions. However, in insisting that so long as the heart continues beating the person is alive (and only questioning whether or not creating this situation is proper), as a matter of practical Halakhah, R. Weisz cannot recognize "brain death" as death.

Rabbi Shemuel ha-Levi Wosner

Rejecting "brain death" as halakhically meaningful in several responsa, R. Wosner largely agrees with the analysis and approach of the last two chapters. In one responsum, R. Wosner suggests that organ transplants may be prohibited even after cardiac asystole, as they are outside the permission granted to a physician to heal.[30] R. Wosner resurrects the rejected opinion of R. Bahyah ben Asher,[31] who, commenting on Talmud's exposition[32] of the verse "And he shall surely heal" (*ve-rapo yerape*)[33] as Biblically sanctioning the practice of medicine, argues that this is limited to "external" maladies – excluding ailments of internal organs. While summarily rejected by the halakhic tradition, the notion it conveys, R. Wosner argues, may still have relevance. He claims that this idea excludes actions that "are contrary to the realities of the creation of Man (*pe'ulah neged metziut beri'at ha-adam*) and a complete change of Creation… against the Providence of the Creator in His creating man

---

29 See chapter 4.
30 *Responsa Shevet ha-Levi* 7:235:3.
31 Commentary to *Shemot* 21:19.
32 *Bava Kama* 85a.
33 *Shemot* 21:19.

(*neged hashgahat ha-Borei be-beri'at ha-adam*)." R. Wosner admittedly hedges a bit, noting that without (what he refers to as) the rabbinic consensus opposed to organ donation as a form of murder, this reason alone would be insufficient to prohibit organ transplants. He leaves the issue somewhat vague as to what role these philosophical understandings should play in halakhic discussions.

The ramifications of adopting this approach, however, are somewhat frightening. Who or what determines which medical interventions are in accordance with Providence and synchronous with the Divine plan for a specific individual? Are organ transplants any different from replacing a cardiac valve, implanting a pacemaker, or even starting hemodialysis? It is hard to believe that R. Wosner would oppose any of these treatments on halakhic grounds.

Conclusion

Representing a wide range of approaches to Halakhah, these halakhic decisors are firm in their rejection of "brain death" as constituting the death of the individual. This opposition does not stem from fear of "that which is new," nor is it part of a general conservative attitude, but rather represents an opinion born out of specific halakhic sources and arguments. As a novel and modern concept, the burden of proof is most certainly on those who wish to assign "brain death" halakhic meaning, and these decisors claim that the threshold has simply not been met. The complexity of the matter – of possibly sanctioning the murder of one person to save another – raises profound questions. While all halakhic prohibitions are set aside, and indeed must be set aside, to save even a single life, this principle does not apply to the three "cardinal sins" – idolatry, adultery, and murder.

Balancing saving the recipient's life against the sanctity of the life of the potential donor, even if short-lived, is both monumental and terrifying at the same time. This carefully choreographed dance puts the sanctity of both the donor and recipient's lives at it center and champions it as a halakhic ideal, advocating maximizing life whenever possible. In doing so, these halakhic decisors view the issue as sacrificing one life to save another – requiring the killing of the innocent – something that simply cannot be sanctioned.

This stance is effectively a halakhic restatement of the "Dead Donor Rule," defining the terms in a halakhic context. While debated in the current bioethical literature, the strong moral, ethical, legal, and halakhic consensus is that the "Dead Donor Rule" must be protected at all costs. Innocents may not be killed for a greater good; the ends cannot and do not justify the means. The halakhic tradition already encompasses a definition of death, one that is certainly not amenable to re-examination for utilitarian purposes. In more clearly defining it, these decisors cannot recognize "brain death" as meeting that standard, and by invoking the halakhic "Dead Donor Rule" must thereby forbid "brain death" dependent organ transplants.

Epilogue – In Lieu of a Conclusion

Readers searching for a conclusion regarding the halakhic status of "brain death" will serve themselves best by contacting their personal halakhic authority for a definitive ruling. This conversation, which may be appropriately held amongst discussion of other "end of life" issues, may even be the catalyst for developing such a relationship.

We have seen three very different general approaches to determining death – ICSR, cessation of "vital motion," and the complete death of the entire brain. Each position is developed through integration of the medical facts and the halakhic sources, and each has serious ramifications for the potential permissibility of "brain death" based organ donation. There are eminently qualified halakhists advocating for each one of these approaches. The goal of this discussion was to create a dialogue among them – not only explaining and analyzing how each relates the medical information to the halakhic texts, but also how each position relates to the others. It was not my intention to advocate or adopt any particular approach, and I therefore do not come to any conclusion as to which position is more correct or even most compelling. Deciding which approach to follow and determining practical Halakhah is the sacred task of the halakhic decisor.

Determining the moment of death is clearly no simple task. Identifying this moment so as to permit organ donation pits two pillars of halakhic Judaism against each other – the mandate of *pikuah nefesh* and the cardinal prohibition of murder. As great, important, and all encompassing as the role *pikuah nefesh* is in Halakhah, organ donation requires balancing the *pikuah nefesh* of the potential donor against the *pikuah nefesh* of the recipient. Finding this delicate equilibrium requires halakhic precision, medical understanding, and a comprehensive mastery of the halakhic corpus. Readers should not delude themselves into thinking that this book adequately provides these tools – all vital to arriving at a final and proper halakhic conclusion.

In the end, the issue remains disputed, with some halakhic decisors recognizing "brain death" as halakhic death and others maintaining that "brain dead" patients are still alive. That diametrically opposite positions exist within Halakhah should not come as a surprise; almost all matters of Halakhah are subject to dispute on some level. The fact that Halakhah is not monolithic – even in identifying some of its most basic premises, such as determining what it means to be alive and what it means to be dead – is not a reason for dismay or despair. It rather reflects a certain strength of diversity – the notion that Torah can be properly interpreted along 70 different ways of thinking.[1]

The Talmud wonders: If regarding a single issue, some permit and some forbid, how is anybody supposed to know how to act? The Talmud reassures us that Torah, even in all of its varied interpretations, was given by a single God, the Master of all actions.[2] This idea, the Talmud argues, compels us to acquire for ourselves a sensitive heart to listen, observe, respect, and be sensitive to all positions, even while practically following the rulings of our particular halakhic authority.

Where, then, to go from here? We can either go to continued study, research, analysis, and understanding of the myriad complex scientific and halakhic issues and ideas or to an experienced, learned, and God-fearing halakhic decisor for practical guidance.

The purpose of this book is to provide a framework for understanding how Halakhah goes about defining the moment of death – understanding the science and analyzing the basic sources, and how halakhic decisors integrate them both to arrive at a final decision. Hopefully, some measure of this has been accomplished and the journey was educational and worthwhile.

---

1 *Bamidbar Rabbah* 13:15.
2 *Hagigah* 3b.

Index

A

abdomen, 13, 71, 73, 92, 98n2, 117, 350-1
abdominal aorta, 73, 350n8
abdominal aortic aneurysm, 350n8
Abraham, Dr. Abraham S., viii, 76n15, 190, 197-8, 222, 224, 242n18, 252nn10-11, 311-15, 319n14, 325, 330, 335-6, 341, 376, 383
Abravanel, R. Yitzhak, 171
accident victims, 27, 227, 274, 279, 281, 292-3; *see also* traumatic brain injury
Ad Hoc Committee of the Harvard Medical School to Examine the Definition of Brain Death, xvii, 9-10, 19-20, 25, 35, 39-40, 46, 203, 248, 250; *see also* Harvard Criteria
ADH (anti-diuretic hormone), 31, 48-50, 327
Aldebi, R. Meir, 152, 354
alveoli, 14, 156, 288, 368
Amar, R. Shelomoh, 121, 265, 267n16, 294-5, 318, 388
American Academy of Neurology (AAN), 22, 26, 28, 46, 301, 301n37, 302n41
amyotrophic lateral sclerosis (ALS), 370
Andalusian scholars, 169-72, 176-7
angiography, 26, 299, 305
apnea, *see* respiratory failure
apnea test, 20-22, 24n11, 28, 48, 221n2, 223, 247-8, 288n9, 289, 291n13, 291-3, 302-3
apoptosis, 107, 331
arginine vasopressin, *see* ADH
Aristotle, 147-8, 279, 286
Arizal (R. Isaac Luria), 148
arterial line, 292n13
Asad, R. Yehudah, 122-4, 127-8, 129n24, 137
Aseh Lekha Rav (Responsa), *see* Ha-Levi, R. Hayyim David
Ashkenazi, R. Tzvi, *see Hakham Tzvi*
asmakhta, 84n32
asystole, 59, 64, 66, 193n14, 209, 259, 319, 320-1, 320n18, 325-8, 395; *see also* cardiac arrest; heartbeat
atrial natriuretic peptide, 208
Auerbach, R. Shelomoh Zalman, xxii, 48n8, 63, 84, 84n34, 362n22
 on cessation of heartbeat, 114, 311-2, 315, 318-22, 319n14, 327
 on decapitation, 108, 114, 233n12, 265, 267-8, 294-5, 312, 315-6, 318, 321-2, 326, 331, 337, 343, 345, 376-80

401

definition of "brain death," 114,
        233n12, 263-5, 266n14, 268,
        294-5, 317-8, 322-3, 326-31,
        334-8, 341, 343-5, 384-5
    on diagnosis of "brain death," 319-
        28, 331-3, 336-9, 344
    dual definition of death, 114, 312,
        321, 323, 379-80
    evolution of approach, 309-24,
        341-2
    interpretation of R. Feinstein, 223,
        252-5
    on organ donation, 7, 252-3, 310-
        11, 319-30, 336-42, 340n42,
        362, 387-92, 395-7, 399-400
    Principles and Conclusions, 333-41
    on prohibition of moving a *goses*,
        319, 331-3, 331-2n37, 338,
        344
    on *safek goses*, 319-20, 324, 326,
        332-7, 341
    sheep experiment, xxii, 112, 114,
        312-6, 321-4, 342, 376-80
    on withdrawal of care, 253-4,
        253n12, 329-30, 342
automaticity, 15, 33, 110
autopsy, xxv, 6, 31, 325
autoresuscitation, 64-65, 193n14, 320
avalanche, *see* building collapse

B

Ba'al ha-Ma'or, 100
BAER (brainstem auditory evoked
    responses), 26, 273-4, 279,
    289, 289nn9-10, 294, 298-9,
    305-6

Bartenura, R. Ovadiah of, 98
basar she-ha-rofe gorero, 109, 343
basar she-nifrakh be-tzipporen, 109, 343
Bauby, Jean-Dominique, 360n20
Ben Zazon, R. David, 265, 330n34
Bernat, Dr. James, 24n11, 37-39, 46-50,
    48n8, 58
Biblical proof-text, 71, 75, 82-83,
    85, 90, 165n7, 348, 349n5,
    356n15
bioethics, secular, xvii, xx, xxvi, 3-4, 8,
    17, 35-43, 45-66, 74, 95, 268,
    379, 397
Bleich, R. J. David, viii, xxii, 41,
    72-74, 81-82, 87, 95, 109-14,
    111n42, 118, 121, 123, 136,
    158-9, 178-9, 181, 346-52,
    356-64, 358n19, 361n22, 367-
    8, 370-1, 373, 375n12, 379,
    384, 388
Bondi, Dr. Elliot, viii, 249-50, 263
Brain and Respiratory Death Law –
    2008, xviii, 26, 36-37, 37n81,
    38, 62, 250, 293-5, 295n21,
    298-9, 301n37, 300, 303-6
brain arrest, 19
brain,
    completely rotted, 228, 231-3, 237,
        256, 280, 328
    critical functions of, 47, 50
    dysfunction vs. destruction of, 61,
        107, 109, 113, 204, 228, 230,
        258, 265-7, 288-9, 289n10,
        306
    integrated function of, 46, 48, 58,
        103-5, 108, 119, 267, 377-8

neocortex of, 32
perfusion of, 31-33, 107, 125-6, 229, 230, 232, 299, 302-6, 317, 322, 323n22, 328, 331, 339
as vital organ, 386-7; *see also* brain cells; brain death; brainstem; cerebrum, "higher brain"; hypothalamus; "whole brain"
brain cells, 32, 229, 232, 303, 343
apoptosis of, 107, 331
death of each and every, 114, 125-6, 267, 295, 317-8, 322-3, 326, 331-2, 334, 338-40, 343-4, 384
lysis of, 104, 107, 232-4, 237, 385
necrosis of, 107, 232
non-perfused, 26, 126, 232, 303, 328; *see also* brain death; brain
brain death,
cell damage in, 32, 104, 107, 232-4, 237, 303, 331, 343, 385
in children, 24-25
confirmation of diagnosis, 10, 25, 26-27, 56, 229-30, 264, 301n37
diagnosis of, 10, 20-22, 24n11, 28, 48, 221n2, 223, 247-8, 288n9, 289, 291n13, 291-3, 302-3
gestation of fetus after, 47, 311-17, 316n10, 334, 391-4
legal issues in, xvii-xviii, xxi, xxvi, 4, 9, 25-26, 36-37, 37n4, 38-39, 40-42, 45, 46n4, 51, 61-62, 65n60, 246n2, 248, 250, 268, 293-5, 295n21, 298-9, 300-1, 301n37, 303-6, 340, 397
misdiagnosis of, 27-29, 29n20

neuro-pathology of, 29-33, 49, 104, 204, 232-3, 328, 339, 341, 387
prognosis, xxviii, 23-24, 40, 99, 180, 225-6, 328
as self-fulfilling prophecy, 23, 28, 316n10
survival after, 23-24, 24n11, 53, 57
brain lesion, 16, 117-8, 157, 359
brainstem, 15-17, 22
death/dysfunction of, 20-21, 25, 29, 32-33, 36, 49n16, 54, 54n28, 56, 106, 113, 157, 202, 212, 217, 225-6, 230-1, 234-5, 237, 260, 265-6, 273-4, 278-85, 288-9, 289n10, 298, 301-7, 310, 323, 328, 333-4, 339, 342, 345, 359, 368, 385
reflexes, 20-21, 29, 49n16, 53, 56, 301n37, 302; *see also* BAER; irreversible cessation of spontaneous respiration
breathing, *see* respiration
British Code of Practice, 54
Brody, Dr. Baruch, 58-60
Brooks, R. Moshe Elyakim, 384
building collapse, 69-71, 84-7, 90, 93-94, 168-9 169n15, 206, 211-12, 218, 278, 284, 350-3, 358, 374-5
burial, 53, 59, 168, 319
delay of, 5, 161-7, 162n2, 173-4, 333n39, 363-4
premature, 161-7, 347
proper, xv-xvi, xxv; *see also* short waiting period before death determination

C

carbon dioxide, 14-15, 21, 42, 156, 288, 291n12, 368

cardiac arrest, 1, 6n12, 28-9, 65n60, 83, 99, 106, 112, 118, 133, 193n14, 225-6, 291n13, 376n12; *see also* asystole; cardiopulmonary arrest; heart

cardiac surgery, 17, 80, 111n42

cardiac transplant, *see* heart, transplant

cardiopulmonary arrest, xix, 3, 8-9, 17, 28, 36, 46n4, 63, 104, 225, 315, 321, 326; *see also* heart; irreversible cessation of spontaneous respiration; respiration

Catholic Church, xvii-xviii

cellular metabolism, 8, 11, 14

cerebrum, 10, 21, 25-26, 31-32, 41, 51, 59, 106-8, 121, 125-6, 202, 273, 289n10, 298, 300-6, 318, 328, 387; *see also* brain

Chajes, R. Tzvi Hirsch, 85, 161-2, 162n2, 168n14

Chief Rabbinate of England, xviii

Chief Rabbinate of Israel, xviii, xxi, 26, 271-307, 345

childbirth, death in, 91-93, 192, 195-7, 316, 364-5, 365n28; *see also* fetus

circulation, 8, 13, 14-17, 36, 46, 65-66, 78-81, 79n24, 110-12, 143-4, 152-6, 172, 193n14, 208, 224, 232, 277, 288, 319, 322, 363, 378-9, 385-7, 386

    effective, 81, 81n179, 112, 114, 114n46, 198, 206n6, 357-8,
379; *see also* cardiac arrest; heart; heartbeat; perfusion

Cohen, R. Feivel, 309, 314, 322

Cohen, R. She'ar Yashuv, 275

coma dépassé, 9, 19

communication, capacity for, 19-20, 261, 360-1, 361n22, 370-5, 375n12

conscience clause, 37, 299-300

consciousness, capacity for, 41, 51-56, 297, 360, 370-2

corneal transplant, 6n12, 6n14

corpse, desecration of, xxv-xxvi, 5-7, 6n12

CPR (cardiopulmonary resuscitation), 64-65, 65n60, 193n14, 197, 320, 329; *see also* resuscitation

Crescas, R. Hasdai, 171n23

criteria for death, xvii, xxiii –xxvii, 10, 18, 20-21, 20n5, 24-28, 24n11, 30, 32n29, 36-37, 56, 58-59, 60, 63, 70, 73, 84n34, 100-1, 104-114, 117-18, 121, 129n24, 131, 131n32, 132, 137, 164, 166, 181n35, 201, 211, 219-21, 234-7, 249, 252, 256, 259n4, 258, 263-5, 266, 286, 297, 299, 301n37, 316-7, 321, 328-30, 334, 337, 339, 340, 344-5, 358n19, 363-3, 365, 375n12, 379-80, 388

    cardiac, 76-78, 80-84, 90, 91n46, 93, 95, 105-6, 111-4, 151-8, 172-82, 180n33, 190, 197-9, 206-7, 206n6, 215, 239-41, 267, 296, 315, 318, 348-52, 356, 363, 367, 385

vs. definition vs. tests, 37-43, 46-47, 50-51, 54, 74-84, 87, 90, 95-96, 105, 157-9, 258, 260-2, 286, 296-7, 304-7, 317, 322-3, 326-7, 346-51, 355, 390
functional vs. structural, 108, 303-6, 318, 331, 343
vs. indication, 106-7, 113, 119, 123-5, 125n18, 180-1, 188, 190, 198, 224-7, 241, 260-2, 264-5, 266n14, 288, 293, 295, 297, 313, 375, 375-6n12, 378
neurological, 204, 228-31, 235, 271, 362, 390
respiratory, 93, 105-6, 172-5, 190, 197-205, 218-27, 230, 234-6, 239-43, 250, 256-60, 302-4, 315, 346-9, 351, 356, 363, 367, 370, 376n12, 377-8, 385n4
universal, 370-2; *see also* brain death; cardiopulmonary arrest; decapitation; definitions of death; Harvard Criteria; heart; irreversible cessation of spontaneous respiration; irreversibility; respiration
critical care medicine, 9, 83
CTA (computerized tomography with angiography), 26, 299, 299n31, 302, 305
Culver, Dr. Charles M., 37
cyclosporine A, 10, 246

D
Daniel (Biblical), 98, 170
Danzig, R. Abraham (*Hayyei Adam*), 154

darkei ha-Emori, 163
Dead Donor Rule (DDR), 3-5, 9, 35, 35n1, 60-65, 199, 397
decapitation, 228-50, 262-8
as independent definition of death, 113-4, 114n47, 121, 197-9, 228, 234-8, 256, 263, 312, 315, 321-3, 326, 356-7, 379-80
forceful, 81n27, 228, 231-2, 234, 236-7, 263, 280
physiological, 105-8, 119, 234-9, 262-5, 266n14, 268, 343, 356
reversibility and, 188-90, 189n3, 197-9, 197n21
decisors, 63, 91n46, 137, 150, 154, 157, 195, 280, 399-400
Ashkenazi, 148
early, 120, 204
later, 143-4
modern, 185, 269, 288, 309, 341-2, 345, 362, 383-97
Sephardic, 148n33
definitions of death, xix, xxiii-xxiv, 8-10, 19, 35-43, 45-66, 80-83, 105-7, 116-8, 121, 123, 131, 172, 175, 177, 180, 188-90, 241, 248, 260-6, 266n14, 295, 297, 304, 318, 340-3, 345-7, 356-7, 362, 370-1, 375-6n12, 377, 385, 397
vs. criteria vs. tests, 37-43, 46-47, 50-51, 54, 74-84, 87, 90, 95-96, 105, 157-9, 258, 260-2, 286, 296-7, 304-7, 317, 322-3, 326-7, 346-51, 355, 390

multiple, 113-14, 114n47 117, 121, 127-8n23, 132, 136-7, 197-9, 204, 228, 234-8, 256, 263, 312, 315, 321-3, 326, 356-7, 379-80; see also criteria for death
diabetes insipidus, 31
diaphragm, 13-14, 16-17, 73, 123, 369, 369n4
Dikdukei Soferim, 71n4
do not resuscitate order (DNR), 65, 65n60
donation after cardiac death (DCD), 63-66, 65n60, 320n18, 395
Duke of Mecklenburg-Schwerin, 161
Dunlap, Zack, 27-29
dyspnea, 255

E
EEG (electroencephalogram), 10, 25, 48, 289n10, 361-2n22, 363
EKG (electrocardiogram), 42, 190, 205-6, 205n5, 206n6, 208-9, 209n8, 211, 213, 219-20, 224, 241, 319, 321, 352, 363
electro-mechanical dissociation, 206n6
Eliyahu (Biblical), 149n39, 169-70, 189, 189-90n5
Eliyahu, R. Mordechai, 271, 275, 291n12, 293, 295, 372-4
Elyashiv, R. Yosef Shalom, 309-10, 310n3, 323-4, 346, 383-5
Emden, R. Yaakov, 163
endotracheal (ET) tube, 22, 221n2, 291n12
Engelhardt, Dr. H. Tristam, 57

Erkhin 7a, 91, 192, 293, 311, 314-7, 342
esophagus, 101, 102n19, 116, 131-2, 140, 380
Ettlinger, R. Yaakov, 7
euthanasia, 62-63, 253-5
extra corporeal membrane oxygenation (ECMO), 66
extubation, 221n2, 291n12
Eyebeschutz, R. Yonatan, 120, 130, 143-4, 152-6

F
Feinstein, R. Dovid, 242-3, 252
Feinstein, R. Moshe,
    on decapitation, 188-90, 197-9, 228-50, 256, 262-8
    on heartbeat, 88, 172n25, 186, 199, 203, 205-9, 209n8, 217-27, 239-41, 259
    on ICSR, 199, 200-5, 218-27, 230, 234-6, 239-43, 250, 256, 258-60
    influence of, xxi, 185, 257, 268-9, 296n24
    interpretation of, 202, 210-15, 217-43, 247-9, 252-6, 258-69, 345
    on irreversibility, 63, 188-90, 189n3, 197-9, 197n21, 225-7, 230-1, 235-6, 238, 259n4
    on medical establishment, 186-8, 246-9, 257-8
    on medical tests, 84, 205-9, 211, 213, 228-31, 235-7, 241, 252, 263, 305, 332-3
    on neurological criteria for death, 204, 228-31, 235

oral record regarding, 256
on organ death, 385-8
on organ transplantation, 7, 186-8, 213-5, 217, 223, 235, 243-54, 257-8, 272, 278, 281, 333n39
posthumously printed letter of, 249-56, 263
on prohibition of moving a *goses*, 194-7, 332-3, 333n39
on short waiting period before death determination, 91, 191-7
on *tereifot*, 155
on withdrawal of therapy, 252-5; *see also Iggerot Mosheh*
fetus,
death of, 311-17, 365
formation of, 69, 71, 86
gestation of, 47, 311-17, 316n10, 334, 391-4
removal of, 91-93, 192, 195-7, 316, 364-5, 365n28, 391-4
status of, xxvii, 40
firstborn, 145
Fisher, R. Yisrael Ya'akov, 114n47
Fleishman, Dr. Yaakov, 319n14, 320
fMRI (functional MRI), 26, 299, 360-1

G
Galen, 146-7
gangrene, 106, 109, 343, 285, 286-7
gas exchange, 14-17, 55, 156, 276-7, 288, 368
Ge'onim, 91n49, 195
Gershon b. Shelomoh, 146, 152, 354
Gert, Dr. Bernard, 37
gezeirah (rabbinic prohibition), 194

Gittin 70b, 380-1
Goldberg, R. Zalman Nehemiah, 179-81, 179n32, 215, 275, 343
Goren, R. Shelomoh, 180n33, 271
goses (moribund person), 4, 59n49, 89, 97, 98-100, 253, 254nn15-16, 281, 297, 324, 329, 372
moving/touching a, 4, 89, 99, 194, 319, 331-3, 331-2n37, 338, 344
safek, 93, 99, 319-20, 324, 326, 332-7, 341
Goulon, Dr. Pierre, 9
Gra (Vilna Gaon), xix-xx, 297-8, 372-3
Guide for the Perplexed, 169-73
Gulevsky, R. Chaim Dov Ber, 201, 204-6

H
Hadassah Medical Center, 272, 274, 277-82, 286, 291n12
Hakham Tzvi (R. Tzvi Ashkenazi), xxi, 76-77, 76n15, 80, 120, 127, 139-59, 178, 207-8, 208n7, 259, 353-5, 363, 374, 376n12, 389, 389n15, 390
Halakhah le-Mosheh mi-Sinai, 155, 166, 278
halakhic process, xxiii-xxix, 43, 87, 92, 94n54, 141, 148, 157, 166n7, 205, 344, 349, 373-4, 388, 399-400
Ha-Levi, R. Hayyim David, 78-79, 79n24, 177, 181, 231, 305, 343
Ha-Levi, R. Yehudah, 77, 151, 208, 354

Halevy, Dr. Amir, 58-60
Halperin, Dr. Mordechai, 267, 275, 290, 291n12, 292, 296n24, 312, 324, 326, 341-2
Harvard Criteria, 10, 20, 40, 248, 250; see also Ad Hoc Committee of the Harvard Medical School to Examine the Definition of Brain Death
Hatam Sofer (R. Moshe Sofer), xxi, 5-6, 85, 89-90, 161-82, 204-5, 211-2, 215, 219-20, 232, 239, 273, 275, 278, 282-6, 296-7, 347, 354, 354n13, 363-5, 376n12, 389, 389n15
havdalat olat ha-of, 100n9, 102, 102n19
hayyei sha'ah, 272
Hazon Ish (R. Avraham Yishayah Karelitz), 153-5
health insurance, 37
heart,
    anatomy of, 14-17, 150n41, 156
    automaticity of, 15, 33, 110
    avodah of, 207-8, 208n7, 240-1
    function, xvi, 14-17, 65, 78-80, 84-85, 111-4, 118, 152, 176-7, 181, 206n6, 208-9, 212, 219-20, 223-7, 262, 264, 268, 298, 312-3, 315, 345-65
    rate, 15-16
    transplant, 8-12, 15, 64, 186-8, 214, 245-7, 257-8, 271-2, 275-6, 281, 310n3, 323; see also asystole; autoresuscitation; cardiac arrest; cardiac surgery; cardiopulmonary arrest; circulation; criteria for death, cardiac; heartbeat; heart-beating cadaver; resuscitation
heartbeat, xv, xix, 3, 8, 12, 15, 40, 42, 59, 63-66, 73-81, 93, 95-96
    natural vs. artificial, 9, 17, 275-6, 284, 287-8, 293, 362, 373-4
    perception of, xvi, 42, 72-79, 79n24, 84, 151, 172, 174, 178, 205-7, 208n7, 240, 347, 365
    respiration without, 16-17, 75-77, 207-8, 212, 240-1
    without spontaneous respiration, xvi, 14, 33, 43, 205, 217-26
    regenerated, 65; see also cardiac arrest; EKG; heart; heart-beating cadaver; *libbo*; pulse
heart-beating cadaver, 9, 11
heart-lung machine, 17, 66, 80-81, 111
hemodialysis, xxvn19, 329, 359, 396
hevra kadisha, 177, 347, 365
Hida (R. Hayyim Yosef David Azulai), 95n54
"higher brain," 51-55, 60
Hirsch, Dr. Moshe, 312
hiyyut (life-force), 70, 76, 80, 93, 101n18, 103, 129n24, 151, 207-8, 221-2, 240, 253, 311, 347-8, 349n5, 389
holeh lefaneinu, 6, 335, 337
homeostasis, 31n24, 49n16, 107, 327n25
hotmo, 69-88, 79n24, 90, 91n46, 151, 209, 218, 240, 350-2, 389

hutzu rasheihem, 97, 100-2, 100n9, 102n19, 108, 116, 129-30, 129nn24-25, 131n33
hypotension, 118, 291n12
hypothalamus, 30-33, 123-4, 264-6, 325-31, 335-6, 342, 344
hypothermia, 10, 20, 28, 49n16
hypoxemia, 291n12
hypoxia, 291n12

I

ibn Caspi, Joseph, 171
ibn Ezra, Abraham, 77, 82n30, 151
Irreversible Cessation of Spontaneous Respiration (ICSR), xvi, xix, 21, 33, 36, 54-56, 73-75, 75n13, 80, 91n46, 95, 107, 113, 157, 178, 180-1, 186, 190, 202-3, 205, 214, 217-19, 222-7, 223n4, 230, 234-43, 247, 250, 256, 258-64, 275, 278-89, 294-5, 298, 302-3, 302n41, 306-7, 311, 345-50, 356-63, 367-81, 375-6n12, 384, 390, 399; *see also* criteria for death, respiratory; irreversibility; respiration
Iggerot Mosheh (Responsa),
  Hoshen Mishpat 2:72, 214n11, 245-9, 251, 258
  Yoreh De'ah 2:146, 76n15, 84, 88-89, 88n42, 107, 172n25, 190, 201-15, 219, 226, 240-3, 252, 258, 261
  Yoreh De'ah 2:174, 7, 185-99, 214n11, 218, 225, 235, 249, 258, 394n28
  Yoreh De'ah 3:132, 202-3, 203n3, 217-43, 245, 247, 252, 258-9, 262, 273, 275, 280, 290, 332; *see also* Feinstein, R. Moshe
immunosuppression, 10, 246, 257
intracranial pressure (ICP), 30, 30n23
intubation, 221n2, 255, 291n12
iron lungs, 370
irreversibility, xix, 9, 19-20, 22, 25-30, 33, 36, 40-43, 45, 47, 49, 51-6, 62-66, 73, 76-77, 80-84, 90-93, 106-7, 110-4, 111n42, 118-9, 136, 148, 151-8, 173-4, 176-81, 188-90, 189n3, 197-9, 197n21, 202, 205-6, 211-2, 224-31, 234-9, 247, 250, 259-60n4, 260-1, 264-7, 273, 286-8, 295, 297-8, 301-7, 312, 315, 318-21, 326-7, 345, 347, 352, 355, 357-8, 358n19, 362-4, 367-71, 375, 375-6n12, 377, 381; *see also* irreversible cessation of spontaneous respiration
irreversible apneic coma, 19
ischemia, 11, 11n24, 31-31, 232, 303, 328, 339
ischemic time, 8, 12, 64
Islam, xviii
Israeli Ministry of Health, 271-2, 274, 277, 298-300, 304, 306
Israeli National Transplant Center, 300-1
Iyov, xv

K

Kahana, R. Kalman, 245
Kamenetsky, R. Shmuel, 309

Kaplan-Meier patient survival prediction rates, 247
Karelitz, R. Avraham Yishayah, *see* Hazon Ish
Karlin, R. Yaakov of, 143n16
Karo, R. Yosef, *see Shulhan Arukh*; *Kesef Mishnah*
Kasher, R. Menahem, 82n30
kavod ha-meit, 163
Kesef Mishnah, 88, 133n35, 140-3, 209-12
kidney, 31, 47, 277
  transplant, xxvn19, 4, 11
Klipara, R. Shelomoh, 143
Kook, R. Abraham Isaac, 165n7
Korban ha-Eidah, 86-87
Kunin, Dr. Joshua, 264
Kuzari, *see* Ha-Levi, R. Yehudah

L

Landau, R. Yehezkel, 5-6
Lau, R. Yisrael Meir, 275, 293, 297-8
law,
  American, xvii, 25, 36-37, 62, 250, 301n37, 340
  Israeli, 26, 37n4, 38, 293-5, 295n21, 298-9, 300, 303-6
Leizerson, R. Simcha Bunim, 266n14
libbo, 69-79, 71n4, 79n24, 85, 87-88, 151, 209, 350-2
life-force, *see hiyyut*
lifnei iver, 338-9
live organ donation, 5n7
liver, 47, 109, 237, 277, 287, 386-7
  transplant, 4, 8, 11, 276, 290
Lizza, Dr. John, 57-58

Locked In Syndrome, 359-60, 360n20
Lowe, R. Judah (Maharal), 141, 144
Luria, R. Isaac (Arizal), 148
lysis, *see* brain, lysis of

M

ma'aseh nisim, 167, 212
Ma'aseh Rokeah, 101
Maggid Mishnah, 88, 130
Maharal of Prague, 141, 144
Maharitz Hiyyut, *see* Chajes, R. Tzvi Hirsch
Maharsham, 347
Malakh, Dr. Daniel, 387-8
medical establishment, dissatisfaction with, 181n35, 186-8, 246-9, 257-8
medical professionals, role of, xxvi-xxvii, 18, 36-41, 60, 64
medical reality,
  changing, xv, 3, 12, 42, 228-9, 232, 299, 306
  in pre-modern times, xvi, 3, 42, 70; *see also* science, previous understandings of
medical technology, reliance on, 42, 84, 93, 205-9, 211, 213, 228-31, 235-7, 241, 252, 263, 305, 332-3
Me'iri, 5n5, 71, 73, 167n12, 170
medulla, 15, 328; *see also* brainstem
meguyyad, 97-100, 297, 372-3
melikah, 102n19, 116
Mendelssohn, Moses, 162-3, 166
meninges, 126-8, 128n23
mi'uta de-mi'uta, 167, 205, 220, 353

Miller, Dr. Franklin G., 55-58, 57n40, 60-63
Minhat Hinukh, 5n5
Minhat Yitzhak (Responsa), see Weisz, R. Yitzhak Yaakov
minimally conscious state (MCS), 19, 360-1, 373n8
Mizrahi, R. Eliyahu, 82n30
Mollaret, Dr. Maurice, 9
moribund patient, *see goses*
Moses, Dr. Naftali, 272
Moshe (Biblical), xxvii, 166; *see also* Halakhah le-Mosheh mi-Sinai
motion, coordinated, 30, 147, 206n6, 358, 376-8; *see also* integrated function; *pirkus*
MRA (magnetic resonance imaging with angiography), 26, 299, 299n32

N
Narboni, R. Moses, 171n23
Nathanson, R. Shaul, 156
Naval (Biblical), 169-72
necrosis, *see* brain, necrosis of
neocortex, 32
nerve shrinkage, 227
neveilah, 100, 115-6, 117n1, 127n22, 132-5, 141-4, 152, 156, 384, 286
neveilah me-hayyim, 132-5
New Jersey, 37
New York State Task Force on Life and the Law, 20n4, 23, 37
Nissim, R. Yitzhak, 271
nivul ha-meit, xxv-xxvi, 5-7, 6n12
Noda bi-Yehuda (Responsa), see Landau, R. Yehezkel

nuclide scan test, 228-31, 235-7, 241, 263, 280, 305

O
Ohalot 1:6, 81n27, 97-114, 116, 119, 125, 125n18, 129-30, 129nn24-25, 136-7, 147, 188, 198, 232-6, 262, 264-7, 294, 297, 312, 315, 321, 323, 326-7, 341, 356-8, 362, 372, 375, 377
Oppenheim, R. David, 142-54, 149-50n39, 157, 159
oral record, xix, xxii, 256
Organ Care System, 12, 15
Organ Procurement and Transplantation Network (OPTN), 12
organ procurement organizations (OPO), 12
organ transplantation, xvii, xxiii, 3-12, 59-60, 289
    allocation in, 3, 12, 12n26
    consent to, 7, 7n14, 28, 62-64, 188, 274
    donor, xvi, xxiii, 3-5, 12, 19, 23-24, 24n11, 27-28, 35, 57, 61-65, 65n60, 186-8, 193n14, 217, 248-9, 274, 278, 283, 290, 292, 295n21, 300-1, 306-7, 311, 316n10, 320n18, 336-41
    as double murder, 186-7, 213-14, 235, 245, 247, 248-9, 251, 272, 281
    halakhic validity of, xix, xxv-xxvi, 5-8, 6n12, 7n14, 181n35, 252-3 223, 235, 243, 249-54, 278,

294-6, 296n22, 310-11, 319-30, 333n39, 336-42, 340n42, 362, 387-92, 395-7, 399-400
  in Israel vs. abroad, 281, 290, 337-9, 391
  live, 5n7
  moratorium, 10, 246, 246n2, 257
  process, 11-12, 15, 27-28, 31-32, 64-66, 196n35, 223n4, 319-21
  recipient, xxii, xxiii, xxv, xxvn19, 6, 7n14, 8-12, 15, 64n57, 186-88, 213-4, 245-7, 248, 251, 254, 257-8, 272, 280-1, 283, 285, 290, 292, 332n37, 337-9, 341, 394-7, 399
  survival rates, xxiii, 11, 185-8, 213-4, 245-9, 257-8, 268-9, 272-3, 280, 282-3; *see also* Auerbach, R. Shelomoh Zalman, on organ transplantation; corneal transplant; Dead Donor Rule; donation after cardiac death; Feinstein, R. Moshe, on organ transplantation; heart, transplant; kidney, transplant; liver, transplant; *pikuah nefesh*
oxygen, 8, 11-17, 21-22, 30, 32-33, 42, 66, 80-81, 86, 110, 112, 126, 150n339, 156, 221-3, 254-5, 276, 286-9, 291n13, 293, 295, 303, 319, 339, 368, 374, 381, 389
oxygen tank, 221, 223, 238

P

Pallis, Dr. Christopher, 54n28
pancreas, 11, 277
Pano, R. Menahem Azaryah (*Rama*) of, 150n41
R. Pappa, 70-79, 79n24, 83, 88, 351-2
paralysis, 107, 127n22, 261, 369, 386
Penei Mosheh, 86
perceptible phenomena, 205, 359, 361, 361n22
Peri Megadim, 143
perfusion,
  of brain, 31-33, 107, 125-6, 229, 230, 232, 299, 302-6, 317, 322, 323n22, 328, 331, 339
  of organs, 14, 17, 66, 118, 387
  studies, 31, 229, 302-6, 317, 328, 339; *see also* CTA; nuclide scan test; transcranial doppler
persistent vegetative state (PVS), 19, 56, 202, 248-9, 360-1, 373n8
PET scan (positron emission tomography), 27
phrenic nerve, 15-16, 107, 122-3, 361, 369
phrenic nerve stimulator (diaphragmatic pacer), 369, 369n4
physiological decapitation, 105-8, 119, 234-9, 262-5, 266n14, 268, 343, 356
pikuah nefesh, xxiii, xxv-xxvi, xxvn19, 4-7, 7n14, 70, 88, 164-7, 189, 189-90n5, 192, 220, 224, 252, 332n37, 348, 399
pirkus, 97, 102, 105, 110, 113, 116, 118, 125n18, 147-8, 206n6, 267, 321-2, 356-8, 364, 374-80; *see also* motion, coordinated
pituitary gland, 31, 327

Index

pneumothorax, 291n12
point of maximal impact (PMI), 73
poisoning, 20
polio, 370
President's Commission for the Study of Ethical Problems in Medicine and Biomedical and Behavioral Research, 36, 39, 45-48, 46n4, 52
President's Council of Bioethics, xvii, xix, 13, 18-19, 20n5, 30, 37, 47, 49, 54-57, 57n40, 104, 229, 230, 233, 263, 336
Prostitz, R. Meir, 153
proxy, 37, 46n4, 59, 62, 64, 329, 392
public policy, 35n1, 36, 37n6, 50, 271, 290, 305
pulmonary artery, 156
pulmonary vein, 156
pulse, xvi, 72-73, 78-79, 79-80n24, 171-4, 178-81, 205-6nn5-6, 241, 291n13, 297, 313, 350, 263; *see also* heart; heartbeat; *libbo*; pulselessness
pulselessness, 190, 198

R

Rabbanut ha-Rashit, see Chief Rabbinate of Israel
Rabbeinu Hananel, 71n3, 350,
Rabbeinu Yeruham, 71n3
Rabbinical Council of America (RCA), xix, 84n34, 134, 239n14, 263, 340n42
Raburk, R. Yisrael of, 144

Rama (R. Moshe Isserlis), 91-93, 91n49, 195, 197, 253, 253-4n15, 316n11, 329, 343, 364-5
Rama mi-Pano, 150n41
Rambam, 87-95, 88n42, 91n44, 94n53, 98, 98n2, 100, 103-5, 108, 117n1, 120, 129n24, 130, 131n32, 132-5, 140-1, 141n6, 143-4, 147-8, 167-71, 175-7, 180, 180n33, 191-6, 209, 218, 266-7, 279, 286, 349, 351-2, 354n13, 377, 386n8
Ramban, 71n3, 129-30, 171n24
Ran (Rabbeinu Nissim), 142, 350
Rappaport, R. Shabtai, 253-5
Rashba, 101, 129n24, 142, 316n11
Rashi, 71-77, 80-87, 82n30, 84-85n36, 90, 91n46, 94-95, 94-95n54, 98-103, 101n18, 125n17, 129n24, 146n27, 150-2, 155-8, 167n12, 170, 173, 179, 179n32, 240, 258-9, 347-55, 349n5, 354n13, 355-6n15, 358, 374-5
Reeve, Christopher, 123, 369-71, 369n4, 373, 376-7, 376n12
Reichman, R. Dr. Edward, viii, 77n19, 264
Reish Lakish, 102, 102n19, 108, 116, 129, 129n14, 131n32
respiration,
    failure, xvi, 21, 41, 48, 56, 180, 211, 223, 225-7, 230, 235-7, 241, 258, 288, 301-3, 319, 319n14, 359
    function, xvi, 13-16

413

neurological control of, 14-16, 288
perceivable, 76, 86, 93, 151, 169, 172, 174, 206-7, 240, 347-8
without heartbeat, 16-17, 75-77, 207-8, 212, 240-1; *see also* criteria for death, respiratory; irreversible cessation of spontaneous respiration; ventilator, mechanical
respirator brain, 31, 232
resurrection, 8, 170-2, 176, 189-90, 190n5, 276
vs. resuscitation, 64, 173, 189-90, 321
resuscitation, 23, 64, 65n60, 83, 99, 170, 190, 193-4n14, 197-8, 197n21, 226n7, 313, 320-1, 327, 334, 394-5 ; *see also* autoresucitation; CPR; do not resuscitate order; resurrection, vs. resuscitation
Rif, xxiv, 71n3, 135n43, 350
ritual impurity, *see tum'at kohanim*; *tuma't meit*; *tum'at neveilah*
Rosh, xxiv, 71n3, 98, 135n45, 142, 350
Rosner, Dr. Fred, 340-1, 391-3, 392n24, 394n27

S
Sa'adyah Gaon, 152, 354
safek (doubt), 166, 194, 224, 268, 324, 387
safek de'oraita, 146
safek goses, 93, 99, 319-20, 324, 326, 332-7, 341
safek nefashot le-hakel, 88, 209-10

Sasson, R. Ya'akov (*Ru'ah Ya'akov*), viii, 7n14, 124-6, 125n26, 150n41, 171n24, 253n12, 259n3, 294n20, 296n23, 376-80, 384
Schachter, R. Hershel, vii, 105n28, 114, 294, 346, 372, 379, 385-8, 386n8
Schechter, Dr. Yaakov, 319n14, 320
Schulman, Dr. Robert, 319n14, 320, 323n22, 340-1, 392
Schussheim, Dr. Eli, 391-4
Schwadron, R. Shalom Mordechai (Maharsham), 347, 352
science,
previous understanding of, 144-58, 150n41, 208, 232-3, 259, 354-5, 354-5n13, 356n15
role in determining Halakhah, xix, 39-43, 83, 84n34, 103, 107, 155, 158-9, 164-6, 164-6n7, 264, 306, 314, 317, 342, 344-5, 354, 354n13, 356n15; *see also* medical reality; medical technology, reliance on
Sefer Sha'ar ha-Shamayyim (R. Gershon b. Shelomoh), 77, 146-7, 152, 208, 354
Sefer Shehitot u-Bedikot (R. Yaakov Weil), 144
Sema (*Sefer Me'irat Einayim*), 59n49
Semahot, 4, 89, 163-7, 174, 191, 204-5
SEP (sensory evoked potentials), 25, 289n10, 299, 299n30, 303-4
Shaare Zedek Medical Center, 272
Shabbat, rescue activities on, 69-70, 78, 79n24, 84-85, 87-94,

165, 168, 189-90, 192, 209-10, 209n8, 218, 321, 350-3, 353n11, 364
Shafran, R. Yigal, 312-3
Shakh (R. Shabtai Kohen), 126, 133n35, 194
Shapira, R. Avraham Kahana, 271, 275, 293, 295, 297, 293, 373-4
sheep experiment, xxii, 112, 114, 114n46, 312-6, 321-4, 342, 376-80
shehitah, 102n19, 116, 126-7, 127n22, 132-5, 139-41, 144, 152-3, 380-1, 384-5, 385n4
Sheilat, R. Yitzhak, 78
Sheloush, R. David Hayyim, 275
Shemuel, 101, 101n17, 115-6, 129-30, 191n12
sheratzim, 100-1, 100n9, 101n18, 129n24, 131n32
Shevet Ha-Levi (Responsa), *see* Wosner, R. Shemuel
Shevilei Emunah, 152, 384
Shevut Ya'akov (Responsa), 92-93, 332n37
Shewmon, Dr. D. Alan., 19n3, 23, 24n11, 30n23, 47, 49, 60
Shohet, R. Tzvi, 144-5
short waiting period before death determination, 89-94, 167-8, 180, 191-2, 191n12, 195-6, 218-9, 225; *see also* time to apnea
Shulhan Arukh, xxv, 5, 87, 88n42, 91, 93-95, 95n54, 99, 106, 126-8, 127n22, 133n35, 140-2, 154, 164n5, 194, 218, 349-52, 384-5

Shumway, Dr. Norman, 246-9, 246n2
Shunamit widow, 170-1
simanim, 101-2, 102n19, 108, 116, 130-3, 131nn28-29, 137
slippery slope, 52
social interaction, 51-53; *see also* communication, capacity for
Sofer, R. Moshe, *see* Hatam Sofer
Soloveichik, R. Ahron, 362-3, 362n23
Soloveitchik, R. Joseph B., xxii
Somer, Prof. Hayyim, 305
soul, 8, 82, 82n30, 88, 224
  departure of, xviii, xxiii-xxiv, 5, 89, 97, 114, 135, 167-8, 191n12, 198, 254n15, 262, 329, 335, 343
spinal cord, 53, 101n18, 108, 117-20, 122-31, 127-9nn22-23, 131nn32-33, 136-7, 344
spinal cord trauma victims, 16, 55, 117-19, 361, 369
Steinberg, Dr. Avraham, 70, 73-77, 75n13, 86-87, 157, 157n58, 159, 175, 177-8, 181, 259, 262, 265-7, 275, 294n20, 309, 311-13, 333-8, 371-5, 375-6n12, 383, 389n16
Sternbuch, R. Moshe, 180-1, 215, 346, 388-9, 389nn15-16
suicide, 63, 213

T

tabburo, 69, 71-73, 86, 207, 350
tachycardia, 206n6, 209n8
Tendler, R. Moshe D., 84-85n36, 95, 103-8, 113, 119-21, 124, 127,

127-8n23, 130-1, 136, 179,
202-3, 215, 217-43, 221n2,
245-53, 261-8, 310, 340-1,
340n42, 343, 371, 391-3,
392n24, 394n27
Teomim, R. Yosef (*Peri Megadim*), 143
tereifah,
    animal, 126, 132, 139-45, 141n6,
    143n16, 150-8, 384-6
    human, 4, 5n24, 280-5, 292
Teshuvot ha-Ge'onim, 91n49, 195n17
thermoregulation, 30, 47-49, 264-5,
    327n25
Tiferet Yisrael, 5n5, 98, 98n2, 103, 130,
    131n33
time to absolute certainty, 193-7, 329
time to apnea, 191-7
tissue decomposition, 161, 163, 168,
    173-4, 317
Tosafot, 100, 100n9, 101n17, 120, 129,
    129n25, 142, 145-6, 189, 189-
    90n5, 354n12
Tosafot Rid, 59n49
total brain necrosis, 232, 301
total brain failure, 19, 49, 56, 104
trachea, 13, 16, 101, 102n19, 116, 131-
    2, 140-1, 291n12, 380; *see also*
    endotracheal tube; *simanim*
tracheotomy, 313
Tradition (journal), 263-4, 340-1, 391,
    392n24, 394n27
transcranial Doppler (TCD), 26, 299, 305
traumatic death vs. natural death, 311-5
traumatic brain injury, 211-2, 320
Truog, Dr. Robert, 53, 56-63, 57n40,
    65n58, 301n37, 303, 379n16

tum'at kohanim, 162, 173, 289, 363
tum'at meit, 97, 116, 117n8, 135, 170,
    193, 372
tum'at neveilah, 100, 116, 133-4
Tzarfatit widow, 169-72, 176, 189
tzemah, *see* persistent vegetative state
Tzitz Eliezer (Responsa), *see* Waldenberg,
    R. Eliezer Yehudah
tzorkhei ha-meit, 194

U

Uniform Determination of Death Act
    (UDDA), 36, 45, 49, 301n37
United Kingdom, 54; *see also* Chief
    Rabbinate of England
United Network for Organ Sharing
    (UNOS), 12, 12n26, 27
Unterman, R. Isser Yehudah, 271-2
utilitarianism, xxiii, 9, 50, 60, 66, 397

V

vagus nerve, 15
Veatch, Dr. Robert, 40-41, 51-54,
    65n58
ventilator, mechanical, 9, 16-19, 21-23,
    33, 42, 48, 50, 156-7, 175,
    202-3, 217, 220-31, 221n2,
    223n4, 238-42, 247, 253-5,
    254n16, 259, 265, 275-91,
    291n13, 295, 299-300, 314,
    316n10, 319-21, 323, 325-30,
    334-8, 342, 355, 358n19, 359,
    367-70, 374, 378-9, 389, 393
ventricular fibrillation, 206n6
Vilna Gaon, *see Gra*
Vilna Shas, 70, 350

vital functions, 9, 55, 77, 104, 147, 262, 277
vital motion, 81-83, 110-13, 111n42, 118-9, 121, 123, 136, 357-64, 358n19, 361-2n22, 367-71, 375, 379, 388, 399
vital organs, 62, 147, 280, 386-8

W

Waldenberg, R. Eliezer Yehudah, xxii, 340-1, 346, 352-5, 353n11, 355n15, 365, 365n28, 389-94, 392n24
Weil, R. Yaakov (*Sefer Shehitot u-Bedikot*), 144
Weisz, R. Yitzhak Yaakov, 7, 186, 187n2, 191-2, 199, 346, 394-5, 394n28
"whole brain" approach, 45-50, 46n4, 48n8, 50-51, 53-55, 60, 263
Wijdicks, Dr. E.F.M., 22n8, 23n9, 24n11, 26nn14-15, 29n20, 291n13, 301n37
withdrawal of care, xv, 28, 31, 59, 62-64, 252-5, 253n12, 271, 295, 295n21, 316n10, 329-30, 335, 342-3; *see also* euthanasia
withholding of care, 63, 253, 254n16, 255
Wolf, R. Binyamin, 144n21
Wosner, R. Shemuel, 78-79, 79n24, 353-4, 353n11, 354n13, 363, 395-6

Y

Yaakov (Biblical), 171n24
Yabia Omer (Responsa), *see* Yosef, R. Ovadiah
Yad Sha'ul, *see* Nathanson, R. Shaul
Yated Ne'eman, 310, 323
Yefeh Einayyim, 72
Yerushalmi, 71, 75n13, 85-87, 350
Yisraeli, R. Shaul, 79, 175-8, 181, 191n12, 196-7, 210-15, 226, 258, 275, 296
Yom Kippur, 70, 165n7
Yoma 85a, 69-96, 105, 113, 116, 136, 150-2, 156-7, 164, 168, 172n25, 173-4, 177-9, 198, 204, 206-7, 209, 211-12, 218, 236, 240, 258, 273, 275, 278, 283-4, 286, 293, 296, 346-52, 358, 374, 389
Yosef (Biblical), 171n24
Yosef, R. Ovadiah, 5n5, 6n12, 6-7n14, 84, 84n34, 131, 294-5, 294n20, 296n22

Z

Ziskind, R. Mordechai (Maharam), 153, 156
Zohar, 80, 141, 148-50, 148n33, 149-50nn39-40, 354
Zylberstein, R. Yitzhak, 369, 383-4

www.ingramcontent.com/pod-product-compliance
Lightning Source LLC
Chambersburg PA
CBHW071618170426
43195CB00038B/1358